THE COMPANY THEY KEEP

The Company They Keep

C. S. Lewis and J. R. R. Tolkien

as Writers

in Community

DIANA PAVLAC GLYER

The Kent State
University Press
Kent, Ohio

© 2007 by The Kent State University Press, Kent, Ohio 44242
Library of Congress Catalog Card Number 2006022137

ISBN-13: 978-0-87338-890-0

Manufactured in the United States of America

11 10 09 08 07   5 4 3 2 1

Library of Congress Cataloging-in-Publication Data
Glyer, Diana.
The company they keep : C. S. Lewis and J. R. R. Tolkien as
writers in community / Diana Pavlac Glyer.
    p.   cm.
Includes bibliographical references and index.
    ISBN-13: 978-0-87338-890-0 (hardcover : alk. paper) ∞
    ISBN-10: 0-87338-890-9 (hardcover : alk. paper) ∞
    1. Lewis, C. S. (Clive Staples), 1898–1963—Friends and
    associates. 2. Tolkien, J. R. R. (John Ronald Reuel), 1892–
    1973—Friends and associates. 3. Oxford (England)—
    Intellectual life—20th century. 4. Authors, English—20th
    century—Biography. 5. Fantasy fiction—Authorship. 6.
    Inklings (Group of writers) I. Title.
PR6023.E926Z6642   2006
823'.912—dc22   2006022137
[B]

British Library Cataloging-in-Publication data are available.

gloria in excelsis deo

Contents

There is one myth about writers that I have always felt was particularly pernicious and untruthful—the myth of the "lonely writer," the myth that writing is a lonely occupation, involving much suffering because, supposedly, the writer exists in a state of sensitivity which cuts him off, or raises him above, or casts him below the community around him. This is a common cliché, a hangover probably from the romantic period and the idea of the artist as Sufferer and Rebel. . . . I suppose there have been enough genuinely lonely suffering novelists to make this seem a reasonable myth, but there is every reason to suppose that such cases are the result of less admirable qualities in these writers, qualities which have nothing to do with the vocation of writing itself. . . . Unless the writer has gone utterly out of his mind, his aim is still communication, and communication suggests talking inside community.

—FLANNERY O'CONNOR

Acknowledgments

In *The Allegory of Love*, C. S. Lewis writes, "But when all is said and done, doubtless I have failed to mention many giants on whose shoulders I have stood at one time or another. Facts and inferences and even turns of expression find a lodging in a man's mind, he scarcely remembers how; and of all writers I make least claim to be αὐτοδίδακτος" (viii). Here are some of the giants on whose shoulders I have stood:

The Mythopoeic Society, especially local discussion groups Midgewater Marshes (1974–78) and The Place of the Lion (1988–91), for providing a supportive, challenging place to discover and discuss the Inklings;

Janice Coulter, John D. Rateliff, and Taum Santoski, who waited for me in Amtrak stations, provided invaluable insight into the Tolkien and Barfield material, and helped me pillage every single bookstore in the state of Wisconsin;

Aubrey Pierson, Erin Wood, Loisa Wright, Ann Wilson, Lee Speth, David Weeks, Andrew Petersen, and Chris Lewis, who provided research assistance;

Linda Sherman Spitser, who not only made this a better book but also made me a better writer;

Josh Long, who ran the last few miles of this marathon with me, editing and encouraging and making the most extraordinary discoveries as we raced along;

Geri Sullivan, who gave me magic hair;

David Jolliffe, who believed in this project from the first;

Robert J. Connors, Donald M. Murray, David Scholer, Paul Ford, Verlyn Flieger, Alan Padgett, and Steve Wilkens, whose example as writers and scholars has meant more than words could ever express;

Wayne Hammond, Christina Scull, and Douglas A. Anderson, for providing unparalleled scholarly resources, and also for their kind and generous responses to pesky questions;

The Marion E. Wade Center, Wheaton College, Wheaton, Illinois, and everyone associated with it for offering a wealth of resources and unflagging encouragement. Special thanks must be given for the Clyde S. Kilby Grant (1997), which provided practical help to make this book possible;

The dedicated staff at the Huntington Library, San Marino, California, especially Jack, Sarkis, and Dorothy, whose efficiency was constantly enriched with warmth and good humor, and Chris, who produced needed work space and books out of thin air;

Terry Franson, who taught me to climb a mountain one step at a time;

The Faculty Development Council and Faculty Research Council at Azusa Pacific University, Azusa, California, and the generous support of James Hedges, David Weeks, Pat Anderson, and Michael Whyte, who provided release time to work on this manuscript;

Colleagues at Azusa Pacific University who endured my worrying and whining and cheered me on to the finish line;

Karen Miller, Pat Hargis, David Esselstrom, Sharon Hinton, James Sainsbury, Joe R. Christopher, Alene Campbell, and Corbin Scott Carnell, who plowed through nearly unreadable drafts with remarkable good cheer, providing real faces to write for when the computer screen became unbearably cold company;

Charles Huttar, who took infinite pains with the manuscript and labored with uncommon grace to look past what I said and figure out what I meant;

David Bratman, whose 26 pages of commentary on my 123-page dissertation stimulated new thoughts and serious revision to every page. You have been resonator, opponent, editor, collaborator, and referent at every stage of the development of this book. Special thanks for compiling an index that is not only accurate and comprehensive but genuinely useful;

Berni Phillips, who suffered in cheerful silence as David and I quibbled ad infinitum;

Laura K. Simmons, who provided unending faith, hope, and love throughout the seasons of this project, and who gave prompt and felicitous replies to endless questions, particularly about Dorothy L. Sayers;

Prayer warriors from Vineyard Christian Fellowship in Evanston, the United Methodist Annual Conference on Prayer and Healing in Yucaipa, St. James Episcopal Church in Springfield, InterVarsity Christian Fellowship in Point Lookout, the Solomon's Housechurch in Pasadena, and the Niños in the San Gabriel Valley;

Lowell and Virginia Leland, Clyde and Martha Kilby, and Lyle and Mary Dorsett, whose precious friendship is as close as I have ever come to knowing the Inklings themselves;

Adam Bradley, who loved me and prayed for me and found the typos that everyone else missed;

Sierra Grace, who bravely waved bye-bye when Mommy left in the morning to go work on her book. I love you more than the whale loves his spout;

And most especially Mike Glyer, the man I adore. Here at last is the book you asked for.

Introduction
An Intellectual Dilemma

I first read J. R. R. Tolkien's *The Lord of the Rings* in high school. A group of my friends became enchanted by the book, and they started giving names to each other based on the fictional characters. I decided to read the book in self-defense—I didn't like feeling left out—and it wasn't long before I came completely under its spell. I enjoyed Hobbit dinner parties, trembled in the presence of the Black Riders, adored Rivendell, hated Orcs, and wondered where the Entwives could have gone.

I couldn't put the book down. I couldn't stop thinking about it. I read more and more slowly as I neared the conclusion because I did not want it to end. It was wonderfully written. Page after page of it was fresh, alive, and magical.

When my friends found out I'd read it too, they dubbed me Galadriel. I liked that; she was an elf, serene, beautiful, happy, "wise and fearless and fair" (*Fellowship* 356). She was pure in heart, and so she was able to resist the wickedness of Sauron's magic ring. I liked that a lot.

I read more Tolkien, taking up *The Hobbit* next, then "Leaf by Niggle," and then I dove back into *The Lord of the Rings* because nothing else I knew had such power to take me out of this world and immerse me so completely in another. Tolkien's creative power was so compelling that I didn't just *read* about Middle-earth; it was as if every time I opened the book, I went there. Throughout my years in high school, I visited again and again.

I decided to find out more about the author of these books, and I was delighted to learn that Tolkien had been close friends with other important writers. Through his work, I discovered C. S. Lewis, and more magical worlds were opened to me: Narnia, Malacandra, Perelandra, and Glome. My own creative imagination resonated with every Lewis book I read.

Then, looking for more of the same, more of the kind of books I like to read, I picked up *The Place of the Lion* by Charles Williams. Nothing I had ever read prepared me for such a complex, compelling supernatural thriller. I started the book innocently; I finished it wide-eyed with awe.

As I read more about these writers, I discovered Tolkien, Lewis, and Williams met regularly to talk about their writing. Other writers participated, including Owen Barfield, Hugo Dyson, R. E. Havard, David Cecil, Nevill Coghill, and Warren Hamilton Lewis, C. S. Lewis's brother. Many of them were Oxford dons. They read their manuscripts aloud to one another, encouraged and criticized one another, and revised their books based on the feedback they received: Tolkien's *The Lord of the Rings,* Lewis's *Out of the Silent Planet,* and Williams's *All Hallows' Eve* were all created in this context. They gathered at different times in different places—notably in Lewis's rooms at Magdalen College, Oxford, and in the Eagle and Child, an Oxford pub—and they held regular meetings for about seventeen years. They called themselves the Inklings.

I started to research the nature and the activities of the group. To my surprise, most scholars claimed that these writers had no influence on each other. Humphrey Carpenter, who has written a book-length biography of the Inklings, is most insistent on this point. He writes, "It must be remembered that the word 'influence,' so beloved of literary investigators, makes little sense when talking about their association with each other" (*Inklings* 160). And in an almost ominous tone, Gareth Knight issues this warning: "We have to be careful however not to attribute influence where none existed" (4).

Other scholars take great pains to emphasize that these men were very different from one another. Mark Hillegas, for example, stresses that "each writer is excellent in his own fashion, unique in style and technique" (xii). William Ready states, "The differences between these men are far more important than the appearance of their likenesses," and he ends his evaluation of Tolkien, Lewis, and Williams by asserting, "Trio they were not" (37, 38).

Why such forthright denial of influence? Why such adamant insistence on individuality? I was mystified. Tolkien, Lewis, Williams, and the other Inklings met regularly, read their works aloud to one another, discussed and critiqued each manuscript, and revised and rewrote their work, and people say they didn't have any influence on each other? That didn't sound plausible.

I dug a little deeper and found more of the same. Some writers discussed the Inklings as a group; others focused on only one of the authors. The claim I found most frequently was that no one had any influence on J. R. R. Tolkien. Knight, for example, writes, "Inklings or not, Tolkien would probably have gone on to do what he did anyway, as a man writing from great depths within himself" (5). In *Imaginary Worlds,* Lin Carter writes, "Whatever criticism the Inklings offered, Tolkien paid no attention," and, stronger still, the Inklings were "unable to influence the writing of *The Lord of the Rings* in any way" (112, 113).

And in *Tolkien: A Look Behind the Lord of the Rings,* he writes, "Though they no doubt discussed it and commented upon it, they did not, apparently, have any appreciable influence on the trilogy as it took shape." He adds with sweeping emphasis, "Everyone concerned seems quite adamant on this point" (18).

Carpenter states the case more fervently, and he considers Williams as well as Tolkien. He writes, "Tolkien and Williams owed almost nothing to the other Inklings, and would have written everything they wrote had they never heard of the group" (*Inklings* 160). And John D. Rateliff agrees: "I think Carpenter is right in saying Tolkien and Williams had no real influence on each other's work" ("'Something'" 51). More recent scholarship continues in the same vein. Candice Fredrick and Sam McBride, for example, claim, "One would *never be tempted to suggest* that the Inklings' reading and critiquing could be appropriately labeled 'collaboration'" (150, emphasis added).[1]

Carpenter, Knight, Hillegas, Carter, Rateliff, Fredrick, McBride, and others generally base their conclusions on statements made by the Inklings themselves. One of the most famous is this declaration by C. S. Lewis: "No one ever influenced Tolkien—you might as well try to influence a bandersnatch" (*Letters* 481).[2] Lewis apparently made his irritation very clear to Tolkien, for Tolkien explained, "Once he said, 'It's no use trying to influence you. You're uninfluenceable!'" (qtd. in Plimmer and Plimmer 2). In a letter written late in his life, Lewis concludes, "I don't think Tolkien influenced me, and I am certain I didn't influence him" (qtd. in Kilby, *Tolkien* 76).

But Lewis is not the only Inkling to deny Inkling influence. When Barfield found out that Lewis had called him his greatest unofficial teacher, he laughed, explaining, "What am I supposed to have taught him? He continues to deny everything I say!" (*Owen Barfield* 150). Tolkien says of Charles Williams, "I do not think we influenced one another at all! Too 'set,' and too different" (*Letters* 209). Robert E. Havard, an Inkling who faithfully attended the weekly meetings, dismisses the notion of influence: "I don't think any of us were much affected by the criticism or altered what had been written."[3] He also downplays any suggestion of group cohesion or group identity. Havard claims, "We really had no corporate existence. In my view we were simply a group of C. S. L.'s wide circle of friends who lived near enough to him to meet together fairly regularly" (qtd. in Carpenter, *Inklings* 161).

The members of the Inklings read each other's work for more than seventeen years. Despite this lengthy and substantial interaction, the members of the group and the scholars who study them seem unanimous in their insistence that the Inklings were nothing more than an informal association of friends. Yet common sense suggests that these men would not have continued to read and critique each other's manuscripts if doing so had not been fruitful and influential. Common sense also suggests that the members of any long-standing group are bound to change each other.

Having wrestled with these statements by Inklings scholars and by the Inklings themselves, I decided to see how the members of other writing groups addressed this question of mutual influence. I read about the Bloomsbury Group, the Transcendentalists, the Brideshead Generation, the Lost Generation. As I considered these accounts, I was struck by how often the members gratefully acknowledged the help they received and how readily scholars took influence for granted.[4]

I looked further, considering scholarly research on creativity, collaborative circles, and composition theory and rhetorical processes. It was clear from all of these research areas that formal and informal writing groups are quite common, and that they thrive in academic and nonacademic settings. And over and over participants and observers alike comment upon the extent to which formal and informal groups change the writers who take part in them.

My own experience confirmed this. When I have participated as a member of a writing group, I have always gained a great deal from the experience. In fact, even when I submit my work to just one reader, it makes a difference. I need the feedback and comments of others in order to shape my text and sharpen my meaning. I rely upon the encouragement that comes when someone is interested in what I have to say. And I genuinely appreciate the criticisms and the disagreements, for even if I don't change my position, I change the emphasis, proportion, or support for my argument to make my point clearer in the face of objections.

My experience in writing groups also confirms my belief that anticipation shapes the creation of my text. When I write with a particular reader in mind, I make changes, large and small. I find myself anticipating questions, bracing against challenges, accommodating interests. In short, if I know David will be reading my story, I will write more and more with David's priorities in mind. If I know Linda will be editing my work, I become particularly alert to the mistakes that catch her eye. If I know Mike will ask how the project is coming along, I am more likely to be motivated and stay on task. Having interested, thoughtful readers has invariably transformed my own writing.

This was my dilemma. Considering my own experience as a writer, my research on composition and the creative process, and my reading about other writing groups, the emphatic denial of influence expressed by Inklings scholars and by the Inklings themselves just didn't make any sense to me. This book is the result of trying to grapple with that tension: the persistent claims that the Inklings did *not* influence each other and my sense that they *must* have.

Did J. R. R. Tolkien, C. S. Lewis, Charles Williams, Owen Barfield, Hugo Dyson, R. E. Havard, David Cecil, Nevill Coghill, Warren Lewis, and the other Inklings influence each other? In what ways? To what extent? What is the evidence? And what are the larger implications for the study of creativity and community? That is the story I tell in these pages.

NOTES

1. Fredrick and McBride deny that collaboration is a valid way to label the interaction of these authors (150). In the pages that follow, I assert that the Inklings did work collaboratively.

2. The Bandersnatch is a mythical beast introduced in Lewis Carroll's "Jabberwocky."

Beware the Jabberwock, my son!
The jaws that bite, the claws that catch!
Beware the Jubjub bird, and shun
The frumious Bandersnatch! (134)

This is the first mention of the Bandersnatch in Carroll's book. However, as Linda S. Spitser has pointed out, Lewis's comment refers to an incident later in Carroll's text (personal correspondence 19 July 2004). When Alice is out of breath from running with the White King and asks him to "stop a minute," he replies, "A minute goes by so fearfully quick. You might as well try to stop a Bandersnatch!" (202).

3. Oral history interview with R. E. Havard, conducted by Lyle W. Dorsett for the Marion E. Wade Center (26 July 1984), page 20.

4. See, for example, S. P. Rosenbaum's study of Virginia Woolf, John Maynard Keynes, Duncan Grant, et al. in *The Bloomsbury Group;* Carlos Baker's study of Ralph Waldo Emerson, Henry David Thoreau, Margaret Fuller, Walt Whitman, Nathaniel Hawthorne, and others in *Emerson among the Eccentrics* (1997); Humphrey Carpenter's study of John Betjeman, Graham Greene, Evelyn Waugh, and friends in *The Brideshead Generation* (1990); and Noel Riley Fitch's *Sylvia Beach and the Lost Generation* (1985). Other useful works include Carpenter's study of Ernest Hemingway, Robert McAlmon, Kay Boyle, and others in *Geniuses Together* (1987); Beach's description of her interaction with James Joyce, Scott Fitzgerald, Sherwood Anderson, André Gide, Ezra Pound, Alice B. Toklas, D. H. Lawrence, Gertrude Stein, Ernest Hemingway, and others in *Shakespeare and Company* (1991); Nicholas Delbanco's study of Joseph Conrad, Stephen Crane, Ford Madox Ford, Henry James, H. G. Wells, et al. in *Group Portrait* (1982); and Michael Farrell's important overview of six creative groups in *Collaborative Circles* (2001).

1

Inklings
Building
Community

In this connection I must say something of the Inklings, a famous and heroic gathering, one that has already passed into literary legend.
  —*Warren Hamilton Lewis*

Fox is a member of our literary club of practising poets—before whom the Hobbit, *and other works (such as the* Silent Planet*) have been read.*
  —*J. R. R. Tolkien*

The best things come, as a general thing, from the talents that are members of a group; every man works better when he has companions working in the same line, and yielding the stimulus of suggestion, comparison, emulation.
  —*Henry James*

C. S. Lewis completed his first science fiction novel, *Out of the Silent Planet,* in the fall of 1937. He submitted the manuscript to J. M. Dent with high expectations. After all, Dent was the publishing house responsible for two of his earlier books: *Dymer* and *The Pilgrim's Regress.* To his surprise, when Dent read his new manuscript, they turned it down flat. Shaken by this rejection, Lewis sought the advice of his friend and colleague, J. R. R. Tolkien. Tolkien had read Lewis's novel, and he was quite enthusiastic about it. He told Lewis to submit it to Allen & Unwin, publisher of *The Hobbit.* Lewis followed his advice, and Tolkien sent along a letter, encouraging Stanley Unwin to give *Out of the Silent Planet* careful consideration. In the letter, Tolkien expresses his own admiration for the work, but he bolsters his personal opinion by invoking a "local club," a group of writers who also knew the book and thought highly of it. Tolkien writes, "Mr C. S. Lewis tells me that you have allowed him to submit to you 'Out of the Silent Planet.' I read it, of course; and I have since heard it pass a rather different test: that of being read aloud to our local club (which goes in for reading things short and long aloud). It proved an exciting serial, and was highly approved" (*Letters* 29).

Tolkien's enthusiastic praise convinced Unwin to give the book a chance, so he sent it to an external reader. But the reader completely denounced it. He called the invented creatures of Malacandra "bunk" and said that the underlying myth stuck in his "gullet." Despite these disparaging conclusions, he thought C. S. Lewis showed promise as a writer: "Mr Lewis is quite likely, I dare say, to write a worth while novel one day. This one isn't good enough—quite" (qtd. in Tolkien, *Letters* 32–33).

Torn between these two opinions, Unwin decided to gather more information. He sent an inquiry to Tolkien, who responded quickly: "Since you ask for my opinion, here it is. I read the story in the original MS. and was so enthralled that I could do nothing else until I had finished it. My first criticism was simply that it was too short" (*Letters* 32). Tolkien continued with a long, detailed discussion of the book. In it, he admitted that in an earlier draft, the story suffered from a number of serious weaknesses, including problems of style ("rather creaking stiff-jointed passages"), narrative inconsistencies, and flaws in "linguistic invention" (32–33). But the book had been significantly revised, and Tolkien's concerns had been satisfactorily addressed. So, as it now stands, the book has much to recommend it: "All the part about language and poetry—the glimpses of its Malacandrian nature and form—is very well done, and extremely interesting, far superior to what one usually gets from travellers in untravelled regions. . . . I found the blend of *vera historia* with *mythos* irresistible" (33). Tolkien continues, praising the novel's language, its poetry, its inventiveness, and its "spice of satire" (33). With a flourish, he concludes, "I at any rate should have bought this story at almost any price if I had found it in print, and loudly recommended it as a 'thriller' by (however and surprisingly) an intelligent man" (34).

Despite the enthusiasm of such a notable critic, Allen & Unwin agreed with the assessment of their external reader and would not publish the book. Still, Tolkien's efforts were not wasted. Although Stanley Unwin had doubts about the novel, he was moved by Tolkien's strong endorsement, so he passed the manuscript along to colleagues at The Bodley Head. They accepted it, and *Out of the Silent Planet* was published shortly thereafter.[1]

The discouragement and delay over this, his first science fiction novel, had caused C. S. Lewis many anxious hours. But this incident and the accompanying correspondence provide us with an important resource: here we find one of the first contemporary references to the Inklings, a writing group that included C. S. Lewis and J. R. R. Tolkien and about a dozen others.

LEWIS AND TOLKIEN

At the core of the Inklings was the interaction of two men, C. S. Lewis and J. R. R. Tolkien.[2] They are generally remembered as authors of creative fantasy, but both men made their daily living teaching at Oxford University. Lewis was a fellow of Magdalen College, serving as a tutor in English Language and Literature; Tolkien was Rawlinson and Bosworth Professor of Anglo-Saxon at Pembroke College, and later became Merton Professor of English Language and Literature at Merton College.

They met at a faculty meeting on 11 May 1926. Lewis's first impression of Tolkien was not favorable. In his diary he describes Tolkien as "a smooth, pale, fluent little chap." Lewis adds, "No harm in him: only needs a smack or so" (*All My Road* 393).

It got worse. As Lewis and Tolkien grew to know one another, it became clear they had a number of fundamental disagreements, including differences in religious convictions and academic loyalties. Lewis writes, "At my first coming into the world I had been (implicitly) warned never to trust a Papist, and at my first coming into the English Faculty (explicitly) never to trust a philologist. Tolkien was both" (*Surprised* 216).[3]

Within months of their first meeting, Lewis and Tolkien found themselves on opposite sides of a curriculum reform measure being hotly debated at Oxford. Tolkien held that the English curriculum should be based on close study of ancient and medieval texts and their languages, believing that if students were given a solid foundation, they could read the full range of modern texts on their own. Lewis, on the other hand, sided with those who favored an emphasis on post-Chaucerian literature (Carpenter, *Inklings* 24–27).

Tolkien was prepared to fight energetically for his curriculum. He decided that the best way to promote it would be to foster a love for Old Norse among his colleagues. So he founded a club he called the Kolbítar (literally "the Coal-biters"), adopting an Icelandic word for "old cronies who sit round the fire so close that they look as if they were biting the coals" (Lewis, *They Stand* 298). They met to read Icelandic sagas and the Eddas in their original language.

Lewis was immediately drawn in. For him, the chance to study these texts was the fulfillment of his life-long devotion to northern mythology. He was only nine years old when he first discovered "Tegner's Drapa" by Longfellow and was "uplifted into huge regions of northern sky" that he "desired with almost sickening intensity" (*Surprised* 17). At twenty-eight, he remained unabashed in his enthusiasm for these ancient texts: "Hammered my way thro' a couple of pages in about an hour, but I am making some headway. It is an exciting experience, when I remember my first passion for things Norse under the initiation of Longfellow. . . . It seemed impossible then that I shd. ever come to read these things in the original. The old authentic thrill came back to me once or twice this morning: the mere names of god and giant catching my eye as I turned the pages of Zoega's dictionary was enough" (*All My Road* 448).[4]

The Coalbiters met regularly, working their way through ancient sagas and thrilling over both the literature and the language. Despite strong initial suspicion and intense professional conflict, Lewis and Tolkien discovered significant common ground. They gravitated toward each other because they shared an interest "in what they called 'northernness,' the linguistic side of it, the heroic side of it."[5] As they talked together, Lewis was slowly won over to Tolkien's view of the English curriculum. And as they worked side by side, they forged a solid friendship. A student at Oxford in the mid-1930s, E. L. Edmonds, remembers, "It was very obvious that [Lewis and Tolkien] were great friends—indeed, they were like two young bear cubs sometimes, just happily quipping with one another" (45).

1929: TOLKIEN SHARES HIS MYTHOLOGY

The transition in their relationship, from initial suspicion to warm, personal friendship, occurred as they pursued a mutual intellectual interest. Lewis himself describes the transforming power of shared pursuits in his book *The Four Loves*. In fact, Lewis defines friends as those who stand "side by side, absorbed in some common interest" (61). According to Michael P. Farrell, who has done extensive research in the life cycle of collaborative circles, this pattern is extremely common. He has found that creative small groups usually begin as "a casual association among acquaintances working in the same discipline" (2). In this early period, the conversation predictably focuses on "peripheral, less threatening, concerns" (20).

However, as intimacy increases and trust grows, the stage is set for a shift. This occurs, as Farrell has discovered, when "one member may risk exposing to the other a wild, half-baked idea or an unfinished work," opening the door to "more intimate disclosures" (151, 280). This is exactly what happened in December 1929, when Tolkien decided to show Lewis the draft of a poem he had been working on. This long narrative poem, *The Lay of Leithian*, is an early version of the most personal and significant story in all of his created mythology: the tale of Beren and Lúthien.[6]

Lewis took Tolkien's manuscript home and read it eagerly. The next day he responded with a brief note, filled with praise: "I can quite honestly say that it is ages since I have had an evening of such delight: and the personal interest of reading a friend's work had very little to do with it. I should have enjoyed it just as well as if I'd picked it up in a bookshop, by an unknown author" (qtd. in Tolkien, *Lays* 151).

Lewis was struck by two qualities in particular: the verisimilitude of Tolkien's sub-created world, and the "mythical value" of the story. But Lewis ends the letter on an ominous note, promising, "Detailed criticisms (including grumbles at individual lines) will follow" (qtd. in Carpenter, *Inklings* 30). Lewis's second letter, full of "criticisms" and individual "grumbles," arrived some weeks later. He questioned large, conceptual matters. He quibbled about small word choices. He requested specific revisions. He even rewrote entire sections of the poem himself.

Tolkien was as cheered by the careful critique as he was by the lavish praise. More than anything else, it meant that he had found someone sympathetic with the nature of his work, and enthusiastic enough to give it a close, attentive reading.[7] Although Tolkien did not agree with all of Lewis's feedback, he did revise the poem extensively, responding to most of Lewis's suggestions in one way or another.[8]

Tolkien had taken a substantial risk; Lewis had offered a generous, detailed response. Now Lewis took the next step. He responded to Tolkien's initiative by sharing some poems of his own. At this point in his life, Lewis had been writing a great deal of poetry. In fact, in these early years Lewis saw himself primarily as a poet, and he fully expected that the most significant accomplishments of his life would be to publish great poetry.[9] His friend Owen Barfield notes that throughout the 1920s, Lewis's "ruling ambition" was "to become a great poet." Barfield adds, "At that time, if you thought of Lewis, you automatically thought of poetry" (*Owen Barfield* 5–6).

Tolkien commented on Lewis's poetry in kind. And it wasn't long before it became a "regular custom" for Tolkien and Lewis to meet together in Lewis's rooms at Magdalen College on Monday mornings to read and criticize one another's work. In a letter to his brother, Lewis calls this regular meeting time "one of the pleasantest spots in the week" (*Collected Letters* 2: 16).

1931: C. S. Lewis Renews His Faith

Lewis's interaction with Tolkien affected more than just his writing; it precipitated a transformation of his faith. Lewis had accepted Christianity as a child, but later abandoned God entirely.[10] In 1916, he explained his position to his childhood friend Arthur Greeves:

> You ask me my religious views: you know, I think, that I believe in no religion. There is absolutely no proof for any of them, and from a philosophical standpoint Christianity is not even the best. All religions, that is, all mythologies to give them their proper name are merely man's own invention—Christ as much as Loki. Primitive man found himself surrounded by all sorts of terrible things he didn't understand—thunder,

pestilence, snakes etc: what more natural than to suppose that these were animated by evil spirits trying to torture him. These he kept off by cringing to them, singing songs and making sacrifices etc. Gradually from being mere nature-spirits these supposed being[s] were elevated into more elaborate ideas, such as the old gods: and when man became more refined he pretended that these spirits were good as well as powerful.

Thus religion, that is to say mythology grew up. (*Collected Letters* 1: 230–31)

As a teenager, Lewis dismissed all religions with this neat and tidy explanation: primitive man simply invented religion in a misguided attempt to make sense of the threats and dangers he observed in the natural world.

But as the years went by, Lewis found it increasingly difficult to remain an atheist, in part because he kept meeting intelligent, articulate men who turned out to be Christians. Lewis became friends with Nevill Coghill, a man Walter Hooper calls "one of the best known and best loved men in Oxford" (*C. S. Lewis* 645). Coghill was recognized as a man of warmth, chivalry, honor, and "gentilesse." Lewis notes, "One could imagine him fighting a duel" (qtd. in *C. S. Lewis* 644). They became friends in George Gordon's discussion class. Despite a promising beginning, Lewis was dismayed when he discovered that even though Coghill was "clearly the most intelligent and best-informed man in that class," he was "a Christian and a thoroughgoing supernaturalist" (*Surprised* 212).

Then two of his most important college friends—A. C. Harwood and Owen Barfield—rejected atheism and became anthroposophists, followers of a spiritual doctrine developed by Rudolf Steiner. Their rejection of rationalism seriously upset Lewis, who writes, "I was hideously shocked. Everything that I had labored so hard to expel from my own life seemed to have flared up and met me in my best friends. Not only my best friends but those whom I would have thought safest; the one so immovable, the other brought up in a free-thinking family and so immune from all 'superstition' that he had hardly heard of Christianity itself until he went to school" (*Surprised* 206). Though distressed by the religious conversions of his friends, it upset Lewis even more to find that many of the authors he loved best were also devout men of faith. The assault, it seemed, was relentless. Tongue in cheek, he writes, "Really, a young Atheist cannot guard his faith too carefully. Dangers lie in wait for him on every side" (226).

The "Danger" became increasingly insistent. In a letter to Barfield, Lewis expressed the gnawing sense that something was closing in on him. He writes, "Terrible things are happening to me. The 'Spirit' or 'Real I' is showing an alarming tendency to become much more personal and is taking the offensive, and behaving just like God." He continues, "You'd better come on Monday at the latest or I may have entered a monastery" (*Collected Letters* 1: 882–83).

Eventually, the old belief system Lewis had constructed with such great care simply collapsed. In an often-quoted passage, he writes, "In the Trinity Term of 1929 I gave in, and admitted that God was God, and knelt and prayed: perhaps, that night, the most dejected and reluctant convert in all England" (*Surprised* 228–29).

This was his conversion to theism, to belief in God. It was two more years before Lewis became a Christian. Many factors contributed to his commitment to Christ, but the turning point came in September 1931, following a long talk with two of his friends. One was J. R. R. Tolkien. The other was Hugo Dyson.[11] Dyson was a man of unusually bold and lively character. Warren Lewis describes him as "a man who gives the impression of being made of quick silver: he pours himself into a room on a cataract of words and gestures, and you are caught up in the stream—but after the first plunge, it is exhilarating" (*Brothers* 97). C. S. Lewis admired Hugo Dyson for his fine mind, vibrant character, and merry laugh. Lewis's descriptions of him generally emphasize his vivacity and quickness of speech, but he also pays him the high compliment of calling him "a man who really loves truth" (*Collected Letters* 1: 918).

On 19 September 1931, Dyson, Tolkien, and Lewis enjoyed dinner together, then went for a walk and talked late into the night. Lewis was confronted about his old anti-Christian biases and was encouraged to consider Christianity as a true myth:

> Now what Dyson and Tolkien showed me was this: that if I met the idea of sacrifice in a Pagan story I didn't mind it at all: again, that if I met the idea of a god sacrificing himself to himself . . . I liked it very much and was mysteriously moved by it: again, that the idea of the dying and reviving god (Balder, Adonis, Bacchus) similarly moved me provided I met it anywhere *except* in the Gospels. The reason was that in Pagan stories I was prepared to feel the myth as profound and suggestive of meanings beyond my grasp even tho' I could not say in cold prose "what it meant."
>
> Now the story of Christ is simply a true myth: a myth working on us in the same way as the others, but with this tremendous difference that *it really happened*. (*Collected Letters* 1: 976–77)

Lewis's commitment to Christ became the central fact of his life. And he acknowledges that the turning point was this specific conversation. In a letter to

Dom Bede Griffiths, he makes it clear: "Dyson and Tolkien were the immediate human causes of my own conversion" (2: 501).[12]

1932: WARNIE COMES HOME

While C. S. Lewis was establishing himself as an academic at Oxford, his brother Warren, three years his senior, was half a world away, serving as an officer at a Royal Army Service Corps (RASC) depot in China. Warren Lewis was only seventeen when he decided to pursue a military career; he began in February 1914 and remained until 1932, when he became eligible for early retirement. Richard C. West explains that "Warren's army service was in supplies and transport, dangerous enough work in wartime when being strafed by enemy planes, and always entailing responsibility for thousands of soldiers" (82–83). Warren Lewis served in England, France, China, and West Africa.

The two brothers were uncommonly close all their lives. As children, they played together, wrote stories of imagined worlds together, and painted pictures and drew maps in creative interaction. When their mother died of cancer in 1908, they became even closer, like "two frightened urchins huddled for warmth in a bleak world" (*Surprised* 19). Both boys attended Wynyard School and Malvern College, and both were tutored by William T. Kirkpatrick. They renewed their commitment to Christ, their attendance at church, and their participation in communion along independent paths, but within the same two-and-a-half-year period. Following Warren Lewis's retirement, they lived together in the same house, the Kilns.[13] And they are buried in the same grave at Holy Trinity Church, Headington Quarry.

Easy-going and affable, Warren Lewis is described in affectionate terms by all who knew him. His tutor Kirkpatrick writes, "He is one of the nicest, best tempered, personally amiable boys I have ever met. To live in the house with him is a pleasure, and no one could sit working along with him so long as I have done without developing an affection for him" (qtd. in Hooper, *C. S. Lewis* 698). John Wain calls him "a man who stays in my memory as the most courteous I have ever met—not with mere politeness, but with a genial, self-forgetful considerateness that was as instinctive to him as breathing" (*Sprightly* 184).

Warren Lewis, also known as "Warnie," was a warm and gentle man and a gifted writer. His books on French history are highly praised: Carpenter says his "readability, wit and good sense almost equalled his brother's work" (*Inklings* 243). Though his histories are quite well-written, in many ways his most important literary masterwork is his diary. Clyde S. Kilby and Marjorie Lamp Mead, who edited and published it, describe his style as "light, quick, and perceptive." They add, "Warren writes in the pages of his journal with

the sensitive eye of the novelist—and yet his is a record of fact, not fiction"
(*Brothers* x). C. S. Lewis writes of his brother, "He's one of the simplest souls
I know in a way: certainly one of the best at getting simple pleasures" (*They
Stand* 489). Carpenter says, "It was largely this quality of getting the best out
of ordinary life that made Warnie Lewis a first-rate diarist" (*Inklings* 38).

After retiring and settling in at the Kilns, Warren decided to complete the
task of editing the Lewis family papers. He loved the work; he calls the project
"one of the most engrossing tasks I have ever undertaken" (*Brothers* 75).[14] He
spent most weekdays researching and writing in Lewis's rooms at Magdalen
College. On Monday mornings, it was only natural for him to join his brother
and Tolkien for literary conversation. Then the three of them would continue
on to the Eastgate Hotel for lunch and a pint of beer.

THE INKLINGS

During this same period in the early 1930s, an Oxford undergraduate named
Edward Tangye Lean decided to start an essay club. "Its procedure was that at
each meeting members should read aloud, unpublished compositions. These
were supposed to be open to immediate criticism" (Tolkien, *Letters* 388). Lean
feared that this group, like most student clubs, would be short lived. He thought
he might extend it by involving some of the Oxford faculty, and so he invited
Tolkien and Lewis to join the group, which he had named "The Inklings."

Despite Lean's best efforts and the clear purpose and talented membership of his group, it lasted only a few terms. Apparently it folded when Lean
graduated from Oxford in June of 1933. Lewis took the name "Inklings" and
transferred it to a different group, "the undetermined and unelected circle" of
writers who had been meeting in Lewis's rooms at Magdalen (Tolkien, *Letters*
388). Though the name was transferred from one group to another, the link
between the two is quite tenuous. The latter group did not replace the former,
nor did it function as a continuation of it. Tolkien makes it quite clear that the
Inklings would have come into being "whether the original short-lived club
had ever existed or not" (388).

Still, the chosen name does tell us something about the group's nature. The
Inklings founded by Lean was not a literary society, nor was it a forum for
general discussion, though both were quite common in Oxford at the time.
This was a weekly meeting of working writers. Members brought works in
progress, read them aloud, received comments and criticisms, and revised
their work in response to what they heard. Tolkien calls the name "a pleasantly
ingenious pun," referring to those who "dabble in ink" (*Letters* 388).[15] In other
words, writing was central.[16]

In addition, as Tolkien points out, the name suggests people "with vague or half-formed intimations and ideas" (*Letters* 388). This suggests a view of texts as fluid: they were drafts in progress, and as such, they were subject to revision in response to criticism and feedback. When Tolkien wrote a story about a fictional writing group much like the Inklings, he called it "The Notion Club," reinforcing the view that they were working with fleeting ideas, or tentative drafts in progress.[17] Indeed, there is evidence of extensive change and revision of manuscripts read to the Inklings, as we will see in later chapters.

The transfer of the name from one group to another serves as a benchmark in the history of the group. Scholars have tended to conflate this event with the group's founding. Kilby and Mead, and Duriez and Porter, for example, give 1933 as the year the group started. But theirs is by no means the only view. Others, notably David Cecil, put the starting point much later, arguing that the group did not really have a critical mass of membership or a regular pattern of meeting until 1939, when several of its most dynamic members began to attend regularly (Trickett and Cecil 561). On the other hand, a much earlier starting date has been suggested by Owen Barfield, who writes, "When can the Inklings be said to have begun? . . . I recall quite a few meetings—enough to constitute a 'series'—in Lewis' room in the twenties between Lewis, Tolkien, and myself, sometimes together with Colin Hardie and at least one with Nevill Coghill. I think it was these foregatherings that ultimately turned into the Inklings" ("Inklings Remembered" 548). This very early date is not corroborated by any of the other Inklings, nor can I find any other scholar who maintains that these gatherings marked the beginning of the group.

Much of the early history of the group is uncertain, and the records concerning its establishment are contradictory. Most of the men who became members of the Inklings had already known one another for some time—C. S. Lewis and his brother, of course, grew up together; Lewis and Barfield met as first-year university students; Coghill and Dyson participated together in the Exeter College Essay Club as undergraduates; Tolkien and Lewis met as faculty colleagues early in their teaching careers. As far as their corporate identity as Inklings is concerned, there is no official starting date, no opening rally, no single catalyzing event. They never wrote any kind of charter or mission statement or manifesto that signaled their establishment as a clearly defined group. And references to the Inklings by that name first occur some five or six years after they had been meeting regularly.[18] Recollections of these early days by the Inklings themselves tend to confuse the matter rather than clarify it. Even the dates of specific events have been contested.

What are we to do with this tangled, even contradictory, evidence? It is most likely, as Farrell suggests, that the emerging pattern of weekly interaction between

Lewis and Tolkien, beginning in about 1929, "became the nucleus of a collaborative circle that profoundly influenced each man's development" (8). Hooper also
calls these morning meetings "the beginnings of The Inklings" (*C. S. Lewis* 731).
This early date is supported by George Sayer, who notes that at the time Lewis
transferred the name from one writing group to another, the members had been
meeting in Lewis's rooms at Magdalen for some time (*Jack* 149).

The specifics can be sifted and cross-checked, but there is a larger lesson to
be learned from this debate. Contrary to popular belief, writing groups and
other kinds of collaborative circles do not typically take shape at a clear and
specific point in time as individuals rally around a common cause or a charis-
matic leader. Instead, a collective identity slowly emerges. Often this happens
among professional colleagues who experience a growing sense of alienation
from the mainstream, a restlessness or uneasiness with the privileged ways
of doing things within their field. Or, as Lewis puts it, effective groups often
emerge from "little knots of Friends who turn their backs on the 'World'" (*Four
Loves* 69). The corporate practices of a group develop slowly and somewhat
haphazardly within this supportive context and, over time, give rise to new
visions and innovative projects.

To the extent that there is one critical moment in the formation of the
Inklings as a group, it seems to be the moment in December 1929 when Tolkien
made the courageous decision to share his created mythology with Lewis. From
there, a casual pattern was established as Tolkien and Lewis began meeting
to read and critique each other's work.[19] These meetings received a boost in
1931, when Lewis renewed his Christian faith, and another when Warren Lewis
retired in 1932 and moved to Oxford.

After that, the group began to grow. All in all, nineteen men are included
in the standard list of the Inklings.[20] They are Owen Barfield, J. A. W. Bennett,
David Cecil, Nevill Coghill, James Dundas-Grant, H. V. D. Dyson, Adam Fox,
Colin Hardie, Robert E. Havard, C. S. Lewis, Warren Lewis, Gervase Mathew,
R. B. McCallum, C. E. Stevens, Christopher Tolkien, J. R. R. Tolkien, John
Wain, Charles Williams, and C. L. Wrenn.[21]

But a typical Thursday night Inklings meeting was fairly small. On the average, six or seven men would show up. This is common, as Farrell points out:
"Collaborative circles usually consist of three to five members; only rarely do
they consist of more than seven or eight" (22). Four of the Inklings—the two
Lewis brothers, J. R. R. Tolkien, and R. E. Havard—attended most faithfully.

Dr. R. E. Havard met Lewis when he was called to the Kilns to treat Lewis
for an attack of influenza. The strong intellectual connection between the two
men is unmistakable. According to Havard, "On my first visit we spent some
five minutes discussing his influenza, which was very straightforward, and

then half an hour or more in a discussion of ethics and philosophy" ("Philia" 350). This is not surprising: Havard was "well-read and keenly interested in the processes of literature and in theology" (Sayer, *Jack* 151).

Havard reports that shortly after his first visit to the Kilns, Lewis invited him to come and join the Inklings, describing it as "a group of us who meet on Thursday evenings and read papers and discuss them."[22] As a physician, Havard might seem like an unlikely candidate for membership in this group of Oxford literary men.[23] But Havard was in fact a skilled and prolific writer. He coauthored and published a number of medical research papers. He wrote an appendix for Lewis's *The Problem of Pain* and provided feedback while the book was being written (Sayer, *Jack* 162). Havard played several other important literary roles. He wrote two important memoirs: a description of Lewis, published in *Remembering C. S. Lewis: Recollections of Those Who Knew Him*, and a description of Tolkien, published in *Mythlore*. Havard also offered significant encouragement to Lewis as he was writing The Chronicles of Narnia, and the second book in that series, *Prince Caspian*, is dedicated to Havard's daughter Mary Clare.[24]

GUESTS AND GATE-CRASHERS

Casual visitors were uncommon in the seventeen years the Inklings met. Attendance was by invitation only, and there was a fixed procedure for inviting and introducing new people. Warren Lewis writes, "Someone would suggest that Jones be asked to come in of a Thursday, and there could be either general agreement, or else a perceptible lack of enthusiasm and a dropping of the matter" ("Memoir" 33–34). It is a common misconception that C. S. Lewis was the only Inkling responsible for identifying and inviting potential members to the meetings. There are many examples that demonstrate otherwise. In this description of the membership procedure, Warren Lewis makes it clear that anyone could suggest a potential invitee, and the group as a whole provided endorsement.

Any violation of this rule of general consensus resulted in open hostility. Those who came to meetings uninvited were called gate-crashers, those who brought unannounced visitors were severely criticized, and those who had the nerve to elect themselves members were considered completely out of line. On one occasion, Warren Lewis was outraged when Tolkien brought an unwelcome guest: "J and I much concerned this evening by the gate crashing of B; Tollers, the ass, brought him here last Thursday, and he has apparently now elected himself an Inkling. Not very clear what one can do about it" (*Brothers* 194).[25]

Tolkien violated protocol more than once, for shortly after this offense, Warren Lewis reports, "Tollers, to everyone's annoyance, brought a stranger with him, one [Gwyn] Jones, professor of English at Aberystwyth" (*Brothers* 200). This time, though, the stranger "turned out to be capital value; he read a Welsh tale of his own writing, a bawdy humorous thing told in a rich polished style which impressed me more than any new work I have come across for a long time" (200).[26]

Another occasion did not end as happily. According to Daniel Grotta, "Barfield made the mistake of presuming to bring a friend along unannounced—a serious *faux pas* that almost broke up the group when some members approved and others disapproved of the new candidate." Ultimately, "The man was never invited back" (93).

Roy Campbell, a poet who had fought with Franco in the Spanish civil war, was an invited, though volatile, guest. Campbell had made a name for himself as a professional jouster and bullfighter. He met Lewis, Tolkien, and Williams in the Eagle and Child pub on 3 October 1944. The conversation was spirited, and Campbell was invited to join them for an Inklings meeting that Thursday. His poetry, political views, and religious perspectives caused quite a stir.[27]

E. R. Eddison also met with the Inklings. He is best known for *The Worm Ouroboros* (1922), an epic fantasy admired by a number of the Inklings. In addition to his work in fantasy fiction, Eddison shared another interest with the Inklings: he loved Old Norse mythologies in the original languages. Among other accomplishments, he translated *Egil's Saga* from Icelandic into English.[28]

On 17 February 1943, Eddison attended a Wednesday-night dinner party with several members of the group. They talked and read manuscripts late into the night; their interaction was a great success.[29] Eddison returned on 8 June 1944 and joined the Inklings for a Thursday night meeting. He read from a new story called *The Mezentian Gate*. Tolkien, in particular, thought highly of the work, saying it was "of undiminished power and felicity of expression" (*Letters* 84). On 18 August 1945, Eddison died of a sudden heart attack. Although *The Mezentian Gate* was never completed, it was published, and C. S. Lewis wrote a blurb for the cover. In it, he calls Eddison's work "a new literary species, a new rhetoric, a new climate of the imagination." Lewis continues, "These books are works, first and foremost, of *art*. And they are irreplaceable."

CHARLES WILLIAMS

Charles Williams was a latecomer to the Inklings, arriving some six or seven years after meetings had been established. Still, he was one of its most important and influential members. Williams was born and raised in London, and, in contrast to the other Inklings, he was unabashed in his strong preference for city life. He worked as an editor at the London office of the Oxford University

Press. Despite his demanding schedule as a senior literary editor and his work as a literary adviser and anthologist, Williams was a prolific writer. He wrote seven books of poetry, four books of criticism, four of theology, seven biographies, seven novels, and dozens of plays, articles, and book reviews.

John Wain exclaims, "Williams! How many people have tried to describe this extraordinary man, and how his essence escapes them!" (*Sprightly* 147). Wain is right: Williams is very difficult to characterize. A short piece published in 1947 calls him a "poet, mystic, scholar and novelist," and offers the following apt description:

> Williams . . . brought the same intense generosity, integrity and fierce honesty to everything he touched. His lectures, that had something of prophetic utterances about them, were always crammed to the back of the hall, while he waved his long arms at a crowd of dons and undergraduates. He gave one the impression of being able to see heaven and hell quite as plainly as the Bodleian and St. Mary's, was a learned authority on the Black Arts and on salvation, and wrote as no other novelist has ever done of the terror to be found in a soul's self-damnation. . . . He was an astonishing and a very great figure to find in a world that for the most part lacked his double vision, and the seven novels are only a small part of what he left behind; writing of this kind will never be repeated, and the reading of his books is a disturbing experience which should not be missed. (Jones 120)

Descriptions of Williams as intense, honest, fierce, disturbing, astonishing, and prophetic are repeated in one form or another by everyone who he met. His coworker at the press, Gerard Hopkins, emphasized the strength of Williams as a transforming *presence*. By the "sheer force of love and enthusiasm," Williams was able to change the ordinary, everyday workplace into something extraordinary ("Charles Williams" ii). Carpenter explains that Williams had an unusual capacity for friendship: "At a first meeting he would talk as if he had known you for years, and as if it were the most natural thing in the world to discuss poetry or theology with you" (*Inklings* 86).

C. S. Lewis's friendship with Williams began with a serendipitous exchange of their works.[30] In 1935, Lewis completed *The Allegory of Love*, his first significant book of scholarship.[31] He submitted the manuscript to Oxford University Press. Charles Williams read the proofs and was quite enthusiastic about it. This is not surprising. As Knight observes, Williams "found in this scholarly work on the Romantic Tradition in literature an answering chord to his own ideas on romantic theology" (8).

At the same time that Williams was reading *The Allegory of Love*, Lewis happened to be reading a copy of Williams's novel *The Place of the Lion*. Lewis loved the book and wrote a fan letter to Williams on 11 March 1936 to tell him so. He begins his letter somewhat hesitantly, then breaks into unabashed enthusiasm: "A book sometimes crosses ones path which is so like the sound of ones native language in a strange country that it feels almost uncivil not to wave some kind of flag in answer. I have just read your *Place of the Lion* and it is to me one of the major literary events of my life" (*Collected Letters* 2: 183). Lewis continues, noting that there are four things he really appreciates about the book: the pleasure of reading a good fantasy novel, the exploration of real philosophical and theological content, great characters, and "substantial edification" (2: 183). Lewis is impressed not only with the presence of these features, but also the skillful way they are handled. He adds with considerable admiration, "Honestly, I didn't think there was anyone now alive in England who could do it" (2: 183).

Following his personal introduction and enthusiastic praise, Lewis concludes his letter with an invitation, offering both a warm welcome and a very fine description of the Inklings: "We have a sort of informal club called the Inklings: the qualifications (as they have informally evolved) are a tendency to write, and Christianity. Can you come down some day next term (preferably *not* Sat. or Sunday), spend the night as my guest in College, eat with us at a chop house, and talk with us till the small hours. Meantime, a thousand thanks" (*Collected Letters* 2: 183–84). Williams responded the next day, expressing his surprise: "If you had delayed writing another 24 hours our letters would have crossed. It has never before happened to me to be admiring an author of a book while he at the same time was admiring me. My admiration for the staff work of the Omnipotence rises every day" (qtd. in Lewis, *Collected Letters* 2: 184).[32]

Williams answered Lewis's praise for *The Place of the Lion* with praise for *The Allegory of Love*, writing, "I regard your book as practically the only one that I have ever come across, since Dante, that shows the slightest understanding of what this very peculiar identity of love and religion means" (qtd. in Lewis, *Collected Letters* 2: 184). Williams makes it clear that he is particularly drawn to Lewis's interest in both love and religion, romance and theology, two of the most important ideas that occupy his own thinking.

When Lewis and Williams met shortly thereafter, they greatly enjoyed each other's company. They made it a point to get together several times a year. Lewis writes that his friendship with Williams "rapidly grew inward to the bone" (*Essays Presented* viii). Their friendship meant a great deal to both of them. Lewis tries to explain the effect that Williams had on others in the following colorful description: "He is . . . of humble origin (there are still traces of cockney in his voice), ugly as a chimpanzee but so radiant (he emanates more *love* than any man I have ever known) that as soon as he begins talking . . . he is transfigured and looks like an angel" (*They Stand* 500–501). Lewis uses this image more than once, with this clarification: "not a feminine angel in the debased tradition of some religious art, but a masculine angel, a spirit burning with intelligence and charity" (*Essays Presented* ix).

In 1939, at the start of World War II, Oxford University Press moved its London offices to Oxford for safety. Williams moved with the Press, though his wife and son remained in London. It wasn't long before he became a regular, active member of the Inklings. Though Williams had a profound impact on the group as a whole, he and Lewis enjoyed a particularly strong connection. Lewis describes him as "my great friend Charles Williams, my friend of friends, the comforter of all our little set, the most angelic" (*Collected Letters* 2: 652). In the following tribute, Lewis captures the versatility and vigor of an Inklings meeting and the important part Charles Williams played:

> [Williams's] face—angel's or monkey's—comes back to me most often seen through clouds of tobacco smoke and above a pint mug, distorted into helpless laughter at some innocently broad buffoonery or eagerly stretched forward in the cut and parry of prolonged, fierce, masculine argument and "the rigour of the game."
>
> Such society, unless all its members happen to be of one trade, makes heavy demands on a man's versatility. And we were by no means of one trade. The talk might turn in almost any direction, and certainly skipped "from grave to gay, from lively to severe": but wherever it went, Williams was ready for it. (*Essays Presented* x–xi)

In the Inklings, substantial intellect, enormous talent, and powerful personality met. And Williams was completely at home in the center of it all.

RITUAL AND ROUTINE

As the group grew, the members fell into a regular habit of Thursday evening meetings. They gathered in Lewis's rooms at Magdalen College, a setting that Carpenter describes as "rather bleak":

> The main sitting-room is large, and though certainly not dirty it is not particularly clean. . . . [Lewis] never bothers with ashtrays but flicks his cigarette ash . . . on to the carpet wherever he happens to be standing or sitting. He even absurdly maintains that ash is good for carpets. As

for chairs—there are several shabbily comfortable armchairs and a big Chesterfield sofa in the middle of the room—their loose covers are never cleaned, nor has it ever occurred to Lewis that they ought to be. Consequently their present shade of grey may or may not bear some relation to their original colour. (*Inklings* 128)[33]

Members would arrive sometime after dinner, usually around 9:00 P.M. According to Warren Lewis, "There was a tacit agreement that ten-thirty was as late as one could decently arrive." Meetings of the Inklings followed a simple structure, and "the ritual of an Inklings was unvarying."[34] When half a dozen members had arrived, Warren Lewis would produce a pot of very strong tea, the men would light their pipes, and C. S. Lewis would say, "Well, has nobody got anything to read us?" Then "out would come a manuscript, and we would settle down to sit in judgement upon it" ("Memoir" 33–34).

The range of texts read aloud at Inklings meetings was rich and remarkable. Tolkien read *The Lord of the Rings.* He also shared original poetry, excerpts from *The Notion Club Papers,* and sections from *The Hobbit.* Williams read each chapter from "The Noises That Weren't There" and *All Hallows' Eve,* as well as his Arthurian poetry and an occasional play, including *Seed of Adam* and *Terror of Light.* Lewis read *Out of the Silent Planet, The Great Divorce, The Problem of Pain, Miracles,* and others, many of them chapter by chapter as they were written. He read poetry, including "Donkey's Delight," and, at one point, a long section of his translation of Virgil's *Aeneid.*[35] He also read *The Screwtape Letters* to the group, and, according to Havard, "They really set us going. We were more or less rolling off our chairs" (qtd. in Hooper, *Through Joy* 89).

Other members of the group attended less frequently and contributed less often. Nevill Coghill and Adam Fox read poetry, the former light lampoons and the latter more serious lyrics. David Cecil read excerpts from his book *Two Quiet Lives,* a literary study of Dorothy Osborne and Thomas Gray. Colin Hardie read a paper on Virgil. Owen Barfield read a short play on Jason and Medea.[36] John Wain read a number of his own poems and his book on Arnold Bennett.[37]

During the years the Inklings met, Warren Lewis began to write books about seventeenth- and eighteenth-century France, exploring in particular the reign of Louis XIV.[38] His book *The Splendid Century* has become a standard text in its field. The Inklings observed that Warren Lewis often provided the best and most thought-provoking material read at Inklings meetings.

Listening to drafts and offering energetic feedback occupied the better part of every Inklings meeting. Warren Lewis makes it clear that the Inklings were unbiased in their judgments, observing, "We were no mutual admiration society: praise for good work was unstinted, but censure for bad work—or even not-so-good work—was often brutally frank" ("Memoir" 34). Havard adds, "Criticism was frank but friendly. Coming from a highly literate audience, it was often profuse and detailed" ("Philia" 351).

There is nothing unusual about such a procedure. Walter Hooper notes that this habit of reading papers aloud and submitting them for comment was typical of Oxford clubs. He writes, "The usual practice in most Oxford societies—literary or otherwise—is for the speaker to *read a paper*. It is, I think I can safely say, as much the expected thing that a speaker will have a paper to read to his audience as that a student will have an essay in his hand when he goes to a tutorial" ("Martlets" 40).

Extensive reading, careful listening, and thoughtful critique marked these weekly meetings. Tolkien expressed heartfelt appreciation for the liveliness and candor of the group, noting that even though the discussion often became heated, he felt safe from "contention, ill will, detraction, or accusations without evidence" (*Letters* 128).

Tuesdays at the Bird and Baby

One way to get a clearer picture of the nature of the Inklings is to contrast these Thursday meetings at Magdalen with other, more informal gatherings that took place throughout the week. On the one hand, the Thursday writers' group might be described as the defining event or effective center of gravity of the Inklings. It is what catalyzed their identity, defined their membership, justified their name. The focus of the Inklings as a group is quite specific. On the other hand, the activity of the Inklings as members is quite diffuse. They met in smaller clusters to discuss literature, trade manuscripts, give advice, or collaborate on projects at other times throughout the week. They saw one another in many other venues: for lunch, dinner, or beer; on walking tours through the English countryside; for feasts and special events, such as occasional ham suppers and the special weekend celebration to toast the end of the war. Although the Thursday group was fairly stable and predictable, a network of friendships preceded these Thursday meetings and continued long after the regular meetings ended. Their literary influence flourished in many ways and diverse places throughout the years they met.[39]

Of these subsidiary meetings, the best known was the gathering on Tuesday mornings, notable and regular enough to be mentioned in a detective novel by Edmund Crispin.[40] They met at an Oxford pub named the Eagle and Child, though it has long been referred to as the "Bird and Baby" by those who frequent it. These meetings were open and public. Warren Lewis makes it clear that they were separate from and secondary to the Thursday writers group ("Memoir" 35). He also writes, "Of course there was no reading on Tuesday" (qtd. in Duriez and Porter 8). Carpenter makes it clear that "talking, rather than reading aloud, was the habit at these morning sessions in a pub" (*Inklings* 185). And Wain takes pains to contrast the "more serious Thursday evenings" with what he calls the "purely convivial meetings in an Oxford public-house on Tuesdays at mid-day" (*Sprightly* 179).

Nathan Starr attended one of the Tuesday meetings. Recalling it years later, he, too, emphasizes its informality:

> During that evening [Lewis] told me about a gathering of friends he attended regularly at a pub in the town. He asked if I would join him at their next session. Would I indeed!
>
> At noon on the day set I presented myself at a pub called The Eagle and the Child, the name vividly illustrated by a large sign on which was painted Ganymede being borne aloft by the eagle of Zeus. . . . I entered, and after ordering my pint of bitter at the bar, I was directed to the parlor, which the proprietor had set aside for the gathering of Lewis and his friends. . . . The conversation at The Bird and Baby was rather casual and general; I do not recall any sustained serious discussion. It was almost entirely informal, friendly talk among men of like vocations and interests. (122)

Unlike the Thursday meetings, this get-together at the pub can, indeed, be accurately described as just a gathering of friends, an opportunity for informal friendly talk, an assembly of those who had much in common and much to share. Tuesday meetings at the Eagle and Child developed a reputation for being quite boisterous, partly as a result of Lewis's exuberance, partly the equally dynamic presence of men like Dyson, Coghill, and Williams.[41] James Dundas-Grant, one of the lesser-known members of the Inklings, emphasizes the drama and the energy: "We sat in a small back room with a fine coal fire in winter. Back and forth the conversation would flow. Latin tags flying around. Homer quoted in the original to make a point." Even Professor Tolkien, often pictured as reserved and reflective, joined in the fray by "jumping up and down, declaiming in Anglo-Saxon" (371).[42] Lewis wondered what other people made of it all, suggesting, "The fun is often so fast and furious that the company probably thinks we're talking bawdy when in fact we're v. likely talking Theology" (*They Stand* 501).

CONCLUSIONS

As seen in the next chapter, a number of controversies and disagreements have arisen about the nature of the Inklings. But the vitality, intellectual rigor, and intensity of interaction are never in doubt. And the Inklings themselves are clear and unequivocal in their frank appreciation for the group. Warren Lewis calls the Inklings "a famous and heroic gathering" ("Memoir" 33). He describes the talk, particularly his brother's, as "an outpouring of wit, nonsense, whimsy, dialectical swordplay, and pungent judgement such as I have rarely heard equalled" (34). Havard echoes Warren Lewis's sentiment, observing, "The talk was good, witty, learned, high-hearted, and very stimulating" ("Philia" 352). John Wain, generally quick to carp and criticize, says of the Thursday meetings, "The best of them were as good as anything I shall live to see" (*Sprightly* 184).

C. S. Lewis is similarly effusive in his appreciation of the Inklings and their impact. In an almost wistful description directly referring to the Inklings, he asks, "Is any pleasure on earth as great as a circle of Christian friends by a good fire?" He further emphasizes their significance, saying, "What I owe to them all is incalculable" (*Collected Letters* 2: 501). Tolkien expressed his appreciation for the group with characteristic artistry and enthusiasm, writing in imitation of his beloved *Beowulf:* "Hwæt! we Inclinga, on ærdagum searoþancolra snyttru gehierdon." Carpenter provides this translation: "Lo! we have heard in old days of the wisdom of the cunning-minded Inklings." The translation continues, "how those wise ones sat together in their deliberations, skillfully reciting learning and song-craft, earnestly meditating. That was true joy!" (*Inklings* 176).

NOTES

1. This is not the first time that an Inkling saved a Lewis manuscript from the rejection heap. Years earlier, Heinemann had rejected Lewis's long narrative poem *Dymer.* Then Nevill Coghill read it and liked it and gave it to a friend who worked for J. M. Dent. Dent accepted it and published the poem in 1926.

2. Christopher Tolkien says that his father and Lewis became the nucleus of the Inklings, asserting, "It was the profound attachment and intimacy between him and Lewis, [which] was, I think, in some ways the real core of it" (*A Film Portrait*).

3. Joe R. Christopher argues that even though Lewis had an early bias against philologists, he himself had "all the necessary ingredients to be a philologist" (*C. S. Lewis* 30). *Studies in Words* is Lewis's most philological work, though the tendency is evident in *Reflections on the Psalms* and also in his literary criticism. Christopher emphasizes that all of the Inklings "tended in the same direction," and that Barfield and Tolkien published extensively in that field:

Owen Barfield began his authorial career (outside of a children's book and some works in journals) with *History in English Words* (1926) and *Poetic Diction* (1928). Among his later essays are "The Meaning of the Word 'Literal'" (1960) and a small book, *Speaker's Meaning* (1967), which takes its title from a passage in [Lewis's] *Studies in Words* (chap. 1, sec. 4). Likewise, Tolkien produced *A Middle English Vocabulary* (1922), "Some Contributions to Middle-English Lexicography" (1925), "The Name 'Nodens'" (1932), "'Iththlen' in *Sawles Warde*" (1947, in collaboration with S. R. T. O. d'Ardenne), and "Middle English 'Losenger'" (1953). (30)

4. In Lewis's letters and diaries, he generally abbreviates "should," "would," and "could" as "shd," "wd," and "cd." Sometimes he uses a period with these abbreviations; sometimes he does not. His usage is inconsistent but generally clear, so I have let these abbreviations stand as they are in the original text.

5. This quotation is taken from Carpenter's interview in *J. R. R. Tolkien: An Audio Portrait*.

6. Tolkien calls this "the chief of the stories of the *Silmarillion*, and the one most fully treated" (*Letters* 149). In this story, Beren, a mortal, falls in love with Lúthien, the most beautiful and beloved of the elven maidens. The poem tells of Lúthien's choice to relinquish her immortality and commit herself to Beren, a choice echoed in the love story of Arwen and Aragorn in *The Lord of the Rings*. Tolkien drew on a number of personal details in crafting this love story.

7. Farrell explains the importance of this kind of careful reader: "A respected peer who serves as admiring but demanding audience can be a powerful stimulus to creative work. When the mirroring other takes the creative person seriously, attends to small advances, and responds with appreciative criticism, the person becomes more centered and invests more in the creative process" (283). This accurately describes the Inklings in general and Lewis's impact on Tolkien in particular.

8. See chapter 5 for a detailed look at Lewis's comments and Tolkien's revisions to this important poem.

9. For a skillful account of Lewis's accomplishments as a poet, see Don W. King's *C. S. Lewis, Poet*.

10. David Downing's *The Most Reluctant Convert* provides a detailed discussion of Lewis's faith journey.

11. Henry Victor Dyson Dyson, known as Hugo, taught at the University of Reading 1924–45 and Merton College, Oxford, 1945–63. His attendance at Inklings meetings was sporadic through both periods. Still, he had a strong affinity to this intellectual community and had a significant impact on the group due to his unusual strength of character. James Houston observes, "If you think that Lewis was witty and loquacious and always said the last word, you should have seen Dyson. . . . The wittiness, the intense enthusiasm of the man—he was alive to life in a remarkable way" (131).

12. Knight claims that this event, the participation of Tolkien, Dyson, and Barfield in Lewis's conversion, represents the most significant influence of any Inkling upon another. He explains his view in the following lengthy but insightful passage:

[Tolkien] had a profound effect upon Lewis, for it was his insistence on the importance of myth that helped to convert Lewis to Christianity. That is, through the realisation that in the Christ story ancient myths of the saviour hero, sacrificed for the sake of the people, descending into the underworld, and then arising reborn to return to the abode of the gods, had become actually enacted in history. This immediate argument was supported by another friend, Hugo Dyson, and also by Owen Barfield, who, following the teachings of Rudolf Steiner, believed that in the Incarnation of the Christ, something had happened to the soul of the Earth that marked a cosmic event of enormous magnitude. Thus in addition to the later impact of his own work, it could be said that without Tolkien there might well have been no C. S. Lewis as Christian apologist and writer of the science or children's fiction! (112)

13. One of Warren Lewis's most enduring delights was life at the Kilns. He writes, "The view from the cliff over the dim blue distance of the plain is simply glorious" and "the eight acre garden is such stuff as dreams are made of" (*Brothers* 58). George Sayer elaborates: "Both brothers loved the estate almost ecstatically. Warren called it 'a veritable garden of Eden, a lotus island, a faerie land, or any other term that will express sheer loveliness.' Jack loved to wander through the woods during every season of the year and always wrote about the estate idyllically" (*Jack* 143).

14. Warren Lewis worked on these family papers for about four years, roughly from 1930 to 1935 (Kilby and Mead 46). They included transcriptions of letters, diary entries, poems, stories, and various personal and public documents, all carefully edited. He added interpretive commentary in-between these excerpts. He compiled eleven volumes in all, calling them *Lewis Papers: Memoirs of the Lewis Family, 1850–1930*. The original is housed at the Marion E. Wade Center, Wheaton College, Wheaton, Illinois; microfilm copies are housed at the Bodleian Library, Oxford, and the Southern Historical Collection in Chapel Hill, North Carolina.

15. Mitzi Brunsdale affirms that the name "Inklings" is suitable for this group primarily because all of the members were writers, but she points out another facet: this name "also suggests the Old Norse 'Yngling,' the name for a member of the ancient royal Scandinavian dynasty which claimed descent from the fertility god Yng" (170). Though it is unlikely that the Inklings placed much significance on this tenuous connection, they probably enjoyed this remote link with northernness.

16. In light of the central place writing held, it is unfortunate that the literature on the Inklings tends to emphasize discussion and conversation rather than writing. Kilby claims that the Inklings "was primarily a friendship" (*Tolkien* 67). McClusky states that the group was founded to "discuss literature" (35). Knight defines them as "an informal society that used to meet for convivial discussion" (1). Sebastian Knowles writes, "These men shared a willingness and ability to discuss any subject whether under the sun or not" (132). Hooper says, "The Inklings were a group of friends who met regularly over beer and pipes in Lewis's college rooms" (*Mark vs. Tristram*). Carpenter claims, "They were no more (and no less) than a number of friends, all of whom were male and Christian, and most of whom were interested in literature" (*Tolkien* 149). Melanie M. Jeschke writes, "The meetings often had no other agenda than good conversation and rich fellowship" (xvii). Most wrongheaded of all, Lin Carter remarks, "It was the pleasant custom of the Inklings to read aloud from their current works-in-progress whenever the conversation lagged" (*Imaginary* 111). All of these authors, and a significant majority of others who write about the Inklings, put conversation front and center, and relegate original manuscripts to the margins.

17. Tolkien's incomplete novel *The Notion Club Papers* is published in *Sauron Defeated*, volume 9 of *The History of Middle-earth*. For further discussion of this work, see chapter 7, "Referents."

18. The earliest known contemporary reference to the Inklings appears in a letter from C. S. Lewis to Charles Williams dated 11 March 1936, inviting him to attend a meeting of the group (*Collected Letters* 2: 183–84).

19. Farrell emphasizes the importance of pairs or dyads to the identity and productivity of small groups. He writes, "Regardless of group size, as knowledge of one another's values, abilities, and personalities deepens, each member is likely to pair off and work more closely with one other person. . . . Most episodes of creative work occur within these pairs" (22–23). Citing such important collaborators as Monet and Renoir, Davidson and Tate, and Conrad and Ford, he writes, "Most of the fragile insights that laid the foundation of a new vision emerged, not when the whole group was together, and not when members worked alone, but when they collaborated and responded to one another in pairs" (114). He elaborates:

> This kind of interpersonal environment seems to nourish creative work for two reasons. First, for each member of the pair, the attentive support from an idealized partner releases

the energy and courage to explore one's most tentative ideas. Being taken seriously by an idealized friend leads one to take one's inner world more seriously. . . . Second, thinking aloud together, the collaborative partners draw on one another's memories, ideas, and thought processes. . . . Sharing one another's "hard drives" and "software," the members of the pair develop solutions to problems that neither would have conceived alone. (285)

Lewis also understood the importance of dyads. In *The Four Loves,* he writes, "What we now call 'the Romantic Movement' once *was* Mr. Wordsworth and Mr. Coleridge talking incessantly (at least Mr. Coleridge was) about a secret vision of their own" (68).

20. See the appendix for biographical and bibliographical information on each of these nineteen members.

21. It has been mistakenly thought that Dorothy L. Sayers, author of detective stories, plays, and theological works, was one of the Inklings. She was not, though she knew a number of the members well. She was friends with Charles Williams, and he was the one who introduced her to Dante's *Divine Comedy.* When she began her translation of this work, she wrote to Williams, saying, "I have embarked upon an arduous enterprise for which you are entirely responsible" (Sayers, *Letters* 3: 45).

Sayers also knew C. S. Lewis and Joy Davidman. Davidman's son Douglas Gresham has noted, "Dorothy Sayers and Jack (and my mother) were good friends, and one of the rare times I saw Jack deeply upset (other than his grief for my mother) was when he received the news that Dorothy had died" (MereLewis Listserve Archives, 27 June 1996 14:47:41). In 1963, when Lewis was asked which Christian writers had helped him most, he named four: G. K. Chesterton, Edwyn Bevan, Rudolf Otto, and Dorothy L. Sayers ("Cross-Examination" 260).

Despite their sympathy of interest and outlook, and her close friendship with Williams and Lewis, Sayers never met with the Inklings as a group. As Ruth Cording makes clear, "Certainly no woman entered this strictly male bailiwick" (44). This fact has led some to criticize the group and accuse it of misogyny, notably Fredrick and McBride in *Women among the Inklings.* However, it is worth emphasizing that single-sex groups were a long-established fact of Oxford life at that time. Derek Brewer's description of men's self-improvement groups in Oxford emphasizes the point: groups such as the Inklings "depend on a profound sense of masculine comradeship, engendered in worlds in which women could not by definition in those days enter: the fighting services, Oxford and Cambridge colleges, rugby teams, pubs with 'gentlemen only' snugs [private back rooms], and so forth" (147).

Though Sayers was not an Inkling, she did actively participate in the Socratic Club along with a number of the Inklings: C. S. Lewis (who served as president for thirteen years), Charles Williams, Owen Barfield, Gervase Mathew, and R. E. Havard. This Oxford group was founded in order to provide a forum for atheists and Christians to publicly debate the Christian religion. They met each Monday on campus during term time, and Lewis presided over "more than 200 meetings" of the club (Mitchell, "University Battles" 330).

Sayers addressed the Socratic Club on 3 June 1954 with a paper entitled "Poetry, Language, and Ambiguity." This paper was later published in *The Poetry of Search.*

22. Oral History Interview with R. E. Havard, conducted by Lyle W. Dorsett for the Marion E. Wade Center (26 July 1984), page 15.

23. Havard not only was a gifted reader, writer, and supporter of his friends' work but also had a propensity for attracting nicknames. Lewis dubbed him "the Red Admiral" (for the color of the beard he wore while in the navy), and Tolkien and the others frequently refer to him as "U. Q.," short for "useless quack." Dyson called him Humphrey or Honest Humphrey. This is not only the most common of his numerous nicknames, but it is also the one Lewis chose when he included Havard as a character in *Perelandra.*

24. A wonderful letter from Mary Clare Havard about The Chronicles of Narnia can be found on pages 758–59 of Walter Hooper's *C. S. Lewis.*

25. Characteristically, Warren Lewis uses nicknames here. The Lewis brothers commonly referred to Tolkien as "Tollers." Tolkien himself signed most of his personal letters "Ronald," particularly in his later years. From childhood, Lewis had disliked the name "Clive." At the age of three, he "suddenly announced that his name was 'Jacksie' and refused to answer to any other. Shortened to Jack, this was the name by which he was always known to his close friends" (Sayer, *Jack* 15). In Warren's diary, this is further shortened to "J."

26. The word "bawdy" has caused some misunderstanding. Here and elsewhere, the word does not refer to off-color, explicitly sexual, or obscene material but to "old-fashioned barrack-room jokes and songs and puns" (Carpenter, *Inklings* 55). C. S. Lewis believed that in order to be acceptable, "bawdy must have nothing cruel about it" and "must not approach anywhere near the pornographic." He adds, "Within these limits I think it is a good and wholesome *genre*" (*Collected Letters* 2: 28).

27. Tolkien describes the encounters with Roy Campbell at some length in a letter to his son Christopher dated 6 October 1944, concluding, "It is not possible to convey an impression of such a rare character, both a soldier and a poet, and a Christian convert" (*Letters* 96). Lewis's *Collected Poems* includes two poems written to him: "To the Author of *Flowering Rifle*" and "To Roy Campbell" (79, 80–81). For more information, see Joe R. Christopher's "Roy Campbell and the Inklings."

28. The full title of Eddison's translation is *Egil's Saga: Done into English out of the Icelandic with an Introduction, Notes, and an Essay on Some Principles of Translation.*

29. A brief discussion of Eddison's dinner party with the Inklings on 17 February 1943 can be found on pages 553–54 of volume 2 of C. S. Lewis's *Collected Letters.* His invitation to attend a Thursday night Inklings meeting can be found on page 613.

30. In the dedicatory letter to *A Preface to Paradise Lost,* Lewis tells Williams, "Far from loving your work because you are my friend, I first sought your friendship because I loved your books" (v).

31. Before Williams and Lewis met, Williams contributed at least one significant change to this text. Lewis had originally titled the work *The Allegorical Love Poem,* but the staff at OUP observed that the word "allegorical" tended to "put people off," and they urged Lewis to change it. Lewis suggested a number of alternatives, including *The House of Busirane.* The publishers, "including Charles Williams," chose *The Allegory of Love* instead (Green and Hooper 134–35).

32. Throughout his life, Williams referred to God in terms of his attributes, including the Omnipotence, the Mercy, the Protection, the Permission, and the One Mover.

33. In *Organizing Genius,* Bennis and Biederman point out that shabby surroundings are the norm, not the exception, in the groups that they studied: "For reasons still to be discovered, creative collaboration seems to be negatively correlated with the plushness of the office or the majesty of the view. Awful places have come to be seen as almost a requisite for a Great Group" (127).

34. Warren Lewis's use of the word "Inklings" in this fashion is typical: he does not generally say "We had an Inklings meeting" but rather "We had an Inklings" or else refers to an event as taking place "at an Inklings." Here and elsewhere, I have retained his idiomatic usage.

35. According to Carpenter, Lewis's translation of *The Aeneid* was never published (Tolkien, *Letters* 440). In *The Christian Century* (6 June 1962), Lewis mentions *The Aeneid* as one of the top ten books that most shaped his vocational attitude and philosophy of life. The other nine are *Phantastes* by George MacDonald; *The Everlasting Man* by G. K. Chesterton; *The Temple* by George Herbert; *The Prelude* by William Wordsworth; *The Idea of the Holy* by Rudolf Otto; *The Consolation of Philosophy* by Boethius; *Life of Samuel Johnson* by James Boswell; *Descent into*

Hell by Charles Williams; and *Theism and Humanism* by Arthur James Balfour (Ford, "Books" 103–4). It is interesting to note that one of the ten books on the list was written by fellow Inkling Charles Williams.

36. Barfield's play *Medea* was never published. In "Owen Barfield: A Short Reading List," Rateliff describes it as "A play of which little is known other than that Barfield read it to the Inklings, who highly approved of the work" (25).

37. There is no evidence that Hugo Dyson, one of the most dynamic and outspoken members of the Inklings, ever read any text at these meetings. But we do know that C. S. Lewis read the proofs of *Augustans and Romantics,* a book Dyson wrote in collaboration with John Butt. In a letter written to his brother, Lewis says *Augustans and Romantics* is "almost too bright, but some of the sparks are admirable" (*Collected Letters* 1: 989).

38. Lewis writes, "My brother's lifelong interest in the reign of Louis XIV was a bond between Williams and him which no one had foreseen when they first met. Those two, and Mr. H. V. D. Dyson of Merton, could often be heard in a corner talking about Versailles, *intendants,* and the *maison du roy,* in a fashion with which the rest of us could not compete" (*Essays Presented* v–vi).

39. The Inklings enjoyed significant interaction with other prominent writers of their day. W. H. Auden met Charles Williams through their mutual affiliation with Oxford University Press, and while Auden had little sympathy for Williams's *Taliessin* poetry, he was enthusiastic about *The Figure of Beatrice,* Williams's study of Dante. He considered *The Descent of the Dove* to be Williams's masterpiece, and he wrote the introduction for the Living Age Books edition. Auden also admired Tolkien and wrote two enthusiastic reviews of *The Lord of the Rings* for the *New York Times.*

Another writer known to the group was William Butler Yeats. Lewis met him on several occasions. In the preface to *Dymer,* Lewis admits, "The physical appearance of the Magician in vi. 6–9 owes something to Yeats as I saw him" (6). Some have speculated that the appearance of Merlin in *That Hideous Strength* is also based in part on Yeats (see, for example, Carpenter, *Inklings* 157). For more information on their interaction, see Joe R. Christopher's "From the Master's Lips."

The Inklings also knew T. S. Eliot, who was a great admirer of Charles Williams. Several scholars have done excellent work on the important parallels between Eliot and Williams, including Suzanne Bray, David W. Evans, David Lenander, Janet Matthews, Charles Moorman, Rossell Hope Robbins, and Lois G. Thrash.

40. Bruce Montgomery wrote nine detective novels under the pen name Edmund Crispin. In *Swan Song* (also published as *Dead and Dumb*), a detective named Gervase Fen is enjoying a beer at the Eagle and Child when he remarks, "There goes C. S. Lewis. . . . It must be Tuesday" (60). Three pages later, Fen observes "There goes C. S. Lewis again" (63).

41. An accurate view of Lewis's emphatic personality helps clarify the nature of these meetings. Luke Rigby observes, "[Lewis] was a man with friends—this is well known. Though I was in a different league, I know why he had friends. The kindness, the sensitivity, the zest for life, the fun, the deep sense of humour, the seriousness, the depths, the unexpectedness—they combined to make a man who was exhilarating to be with" (114).

Rigby and others who knew Lewis are completely consistent in their description of him as a hearty, robust, spirited, and exuberant man. Green and Hooper observe, "Whether one had read any of his works or not, the first sight of C. S. Lewis was always a surprise." They continue, "There strode in a big man with a large red face and shabby clothes, looking like nothing so much as a prosperous butcher, who began addressing his audience in a loud, booming voice and with tremendous gusto" (140).

Others who knew Lewis also place particular emphasis on the fact that he was a living contradiction to the stereotypical image of an Oxford academic. Peter Philip, for example, observes, "When I went up to Oxford I had certain fixed ideas about how a don should look—elderly, thin, pale, austere, scholarly and rather aloof. Lewis, therefore, came as a shock" (93). W. R. Fryer also contrasts Lewis with the pale and quiet presence of an earlier era. Given such firmly entrenched expectations, Fryer emphasizes, "After too many people like this, it was both a shock and an excitement to find the already famous Mr. Lewis . . . whose face was brilliant with color, whose voice was deep and loud, whose greeting was positively enthusiastic, whose step was firm and noisy . . . who used to carry all this formidable apparatus of masculinity right into the College Chapel and right into the near proximity of God's altar; to be its own self there, just as much as anywhere else" (34).

Whether we are trying to picture Lewis in particular or the Inklings in general, these descriptions serve as a useful corrective. It is common to associate university men and scholarly writers like the Inklings with a certain asceticism and stiff decorum. These descriptions of Lewis—burly, loud, merry, and brilliant—not only help us to picture Lewis more accurately, but also help us to capture the electric atmosphere of a typical Inklings meeting.

These descriptions also offer a useful corrective to the formal, stiff, and staid Lewis portrayed by Anthony Hopkins in the 1993 film *Shadowlands*. As Sayer observes, "C. S. Lewis was quite unlike the person described in some recent biographies and hardly to be recognized as the man depicted in *Shadowlands* and other films"—more helpful details about Lewis as a person can be found in Sayer's article "C. S. Lewis: The Man" in Schultz and West, *The C. S. Lewis Reader's Encyclopedia,* pages 246–47.

42. Those who have difficulty picturing the "reserved" Professor Tolkien carrying on like this would do well to look at the description offered by his children in *The Tolkien Family Album.* There John Tolkien and Priscilla Tolkien emphasize that both of their parents "had a gift for enduring friendships" (67). In fact, Tolkien was so sociable that he had a bit of trouble as a student: "Back at college the next term it became clear that Ronald's great sociability and extra-curricular university activities were resulting in neglect of his studies. As well as playing rugby, and being a member of the college Essay Club, the Dialectical Society, and the Stapeldon (the college debating society), he also started his own club—the Apolausticks—devoted to 'self-indulgence'" (*Tolkien Family Album* 32). Tolkien was the member of a great many groups throughout his life, and he was the founder or organizing force for most of them.

Another account of Tolkien's exuberance is given by Nevill Coghill, who reports, "In his Valedictory Lecture he entered the lecture-hall shouting, in full spate, the opening lines of *Beowulf:* 'HWAET, We Gardena in geardagum / theodcyninga thrym gefrunon / hu tha aethelingas ellen fremedon.!'" ("John Ronald" 31).

2

Influence
Assessing
Impact

*Charles Williams certainly influenced me and I
perhaps influenced him.*
  —C. S. Lewis

We owed each a great debt to the other.
  —J. R. R. Tolkien, writing of C. S. Lewis

We are necessary to each other.
  —Charles Williams

*When a tree grows by itself it spreads out, but does
not grow tall. When trees grow together in the for-
est, they help push each other up towards the sun.*
  —Buddhist Monastic Saying

The Inklings met as a writing group for about seventeen years, starting early
in the 1930s. The end of the group was as gradual and unremarkable as its beginning. By 1945, the year Charles Williams died, the group had begun to slip
away from its moorings. Reading and critiquing manuscripts had become less
central, and their focus and purpose had become less clear. Vitality declined,
and attendance faded. Then, without fanfare, meetings simply came to a halt.
On Thursday, 27 October 1949, Warren Lewis wrote in his diary, "Dined with
J at college. . . . No one turned up after dinner, which was just as well, as J has
a bad cold and wanted to go to bed early" (*Brothers* 230, ellipsis in the original). It was the end of the Thursday night Inklings, but only the beginning of
controversy about the nature and significance of the group. Many of the key
disputes were waged while most of the members were still alive, and so the
Inklings themselves were drawn into battle.

In 1959, Marjorie Wright completed the first extended treatment of the
Inklings, a doctoral dissertation at the University of Illinois.[1] The early date of
her work is significant: Wright completed her research only ten years after the
group folded, and only four years after *The Return of the King* was published.

In her dissertation, Wright emphasizes the conformity of the members. She explains, "The similarity is one not only of idea and theory but of common atmosphere. They belong to, indeed have made, a common world, a world of myth" (11). She further argues that "the mythic realms mapped out by Lewis, Williams, and Tolkien . . . all follow basically the same pattern" and she explains that this is to be expected given "the similar orientation of the three Mythmakers" (65).

In an article written in 1961, W. R. Irwin follows a comparable path. He describes the work of the Inklings as "essentially uniform," and he puts a great deal of emphasis on their common source material (577). As one reads the Inklings, he argues, one perceives a "steady flow" of the following source materials: "Neo-platonic, Hermetic, Teutonic, Scandinavian, Nibelung, Arthurian, Celtic, Anglo-Saxon, Paracelsian, Miltonic, Swedenborgian, Blakean, Rosicrucian associations are liberally to be found. Likewise echoes of Novalis, William Morris, George Macdonald, H. Rider Haggard, Maeterlinck, Wells, Chesterton, Arthur Machen, Rex Warner, and Kafka" (575).

This view of the Inklings as a fairly uniform group with common ideas, theories, moods, created worlds, approaches, patterns, and sources intensified when John Wain published *Sprightly Running: Part of an Autobiography* in 1962. Wain had been a student at Oxford, and C. S. Lewis had been his tutor. At Lewis's invitation, Wain attended Thursday night Inklings meetings "for two or three years," roughly from 1946 to 1949 (*Sprightly* 179).

In his book, Wain claims that group members shared one single outlook. He writes, "The group had a corporate mind," a mind both "powerful" and "clearly defined." And its nature? "Politically conservative, not to say reactionary; in religion, Anglo- or Roman Catholic; in art, frankly hostile to any manifestation of the 'modern' spirit" (*Sprightly* 180–81). Wain takes the matter a step further and claims that the group's strong focus was not only radical but quite intentional. He describes the Inklings as "a circle of instigators, almost of incendiaries, meeting to urge one another on in the task of redirecting the whole current of contemporary art and life" (181).

Lewis read *Sprightly Running,* and he was outraged. He published a rebuttal in *Encounter,* seeking to set the record straight. Lewis states in no uncertain terms, "The whole picture of myself as one forming a cabinet, or cell, or coven, is erroneous. Mr. Wain has mistaken purely personal relationships for alliances" ("Wain's Oxford" 81). Lewis's attitude toward such things could not be more clear, for elsewhere he writes, "I hated the Collective as much as any man can hate anything" (*Surprised* 173).[2] As seen in chapter 1, the claim that the Inklings gathered together under the banner of some "incendiary" purpose cannot be substantiated. The Inklings were not men of one mind, they did not subscribe to an overarching purpose, and they did not envision themselves as the leaders of a countercultural revolution.

But despite Lewis's emphatic protests, early writers continued to portray the Inklings as a homogenous group, a "cabinet" or "corporate mind" with a clear and reactionary purpose. For example, in 1964 Roger Sale followed closely in John Wain's footsteps, using the terms "coterie" and "cult" freely in his article about the literary techniques used by the Inklings.[3] His article is highly critical. He refers to Lewis as an "amateur" and calls the Ransom trilogy "tinny and preacherly" (209–10, 208). He denounces *The Lord of the Rings*, and he concludes his cutting remarks with this comment: "Tolkien is very fond of these cozy little people with their tobacco and beer and good humor" (217). Even though Sale is clearly referring to Tolkien's hobbits, one gets the impression that he is attempting to characterize Tolkien and the Inklings as cozy and insular as well.

The tendency to describe the group in terms of uniformity reached its peak in 1966 when Charles Moorman published *The Precincts of Felicity: The Augustinian City of the Oxford Christians*. Moorman surveys the "common ground" inhabited by Lewis, Tolkien, and Williams, summarizes "the major themes and images of each," and charts "the lines of influence among them." In his conclusion, he affirms uniformity in unequivocal terms, writing, "One is impressed again by just how much these writers have in common and by the degree to which their expressions of their mutual concerns resemble one another" (137).

In early 1967, Warren Lewis took Moorman to task. He writes, "One Mr. Moorman whom I remember as an occasional correspondent of [Jack's] has sent me his book, *The Precincts of Felicity,* a critique of the works of Charles Williams, CSL and Tollers." Warren Lewis quickly shifts from describing the book to evaluating it: "It is not a stupid book, nor a dull one, but I think a silly one" (*Brothers* 268). He criticizes Moorman on a number of points. For one thing, he finds the label "Oxford Christians" misleading.[4] He does not deny the fact that a common Christian faith played an important role in the nature of the group, affirming that Moorman is literally correct in that the Inklings "nearly all lived in Oxford and were all believers" (268). As we have seen, C. S. Lewis made a similar observation in his first letter to Charles Williams, telling him that the informal "qualifications" of the Inklings were "a tendency to write, and Christianity" (*Collected Letters* 2: 183). Another member of the Inklings, David Cecil, has also emphasized that "this religious aspect is most important" in understanding the nature of the group (Trickett and Cecil 563).

But despite its appropriate emphasis on the role of Christian faith, Warren Lewis argues that calling them "The Oxford Christians" is problematic. It isn't that the phrase overemphasizes the importance of faith to the group's *identity,* but that it misrepresents the role of faith in the group's *purpose.* He tells us that the name "strikes a wrong note at the outset by suggesting an organized group for the propagation of Christianity" (*Brothers* 268). Again, even though the creative and compelling expression of their Christian convictions was important to each one of the Inklings, the group as a whole had no such unified purpose.

Warren Lewis summarizes his critique of Moorman as follows: "His thesis is that in the Inklings a kind of group mind was at work which influenced the writing of every Inkling, and this he supports by assertions which seem to me very shaky." Then he quips, "I smiled at the thought of Tollers being under the influence of Moorman's group mind, and think of sending him the book" (*Brothers* 268). Warren Lewis, like his brother, rejected the idea of the Inklings as a homogenous circle; apparently Tolkien did too.

THE INKLINGS: VERY DIFFERENT

In Inklings Studies, the tide turned in the late 1970s when Humphrey Carpenter published *The Inklings: C. S. Lewis, J. R. R. Tolkien, Charles Williams, and Their Friends.* Carpenter makes it clear that his book about the Inklings is, in part, a response to an inappropriate emphasis on similarity. Carpenter writes: "When some years later it was noted that *The Lord of the Rings, The Screwtape Letters,* and *All Hallows' Eve* (to name but three of many books) had this in common, that they were first read aloud to the Inklings, it became something of a fashion to study the writings of Lewis, Tolkien, and Williams on the assumption that they were members of a clearly defined literary group with a common aim" (xiii).

Carpenter's collective biography is a deliberate attempt to disprove the "fashionable tendency" of authors who, like Wain, Wright, Irwin, Sale, and Moorman, treat the Inklings as a uniform, unified literary group. Not surprisingly, his book is filled with phrases that emphasize contrast. Carpenter states again and again that there is scant resemblance among them, that they have very little in common, and that on nearly every issue they stand far apart from one another. In contrasting the Christian experience of C. S. Lewis and Owen Barfield, for example, he says their differences are "profound" (*Inklings* 155). In describing the academic life of these men, he says, "Their forms of expertise could scarcely have been more different." In examining the literary scholarship of Williams and Lewis, Carpenter observes that it is "surprisingly hard to find any similarity" and "their attitudes reveal themselves as fundamentally different" (156). In discussing their view of the magical, he says, "[Williams] and Tolkien had nothing whatever in common" (157). Positioning himself in direct opposition to those who stood before him, Carpenter argues that the group had neither a reactionary purpose nor a unified set of convictions. To look for such things, he writes, is to seek "a fox that isn't there" (154).[5]

It is difficult to overstate the impact of Carpenter's conclusions on the field of Inklings Studies. Verlyn Flieger offers the following summary:

> Much of the early criticism of *The Lord of the Rings* was marked by a tendency to link Tolkien with [C. S. Lewis and Charles Williams]—his fellow Inklings and Oxford companions. The basis of this seems to have been their known friendship with one another, their shared Christianity, and superficial similarities in their use of fantasy as a fictional mode. The critical impulse was to link all three as religious fantasy writers with a common goal, a kind of unofficial Christian brotherhood of craftsmen. That this was never the case is made plain by Humphrey Carpenter, who devotes a chapter of his book on the Inklings to investigating, carefully considering, and finally dismissing the idea. (*Splintered* xvii–xviii)

Inklings scholars continue to weigh in on this debate. Most follow closely after Carpenter and emphasize fundamental differences among the members. This approach has much to recommend it. Carpenter is right, it seems, in downplaying the idea of a deliberate and unified goal or purpose. He is also wise to stress that in matters of faith, academic specialty, and literary taste, and in their views on myth, magic, and the occult, there are notable, even irreconcilable, differences.

On the other hand, one of the results of Carpenter's approach is to perpetuate an unnecessary and somewhat misleading debate. Are the Inklings mostly alike? Are they mostly different? Are their similarities more significant than their differences? Are their differences more significant than their similarities? The inevitable outcome is a debate between those who assert that there are more (or more significant) similarities, and those who assert that there are more (or more significant) differences. It creates an endless circle.

But similarities and differences are important aspects of the Inklings, and both contribute to the coherence and effectiveness of the group. The Inklings shared a passionate concern for a rather unusual constellation of interests: Christianity, myth, imaginative literature, linguistics, and history.[6] However, within each of these interests, they held very different points of view. The dynamism and, to some extent, the longevity of the group depended upon the dramatic tension between their common interests and their contrasting opinions. To say the Inklings were close friends despite their differences or to say they were effective collaborators despite their differences is to deny a fundamental truth:

these connections are generally effective as a direct result of personal differences. In other words, these cooperative relationships thrive because of the ways in which opposites attract and then enhance one another.

Lewis elaborates this very idea in *Surprised by Joy*. He starts by expressing warm appreciation for a "First Friend," the one who shares all of your "most secret delights." With this kind of like-minded person, "there is nothing to be overcome in making him your friend; he and you join like raindrops on a window" (199). But in addition to the treasured "First Friend," Lewis expresses far greater enthusiasm for what he calls a "Second Friend": "He has read all the right books but has got the wrong thing out of every one. It is as if he spoke your language but mispronounced it. . . . When you set out to correct his heresies, you find that he forsooth has decided to correct yours! And then you go at it, hammer and tongs, far into the night, night after night, or walking through fine country that neither gives a glance to, each learning the weight of the other's punches" (199–200). There could hardly be a better description of the fierce intensity and critical engagement that characterized the members of this group. Lewis concludes his reflection on friendship with a statement which might be considered an epigraph for the Inklings themselves: "Out of this perpetual dogfight a community of mind and a deep affection emerge" (200).

This idea of a varied, dynamic, effective community describes the Inklings; it is also a key concept that the Inklings expressed in their fiction. In his novel *That Hideous Strength,* Lewis creates a lively and diverse household, alternately referred to as a company, society, organization, and army. It includes professors, students, housewives, gardeners, jackdaws, cats, angels, a bear, the Fisher King, and even Merlin himself. But the household Lewis describes at the Manor at St. Anne's is only one such example. As Nancy-Lou Patterson explains, "Clearly, this company [at St. Anne's] is like the Fellowship of the Ring in Tolkien's great work *The Lord of the Rings,* with its elf, dwarf, wizard, hobbit, and human members ranged against the awesome power of Sauron, and like the Company of Logres in Charles Williams' Arthurian poem cycle, *Taliessin through Logres* (1938) and *The Region of the Summer Stars* (1944)" (247). Each group is made up of distinct individuals, clearly joined together into effective communities. In each case, the parts work together *because* they are different, not in spite of their differences. Her summary is illuminating. Patterson writes, "The collection of differing, even ill-fitted parts to create a coherent whole is a figure for the body, in which each part differs and is meaningless on its own, but is indispensable to the whole" (247–48). She connects this imagery to the description of the Christian church in the New Testament, where unity—one body, one spirit, one hope—is made possible through a diversity of gifts and abilities.[7]

As the Inklings worked together, their differences in personality, perspective, and creative gifts stimulated fresh thought, encouraged risks, and inspired
new directions. Their differences brought their personal convictions into
sharper relief and allowed them to articulate these distinctions with greater
strength and clarity. As Havard emphasizes, "Our differences laid the foundation of a friendship that lasted, with some ups and downs, until [Lewis's] death
nearly thirty years later" ("Philia" 350). The point is clear—Havard does not
say that similarities formed a foundation that allowed friendship to thrive in
spite of their many differences. He says the differences themselves were the
foundation.

In one of his letters, Lewis contrasts his own "bow-wow dogmatism" with
Barfield's "dark, labyrinthine pertinacious arguments" (*Collected Letters* 2:
572). We could add to his list Warren Lewis's generous hospitality, Dyson's
unrestrained exuberance, Havard's thoughtful attentiveness, Tolkien's gentle
precision, and Williams's dramatic intensity. These personality differences
became even more pronounced over time.[8] In these descriptions, we see the
concept of diversity within unity. And we see a spirit of playfulness, even
celebration, in the way these differences are described.

FINDING THE RIGHT FOX

This synthetic view—a diversity of perspectives within a unity of interests—
provides a clearer picture of the nature of the Inklings. It also sets the stage
for a closer look at the nature of influence among the members. Influence
Studies, too, have been subject to a limiting preoccupation with similarity.
Scholars who want to discover where and how the Inklings influenced one
another often start by examining two texts that seem to have something in
common. For example, they may compare Tolkien's *Ainulindalë* side-by-side
with Lewis's *The Magician's Nephew*. Or perhaps they will contrast Barfield's
History in English Words with Lewis's *Studies in Words*. Or they might compare
the choices made in two collections: J. A. W. Bennett's *Poetry of the Passion*
and Charles Williams's *The Passion of Christ*.

In searching for literary influences, scholars typically examine the works and
ask, "Does Author B do the same thing as Author A?" They look for ways these
authors use the same techniques, employ the same images, follow the same patterns, use the same style, rely on the same sources, take the same approach, or
make the same point. In *Critical Terms for Literary Study*, a standard reference
text, Louis A. Renza explains that literary influence is generally discerned by
"spotting certain thematic likenesses or disclosing related verbal patterns" (187).

Renza says that finding this kind of similarity serves as the starting point and initiates the enthusiasm for discussions of literary influence, and it has done so throughout "a major portion of Western literary history" (187).

There is no question: it is exciting to discover similar themes or similar images or similar forms of expression between two texts. In his book on C. S. Lewis, Joe R. Christopher identifies a large number of connections between the works of Lewis and those of Tolkien: both authors refer to "orcs" (*C. S. Lewis* 24); both describe loud drums booming through large caves (97); both "used images of far mountains as a symbol of Heaven" (105); both have a main character who is "met by a shepherdlike guide" (105); both describe God singing the world into existence (111); both refer to a gold tree and a silver tree present at creation (112); and both use walking trees to conclude a battle (115). He also notes a number of characteristics common to Williams and Lewis, including a specific instance of "painters discussing the painting of light," and a reference to the exact same phrase from the Athanasian Creed (105, 61–62).

It does not take much effort to find dozens of other examples. Owen Barfield uses the phrase "daughter of Eve" in a poem entitled "Hagar and Ishmael," and Lewis uses the same phrase throughout The Chronicles of Narnia. Charles Williams wrote a poem entitled "Witchcraft" in which a devil prays to "Our Father who wert in heaven" (*Windows of Night* 114); Lewis wrote *The Screwtape Letters* from one devil to another, full of references to "Our Father Below." To some critics, the most striking examples of similarity in the works of the Inklings can be found in their use of titles and names. Tolkien had a fictional inn at Bree and Lewis a fictional horse named Bree. Tolkien wrote a poem called "The Nameless Land," and Lewis wrote a poem called "The Nameless Isle." Adam Fox published *Old King Coel,* and Lewis published "Young King Cole." Barfield wrote a book called *The Silver Trumpet,* Williams wrote *The Silver Stair,* and Lewis wrote *The Silver Chair.* The names of Lewis's characters Rabadash and Glimfeather of Narnia sound a lot like the names of Tolkien's characters Radagast and Glorfindel of Middle-earth. In the Ransom trilogy, Lewis's Elwin, Eldil, Tor, and Tinidril seem to echo Tolkien's Ælfwine, Eldar, Tuor and Idril.

Identifying this kind of similarity serves as a useful starting point and may lead to a fruitful line of inquiry. However, as these varied examples suggest, this method of comparing texts and finding similarities creates a number of problems. For one thing, any measure of similarity is by nature highly subjective. As Göran Hermerén makes clear, "Our knowledge and expectations determine what similarities (or differences) we notice" (62). Furthermore, even if one is drawn to some apparent point of similarity, how can it be measured with accuracy? How much significance does it deserve? What "weight" should be assigned to it? (62). Finding correspondences and quantifying them with precision is a demanding process.

Another challenge complicates things even more. Studies based on this method of research tend to focus on the small and particular: specific images, common characters, parallel events, invented names. Weightier issues such as purpose, theme, technique, and the like are much harder to compare by looking at textual features side by side. Charles Moorman offers this word of warning: "All too often, studies [of influence] are notable only for the amount of irrelevant minutiae they are able to uncover" (*Precincts* 4).

These problems are by no means insurmountable. Careful scholars have studied the Inklings and identified similarities in larger, more substantial matters. They note the way Lewis incorporates Williams's views of substitution and exchange, or how Tolkien makes use of Barfield's theories of language.[9] They have articulated common themes such as co-inherence, common imagery such as the use of the myth of Arthur, and common plot elements such as the invasion of the supernatural world into the natural world. They have found many common sources, including the Orpheus myth, Norse tales, *Beowulf*, children's books, and fairy stories.

For the student of literary influences, noting resemblances between texts is just the beginning. Having found similarities, small and large, and demonstrated that they are in some way substantial and significant, the next task is to establish causation. As Joe R. Christopher is quick to emphasize, "literally, no number of parallels can prove an indebtedness" (*C. S. Lewis* 118). Other questions must be addressed. Can it be shown that the composition of one work clearly preceded composition of the other? The problem of timing is more difficult to prove than one might think, for publication date is not the same as composition date, and confusing the two causes serious difficulties. Lewis offers this compelling example: "Many reviewers said that the Ring in Tolkien's *The Lord of the Rings* was suggested by the atom bomb. What could be more plausible? Here is a book published when everyone was preoccupied by that sinister invention; here in the centre of the book is a weapon which it seems madness to throw away yet fatal to use. Yet in fact, the chronology of the book's composition makes the theory impossible" ("Modern Theology" 160).

Chronology is one complicated issue, contact is another. Can it be demonstrated that an author had access to another author's work? Here, Lewis's book *The Screwtape Letters* provides us with an interesting illustration. In 1772, a Baptist minister named John Macgowan published a book called *Infernal Conference; or Dialogues of Devils*. It is written entirely from a devil's point of view, and in it, one devil is the uncle of another.[10] Did Lewis know about this book? Is this where his idea for *The Screwtape Letters* came from? It certainly seems likely. But there is no record that Lewis was aware of it.[11] Contact has not been established. In fact, Lewis's account of the conception of *The Screwtape Letters* emphasizes the complete spontaneity of his idea:

> I have been to Church for the first time for many weeks owing to the illness, and considered myself invalid enough to make a mid-day communion. . . . Before the service was over—one cd. wish these things came more seasonably—I was struck by an idea for a book wh. I think might be both useful and entertaining. It wd. be called *As One Devil to Another* and would consist of letters from an elderly retired devil to a young devil who has just started work on his first "patient." The idea wd. be to give all the psychology of temptation from the other point of view. (*Collected Letters* 2: 426–27)

If it is true that Lewis was completely unaware of Macgowan's work, how does one explain the striking similarities in these two books? Hermerén points out that any number of explanations may be offered when similarities are discovered:

> In that case the similarities noticed between *X* and *Y* may depend on the fact that the two artists who created *X* and *Y* depict or describe similar objects or events; or that they illustrate the same story or text; or that they express similar feelings, emotions, or moods; or that they are working in the same genre or with the same material (clay, marble, and so forth); or that they have had similar experiences in the past; or that they have had the same or similar background (training, education, and so forth); or that they are living in the same political, social, or intellectual milieu. (222)

Similarities of subject, mood, material, or context account for many instances of overlap. Frequently, similarities between texts simply indicate that both authors have been influenced by another, different source. Warren Lewis was well aware of this possibility, and expressed it in his critique of Charles Moorman: "What he chiefly harps on is their common belief that there is a transitional state between death and our resurrection. Thus [Jack] 'borrowed' the framework of his *Great Divorce* from Charles's *All Hallows' Eve* and so on" (*Brothers* 268). Warren Lewis dismisses all of this by pointing out that believing in this kind of transitional state is not in any way unique to the Inklings. He scoffs, "Just as if this speculation about a transitional state must not have occurred to hundreds of Christians who didn't even know of each other's existence" (268). C. S. Lewis and Charles Williams did not get the idea of a transitional state between death and heaven from one another; they were both influenced by the same Christian tenet.[12]

Other examples are easy to find. Lewis's Psyche and Tolkien's Gandalf sacrifice their lives and then later reappear. Both authors are using a sacrifice, death, and resurrection motif quite common in Christian and pagan mythologies. Furthermore, Lewis, Barfield, and Williams all write of large, symbolic lions. The idea of the lion as an embodiment of strength and royalty is very common, and Christ is designated "Lion of the tribe of Judah" in Revelation 5:5. In each of these instances, the Inklings are probably referring back to these sources, and not to one another.[13]

There are many different ways to explain the similarity between two works, including the possibility of sheer coincidence. In short, two artistic works may show marked similarities, and yet there may be absolutely no relationship between the two, nor any direct influence.

To complicate matters, the opposite is also true. Two literary works may be very different from one another, and yet one may be clearly and directly influenced by the other. For example, when *Out of the Silent Planet* by C. S. Lewis is compared to *A Voyage to Arcturus* by David Lindsay, it is difficult to find any significant parallels. The books are very different in style, tone, imagery, philosophy—in fact, in nearly every way imaginable. Despite these radical differences in the final product, we know that *A Voyage to Arcturus* influenced Lewis because he tells us that it completely transformed his thinking. Lewis recognizes his debt to Lindsay and calls him "the real father of my planet books." Lewis continues, "It was Lindsay who first gave me the idea that the 'scientifiction' appeal could be combined with the 'supernatural' appeal." This is not to say that Lewis completely agrees with Lindsay's approach. He hastens to label Lindsay's own spiritual outlook "detestable, almost diabolist." Still, Lewis explains, "He showed me what a bang you cd. get from mixing these two elements" (*Collected Letters* 2: 630). The case of Lewis and Lindsay further illustrates that the search for influence must be more than a simple search for similarity.

NEGATIVE INFLUENCE

We've seen some of the limits of similarity as a measure of influence. Two works may be alike, yet unrelated; two works may be quite different, yet closely tied. Another complication is presented by the possibility of negative influence, that is, a situation where one work is created in deliberate opposition to another. Clearly, in such a case the end products will be very different. Hermerén gives the following illustration to help readers understand how negative influence

works: Suppose an artist visits an exhibition of paintings, and he strongly dislikes the work he sees. He leaves the exhibition agitated and angry, and then
"he walks home and makes some paintings in protest" (48).

Individual artistic works, comprehensive artistic series, even entire artistic
movements have been created through this kind of direct, even hostile, opposition to the work of others. Such "reaction against" is also a common trait
of collaborative circles. Farrell explains that, especially in the early stages of a
circle, the members are "deliberately provocative toward those in authority"
(14). This reaction is clearly a form of influence, and yet it does not result in
work that is imitative or similar.

Negative or reactive influence can happen in a number of ways, both large
and small. Much of Lewis's critical work is reactive or remedial in impulse.
A Preface to Paradise Lost and *An Experiment in Criticism,* for example, are
each presented as correctives to prevailing theories. *The Pilgrim's Regress* is
reactive in many senses of the word. And the first third of *The Abolition of
Man* is presented as an explicit counter-argument to the position of "Gaius
and Titius," authors of what he calls *The Green Book.*[14]

We see this same impulse in Lewis's poetry as well. Lewis had a strong
preference for traditional poetic forms; he expressed contempt for modern
poetic trends in general and free verse in particular.[15] Reacting against the
mainstream, Lewis redoubled his efforts to show the value of traditional forms,
and he made a conscious decision to write and publish more poetry using
them.

One place where this is particularly evident is in a poem called "Spartan
Nactus."[16] Don W. King calls this poem Lewis's "sharpest attack on modern
misuse of language." Lewis writes in rhyming couplets, using this traditional
form "as his platform from which he attacks modern poetry, particularly that
of T. S. Eliot" (*Poet* 182). In part, the poem reads,

> For twenty years I've stared my level best
> To see if evening—any evening—would suggest
> A patient etherized upon a table;
> In vain. I simply wasn't able. (*Collected Poems* 15).

In his commitment to traditional poetic forms in general and in his composition of this poem in particular, Lewis was working in opposition to other
writers, and, therefore, was influenced by them.[17]

In the context of the Inklings as a group, one clear example of negative
influence is described by Robert Murray. He explains that when Tolkien gave
him a copy of *Smith of Wootton Major,* Tolkien described the story as "a little

counterblast to Lewis" (879). This is negative influence: in this instance, Tolkien was influenced by Lewis because he was deliberately reacting against him.

More than Similarity

When we recognize that similarity and influence are not synonymous, it becomes easier to untangle some of the common statements used to downplay any notion of influence among the Inklings. For example, when Hillegas takes pains to emphasize that "each writer is excellent in his own fashion, unique in style and technique," he is not denying influence per se (xii). He is simply saying that these writers are not the same. Ready's comment that "the differences between these men are far more important than the appearance of their likenesses" makes the same point (37). In fact, many observations by Carpenter, Knight, and other Inklings scholars that seem to deny influence are better understood as comments on similarity or imitation.

More significantly, this awareness helps us to clarify some of the comments that the Inklings themselves make about their mutual influence. For example, when Hooper asked C. S. Lewis "what he thought of the current vogue for tracing the 'influence' of Williams in his work," this is how Lewis replied: "I have never been *consciously* influenced by Williams, never believed that I was in any way imitating him" (qtd. in Green and Hooper 184). Here, Lewis does not deny influence. What he denies is conscious imitation.

The same underlying assumptions are at work in a long letter that Lewis wrote to Charles Moorman. Since this letter addresses the issue of Inkling influence head on, it is often used as the definitive statement on the subject. Lewis recommends that Moorman abandon his planned research project on the mutual impact of the group, explaining that there are only a few meager instances of Inkling influence. But then he concludes, "To be sure, we had a common point of view, but we had it before we met" (*Letters* 481). Throughout this important letter, Lewis has been articulating the limits of their commonality, not the extent of their mutual impact.

Commonality is also the theme of an oft-quoted statement by Tolkien. He writes, "I do not think we influenced one another at all!" His comment seems altogether straightforward, and it is often taken at face value. But this sentence is only the first part of his view on the matter. The complete quotation is as follows: "But I do not think we influenced one another at all! Too 'set,' and too different" (*Letters* 209). Again similarity, not influence, is the issue.

The same pattern is seen as we reconsider Owen Barfield's comment, "What am I supposed to have taught [Lewis]? He continues to deny everything I say!" (*Owen Barfield* 150). Barfield is right: while they learned a great deal from one another, the two men remained different in many of their most central convictions. But that does not in any way disprove strong mutual influence.

MORE THAN A BANDERSNATCH

Distinguishing questions of influence from questions of imitation leads us to a broader sense of what counts as influence.[18] And studying the influence of those who actively participate with one another in the process of creating a work directs us to a more encompassing methodology. Traditionally, when scholars are searching for evidence of influence, they place published texts side by side and compare them. For example, if they want to study the influence of Jack London on Ernest Hemingway, they might begin by looking at a copy of *The Call of the Wild* and comparing it with a copy of *The Sun Also Rises*.[19]

On the other hand, if they want to examine the influence of Gertrude Stein on Ernest Hemingway, different materials and methods are required. Stein writes that she and Hemingway "used to walk together and talk together a great deal" (qtd. in Carpenter, *Geniuses* 68). Their published works are very different, and those who are unaware of their well-documented personal interaction are not likely to make a connection between these two writers. But Stein and Hemingway did walk and talk together, share meals, have drinks, draft creative works in tandem, read their work aloud to one another, and argue late into the night. And in studying this literary relationship and the work of others like them, their interaction itself becomes an informative "text." Source materials such as diaries, journals, letters, and interviews add as much to the study of their mutual influence as do the manuscripts and published works themselves.

In examining these various materials, we find substantial evidence to support Karen Burke LeFevre's assertion that "the thinking and inventing of any man or woman happens in large part because of the ways each has interacted with others and with society and culture" (139). In *Invention as a Social Act*, LeFevre provides a rich theoretical background for studying what happens as texts are created in community. She also provides practical starting points for researchers. In a chapter describing the social aspects of invention, she asserts that "writers often invent by involving other people" (34). Then she articulates four specific roles that are common whenever writers work together. Writers in writing groups function as resonators, opponents, editors, and collaborators.

Resonators

Writers depend on the motivation and encouragement that come from having a supportive, interested audience. LeFevre calls them "resonators."[20] When readers function in this way, they "provide a supportive social and intellectual environment that nurtures thought and enables ideas to be received, thus completing the inventive act" (65). Resonators nourish both the inventor and the project, instilling the writer with self-esteem and encouraging the writer to persist through discouragement, doubt, anxiety, impatience, fatigue, and other obstacles. They praise specific projects and validate creative risks. They may spur one another on, providing pressure to perform, or even engage in healthy competition. They may make specific suggestions that launch a whole new project or give advice that takes a piece in a whole new direction. They may offer practical help, such as financial support or work space or resource materials. Resonators may also serve the important function of encouraging wider distribution of a text, helping the writer make the shift from private to public discourse.

Opponents

Readers may also serve as opponents, expressing disapproval of a premise, a character, an action, or some other aspect of a project. As a result, the work may be altered or even abandoned. On the other hand, such negative influence may motivate writers to dig in their heels and strengthen their resolve on a particular matter, or even react against a comment and move decisively in the opposite direction. At its best, such feedback improves the quality and effectiveness of an author's work. But sometimes healthy criticism erupts into accusations and misunderstandings, resulting in personal conflict and hurt feelings.

Editors

Readers may make specific suggestions that shape the text in a number of ways. They offer ideas, ask questions, give instructions, and in other ways comment upon drafts, which leads to further revision. Editing is especially powerful when writers share their work section by section as they write. Such comments may change minor aspects, such as the name of a character or a feature of the setting or the way a point is phrased. Or they may change major aspects, such as the genre or length of a work, sometimes completely changing the direction, mood, or emphasis of a text. Editors may suggest specific wording that becomes a permanent part of the final text. They may also proofread final drafts, catching errors and making corrections.

Collaborators

When readers serve as either resonators or editors, they offer assistance to an individual who serves as the primary author. In contrast, writers may also influence one another by planning and composing text collaboratively—producing a final text by consensus and publishing it under more than one name. John Trimbur and Lundy A. Braun observe that researchers are starting to uncover more and more examples of collaboration: "The traditional literary view of the single author has obscured the fact that coauthorship is the norm in many academic and professional fields, and . . . investigations have started to chart the ways writing in business, industry, government, the professions, and in technical and scientific research actually gets produced through multiple contributions of individuals in complex divisions of labor" (21). Trimbur and Braun might have noted that coauthorship is also the norm in many literary endeavors. Literary collaborations include coauthoring creative works, scholarly editions, and essay collections. They also include such activities as composing alternate sections of a single poem, creating a serial piece of prose or poetry, writing companion essays, or gathering with a larger circle of writers and publishing an interactive collection.

CONCLUSIONS

LeFevre's model is based on extensive research into theories of language and the behavior of writers in social contexts. Her work provides the framework for answering the questions that initiated this study: What difference did it make that C. S. Lewis, J. R. R. Tolkien, Charles Williams, and the other Inklings wrote in association with one another? What comments, suggestions, connections, ideas, or criticisms did they share with one another? What part did encouragement and criticism play in the completion of their texts? How did their relationship affect the amount of material each man produced? Were there any joint projects or books prepared collaboratively? What impact did they have on the reception of each other's work by those outside their circle?

In the next four chapters, I consider how the Inklings served in reciprocal roles as resonators, opponents, editors, and collaborators. In addition, I discuss some of the varied, interesting, and playful ways the members of the group included one another as characters in their stories, as subjects in their poetry, and as resources for their scholarship. I call this fifth role "referents." Finally, I conclude this book with a chapter on the creative process, affirming a positive approach to influence, clarifying the way the Inklings viewed creativity, and underscoring their deep appreciation for the value of community.

The Inklings were not a cult or a coterie or a cohesive literary movement, but neither were they just a loose-knit group of friends. They were members of a writing group, knowledgeable peers who met on a regular basis to discuss written works in progress. They read their work aloud to one another and offered specific, substantial suggestions. In doing so, they influenced one another and one another's writing.

NOTES

1. Marjorie Wright was killed in an automobile accident in 1959. At the time, her dissertation was "all but completed" and had already been approved by her director, A. Dwight Culler (Milligan). She was awarded her doctoral degree posthumously in May 1960.

2. Owen Barfield elaborates Lewis's attitude toward groups in these comments: "He was not ever interested in collectivity of any sort. It wasn't real to him. He was not interested in races, civilizations as a whole, nations and the differences between them, societies, groups; still less in movements of any sort. He always came back to the individual soul" (*Owen Barfield* 112).

3. Lewis was known to have "a holy terror of coteries" (*Collected Letters* 1: 450). He explains his perspective decisively in this comment from *The Screwtape Letters,* written from one devil to another: "Any small coterie, bound together by some interest which other men dislike or ignore, tends to develop inside itself a hothouse mutual admiration, and towards the outer world, a great deal of pride and hatred which is entertained without shame because the 'Cause' is its sponsor and it is thought to be impersonal. Even when the little group exists originally for the Enemy's [i.e. God's] own purposes, this remains true" (32–33).

4. In an interesting variation on Moorman's attempt to categorize these authors, Joe R. Christopher suggests that C. S. Lewis and Charles Williams, along with Dorothy L. Sayers and Christopher Fry, might be usefully grouped with the Anglican Revival of the early twentieth century, a term "invented to refer to figures like T. S. Eliot, W. H. Auden, and Edwin Muir" (*C. S. Lewis* 129).

5. Having dismissed commonality as the link that binds the Inklings together, Carpenter asserts that Lewis was at the center (171). As I discussed in chapter 1, I am convinced that no individual is the founder or the center of the group. The Inklings grew in the transactional space between Lewis and Tolkien as they shared their original drafts with one another, and the most accurate way to understand the essential nature of the group is not as a circle of friends or a literary movement but as a writing group. For an extended discussion of the mistaken notion that Lewis was the center of the Inklings, see my (forthcoming) article on the Inklings as a model of dialogical mode.

6. An elaboration of this idea is found in "What Makes an Inkling an Inkling?" an unpublished paper presented by Pat Hargis at the Sixteenth Annual Convention of the Mythopoeic Society ("Mythcon"), held 26–29 July 1985 at Wheaton College, Wheaton, Illinois. Hargis writes, "It is not one distinct belief or idea that pulled the Inklings together and distinguished them from all other groups. It was rather their peculiar concern for Christianity *and* myth *and* Romanticism *and* language *and* writing (both scholarly and popular) *and* education, *and,* finally, history that attracted them to one another" (4).

7. Patterson draws primarily from Paul's letter to the Ephesians, particularly chapter 4.

8. A perceptive observation from the five authors of *Habits of the Heart* skillfully expresses this tendency for strong groups to enhance individuality. Robert N. Bellah, Richard Madsen, William M. Sullivan, Ann Swidler, and Steven M. Tipton write,

> The book is the product of all of us, and none of us could have done it alone. But, as subsequent individual monographs should make clear, we have not been homogenized. Each of us has learned to speak better in his or her own voice. Our experience together has confirmed for us one of the central arguments of our book, that the individual and society are not in a zero-sum situation; that a strong group that respects individual differences will strengthen autonomy as well as solidarity.

Based on their research and their collaborative experience, they arrive at this emphatic conclusion: "It is not in groups but in isolation that people are most apt to be homogenized" (307).

Lewis uses different imagery to express a similar notion in *The Four Loves,* observing that each member of a group brings out unique aspects of the others. He writes, "By myself I am not large enough to call the whole man into activity; I want other lights than my own to show all his facets" (61).

9. Those who read even a small selection of work by the Inklings are likely to notice such similarities. Some of the most important ones are the result of insights they learned from one another. The conversation with Tolkien and Dyson that led Lewis to a new understanding of myth is only one example. This is an important aspect of the Inklings dynamic, and one that has received significant attention by scholars in the field. I will return to this subject in chapter 7.

10. *Infernal Conference* purports to be a transcript of a conversation between two devils named Avaro and Fastosus; eventually they are joined by others with names like Infidelis and Discordans. They engage in eighteen dialogues, describing various interactions with humans.

11. Duriez and Porter state with finality that C. S. Lewis "never read" Macgowan's book (151). Lewis does mention "a debt to Stephen McKenna's *Confessions of a Well-Meaning Woman* (1922) which contains 'the same moral inversion—the blacks all white and the whites all black—and the humour which comes of speaking through a totally humourless *persona*'" (qtd. in Hooper, *C. S. Lewis* 269). It is also possible that Lewis was influenced by *Letters from Hell,* a book by Valdemar Adolph Thisted. This book was published in 1887, and it featured an introduction by George Macdonald, one of Lewis's favorite authors. We know that Lewis read *Letters from Hell;* in fact, Lewis wrote to tell Arthur Greeves that he was so disappointed by this book that he donated his copy to a "jumble sale" (*They Stand* 151).

12. One line of influence on Lewis's *The Great Divorce* is clear and well-documented. Hooper records, "In August and September 1931 [Lewis] read the works of the seventeenth-century Anglican divine, Jeremy Taylor. In Taylor's sermon on 'Christ's Advent to Judgement' he came across the idea of the *Refrigerium,*" that is, the idea that souls which are suffering in hell may sometimes have a brief time of "remission and refreshment" (*C. S. Lewis* 279). C. S. Lewis and Warren Lewis both credit Taylor as a source for *The Great Divorce.* As for Taylor, he says he encountered the idea of the *Refrigerium* in the work of Prudentius Aurelius Clemens (279).

13. Other scholars have suggested different explanations for these recurring images. Maud Bodkin, J. G. Frazer, Northrop Frye, Joseph Campbell, Carl Jung, and others have noted the repeated use of archetypes—certain patterns in narrative design, character types, or images—found in literature, myths, dreams, and even in ritualized modes of social behavior. These patterns are pervasive, and they can be found in the work of authors who have no relationship to each other.

Using a different approach, one that highlights a social understanding of the creative act, Silvano Arieti, Charles Edward Gray, Alfred Kroeber, and others have written about the way genius seems to "cluster" at specific points in history, and how certain cultural contexts seem ripe for the discovery of great ideas or the composing of great works. For more on this concept, see especially Arieti's *Creativity.*

14. Hooper identifies *The Green Book* as *The Control of Language* (1940) by Alec King and Martin Ketley (*C. S. Lewis* 331–32).

15. Describing Lewis's poetic tastes, George Sayer writes, "Until very late in his career, he took no interest at all in free verse, and, even then, perhaps only in a little poetry by Edith Sitwell and T. S. Eliot. He tended to regard the new poetry with its formlessness and lack of poetic diction as a revolutionary movement deliberately directed against the traditions of English poetry" (*Jack* 122).

16. "Spartan Nactus" was originally published in *Punch,* December 1954. The title means "Spartan having obtained" (D. King, *Poet* 347). It was retitled "A Confession" and reprinted in *Poems* (1964) and again in *The Collected Poems of C. S. Lewis* (1994), both edited by Walter Hooper.

17. Charles A. Huttar offers a useful discussion of Lewis's response to "The Love Song of J. Alfred Prufrock" in his article "A Lifelong Love Affair with Language."

18. Hermerén believes that the most basic measure of influence is not whether two works are alike, but this more precise formulation: "If X influenced the creation of Y with respect to *a*, then Y is with respect to *a* different from what it would otherwise have been" (246). For Hermerén's discussion of this definition, including its strengths and weaknesses as a model for measuring artistic influence, see chapter 2 of *Influence in Art and Literature.*

19. In *Geniuses Together,* Carpenter says that as a young author, Hemingway "had read scarcely any good modern fiction and knew almost nothing worth imitating other than Jack London's *The Call of the Wild*" (57).

20. LeFevre adopts the term from Harold Lasswell, who articulates this concept in his article "The Social Setting of Creativity."

3

Resonators
Supporting
Progress

Your essay is magnificent.
    —C. S. Lewis to Owen Barfield

This is a thundering good book.
    —C. S. Lewis to Charles Williams

I do like my peers to like me.
    —Charles Williams

*Whenever you write a book, you need
someone to say yes to it.*
    —Gertrude Stein

No matter how accomplished writers become, they still struggle with discouragement. Charles Williams, for one, was well acquainted with disappointment and apprehension. When *All Hallows' Eve* was released, he waited anxiously for the public response. In a letter to his wife, he admits, "The novel really gnaws me. I feel as if everyone would sneer at it. This is silly, because you liked a lot of it, and [T. S. Eliot] liked it, but there it is! You must forgive me and be kind" (*To Michal* 242).

Then, after two weeks of anxious waiting, Williams opened the *Daily Herald* and found an enthusiastic review, written by John Betjeman:

> A book by Charles Williams is an event.
>
> He is considered by some people our greatest living writer. I do not think he will ever be a popular writer, yet I venture to say that his work will go on steadily selling in a century's time when you and I and the book of that title have *Gone with the Wind*.
>
> As it is, he is more talked about in literary circles than he is read. He is uninviting, for his prose style is like glue and you stick fast in it un-

less you exercise the will power that the soaring majesty of his themes demands. The publishers say that *All Hallows' Eve* may be read as an ordinary thriller. I do not think this is so, but I would say that whatever your opinions, if you have a clear brain or one that likes flights of the imagination, this story is worth the effort it demands.

> You will find yourself walking on air and seeing the world in perspective and from a great height. (2)

Williams was greatly encouraged. His book was labeled "an event"; his themes were said to possess "soaring majesty"; and he was referred to as "our greatest living writer." He forwarded a copy of this review to his wife with this note attached: "I send you the *Herald Review*, which has just reached me. I admit that, except for one sentence (and I don't defend the style!), it could hardly be better. . . . All my love, & thank you for supporting *A. H. E.*" (*To Michal* 243–44).

Like Williams, C. S. Lewis also struggled with discouragement. After reviewing the proofs of his narrative poem *Dymer,* Lewis agonized, "I never liked it less. I felt that no mortal could get any notion of what the devil it was all about" (*Letters* 223). He expresses similar doubts early in the writing of *Perelandra,* telling his friend Sister Penelope, "I may have embarked on the impossible" (*Collected Letters* 2: 496). And again, after working for more than ten years on *English Literature in the Sixteenth Century, Excluding Drama,* Lewis confides to an American correspondent, "The book really begins to look as if it might be finished in 1952 and I am, between ourselves, pleased with the manner of it—but afraid of hidden errors." He continues, expressing a foreboding that will sound familiar to every scholar: "A mistake in a history of literature walks in silence till the day it turns irrevocable in a printed book and the book goes for review to the only man in England who wd have known it for a mistake" (*Letters* 415).

Lewis understood anxiety, discouragement, fear, and doubt, and he saw them as inevitable aspects of the creative process. Moreover, he did not attribute this stress and fear to human weakness or devilish interference. Instead, he believed that God is responsible for the fact that disappointment occurs "on the threshold of every human endeavour." He observes, "In every department of life it marks the transition from dreaming aspiration to laborious doing" (*Screwtape* 7). And he firmly believed that the purpose of such strife is to foster personal strength and spiritual maturity.[1]

As these examples from Charles Williams and C. S. Lewis illustrate, the writing life can be an emotional roller coaster ride. The excitement of creating is followed by desperate self-doubt. A bright light of affirmation comes right on the heels of the long, dark night of the soul. Day after day, courage and creativity square off against discouragement and despair. For artists in general and for writers in particular, one of the most valuable resources in the midst of these challenges is the presence of resonators.

The term "resonator" refers to anyone who acts as a friendly, interested, supportive audience. Resonators fulfill many roles: they show interest, give feedback, express praise, offer encouragement, contribute practical help, and promote the work to others. LeFevre stresses that the presence of resonators is one of the most important factors that differentiates the successful writer from the unsuccessful.[2] Without resonators, she says, writers are very likely to succumb to the "dampening influence" of their environment (65). Vera John-Steiner concurs, emphasizing that "creative work requires a trust in oneself that is virtually impossible to sustain alone. Support is critical, as the very acts of imaginative daring contribute to self-doubt" (8).

Resonators function by showing interest in the text—they are enthusiastic about the project, they believe it is worth doing, and they are eager to see it brought to completion. In addition, resonators show interest in the writer—they express confidence in the writer's talents and show faith in his or her ability to succeed. In LeFevre's words, they "nourish and sustain the inventor as well as the invention" (34).

Resonators may read drafts in progress and give feedback about the style or the content. This feedback may be very important; in fact, it may have a transforming effect on the shape and direction of the work. But the primary gift that the resonator gives to the writer is encouragement. Tolkien praises this important gift, expressing gratitude for the role C. S. Lewis played in *The Lord of the Rings*. Tolkien says of Lewis, "He was for long my only audience. Only from him did I ever get the idea that my 'stuff' could be more than a private hobby. But for his interest and unceasing eagerness for more I should never have brought [*The Lord of the Rings*] to a conclusion" (*Letters* 362).

Tolkien uses absolute terms when he describes Lewis's important role as a resonator. Lewis was, Tolkien says, his *only* audience. *Only* Lewis encouraged him to seek a wider audience. Without him, Tolkien asserts, the book would *never* have been written. The critical importance of resonators is worth emphasizing. Writing projects may be slowed, stalled, or even completely abandoned if such support is lacking. This form of influence is more than helpful, handy, or somewhat useful. In many cases, encouragement is absolutely essential to the very existence of the work. Without it, the writer may lack the courage to start or the persistence to finish. As Charles Williams puts it, "If no-one says to [the writer], 'My dear, how marvellous,' he will pretty soon tire" (qtd. in Hadfield, *Charles Williams* 114).

In expressing his gratitude to Lewis, Tolkien does more than underscore the importance of resonators. He also suggests several of their most important functions. Resonators serve as an interested audience. They help move the text from the private to the public sphere. As they eagerly anticipate new chapters, they inspire—or compel—the writer to produce new text in response. And they coerce the writer to bring long-term projects to a conclusion.

PRAISE FOR GOOD WORK

Resonators offer support in a number of forms, and the most obvious is praise. Lewis firmly believed that praise should be an integral part of daily life. He asserts, "All enjoyment spontaneously overflows into praise." He continues, "The world rings with praise—lovers praising their mistresses, readers their favourite poet, walkers praising the countryside, players praising their favourite game—praise of weather, wines, dishes, actors, motors, horses, colleges, countries, historical personages, children, flowers, mountains, rare stamps, rare beetles, even sometimes politicians or scholars." For Lewis, praise is not only a natural part of life but also one of the most important traits of a healthy mind. He observes, "The humblest, and at the same time most balanced and capacious, minds praised most, while the cranks, misfits and malcontents praised least." This attitude is made evident in the most mundane experiences: "The healthy and unaffected man, even if luxuriously brought up and widely experienced in good cookery, could praise a very modest meal: the dyspeptic and the snob found fault with all." He sums it up this way: "Praise almost seems to be inner health made audible" (*Reflections* 94).

Since Lewis viewed praise as an indication of good mental health, it is not surprising that he defined good literary criticism as that which is fundamentally positive: "The good critics found something to praise in many imperfect works; the bad ones continually narrowed the list of books we might be allowed to read" (*Reflections* 94).[3] In many ways, the Inklings cultivated the habit of seeking and supporting what is good. In his description of the group, Warren Lewis asserts, "Praise for good work was unstinted" ("Memoir" 34). His own response to Tolkien's poem "Errantry" illustrates this positive, generous approach. He calls the poem "excellent in itself" and calls the structure "very interesting as being in an entirely new metre." He concludes with enthusiasm: "I think it a real discovery" (*Brothers* 126).

Warren Lewis's response to *The Lord of the Rings*, sometimes called "the new Hobbit," was even more effusive, and it continued over a period of years:

10 October 1946 Tollers continued to read his new Hobbit: so sui generis, so alive with the peculiar charm of his "magical" writing, that it is indescribable—and merely worth recording here for an odd proof of how near he is to real magic. (*Brothers* 195)

24 October 1946 Tollers read us a couple of exquisite chapters from the "new Hobbit." Nothing has come my way for a long time which has given me such enjoyment and excitement; as [Jack] says, it is more than good, it is great. (196–97)

4 July 1947 After dinner I read about half of the batch of [the new] Hobbit which Tollers sent me: how does he keep it up? The crossing of the marshes by Frodo, Sam and Gollum in particular is magnificent. (204)

12 November 1949 The inexhaustible fertility of the man's imagination amazes me. It is a long book, consisting very largely in journeys: yet these never flag for an instant, each is as fresh as the one before, new colours available in profusion, whether the journey be beautiful or terrible. Some of the scenes of horror are unsurpassed, and there is wonderful skill in the way in which the ultimate horror—the Dark Lord of Mordor—is ever present in one's mind, though we never meet him, and know next to nothing about him. The beauty of Lothlorien, and the slightly sinister charm of Fangorn are unforgettable. Frodo's squire, Sam Gamgee[,] and the dwarf Gimli are I think the two best characters. What is rare in a story of this type, is that there is real pathos in it; the relationship between Sam and Frodo in the final stages of their journey moved me greatly. (231)

Praise for stories, poems, plays, and essays is sprinkled throughout the letters and diaries of the Inklings. Their evaluations contain memorable imagery, and some qualify as literary expressions in and of themselves. In a letter to Charles Williams, C. S. Lewis expresses gratitude for the novel *Descent into Hell*. Lewis observes, "In sheer writing I think you have gone up, as we examiners say, a whole class. Chapter II is in my opinion your high water mark so far. You have completely overcome a certain flamboyance which I always thought your chief danger: this is crisp as grape nuts, hard as a hammer, clear as glass." Lewis calls *Descent into Hell* "a thundering good book and a real purgation to read." He adds, "I shall come back to it again and again. A thousand thanks for writing it" (*Collected Letters* 2: 219). In another letter, Lewis characteristically begins with lavish and poetic praise: "Though I have not yet finished it I feel I must write and congratulate you on producing a really great book in your *He Came Down from Heaven*. It is thickly inlaid with patins of bright gold" (2: 227). Lewis goes on to praise specific pages and phrases. He congratulates Williams for "every word on p. 25" (2: 227–28). He praises one sentence in particular, exclaiming, "This is really overwhelming. I honestly think it quite likely that when we are in our graves this may become one of the sentences that straddle across ages like the great dicta of Plato, Augustine, or Pascal" (2: 227).[4] Then there is a clever backhanded compliment: "And it's so *clear,* which at one time I should never have expected a book of yours to be" (2: 228).

Praise was lavishly expressed and gratefully received. Williams clearly appreciated Lewis's enthusiasm—he comments in his letters that Lewis is the one reader who really understands him. He writes, "Lewis says that my last Monday's address on the Comus-Chastity was 'the most important thing that has happened in the Divinity Schools for a hundred years, or is likely to happen for the next hundred'" (*To Michal* 44). It may seem that Williams is exaggerating Lewis's response, but Lewis's own account of the same event suggests that he is not. Lewis describes the event memorably: "On Monday C. W. lectured nominally on *Comus* but really on Chastity. Simply as criticism it was superb—because here was a man who really started from the same point of view as Milton and really cared with every fibre of his being about 'the sage and serious doctrine of virginity' which it would never occur to the ordinary modern critic to take seriously. But it was more important still as a sermon." Lewis continues, describing the effect on the students: "It was a beautiful sight to see a whole room full of modern young men and women sitting in that absolute silence which can *not* be faked, very puzzled, but spell-bound." In an echo of Williams's report of the event, Lewis continues, "It was 'borne in upon me' that that beautiful carved room had probably not witnessed anything so important since some of the great medieval or Reformation lectures." He concludes, "I have at last, if only for once, seen a university doing what it was founded to do: teaching Wisdom" (*Collected Letters* 2: 345–46).[5]

C. S. Lewis writes movingly about Williams on a number of occasions, but he was by no means Williams's only fan. Warren Lewis greatly appreciated him, writing the following letter to him in September 1937, quite early in their friendship:

This letter, though emanating from the above seat of learning [Oxford], is not from Lewis the English Tutor, but from his fat brother,—whom you may remember to have met on a couple of pleasant occasions, and who is glad to hear that there is a prospect of seeing you down here some time this term.

I wanted to tell you how much I have enjoyed "Descent into Hell": though on second thoughts perhaps "enjoyed" is hardly the right word: I should rather say how much I appreciated it. Up to this I have always thought that the death of Sir Giles Tumulty [in *Many Dimensions*] was

your high water mark, but the Descent seems to me far in a way better—it
will be a long time before I forget those footsteps pattering through
Battle Hill at night!!

This gracious and appreciative letter continues with more compliments, balanced with gentle criticism: "The only character whom I thought did not
perhaps altogether pull his weight was the playwright: I don't quite know why,
but he did not seem to me strong enough. All the rest I thought magnificent"
(unpublished letter, 19 October 1937).

Late in his life, at Christmastime in 1967, Warren Lewis notes in his diary
that he had "just finished re-reading Charles's *All Hallows' Eve.*" He remains
quite taken with the work, and writes, "It is so plausible that I found myself
wondering if it could possibly have been written under inspiration; why should
not death be the gradual process which he imagines it to be? Anyway, golly
what a book!" (*Brothers* 267).

Warren Lewis appreciated Williams as an author, and also as a friend.
When Williams died, Warren Lewis expressed his shock: "One often reads of
people being 'stunned' by bad news, and reflects idly on the absurdity of the
expression; but there is more than a little truth in it. I felt just as if I had slipped
and come down on my head on the pavement." In his reflection on this event,
Warren Lewis emphasizes the closeness he felt to Williams: "I knew him better than any of the others, by virtue of his being the most constant attendant.
I hear his voice as I write, and can see his thin form in his blue suit, opening
his cigarette box with trembling hands." Fittingly, he adds, "These rooms will
always hold his ghost for me" (*Brothers* 182–83).

Other Inklings also wrote appreciatively of one another. C. S. Lewis and
Nevill Coghill read one another's poetry and provided detailed feedback. Encouragement played a significant part in their exchange. When Coghill wrote an
enthusiastic response to *Dymer,* Lewis responded to express his gratitude. "My
dear Coghill," he writes, "It is as if you had given me a bottle of champagne—a
dangerous moment and difficult to reply to" (*Collected Letters* 1: 663).

Lewis and Barfield, who had known one another since their days as undergraduates, also exchanged manuscripts and critiques regularly, and these
letters include high praise. In 1930, for example, Barfield sent Lewis an essay,
along with a letter expressing doubts about the work and asking specifically for
some honest feedback. Lewis assured him, "Don't think it has failed either *per
se* or in its effect on me. It is bathed in a golden cloud & drips with honey—well
worth doing a good bit more on" (unpublished letter, dated circa February
1930). Such encouragement is typical of Lewis's feedback to Barfield, which
at times is downright extravagant. For example, when Barfield sent him one

particular draft of a poem, Lewis declared, "I have no doubt at all that you are engaged in writing one of the really great poems of the world" (unpublished letter, dated circa fall 1926).[6]

Barfield himself confirms that Lewis thought highly of his work: "When he read *Saving the Appearances,* he called it a 'stunner'; *Worlds Apart,* when it first came out, he said he found so exciting that he was in danger of reading it too quickly; and shortly before his death, when he was confined to his bed, he wrote to me that the two things that consoled him most were reading that book, *Worlds Apart,* and the *Iliad.*" Barfield adds modestly, "So you see he knew how to couple in a flattering way" (*Owen Barfield* 106).

Not all of their critiques were this effusive, or extensive. When Lewis finished writing a poem called "The Birth of Language," he sent it off to Barfield with a request for feedback, as was his custom. Barfield writes, "I have a very vivid memory of receiving it by post. I was very busy at the time and quite immersed in a non-literary milieu. I seized a postcard, wrote the one word 'Whew!' on it and dropped it in the letter box!" (qtd. in Huttar, "Lifelong Love" 108).

Even though Tolkien was known to grumble, he could also be enthusiastic and generous in his praise of the work of his friends. As we have seen, he wrote two long letters to Stanley Unwin in strong support of Lewis's *Out of the Silent Planet.* Tolkien also respected *Perelandra,* telling his daughter, Priscilla, that he considered it "a great work of literature" (qtd. in Carpenter, *Inklings* 182). Tolkien wrote a long description of Lewis's "Myth Became Fact," praising it highly and calling it "a most interesting essay" (*Letters* 109). He was enthusiastic about *Letters to an American Lady,* saying that he found it "deeply interesting and very moving" (qtd. in Kilby, *Tolkien* 77). He was bothered by *That Hideous Strength,* but he expressed sincere appreciation for it nonetheless. As Carpenter notes, "When Tolkien had heard it right through he remarked that though it was scarcely a proper conclusion to Lewis's trilogy it was certainly 'good in itself'" (*Inklings* 198). Tolkien also called *English Literature in the Sixteenth Century* "a great book," though he qualified it by saying it was "the only one of his that gives me unalloyed pleasure" (qtd. in Sayer, *Jack* 197).

Tolkien's response to C. S. Lewis's work is somewhat mixed, but he had nothing but praise for the writing of Warren Lewis. In his letters, Tolkien calls the histories witty and learned, "very good," and "very amusing" (71, 83, 84). Tolkien admits he is not inherently interested in the subjects that Warren Lewis explores. Even so, he is captivated by the skill and grace of the writing itself.

Tolkien enjoyed the give and take of praise among the Inklings, and he also found praise a beneficial aspect of his spiritual practice. He advises his son Christopher to "make a habit of the 'praises,'" adding, "I use them much (in Latin): the Gloria Patri, the Gloria in Excelsis, the Laudate Dominum; the

Laudate Pueri Dominum (of which I am specially fond), one of the Sunday psalms; and the Magnificat; also the Litany of Loretto (with the prayer Sub tuum præsidium). If you have these by heart you never need for words of joy" (*Letters* 66). In spiritual matters and in literary ones, in corporate gatherings and in private moments, the Inklings appreciated the importance of praise.

All of the Inklings encouraged one another, but Charles Williams seems to have been uniquely gifted as a resonator. John Wain explains, "Williams was a lover and praiser. If he announced a course of lectures on a poet, you knew that you were in for a tremendous paean in praise of that poet. He never tried to point out weaknesses or to cut his subject down to a more manageable scale. If he attempted a 'revaluation,' it was invariably a revaluation *upwards*" (*Sprightly* 150). Dorothy L. Sayers noted much the same quality, writing, "He had the great gift of making every author he touched alive and relevant, so that the great dead were never pushed back into a historical past but remained in his writing quick and vibrating with their own vitality and meaning" (*Letters* 3: 340).

Williams's positive, generous approach was not limited to academic discussions of famous poets. His biographer, Alice Mary Hadfield, explains that Williams had this effect on everyone, whether a stranger at a bus stop or an old, familiar friend. She summarizes his impact as follows: "C. W. could make each one seem important and interesting, a vital gift to most of us, but even more than that, he could make life important and interesting, not some life removed from us by money, opportunity or gifts, but the very life we had to lead and should probably go on leading for years" (*An Introduction* 70). W. H. Auden highlights this again when he says, "In his company one felt twice as intelligent and infinitely nicer than, out of it, one knew oneself to be" (*Descent of the Dove* v).

Williams brought a unique quality of vitality and vision to the Inklings, to the classroom, to personal relationships, and to his workplace. What was the exact nature of this transforming presence? Gerard Hopkins puts it this way: "He found the gold in all of us and made it shine" ("Charles Williams" ii). Although all of the Inklings were quick to praise, Charles Williams charged the very atmosphere with praise and encouragement wherever he went.

PRESSURE AND PERSEVERANCE

Generally, resonators give feedback and provide encouragement in a positive, nurturing way. But there is another mode of encouragement that is more forceful, even coercive, in nature. Caroline Gordon provides an illustration, describing the influence of Ford Madox Ford as follows: "Ford took me by the scruff of the neck . . . set me down in his apartment every morning at eleven o'clock and forced me to dictate at least five thousand words of my novel to him. If I complained that it was hard to work . . . he observed 'You have no passion for your art. It is unfortunate' in such a sinister way that I would reel forth sentences in a sort of panic" (qtd. in LeFevre 69–70). The intimidation described in this situation is unusually severe. Yet this approach is not at all uncommon. Williams, for example, relied a great deal on his wife for this kind of necessary pressure. Separated after his move to Oxford, Williams writes to her admitting, "An infinite distaste of writing is on me." Then he laments, "Why are you not here to give me a cup of tea, & then *make me* do some work?" (*To Michal* 253, emphasis added).[7]

At times a similar dynamic is evident in the interaction between Lewis and Tolkien. Tolkien explains that when he produced text that was not up to par, Lewis would say, "You can do better than that. Better, Tolkien, please!" Tolkien writes, "I would try. I'd sit down and write the section over and over" (*Letters* 376). Lewis admits that his part in Tolkien's writing process often "carried to the point of *nagging*" (qtd. in Kilby, *Tolkien* 76, emphasis added).

Tolkien needed the presence of others in order to keep writing. *The Hobbit* is a prime example. Tolkien drafted most of it in 1930 and 1931. He wrote it rather quickly up to the point where Smaug the dragon is about to die. There he stopped, and the story fragmented into rough notes and remained incomplete. He read it to his sons. He also showed it to C. S. Lewis, who had a "delightful time" reading it and declared that, apart from the rough ending, he thought it "really *good*" (*Collected Letters* 2: 96). Early in 1936, some staff members at Allen & Unwin learned of the unfinished story and urged Tolkien to finish it. Responding to their interest, he completed the book and submitted it on 3 October 1936. The book was published about a year later. A publisher, a deadline, and a specific request were the ingredients Tolkien needed to bring that project to a close.

Pressure continued to play an important role in Tolkien's productivity. Gratified by the reception of the book, Stanley Unwin told Tolkien, "A large public will be clamouring next year to hear more from you about Hobbits!" (qtd. in Carpenter, *Tolkien* 182). Unwin and Tolkien met to discuss future projects. Tolkien gave him rough manuscripts of *The Silmarillion, Mr. Bliss, Farmer Giles of Ham, Roverandom,* and *The Lost Road.* All were rejected. Unwin and the public "clamoured" for Hobbits instead.

On 19 December 1937, Tolkien recorded cautiously, "I have written the first chapter of a new story about Hobbits—'A long expected party'" (*Letters* 27). He struggled to make progress, and as he wrote, the story began to change, gaining darker elements and extending into much longer narrative segments and far greater complexity. On 31 August 1938, Tolkien told Unwin that the book was "getting quite out of hand" (40). The project that had begun rather simply as another Hobbit story—suitable for children and filled with picnics, parties, riddles, and pranks—had become richer, more complex, and much more challenging to write.

By the winter of 1942, Tolkien became discouraged (*Treason* 1). The reasons are complex. He was uncertain about the direction of the story, explaining that he "did not know how to go on" (*Letters* 321). Furthermore, as Carpenter writes, "Two of his sons, Michael and Christopher, were called up into the armed forces, and his anxiety about them certainly distracted him from the task" (*Souvenir Booklet*). Also, at the height of World War II, Tolkien served as an air raid warden, and while this did not occupy a great deal of his time, it demanded significant emotional energy (*Letters* 437).[8]

Another factor also weighed him down: Tolkien was beginning to doubt that his book would ever be published. In December 1942, he wrote to Stanley Unwin, asking, "Is such an 'epic' possible to consider in the present circumstances?" He clarifies, "It is a question of paper, bulk, and market!"(*Letters* 58). Given the shortages and distractions of wartime, Tolkien had begun to wonder if the publication of such a long book was even a possibility. Despite these deep misgivings, Tolkien told Unwin he hoped to finish the book within the next few months (58). Instead, he abandoned it altogether, and "not a line on it was possible for a year" (86).

Tolkien was "*dead stuck*" (*Letters* 321). Then, on 29 March 1944, he had lunch with Lewis. Lewis provided encouragement in two different ways. First, he shared his own work in progress. Tolkien records, "The indefatigable man read me part of a new story!" (68). In the act of reading his own work out loud, Lewis challenged Tolkien, providing a hint of friendly rivalry.[9] But Lewis also goaded him directly, urging him to get back to work and finish his book. In a tone both grumbling and appreciative, Tolkien writes, "He is putting the screw on me to finish mine. I needed some pressure, & shall probably respond" (68).

It is tempting to try to re-create what these men said that day. But whatever the content or mood may have been, this single conversation proved to be a critical turning point. Five days after the meeting, on 3 April 1944, Tolkien writes, "I have begun to nibble at [*The Lord of the Rings*] again. I have started to do some (painful) work on the chapter which picks up the adventures of Frodo and Sam" (*Letters* 69). And two days after that, Tolkien writes, "I have seriously embarked on an effort to finish my book, & have been sitting up rather late: a lot of re-reading and research required. And it is a painful sticky business getting into swing again" (70). From that time, Tolkien reports steady, significant progress and records that Lewis and the others offered frequent praise for sections of the text he read at Inklings meetings.

This example of Tolkien's work on *The Lord of the Rings* highlights the important role resonators play. It also illustrates one of the difficulties in identifying this form of influence. Although it is clear that resonators exert a profound influence on writers and their work, it can be very difficult to recognize the extent of their contributions. On the surface, the writer appears to be continuing in the same direction that he or she has been moving all along. The following example from Hermerén helps to clarify the difficulty of trying to measure such influence: "Suppose that an artist has a long and homogeneous production behind him. At a certain time he becomes involved in a series of tragic accidents which result in a crisis of personality. This crisis would have brought about a radical change in his painting, if he had not come into contact with the paintings of his colleague *A* at this very moment. This contact gives him inspiration and strength to continue to paint in roughly the same way as before. In this case there appears to be a clear example of artistic influence but no change" (245).

Hermerén's illustration presents a fairly drastic case. However, it is easy to picture a less drastic, more common scenario. Rather than experiencing a full-blown "crisis of personality," a writer may simply grow discouraged, lose interest, get tired, or turn his or her attention to other projects. This is where resonators make all the difference: through encouragement, praise, or pressure, they often become the crucial element that propels the work forward. As LeFevre observes, "Certain acts of invention—or certain phases of inventive acts—are best understood if we think of them as being made possible by other people" (65).

Many authors writing about the composition of *The Lord of the Rings* have noted how much Tolkien relied on the Inklings as resonators. Joan McClusky writes, "Tolkien was devoted to these good friends. Without their encouragement, support, and shared interest in mythology, *The Lord of the Rings* might never have been written" (32). Tom Shippey asserts, "I don't think Tolkien would ever have finished *Lord of the Rings* without Lewis's encouragement," and again, "I am sure that Tolkien would never have finished *The Lord of the Rings* without Lewis continually encouraging him and urging him on and talking to him and generally smoothing the way for him."[10] Carpenter says that Tolkien nearly abandoned the whole project, and that his decision to press on was "chiefly due to the encouragement" of C. S. Lewis, "one of the handful of people who were reading the book, or hearing it read aloud to them, as it was being written" (*Souvenir Booklet*). This testimony should be taken very seriously, since Tolkien was a notorious non-finisher.[11]

Ultimately, Tolkien is the one who makes it clear that Lewis's input was of critical importance to his work. He writes, "But for the encouragement of C. S. L. I do not think that I should ever have completed or offered for publication *The Lord of the Rings*" (*Letters* 366). And again, "Only by [Lewis's] support and friendship did I ever struggle to the end of the labour" (184). And again, "I owe to [Lewis's] encouragement the fact that in spite of obstacles (including the 1939 war!) I persevered and eventually finished *The Lord of the Rings*" (303).

THE WAGER

Tolkien finished *The Lord of the Rings* in 1949, but for Tolkien and Lewis, encouragement and rivalry began much earlier in their friendship. In 1936, Tolkien and Lewis were largely unknown and unpublished authors, even though they had been writing all of their lives. Then Lewis read *The Place of the Lion* by Charles Williams and *A Voyage to Arcturus* by David Lindsay. These two novels could hardly be more different from one another, but each of them offers a skillful blend of popular fiction and spiritual ideas. Lewis found the combination compelling, but he was hard-pressed to find other books that succeeded in quite the same way. With this in mind, he approached Tolkien with a proposal: "Tollers, there is too little of what we really like in stories. I am afraid we shall have to try and write some ourselves" (qtd. in Tolkien, *Letters* 378). Tolkien says that he and Lewis "tossed up," and it was determined that Lewis was to write about space travel and Tolkien was to write about time travel (347). Tolkien elaborates the details of their mutual charge when he writes, "We originally meant each to write an excursionary 'Thriller': a Space-journey and a Time-journey (mine) each discovering Myth" (29).[12]

Lewis wrote *Out of the Silent Planet,* and despite some initial difficulty, it was published by The Bodley Head and has garnered praise and affection ever since. It was followed by two other important works, *Perelandra* and *That Hideous Strength.* The three novels constitute Lewis's Ransom trilogy.

Tolkien's effort, which he called *The Lost Road,* was less successful. He writes, "I began an abortive book of time-travel of which the end was to be the presence of my hero in the drowning of Atlantis" (*Letters* 347). It was never completed: "My effort, after a few promising chapters, ran dry: it was too long a way round to what I really wanted to make, a new version of the Atlantis legend" (378). The fragment and Christopher Tolkien's illuminating commentary upon it have been published in *The Lost Road and Other Writings.*

Although Tolkien did not make much progress with *The Lost Road,* this draft and the wager that inspired it still proved fruitful. Christopher Tolkien has argued that the composition of *The Lost Road* is "intimately connected" with another project, "The Fall of Númenor" (*Lost Road* 9). In fact, it is not only the basis for the work itself, but also for the larger concept behind it. Christopher Tolkien writes, "I conclude therefore that 'Númenor' (as a distinct and formalised conception, whatever 'Atlantis-haunting,' as my father called it, lay behind) arose in the actual context of his discussions with C. S. Lewis in (as seems probable) 1936" (9).

It is also noteworthy that in a letter to a reader, Tolkien contrasts Lewis's rapid work on the Ransom trilogy with his own slower composition of *The Lord of the Rings,* and, in doing so, traces both projects back to this famous wager. "Being a man of immense power and industry, his 'trilogy' was finished much sooner amid much other work; but at last my slower and more meticulous (as well as more indolent and less organized) machine has produced its effort. The labour! I have typed myself nearly all of it *twice,* and parts more often; not to mention the written stages! But I am amply rewarded and encouraged to find that the labour was not wasted" (*Letters* 209).

Out of the Silent Planet, Perelandra, That Hideous Strength, The Lost Road, "The Fall of Númenor," *The Lord of the Rings:* each of these works has a long and intricate history.[13] But each one has its genesis in the same place. They were born out of a specific conversation, a friendly competition, and a deliberate decision to write fiction along similar lines.

"Think of a Subject"

The Inklings received ideas and motivation from a number of sources—Tolkien's publisher asking for another Hobbit book and Lewis's publisher asking him to write on the problem of pain are two examples. Williams regularly sought suggestions, too, and on 21 June 1940, Charles Williams writes to tell his wife that he is wrapping up a number of projects. He says with some urgency, "Think of a subject for a new novel, I beg you; let it be supernatural this time, because I am more certain there" (*To Michal* 73). The Inklings also regularly helped one another generate ideas for new projects. For example, in the late 1930s, Barfield wrote a poetic drama called *Orpheus,* and he credits Lewis as the instigator of the project. In the introduction to the play, Barfield speculates that readers might be interested to know the history of the project. He recounts: "I had casually remarked to my friend C. S. Lewis that I seemed to be feeling an impulse to write a play in verse and was wondering about a subject. . . . I recall the occasion very clearly and, though I am not reproducing his exact words, he said in effect: 'Why not take one of the myths and simply do your best with it—Orpheus for instance?' To which my mental reaction was, after some reflection: Well, why not? And so, in the event, I got down to it in the limited spare time then at my disposal" (7). The mood of this conversation is comfortable and low key: Barfield asks for an idea, Lewis offers a suggestion, Barfield says, "Well, why not?" and gets to work. Also, Lewis's suggestion is very, very specific: he recommends the myth of Orpheus in particular. Both the ease and the specificity are typical of the interaction of these two Inklings and quite characteristic of the way group members interact.

Barfield wrote the play *Orpheus,* and Lewis was enthusiastic about the result. In a letter to Barfield on 28 March 1938, he offers a long comment on the unpublished draft, noting specifically, "Act II is simply superb. It brought tears to my eyes" (*Collected Letters* 2: 223). In August 1948, Lewis wrote a blurb for a production of the play, and he begins, "I await with great interest the public reaction to a work which has influenced me so deeply as Barfield's *Orpheus*" (2: 872).

Lewis played an important role in another Barfield piece, a two-part poem titled "A Visit to Beatrice." Barfield explains that he wrote the first section of the poem, forty-two lines in rhyming couplets, after reading the novel *Moll Flanders (Barfield Sampler* 177). Flanders narrates the poem in the first person. She introduces herself to Beatrice and chats with her about mutual acquaintances. When Barfield finished, he sent it to Lewis and told him to share it with the Inklings. He also suggested that someone in the group should write the second section of the poem, containing Beatrice's reply (177).

Barfield's open attitude toward his poem is noteworthy—he is eager to find a collaborator to work with, and he does not specify or limit who that collaborator should be. Lewis, however, had a different idea. He told Barfield to write the second half of the poem himself. And so he did. Hunter and Kranidas write, "When Barfield sent Lewis the Beatrice section, he received enthusiastic approval; but, Lewis added, the second part had rendered the first part worthless!" (177).

Lewis also welcomed input at all stages of his composing process, including suggestions for new projects. In one instance, an idea from Humphrey Havard became the basis of a series of poems.[14] These five sonnets deal with the topic of despair, and, as Don W. King observes, "For the most part he reflects a biblical understanding of the way to deal with despair; eschewing either casual, flippant dismissal or self-indulgent introspection, he suggests facing it fully and working through it to the other side" (*Poet* 199).

In his exploration of this theme, Lewis uses the comparison of a bee buzzing against a window pane in the fourth and fifth sonnets in the sequence. Owen Barfield tells us that the comparison itself was "suggested in conversation with his physician [and fellow Inkling] Dr. Havard" (*Owen Barfield* 15). A section from the end of the fourth sonnet reads:

> . . . if we once assent
> To Nature's voice, we shall be like the bee
> That booms against the window-pane for hours
> Thinking that way to reach the laden flowers.

The image appears again at the beginning of the fifth sonnet, and Havard's voice is added directly to the work:

> "If we could speak to her," my doctor said,
> "And told her, 'Not that way! All, all in vain
> You weary out your wings and bruise your head,'"[15]

But in the poem, the determined bee refuses to perceive the glass:

> "Might she not answer, buzzing at the pane,
> 'Let queens and mystics and religious bees
> Talk of such inconceivables as glass;
> The blunt lay worker flies at what she sees,
> Look there—ahead, ahead—the flowers, the grass!'" (*Collected Poems* 141)

In this series of poems, Havard's suggestion provided the central image of the buzzing bee, and his contribution is directly recognized by Barfield and by Lewis as well.

A suggestion for another project is documented by James Dundas-Grant.[16] Lewis was ill, and Dundas-Grant went to visit him in an Oxford nursing home. He recalls,

> I leaned over the end of the bed and watched him, obviously under drugs. One eye opened. "Hullo, D.G. Nice to see you." He drowsed off again, and as I was about to slip out I heard him say, "Not going yet, are you?" and he stirred up fully awake.
>
> After a brief chat, I said, "Jack, I wish you'd write us a book about prayer." "I might," he said, with a twinkle. Then he dozed off again. I'm sure many people must have suggested this, but his last book, published posthumously, was *Letters to Malcolm*. (372)

Dundas-Grant admits he was probably not the only one to suggest that Lewis write a book on prayer. No direct line of cause and effect can be established. Still, this anecdote makes it clear that the Inklings were completely comfortable making suggestions in a wide variety of structured and unstructured settings. It is also clear that such suggestions were warmly welcomed.

MODELING

Warren Lewis, one of the most active and talented members of the Inklings, benefited greatly from the group. He became a published writer as the direct result of their encouragement and example. Warren had worked on different writing projects throughout his life. As a child, he wrote imaginative tales of India, and as an adult he kept a diary that shows his talent for graceful prose. His first extended writing project was to compile and edit his family papers. He describes it as follows:

> My father died in 1929 . . . and when we came to examine his papers we found that he had never destroyed *anything*—not even the stubs of his used cheque books. All this material was shipped over to my brother's rooms in Magdalen College, Oxford, and we decided vaguely to sort it out at some future date. I retired in 1931 and came to live in Oxford myself. I had not begun to write in those days and wanted some occupation, so I went through this mass of documents, and decided—more or less as a joke—that I should compile and type 'The Lewis Papers.' This I did, including diaries in addition to letters, and covering a period 1850–1930.[17] (unpublished letter, 22 October 1968)

Warren Lewis spent a little more than four years selecting, arranging, and typing these materials, and he ended up with eleven bound volumes of *Lewis Papers*. On 2 June 1933, he writes, "The first volume of the Lewis papers arrived from the binders yesterday, and [my brother and I] both pronounce it a great success: I am delighted with it" (*Brothers* 103). The entire collection is a wonderful achievement and an indispensable aid to Inklings scholarship.

Despite these writing experiences, it was not until some time later that Warren Lewis thought of writing and publishing books, even though he had been collecting notes on French history for many years. In 1934, he started to work with the material more deliberately, but he saw little value in the exercise. He notes in his diary, "I now write from time to time, a doggerel history of the reign of Louis XIV, to my own intense amusement, and, being under no illusions as to its practical value, do not see any danger in so doing" (*Brothers* 147).

What inspired this retired army officer to take his work more seriously? He responded to the ongoing example and support of the Inklings. On 13 April 1944, Tolkien sent a report of an Inklings meeting to his son Christopher. He tells him that Warnie is writing a book, then adds with apparent pride, "It's catching." Tolkien was more than enthusiastic—he calls Major Lewis's projected book the best entertainment of the evening (*Letters* 71). This literary dabbler became an active, accomplished author as a result of the modeling of the group.

In all, Warren Lewis published seven books on seventeenth-century France. One of these, *The Sunset of the Splendid Century,* earned an accolade from Edwin Morgan, who writes, "This book has not only scholarship; it has wit and a warm insight into human nature—endowments which are not always found in an historian" (383). Other readers have been equally appreciative of these histories. In his later years, Warren Lewis began a long correspondence with Dr. Blanche Biggs, a missionary serving in Papua New Guinea.[18] Their correspondence is interesting in a number of ways, particularly as an indication of his deep devotional life and extensive writing skill. After corresponding with her for some time, he sent Biggs a copy of his edition of *Memoirs of the Duc de Saint-Simon.* She replied, "Knowing that you and your brother wrote such imaginative things as boys, I wonder that I ever expected your writing to be statistical and unimaginative. You must have had a lot of fun reading up all these old records, letters, etc., and then breathing your own kind of life into them. It makes excellent reading" (unpublished letter, 22 March 1970).

In these letters, Warren Lewis describes the beginnings of his writing career; he also shows his eagerness to support the writing of others. He writes to Biggs on 22 October 1968: "As regards your own material I would strongly urge you neither to burn it or hand it over to anyone else, but retain it and when you retire, have a go at making a book out of it yourself. I can see from your letter that you are the kind of person who would have no difficulty in writing" (unpublished letter). In this and other letters, Warren Lewis encourages Biggs as a writer, much as he had been encouraged by the Inklings. And apparently his kind words had their intended effect. In 1987, Biggs published *From Papua with Love,* a book of personal reflection on her mission experience. The book includes selections from 110 newsletters, along with various drawings, maps, and photographs. In structure, tone, and purpose, it is much like Warren Lewis's work of assembling the Lewis family papers.

Biggs also encouraged Lewis to continue his good work, writing, "I admire *your* courage in launching out into authorship at a fairly late age and successfully producing seven of them. Why stop at the age of 73?" (unpublished letter, 7 December 1968).

The example of the other Inklings made a significant difference to Warren Lewis. Late in his life, he observed with some wonder, "Since I began writing in 1953 my earnings come to a total of £9,766-10. Not so bad for a complete amateur who was over fifty eight when he turned author!" (*Brothers* 300). Warren tells us that his brother had urged him to try his hand at writing something much earlier, in 1931 (81).[19] But as it turned out, his writing was to flourish later, within the context of a supportive and active writing group. As LeFevre asserts, the myth of the solo artist working away in complete isolation is not only false but also highly destructive. She advises writers and other creative artists to be deliberate in surrounding themselves with resonators in order to create "communities that foster invention" (124).

LeFevre offers the following illustration of this principle, an illustration that is not only a powerful metaphor for the creative process but also an admonition that might be taken as the theme of this whole book:

> There will always be great need for individual initiative, but no matter how inventive an individual wants to be, he will be influenced for better or for worse by the intellectual company he keeps. On top of Mt. Mansfield in Vermont, there are thirty-year-old trees that are only three feet tall. If a tree begins to grow taller, extending beyond the protection of the others, it dies. The moral for inventors: Plant yourself in a tall forest if you hope to have ideas of stature. (124–25)

This is exactly what the Inklings did.

ANTICIPATION AND ACCOUNTABILITY

There is another way resonators shape text, a way even more subtle and harder to trace, which may be more profound than the influence of praise, pressure, competition, or modeling. When writers meet regularly, their established meeting times provide accountability. Most writers find it easier to respond to specific deadlines. Thursday after Thursday, the Inklings knew they would be facing the same question: "Well, has nobody got anything to read us?" This motivated them to make regular progress on their manuscripts.

Furthermore, when writers are part of an established group, they may begin to write in anticipation of particular kinds of comments, working deliberately to attract certain kinds of compliments and avoid known forms of criticism. It is exceedingly difficult to ascertain how significant a part this played within the group. It certainly seems likely that as C. S. Lewis sat at his writing desk, his thoughts might have run something like this: "If I put it that way, it might offend Charles; if I leave that out, I'll annoy Colin; if I don't define this term, I'll catch it from Owen." Surely the Inklings adjusted what they said and how they said it in anticipation of the questions, concerns, biases, and tastes of this ever-present audience. In fact, Owen Barfield admits to just this kind of anticipatory thinking. In an interview, he says, "If I'm writing anything to do with the theory of knowledge, with the nature of thought, I find myself always putting it in the form of a question to myself: Is this something that Jack could knock down? Is it something which is proof against any objection he would raise?" (*Owen Barfield* 127).

Was this kind of anticipation also important to Tolkien? I believe it was. One indication may be the distinct difference between *The Silmarillion* and *The Lord of the Rings. The Silmarillion* was not initiated by external readers, nor was it composed in the context of an interested audience. It is in *The Silmarillion* that we see most clearly what Tolkien means when he refers to his mythology as "a private hobby" and "my stuff" (*Letters* 362). It is here that we find what composition theorist Linda Flower calls "writer-based prose."[20] Tolkien wrote it for his own amusement; he found the myths and languages of Middle-earth endlessly fascinating. *The Lord of the Rings,* in contrast, was initiated externally, as we have seen, to satisfy an eager publisher. In fact, as Carpenter says, "Tolkien began writing the book under pressure, almost unwillingly" (*Souvenir Booklet*). And then it was drafted within the context of interested readers, and most of it was read aloud chapter by chapter as it was written.[21]

Tolkien was completely aware of the essential difference between these texts. He writes, "*The Silmarillion* is quite different [from *The Lord of the Rings*], and if good at all, good in quite another way" (*Letters* 366). The nature of this difference is effectively summarized by Randel Helms in his book *Tolkien and the Silmarils:* "It is very fine, but it lacks certain qualities, chief among them a humanizing sense of humor and a sense of developing personality among its characters" (80). *The Silmarillion* contains some of the most beautiful passages Tolkien has ever written. But the quality is not sustained, and, overall, the book lacks a compelling narrative flow. As David Bratman observes, Tolkien's style in *The Silmarillion* may be described as "desiccated, overly abbreviated, and somewhat fussy" ("Literary Value" 72).

The lack of a deliberate connection between the writer and his readers may be one of the factors that makes *The Silmarillion* demanding to read, challenging to connect with, and less popular than *The Lord of the Rings.* I suggest that *The Lord of the Rings* might have been much more like *The Silmarillion* in structure and style if it had not been so strongly influenced by the "humanizing" effect of the Inklings. Knight characterizes the influence of the Inklings this way: "Tolkien began to come out of his Silmarillion shell and opened up gradual access to that world, first with *The Hobbit,* and then, like the slow opening of a flower, *The Lord of the Rings*" (244).

There is something of a parallel between Tolkien's *Silmarillion* and Lewis's *Pilgrim's Regress* in that both are among their author's least approachable, that is, least reader-friendly texts, and both were written apart from the Inklings. J. I. Packer notes that *The Pilgrim's Regress* was written long before Lewis became a popular author and that Lewis actually subtitled it "*or Pseudo-Bunyan's Periplus*," which "shows how little he saw himself as writing for the general Christian public." Packer concludes, "We should be glad his first publisher cut that bit out" (30).

Lewis himself recognized the inaccessibility of this book. In a letter to Mrs. Edward A. Allen, Lewis says, "I don't wonder that you got fogged in *Pilgrim's Regress*. It was my first religious book and I didn't then know how to make things easy. I was not even trying to very much, because in those days I never dreamed I would become a 'popular' author and hoped for no readers outside a small 'highbrow' circle. Don't waste your time over it any more" (*Letters* 430). We can credit the Inklings, the presence of an interested and critical audience, for some of the differences between these early writer-based works and later reader-based ones.

PRACTICAL HELP

So far, this chapter has emphasized the ways in which several forms of encouragement had a positive impact on the Inklings, increasing their productivity and shaping the direction of their work. There is another way resonators can offer support, and that is by providing practical help. Such help can take many different forms, including such acts of kindness as meeting financial needs, running errands, providing meals, handling mundane chores, typing or retyping texts, sharing research materials, and providing work space.

For example, during the time that Williams lived in Oxford, both his living space and work space were cramped. Hadfield notes, "There was a severe loss of privacy, for he had to gather with others round the sitting room fire, among the general activity which regularly included a typewriter, and write on his little pad on a crossed knee" (*Charles Williams* 179). If his personal quarters were uncomfortable, his office was worse: his employer created an office for him in an unused bathroom. Apparently he made the best of it: "It was a large roomy bathroom, leading off the first-floor landing and overlooking the entrance. The covered bath made a good shelf for piles of manuscripts and books" (179).

Sensitive to his friend's needs, C. S. Lewis encouraged Williams to use his rooms at Magdalen College as a more congenial place to work. Williams reports to his wife in a letter: "It is all very still. I have fled to Lewis's rooms; the College is silent all round me. I shall only go back to supper. He is [a] great tea-drinker at any hour of night or day, and left a tray for me with milk & tea, & an electric kettle at hand. Sound man! You must come here one day and see my refuge" (*To Michal* 18). It is clear that Williams appreciated Lewis's thoughtfulness. He was grateful for the practical assistance and the cheer of a good cup of tea.

Lewis's rooms at Magdalen served as a refuge for Warren Lewis as well. Their house, the Kilns, was a lively household, consisting of the Lewis brothers, Janie Moore, her daughter Maureen, Fred Paxford the gardener, and a variety of cooks, housekeepers, and other help. They also kept a number of animals, including dogs and cats.[22] Warren Lewis described it as "a house which was hardly ever at peace for 24 hours, amid senseless wranglings, lyings, back-bitings, follies, and *scares*" (*Brothers* 265). Consequently, Warren kept most of his books in his brother's rooms at Magdalen and spent his mornings there, researching and writing. One of Lewis's students, Helen Tyrrell Wheeler, offers this description:

> My other tutors, Dame Helen Gardner and Lord David Cecil, lived in elegant, orderly eighteenth-century rooms which always seemed full of brightness: sunshine or firelight or both. Quite different was Lewis's. There were of course books everywhere, but that was true of every room one went into in Oxford. These books had *taken over*—so that comfort had long departed. It was quite a business to find seats. . . . And the room was curiously shadowy, with what I think were heavy dark curtains over other mysterious doors. . . . Through these obscure entries there would, now and again, appear a very stealthy figure, who with a mur-mured greeting would track down a wanted book and disappear again into limbo. This, we gathered, was Lewis's brother. Informed opinion in Oxford at the time held that he was the world's greatest authority on all those families of that French aristocracy who had suffered during the Revolution; and that he knew the tiniest detail of their disastrous lives. I have no idea if this interesting belief is correct. (48–49)

Another Inkling who benefited from the practical help of others was J. R. R. Tolkien. He was particularly grateful to his son Christopher, who played multiple roles and exerted an important influence on his father's work. Christopher Tolkien was also an Inkling, the youngest member of the group. His father made his status clear in a letter dated 9 October 1945, telling him that the Inklings proposed "to consider you a *permanent member,* with right of entry and what not quite independent of my presence or otherwise" (qtd. in Carpenter, *Inklings* 205). At the time this invitation was extended, Christopher Tolkien was twenty years old.

Christopher Tolkien helped his father in a number of ways, most significantly as a reader who motivated the creation of text and as a critic who evaluated the text. But he also did simple clerical work. On 5 April 1944, Tolkien expressed his gratitude to his son, saying, "What a lot of work you put into the typing, and the chapters written out so beautifully! I wish I still had my amanuensis and critic near at hand" (*Letters* 70). On 11 May 1944, he wrote again to tell Christopher how much he was missed and appreciated: "I wish I had you here, doing something useful and pleasant, completing the maps and typing" (79).[23]

Carpenter comments on one other role Christopher Tolkien played in the group: "Once Christopher had become an Inkling it grew to be the custom that he, rather than his father, should read aloud any new chapters of *The Lord of the Rings* to the company, for it was generally agreed that he made a better job of it than did Tolkien himself" (*Inklings* 205). J. R. R. Tolkien spoke in a rapid, indistinct voice, a quality that hampered his reputation with his students and tried the patience of some of the Inklings. On 6 February 1947, Warren Lewis noted in his diary, "Chris then gave us an admirable chapter of the '[new] Hobbit,' beautifully read" (*Brothers* 198). Such simple acts are frequently acknowledged as these writers describe their time together.

PROMOTION

Through praise, encouragement, challenge, example, and practical help, resonators increase a writer's persistence and productivity. In addition, resonators may also serve to promote an author's work. This may be something as simple as purchasing copies of their books. We know, for example, that John Wain's first book, a slim collection of nineteen poems, was printed in a limited edition of 120 numbered copies and both Lewis and Tolkien are named on the list of "subscribers before publication" (Hatziolou 58). The Inklings also shared books with one another. Nevill Coghill's decision to give Lewis his copy of Williams's novel *The Place of the Lion* is a typical act of promotion, and a powerful one, for it ultimately paved the way for Williams to join the group. Lewis lent Tolkien his copy of *The Silver Trumpet,* a fairy tale written by Barfield. Sometime later, Lewis wrote to Barfield to tell him of the enthusiastic reception: "It is the greatest success among [Tolkien's] children that they have ever known. His own fairy-tales, which are excellent, have now no market: and its first reading—children are so practical!—led to a universal wail 'You're not going to give it back to Mr. Lewis, are you?'" (*Collected Letters* 2: 198). The letter ends with this quick comment: "Cecil now has *The Place of the Lion:* get it out of him before he returns it to me" (2:199).

Furthermore, the Inklings often recommended books to others. For example, Williams tells Lois Lang-Sims, "You must read CSL's *Allegory of Love*—a great book on European poetry from Rome to Spenser: you might, I think, like it" (*Letters to Lalage* 66). Lewis tells a student to read *Sir Gawain and the Green Knight,* but makes it clear that he should use the Tolkien/Gordon edition and no other (*Letters* 285). Lewis asks Sister Penelope, "Do you know the works of Charles Williams? Rather wild, but full of love and excelling in the creation of convincing *good* characters" (322). At a very young age, Christopher Tolkien tried to do his part to boost his father's sales. He writes, "In December 1937, two months after publication, I wrote to Father Christmas and gave *The Hobbit* a vigorous puff, asking him if he knew of it, and proposing it to him as an idea for Christmas presents" (Foreword).

Promoting one another in the larger public arena was a significant aspect of the mutual influence of the Inklings. The effort of Lewis and Tolkien to promote Charles Williams is probably the clearest example. Readers often discover Williams indirectly, as a result of his relationship with the other Inklings. This is true now, as the blurbs on his books will testify. This was also true in his own day. A former student at Oxford, Erik Routley, observes, "In a sense [Lewis] mediated Charles Williams to ordinary people." Routley adds, "Williams was a genius, of course" (108).

Genius, perhaps. Dramatic, no doubt. But Williams's work *is* difficult: his themes are lofty, his thought process complicated, his use of symbolism complex, his expression obscure. For these reasons, when Williams lived in London, he was not well known, even though by 1939 he had already published more than 30 books. They had received significant critical acclaim but found a very modest audience. Gareth Knight says that at this time, Williams was "to all intents and purposes a partially failed novelist" (243–44).

Moving from London to Oxford and associating with the Inklings changed Williams's life. Lewis promoted Williams with characteristic enthusiasm, opening all sorts of doors for meeting people, giving talks, and getting published. As Hadfield puts it, "What intellectual virtue and generosity there was in Lewis. Warmhearted and highly intelligent, he was to give immense help to Charles in wartime Oxford" (*Charles Williams* 188). The extent of this influence was clear to Tolkien, who wrote the following humorous rhyme:

The sales of Charles Williams
Leapt up by millions,
When a reviewer surmised
He was only Lewis disguised. (qtd. in Carpenter, *Inklings* 187)

Hadfield expresses the effect of his new fame this way: "Charles's life was being burst open by the university and town contacts that were increasingly pressing in on him. In prewar days it had been circumscribed, his days mainly occupied with a handful of people he had known for years. Now he lived almost wholly in public, even in his lodging, where strangers came and went and ate and spent evenings together" (*Charles Williams* 218).

In the years 1943 through 1945, Williams gave forty-nine public lectures, many of them under the sponsorship of Lewis and Tolkien (Hadfield, *Charles Williams* 188).[24] His accomplishments as a lecturer led to other opportunities. He was invited to contribute a book to the Christian Challenge series, which was initiated by Ashley Sampson "with the purpose of introducing the Christian faith to people outside the Church" (Hooper, *C. S. Lewis* 294). Lewis had written *The Problem of Pain* (1940) for the series. Williams contributed *The Forgiveness of Sins* (1942). Both books were read aloud in Inklings meetings as works in progress and both books were dedicated to the group.

The Inklings tried their best to promote Williams's work. Publishers were encouraged to keep his work in print, which was no mean task. Hadfield records that an internal memo at Oxford University Press asked, "How CAN we put CW over? Shall we try announcing him as the most unsaleable of all Oxford authors?" (*Charles Williams* 79).

C. S. Lewis remained Williams's strongest supporter, and his efforts to promote Williams's work did not end when his friend died. In the autumn of 1945, he gave a series of lectures at Oxford about Williams's Arthurian poem cycle. On 11 February 1949, he gave a radio talk at the BBC to discuss his friend's work, explaining to the producer that even though he was "v. busy and not v. well," he "wd. not miss a chance of helping C. W.'s sales" (qtd. in Phillips 279).[25] And in 1955, Lewis and Dorothy L. Sayers signed a brief letter appearing in the *Times* of London, announcing that public meetings were being arranged in honor of the tenth anniversary of Williams's death and suggesting that "his disciples and students of his works elsewhere should take steps to pay tribute in some fashion wherever they may be" (9).[26] Considering the ongoing difficulty publishers have had promoting Charles Williams, the impact of Lewis and the other Inklings on the awareness and critical reception of his work, then and now, is profound.

CONCLUSIONS

The Inklings engaged in a wide range of supportive activities as they worked together. They expressed faith and hope. They offered praise and encouragement. They applied pressure, admonishing one another to persevere. They provided accountability and established literary expectation, some spoken, some unspoken. They modeled the habits and creative techniques of productive writers, offering inspiration through their example. They provided resources and practical aid. They served as advocates for one another's work, assisted with publishing, and helped promote the finished product to the wider public.

The Inklings strongly influenced one another through encouragement, but this point is typically diminished, denied, or overlooked. Careful consideration of the following passage helps to emphasize this point. In discussing the mutual influence of the Inklings, Daniel Grotta writes:

> The Inklings existed for a quarter century; during that time Lewis and Tolkien remained prominent members (Charles Williams died in May, 1945). Lewis freely acknowledged the positive influence they had on him, both as a writer and a Christian. . . . Lewis even "borrowed" from Tolkien's writings in his *Silent Planet* trilogy. In one instance, he writes about Numinor, "a misspelling of Númenor which . . . is a fragment from a vast private mythology invented by Professor J. R. R. Tolkien." (98)[27]

Here Grotta makes a good start. He emphasizes that the Inklings met over a very long period and that Lewis expressed gratitude to the Inklings for their friendship and support. He also notes a specific instance of textual influence, a place where Lewis borrowed a single concept directly from Tolkien.

Although Grotta makes several good observations and expresses them well, he quickly takes a wrong turn. Having acknowledged that Lewis was influenced by the group, he writes, "On the other hand, although Tolkien received encouragement, he was influenced by neither Lewis nor the other Inklings" (98). Grotta minimizes the importance of encouragement and, furthermore, fails to recognize it as a form of influence.

Grotta may be basing his conclusion on Tolkien's own comment: "The unpayable debt that I owe to [Lewis] was not 'influence' as it is ordinarily understood, but sheer encouragement" (*Letters* 362). Here Tolkien is very careful in his wording: he does not say that encouragement is not influence. He says that encouragement is not influence *as it is normally understood*. That is a critical difference. Considering the profound impact that resonators have on texts, it is time that encouragement and support be accepted as transforming aspects of influence.

NOTES

1. The relevant passage, from a devilish point of view, is as follows:

The Enemy [i.e., God] allows this disappointment to occur on the threshold of every human endeavour. It occurs when the boy who has been enchanted in the nursery by *Stories from the Odyssey* buckles down to really learning Greek. It occurs when lovers have got married and begin the real task of learning to live together. In every department of life it marks the transition from dreaming aspiration to laborious doing. The Enemy takes this risk because He has a curious fantasy of making all these disgusting little human vermin into what He calls His "free" lovers and servants—"sons" is the word He uses, with His inveterate love of degrading the whole spiritual world by unnatural liaisons with the two-legged animals. Desiring their freedom, He therefore refuses to carry them, by their mere affections and habits, to any of the goals which He sets before them: He leaves them to "do it on their own." And there lies our opportunity. But also, remember, there lies our danger. If once they get through this initial dryness successfully, they become much less dependent on emotion and therefore much harder to tempt. (*Screwtape* 7–8)

2. LeFevre highlights the intrinsic value of group support in her observation that women have often been excluded from professional organizations and, as a consequence, have been hampered in their productivity:

If, for example, it is (or has been) a "social fact" that women can't invent, then it follows that men needn't allow women into professional organizations. If women don't have such affiliations, they are indeed less likely to invent when they lack the benefits of membership, such as the chance to work collaboratively, to present ideas in a forum, to publish, and to seek awards to support research. When women then do *not* invent, the social fact is confirmed: women can't invent. (We knew it all along.) Such has been the experience for many women in literature and science, to name but two examples. (84–85)

In addition to LeFevre's helpful discussion of women in writing groups, I recommend Anne Ruggles Gere and Laura Jane Roop's "For Profit and Pleasure" and Gere's *Writing Groups*.

3. As Joe R. Christopher explains, Lewis's approach to personal relationships and his approach to literary criticism were the same: "The first thing to do is to surrender to the experience; later, if necessary, one can judge" (*C. S. Lewis* 58). Further discussion of Lewis as literary critic can be found in Bruce L. Edwards's article "An Experiment in Criticism" and in his book *A Rhetoric of Reading*.

4. Here is the sentence that Lewis says will "straddle across the ages": "If, *per impossibile*, it could be divinely certain that the historical events upon which Christendom reposes had not yet happened, all that could be said would be that they had not *yet* happened" (Williams, *He Came Down* 6).

5. For his part, Williams was encouraging, if somewhat restrained, in his assessment of Lewis's lectures on Milton. He writes, "Lewis was very good on Tasso & Milton this morning; it is years since I have heard anyone talk intelligently on poetry." He adds, "Even [T. S. Eliot] is unsound on Milton" (*To Michal* 27).

6. G. B. Tennyson believes that the poem Lewis refers to here is an unpublished one entitled "The Tower" (personal correspondence, 10 February 2005). Lewis quotes from "The Tower" in his published work and praises it in personal notes. In a diary entry dated 21 June 1922, Lewis says it is "full of magnificent material and never a dead phrase: the new part strong and savage" (*All My Road* 53). Writing to Leo Baker in March 1921, Lewis says of this poem, "I am amazed at its power and feel that we have never yet treated him with sufficient respect" (*Collected Letters* 1: 522).

7. Charles Williams's wife, whom he called Michal, elaborates:

He had a habit of waking me at any hour of any night when he was writing a book. I would wake from sleep to hear him saying "What about a cup of tea, darling, then I should like to read you what I have written this evening."

When he wrote the play *Thomas Cranmer of Canterbury* for the Canterbury Festival of 1936, I was awakened at mid-night to go to the death-bed of Henry VIII. Round about midnight too, I was called from my bed to hear of Damaris Tighe's adventure with the pterodactyl in *The Place of the Lion*. I am not brave when I hear a mouse, whether by night or day, and to hear about the pterodactyl at such an hour was indeed alarming. . . . I heard the last two chapters of *The Greater Trumps* at 3:00 A.M. I loved those nocturnal readings and the ritual that went with them. Making tea and cutting wafer-like sandwiches to refresh my tired husband. Then the reading and discussion, and of course more tea making. I spent considerable time in making tea. (262)

8. Carpenter describes his responsibilities: "Tolkien took turns of duty as an air raid warden, sleeping in the damp little hut that served as the local headquarters. There were, however, no German air attacks on Oxford; nor was Tolkien required, as were a number of dons, to undertake work for the War Office or other government departments" (*Tolkien* 193). Although Tolkien's actual wartime service may have been minimal, it did preoccupy his mind, and this burden provided him with yet another obstacle to progress on his book.

9. A very early reference to this kind of competition in an Inkling's life is found in a letter from Lewis to Arthur Greeves. Lewis writes to say that he is just about to finish writing his narrative poem *Dymer*. Then he issues the challenge: "After that I shall expect something from you" (*Collected Letters* 1: 269).

10. The first quotation is from http://www.tolkien.co.uk/frame.asp (accessed May 2005), and the second is from *Beyond the Movie: The Lord of the Rings*, directed by Lisa Kors.

11. Carpenter gives a number of reasons for Tolkien's ongoing habit of not finishing his work, including his perfectionism, his preference for working on his invented languages, and the constant burden of his professional and family responsibilities. Carpenter also emphasizes his real and abiding need for encouragement, accountability, and collaboration, a point that deserves some emphasis. For Carpenter's discussion of Tolkien as non-finisher, see his *Tolkien*, pages 137–42.

12. The wager was so important to Tolkien that he mentions it five times in his letters. The dates for these letters are 18 February 1938, 3 March 1955, November/December 1963, 16 July 1964, and 8 February 1967. Warren Lewis also describes it in his diary entry for 24 May 1948 (cited in Sayer's *Jack*, page 153). Rateliff notes, however, "So far as I can discover, [C. S.] Lewis left no account of the bargain that resulted in three of his most famous books, nor of Tolkien's part in their inception" ("Time Travel" 200).

13. John D. Rateliff adds The Chronicles of Narnia, *The Screwtape Letters*, and *The Great Divorce* to the list of works that eventually grew from the trunk of this same tree ("Time Travel" 215). His comments on the importance of this wager and the significant creative interaction of Tolkien and Lewis are found in his article "*The Lost Road, The Dark Tower*, and *The Notion Club Papers*: Tolkien and Lewis's Time Travel Triad."

14. Don W. King discusses these sonnets on pages 197–99 of *C. S. Lewis, Poet*. He notes that this sequence is undated.

15. Lewis uses a similar image in a poem entitled "Caught." Here, Lewis imagines himself as a bird: "But you have seized all in your rage / Of Oneness. Round about, / Beating my wings, all ways, within your cage, / I flutter, but not out" (*Collected Poems* 130).

16. James Dundas-Grant participated in Inklings meetings after he was posted to Magdalen in 1944. Like Warren Lewis, he was a military man. Like Tolkien, he was a devout Roman Catholic. And like Dr. Havard, he sometimes felt a little awkward in the midst of these academics. Hooper writes, "Most of the Inklings were specialists in some academic field, and this inevitably led to Dundas-Grant being asked which one he worked in. 'I dinna work in any *field!*' he would exclaim" (*C. S. Lewis* 650).

17. The dates are somewhat confusing, particularly since Warren Lewis is mistaken in his recollection here. He made the decision to edit the *Lewis Papers* in May 1930, while in Ireland after his father's death. He began working on the project in December 1930, while home on leave. He retired in December 1932 and moved into the Kilns. He started work in earnest early in 1933.

18. These unpublished letters are available to researchers at the Marion E. Wade Center. C. S. Lewis's book *Letters to an American Lady* is delightful reading and an invaluable resource; perhaps some enterprising publisher will see the potential in Warren Lewis's fascinating *Letters to a Papuan Lady.*

19. Warren Lewis had also encouraged Jack Lewis's writing early on. On 24 August 1930, Warren Lewis writes that he has just "re-read J's fragment of his Ulster novel and found it so good that I urged him to take it in hand again, and he did not at any rate turn down the suggestion: I have hopes that he may yet do something with it" (*Brothers* 64). Despite his brother's urging, C. S. Lewis did not do any more work on this novel; the nine-page fragment can be found in *Lewis Papers: Memoirs of the Lewis Family, 1850–1930,* volume 9, pages 291–300. Extended description and analysis of this novel is found in chapter 4 of *The Backward Glance,* by Ronald W. Bresland.

20. For an excellent discussion of the important differences between inner-directed (or writer-based) prose and outer-directed (or reader-based) prose, I recommend Linda Flower's article "Writer-Based Prose: A Cognitive Basis for Problems in Writing."

21. Similarly, *The Hobbit, Roverandom, Mr. Bliss, Farmer Giles of Ham,* and *The Adventures of Tom Bombadil* were written within the supportive context of his family.

22. Again, the 1993 movie *Shadowlands* has given many people the false impression that the Lewis brothers lived lives of serene isolation. To the contrary, the Kilns was a noisy, busy place. Warren Lewis gives an extensive and rather bitter description of their household in a diary entry dated 17 January 1951, emphasizing the extreme turmoil of the house and the constant, interruptions (*Brothers* 236–39). A different kind of disruption, this one far more playful, is described by Walter Hooper:

> One summer morning when Lewis was writing at his desk by the open window, Snip [a Siamese cat which Lewis had inherited from his wife] took a great spring and shot through the window. She landed with a great thump on top of his desk, scattering papers in all directions, and skidded into his lap. He looked at her in amazement. She looked at him in amazement. "Perhaps," he told me, "my step-cat, having finished her acrobatics, would enjoy a saucer of milk in the kitchen." I opened the door for poor Snip and she walked out, embarrassed, but with the best grace she could manage. (*Past Watchful Dragons* 16)

23. Further discussion of Christopher Tolkien's indispensable work on the history of Middle-earth can be found in chapter 6.

24. Lyle W. Dorsett writes, "Williams certainly gave as much to the Inklings as he received. He possessed an animated and original mind, and his contributions enlivened the meetings. He published some of his new colleagues' manuscripts and helped launch a monograph series with Lewis and Tolkien as general editors" (*Essential C. S. Lewis* 11).

25. This eighteen-minute talk is one of only five surviving recordings of Lewis's voice in the BBC Sound Archives (Phillips 301–2).

26. I am indebted to David Bratman for calling this elusive notice to my attention.

27. Grotta is quoting from a 2 October 1952 letter by C. S. Lewis to Charles Moorman, published on pages 425–26 of *Letters of C. S. Lewis*. The second ellipsis is original to Grotta's text.

4

Opponents
Issuing Challenge

You can't really argue keenly, eagerly, without being a bit aggressive.
  —Owen Barfield

No mind was so good that it did not need another mind to counter and equal it, and to save it from conceit and blindness and bigotry and folly.
  —Charles Williams

I hope you don't mind me telling you all this? One can learn only by seeing one's mistakes.
  —C. S. Lewis

They read papers to each other, they read bits of their books to each other, they argued, they were a bit critical—a bit too critical for my father's taste.
  —Christopher Tolkien

Criticism may not be agreeable, but it is necessary.
  —Winston Churchill

All this talk about praise, encouragement, and mutual admiration is a little bit misleading. While the Inklings were quick to praise one another, they were also bold to challenge and criticize one another. In fact, if there is anything the Inklings express more often than humble gratitude for encouragement, it is healthy respect for opposition. As we have seen, Warren Lewis presents encouragement and opposition as two sides of the same coin: "Praise for good work was unstinted, but censure for bad work—or even not-so-good work—was often brutally frank" ("Memoir" 34). Critique was a significant part of Inklings meetings. Havard expresses it best: Lewis "read *The Screwtape Letters* to us. And very hilarious evenings they were. And we enjoyed them very much. But he had no need to ask, 'What did we think of it?' We were all too ready to say what we thought of it. *This was the ethos of the whole thing. That criticism was free*" (emphasis added).[1]

Criticism was free, and it could be ferocious. Warren Lewis describes the conversation as "dialectical swordplay" and tells us, "To read to the Inklings was a formidable ordeal" ("Memoir" 34). We get some idea of just how formidable in a comment made by Ruth Pitter. Though not an Inkling, this gifted writer and poet knew several of the members quite well. When C. S. Lewis asked her to read and criticize his poems, she exclaimed, "That would be like a lion asking a mouse to criticize his roar" (qtd. in Gibson 12).[2]

Though Pitter shied away from the lion's roar, the Inklings never did. Instead, the language of warfare is evident throughout their interaction.[3] Lewis in particular emphasizes that an aggressive approach is an ingrained part of his conversational style. Some see this tendency as an inborn aspect of his personality. Others have suggested that his approach stems from the fact that his father was a lawyer. But Lewis attributes it to his academic training. Addressing E. M. W. Tillyard, Lewis declares, "We have both learnt our dialectic in the rough academic arena where knocks that would frighten the London literary coteries are given and taken in good part; and even where you may think me something too pert you will not suspect me of malice. If you honour me with a reply it will be in kind; and then, God defend the right!" (Tillyard and Lewis 69). Lewis's training under the "Great Knock," William T. Kirkpatrick, was undoubtedly a major aspect of the "rough academic arena" that played such an important part in developing Lewis's keen appetite for intellectual argument.

In fact, even praise was sometimes expressed using physical, combative language. In one notable situation, Lewis tells Williams, "You go on getting steadily better ever since you first crossed my path: how do you do it? I begin to suspect that we are living in the 'age of Williams' and our friendship with you will be our only passport to fame." Then Lewis adds, "I've a good mind to punch your head when we next meet" (*Collected Letters* 2: 228).

Reports of Inklings meetings describe powerful minds equaling and countering one another in intellectual confrontation. Tolkien, for example, describes one particular meeting that he calls "a great event." It took place in November 1944. Williams, Havard, Barfield, and Lewis were there, and "C. S. L. was highly flown, but we were also in good fettle." Lewis and Barfield had at it, and Tolkien writes, "The result was a most amusing and highly contentious evening, on which (had an outsider eavesdropped) he would have thought it a meeting of fell enemies hurling deadly insults before drawing their guns." Their joy in witty repartee is evident here, too. Tolkien continues, "Warnie was in excellent majoral form. On one occasion when the audience had flatly refused to hear Jack discourse on and define 'Chance,' Jack said: 'Very well, some other time, but if you die tonight you'll be cut off knowing a great deal less about Chance than you might have.' Warnie: 'That only illustrates what I've always said: every cloud has a silver lining'" (*Letters* 103).[4]

At another meeting, an argument arose about the proper interpretation of Matthew 7:14, which reads, "Because strait is the gate, and narrow is the way, which leadeth unto life, and few there be that find it." Lewis writes, "I had a pleasant evening on Thursday with Williams, Tolkien, and Wrenn, during which Wrenn *almost* seriously expressed a strong wish to burn Williams, or at least maintained that conversation with Williams enabled him to understand how inquisitors had felt it right to burn people. Tolkien and I agreed afterwards that we *just* knew what he meant: that as some people at school, coll. punts, are eminently kickable, so Williams is eminently combustible" (*Collected Letters* 2: 283). The juxtaposition of moods is particularly interesting: in the context of a pleasant evening and agreeable conversation, which happened to be about the proper interpretation of a passage of scripture, the discussion gains such intensity that Williams is deemed "combustible" by a group of his dear friends. Regarding the debatable passage, Lewis says that the group concluded, "Our Lord's replies are never straight answers and never gratify curiosity, and that whatever this one meant its purpose was certainly not statistical" (2: 283).[5]

GREAT WAR

This agonistic quality, so evident in Inklings meetings, is also apparent in more personal settings. For example, on 26 January 1923, C. S. Lewis was just sitting down to dinner when he was surprised by a knock at the door. It was Owen Barfield. "The unexpected delight gave me one of the best moments I have had," Lewis writes. "We went at our talk *like a dogfight*: of Baker, of Harwood, of our mutual news" (*Letters* 179, emphasis added). As we saw in chapter 2, Lewis also uses the image of a "dogfight" in his description of Barfield as a Second Friend, "the man who disagrees with you about everything" (*Surprised* 199).

Apparently, benevolent conflict erupted often when Barfield and Lewis got together. According to Tolkien, Barfield "tackled" Lewis, "making him define everything and interrupting his most dogmatic pronouncements" (*Letters* 103). Over time, this intellectual conflict took a formalized turn. For about nine years, roughly from 1922 to 1931, they exchanged a series of letters that they called the "Great War."[6] It has never been published.[7] The focus is primarily philosophical. And it is very early, even seminal, in Inklings history.

Lewis characterizes the exchange as "an almost incessant disputation, sometimes by letter and sometimes face to face, which lasted for years" (*Surprised* 207). The extant letters are not letters per se but extended essays. Their tone is academic and their diction is precise and impersonal. Some are thickly illustrated with charts and diagrams, and many include numbered lists as the opponents enumerate specific points of contention. This complex correspondence is rife with references to literature, history, theology, and philosophy—both Lewis and Barfield constantly summarize, quote from, and allude to other thinkers and writers. Lewis's longest contribution is a two-part essay entitled, "*Clivi Hamiltonis Summae Metaphysices contra Anthroposophos,*" after Aquinas (Adey, "*Great War*" 12).

The issues at stake have their basis in the essential differences between anthroposophy and orthodox Christianity. Lionel Adey says their central disagreement was "whether subject and object were ever one or always distinct" (*"Great War"* 22). He explains, "Lewis maintained the poet's separateness from, and health-giving requirement to attend to, the object. Barfield has persistently and with increasing elaboration argued the case for the underlying oneness of subject and object, sometimes by adducing evidence of the human body's material identity with its environment, sometimes by pointing to modern notions of matter, mind and feelings as systems of opposed energies or impulses" (22).

Their arguments about these questions were not orderly or comprehensive. Instead, they were narrowly directed toward the specific questions, perspectives, concerns, and experiences of the two participants. In addition, their arguments were not conclusive. In fact, as Tennyson explains, "Each credits the other with superior intellectual acuity; each insists that the other regularly prevailed" (Introduction xvi).[8] Each also regularly insists that he was influenced much more than the other. Though the materials are incomplete and the outcome unresolved, this whole exchange—not just these written documents, but the conversations in which they were embedded and the publications that flowed, directly or indirectly, from this disagreement—made a powerful and lasting difference. Both Barfield and Lewis clarified their understanding of their own convictions. Perhaps more importantly, they also experimented with the most effective means of asking and answering serious philosophical questions.

The impact on Lewis was profound. Adey believes that Lewis could not "have developed as religious apologist, novelist or literary historian and expounder of the medieval *Weltanschauung* but for the stimulus of his controversies with Barfield" (*"Great War"* 18). The importance of this exchange to Barfield deserves particular emphasis. Commenting on the effects of the Great War, Barfield asserts that Lewis is the one who taught him "how to think" (*Owen Barfield* 9). This is illustrated with particular clarity by the fact that many of the ideas expressed in his BLitt. thesis (1926–27), revised and published as *Poetic Diction* (1928), were forged and refined in the process of this long debate. Also, Adey documents two specific contributions Lewis made to this book. He "supplied Barfield with the frontal quotation from Aristotle's *De Anima* on active and passive reason (*poiein* and *paschein*), which Barfield re-interpreted as poetic and prosaic consciousness." He also "supplied 'felt' in Barfield's definition of a poem's first effect, 'a felt change of consciousness' in the reader" (*"Great War"* 13).

After Lewis read Barfield's thesis, he made a "lengthy and detailed analysis" of it (Adey, "*Great War*" 13). These notes have been lost, so it is impossible to demonstrate a direct line of cause and effect. But we do know that Lewis thought chapter 7, "The Making of Meaning," was one of the "weakest portions" of the book (13). After Barfield read Lewis's comments, he added a new introduction and a whole new chapter, chapter 8, "The Making of Meaning II."[9] It would seem that Lewis's contribution to these changes was substantial. Barfield dedicated the work to C. S. Lewis, adding the Blakean maxim "Opposition is true friendship."

The Great War provides evidence for many aspects of Inklings influence. The letters themselves constitute a collaborative text, a kind of interaction that will be treated in some detail in chapter 6. The process of extended debate and disagreement shows the shaping of ideas and the mutual sharpening of intellectual abilities. And their discussion was followed by a clearly documented change in a specific text: revision to *Poetic Diction*.

In this particular situation, the influence continues in widening circles, for *Poetic Diction* proved enormously influential to Tolkien as well. Tolkien once said that the concept of ancient semantic unity—the central thesis of Barfield's book—had "modified his whole outlook" (qtd. in Carpenter, *Inklings* 42). Verlyn Flieger finds clear evidence for the impact of Barfield in two of Tolkien's critical essays: "Sigelwara Land," which was written six years after he first read Barfield, and "On Fairy-Stories," composed eight years later (*Splintered* 41). She adds, "Barfield's concept could not have affected Tolkien's philological and scholarly outlook without at the same time coloring his creative work, so much of which was built on and of language" (41). She illustrates this by noting that "this same attitude toward words is at the heart of the concept which lies behind The Silmarillion, a work of fantasy which strikingly illustrates the very kind of development and fragmentation of language and perception which Barfield's theory describes" (41).[10] And even more, she observes, "The languages of Middle-earth, in their development, are so striking an illustration of Barfield's thesis that one might almost think Tolkien had kept *Poetic Diction* at his elbow as he worked" (65).

Censure Was "Brutally Frank"

The Great War is a particularly fruitful illustration; most instances of opposition do not leave written records that are quite this easy to trace. Although a quick survey of their letters shows that the Inklings made plenty of negative comments about one another's work, a number of factors make it hard to assess the ultimate impact of those comments. For one thing, many of them are recorded privately. In his description of one Inklings meeting, for example,

Warren Lewis reports that Colin Hardie "read an interminable paper on an unintelligible point about Virgil" (*Brothers* 198). Apparently Warren Lewis wasn't the only one who disparaged this particular work. After the reading, John Wain remarked, "To say I didn't understand it is a gross understatement" (qtd. in *Brothers* 198). In another instance, Warren Lewis criticizes Barfield for issuing "withering discourse on the nothingness of the utterness" (257).[11] These comments tell us something about the effect of the text on the hearers, but nothing about the effect of the feedback on the author.

Other criticisms appear in letters written some time after a book had already been published. For example, Barfield gives this account of a letter he wrote criticizing *Perelandra*:

> When his novel *Perelandra* appeared, I wrote [to Lewis] praising it highly but making one minor adverse criticism. There is a passage near the beginning of the book where Ransom, the returned space traveler, is endeavoring to describe his feelings about the Green Lady. In order to achieve this, the character in the book makes use of three or four similes one after the other.[12] I complained in my letter that I thought these held up the narrative and were more appropriate for an essay or lecture than a novel, all the more so because the last of the three similes was introduced with the words, "One way of putting it would be . . ."[13]

Lewis responds to Barfield's comments with ready agreement: "The devil of it is, you're largely right. Why can I never say anything *once?*" He continues his letter with an illustration, and a shrug of resignation: "'Two and two make four. These pairs, in union, generate a quaternity, and the duplication of duplicates leaves us one short of five.' Well, all's one." Lewis continues in lighthearted self-mockery, using this same deliberate repetition in two other places in the letter. He concludes these mild and agreeable comments with a quick jab: "And take that grin off your ugly face" (*Collected Letters* 2: 574–75).[14]

Lewis criticized Barfield's work in turn, challenging him about specific features of his writing. In a letter written in 1962, he critiques Barfield's latest book, *Worlds Apart.* Characteristically, Lewis begins his commentary with lavish praise, emphasizing his enthusiasm for the work. He writes, "My trouble is that [it] is to me so exciting that I can't help reading it far too quickly. I must presently tackle it again and less greedily." Without transition or any other fanfare, Lewis launches directly into criticism: "Your language sometimes disgruntles me. Why must it be *polyvalence* instead of *multivalence*? And why do you use *base* as an intransitive verb—'He bases on' meaning 'He bases his argument on' or 'starts from'?" (unpublished letter, 29 March 1962). In these critiques of *Perelandra* and *Worlds Apart,* the comments are both direct and precise. They are primarily directed at stylistic matters, focusing on word choice and expression.[15]

Other critical comments found in letters and diary entries simply serve to illustrate that the Inklings did not like all they found in one another's books. For example, when Warren Lewis read *The Problem of Pain,* he did not find the arguments compelling, nor did he find the conclusion convincing. In a letter to Edward A. Allen, Warren Lewis writes, "I've never seen any explanation of the problem of pain (not even my brother's) which came near to answering the question for me" (unpublished letter, 2 July 1970). If *The Problem of Pain* proved unsatisfying, two other C. S. Lewis books proved simply unreadable. In compiling a list of devotional readings for the Lenten season of 1967, Warren included several of his brother's works. Although he read and enjoyed *Letters to Malcolm* and *Reflections on the Psalms,* he could not make his way through *Christian Reflections.* He says the essays in the book were "far above" his head (*Brothers* 273). Warren Lewis also struggled hard to make his way through Lewis's *Studies in Words.* He simply couldn't do it. He writes, "I've also (I'm afraid the only word is 'waded') half through J's *Studies in Words* but have had to abandon it—far too abstruse for me" (275).

Charles Williams also received his share of criticism. Havard, for example, describes *Taliessin through Logres* disparagingly as "a poem of epic dimensions, very Welsh and of an obscurity beyond belief" ("Philia" 351). He admits that "when it came to reading his work, I couldn't understand a word of it."[16] Hugo Dyson, never one to mince words, referred to Williams's work as "clotted glory" (qtd. in Lewis, *Collected Letters* 2: 501).[17]

The Inklings were not the only ones who struggled with Williams's poetry: both W. H. Auden and T. S. Eliot liked Williams and admired his work, but even they acknowledge that reading Williams is a challenge. In the introduction to Williams's history *The Descent of the Dove,* Auden writes, "I must confess that, when I first tried to read his poetry, though as a fellow verse writer I could see its great technical interest, I could not make head or tail of it" (ix–x). And after reading and rereading one of Williams's books in manuscript, Eliot urged Williams to revise the table of contents and the introduction, saying that the complex imagery was so difficult that it would frighten the readers away.[18]

Lewis also criticized Williams, saying that he labored under "an almost oriental richness of imagination" (*Collected Letters* 2: 501). Lewis had set the precedent for being perfectly honest in his second letter to Williams, written before the two men had met. Williams sent Lewis some of his poetry, and Lewis told him, "You will not be surprised to learn that I found your poems excessively *difficult.*" In his letter, Lewis discusses several of the poems, offering praise. Then he continues, "*Presentation* I liked, and the bit in *Gratia Plena* about the provincial dialect. *Orthodoxy* and *Ecclesia Docens* I definitely disliked." Lewis concludes this thought unequivocally: "I embrace the opportunity of establishing the precedent of brutal frankness, without which our acquaintance begun like this would easily be a mere butter bath!" (*Collected Letters* 2: 186–87).[19] The Inklings were committed to avoiding this "butter bath," and they were intentional in giving real, substantial critique. C. S. Lewis assured Barfield, "Don't imagine I didn't pitch into C. W. for his obscurity for all I was worth" (2: 819).[20]

Tolkien expressed dislike for a number of Lewis's books.[21] He took serious issue with several key points in *Christian Behaviour.*[22] He challenges Lewis primarily on the basis of logical inconsistency, a "confusion of thought" within the book itself. That is, Tolkien attacks him in terms of his argument, an area where Lewis is generally seen to be particularly strong. Tolkien also didn't care for *The Great Divorce.* "I did not think so well of the concluding chapter of C. S. L.'s new moral allegory or 'vision,'" he writes (*Letters* 71). Tolkien never elaborates his reasons. It may be significant that he refers to it as a moral allegory, for he has said bluntly, "I dislike allegory wherever I smell it."[23] Or it may be a reflection of his distaste for the use of a dream vision as a framing device, an important feature of the book's last chapter. Tolkien criticized several other Lewis books as well. He was irritated by *Studies in Words,* writing, "Alas! His ponderous silliness is becoming a fixed manner" (*Letters* 302).[24] Tolkien called *Letters to Malcolm* "a distressing and in parts horrifying work." He adds, "I began a commentary on it, but if finished it would not be publishable" (*Letters* 352).[25]

Tolkien's dislike for some of these works reflects a much larger issue: his general discomfort with Lewis's religious writings. Lyle W. Dorsett writes, "Owen Barfield told me that his friend Jack Lewis received much criticism for his preaching, teaching, and writing on Christian topics. Indeed, J. R. R. Tolkien was embarrassed that *The Screwtape Letters* were dedicated to him. When I inquired why, Barfield said that Tolkien and others, including himself, felt that Jack, being neither a theologian nor an ordained clergyman, had no business communicating these subjects to the public" (*Seeking* 58). Criticism of Lewis as a Christian apologist was widespread among academics in Oxford at the time. Mary Rogers, a student in the 1930s, explains that Lewis's lectures to young RAF personnel and his religious talks on the BBC were grudgingly accepted as war work. On the other hand, "The publication of *The Problem of Pain* in 1940 raised academic eyebrows." Then Lewis really went too far: "When *The Screwtape Letters* were published in 1942, with his description as 'Fellow of Magdalen College, Oxford' on its title page, many of his colleagues were outraged. This was a best-seller. He was employed as a literary scholar, not a popular evangelist!" (Rogers 54).

Tolkien was well aware of this reaction; in fact, he articulates it clearly and emphatically. In one letter, he takes note of "the extraordinary animosity that C. S. L. seems to excite in certain quarters" (*Letters* 184). Elsewhere, he elaborates: "No Oxford don was forgiven for writing books outside his field of study—except for detective stories which dons, like everyone else, read when they are down with the 'flu. But it was considered unforgiveable that Lewis wrote international best-sellers, and worse still that many were of a religious nature" (qtd. in Hooper, *Through Joy* 125). Christopher W. Mitchell describes the Oxford sentiment, writing, "The amount of ridicule and scorn [Lewis's Christian writings] fostered among his non-Christian colleagues was especially virulent." Mitchell cites a number of people who were uneasy with Lewis as evangelist, including Tolkien, and also Owen Barfield, who was bothered and embarrassed by it ("Bearing the Weight" 7).

Lewis knew all of this, and it caused him much distress. He once told his friend Harry Blamires, "You don't know how I'm hated" (qtd. in Mitchell, "Bearing the Weight" 7). His determination to express his faith in defiance of academic protocol did more than alienate his friends and colleagues; it proved hazardous to his career. Lewis was passed over for promotion to two "coveted Chairs in English Literature at his university despite his scholarly claim to the appointments" (8). There is virtual unanimity that his religious writing was the reason.

Denouncing Narnia

Though Tolkien attacked a number of Lewis's books of fiction and nonfiction, his strongest antipathy was directed toward The Chronicles of Narnia. In February 1949, Lewis read the early chapters of *The Lion, the Witch and the Wardrobe* to Tolkien. Shortly afterward, Tolkien was talking with a friend and reportedly told him, "I hear you've been reading Jack's children's story. It really won't do, you know! I mean to say: '*Nymphs and their Ways, The Love-Life of a Faun.*' Doesn't he know what he's talking about?" (qtd. in Green and Hooper 241).

What would account for such a brutal reaction? The most common explanation, as Nan C. L. Scott has said, is that "Tolkien expressed distaste for C. S. Lewis' 'Narnia' books because of their allegorical nature" (qtd. in Christopher, "Narnian Exile" 42).[26] Tolkien's dislike of allegory in general and religious allegory in particular is well known. Tolkien is quite clear on the matter. He writes, "I cordially dislike allegory in all its manifestations, and always have done so since I grew old and wary enough to detect its presence" (*Fellowship* xv); "I am not naturally attracted (in fact much the reverse) by allegory, mystical or moral (*Letters* 351); "My mind does not work allegorically" (*Letters* 174); and "Allegory is entirely foreign to my thought" (*Letters* 307). He makes a particular point of rejecting "conscious and intentional" allegory (*Letters* 145).[27] Many scholars who have written about Lewis and Tolkien, including Duriez, Wilson, Murray, and Howard, also see this as Tolkien's primary objection to the Chronicles.[28]

In his biography of Tolkien, Carpenter offers a different explanation. He suspects that two kinds of jealousy might be at issue. For one thing, he believes that Tolkien resented the fact that Lewis seems to have borrowed certain elements from Tolkien's work. Tolkien does complain to Lewis: "It probably makes me at my *worst* when the other writer's lines come too near (as do yours at times): there is liable to be a short circuit, a flash, an explosion—and even a bad smell, one ingredient of which may be mere jealousy" (*Letters* 127).[29]

Carpenter also thinks that Tolkien was jealous that Lewis produced text so quickly and easily while he had to struggle so much to make slow progress with his own work. All seven of the Narnia books were "written and published in a mere seven years, less than half the period in which *The Lord of the Rings* gestated" (*Tolkien* 201). Sayer, also, has argued that this was a key issue, writing, "I think that perhaps he envied Lewis his fluency" ("Recollections" 25). I believe that Tolkien's discomfort with Lewis's haste was not jealousy but rather the conviction that these stories were constructed carelessly. Hooper puts it simply, "Tolkien had very severe standards, and he probably thought the Narnian stories too hastily written, and containing too many inconsistencies" (*C. S. Lewis* 402). As Tolkien observed of his own nature, "I am a pedant devoted to accuracy, even in what may appear to others unimportant matters" (*Letters* 372).

In addition, it seems likely that he objected to the haphazard mixing of widely diverse mythologies. David Graham thinks that Tolkien saw the tale as "a jumble of unrelated mythologies." He elaborates, "To put Aslan, the fauns, the White Witch, Father Christmas, the nymphs, Mr. and Mrs. Beaver and the like—all of which had distinct mythological or imaginative origins—into a single imaginative country seemed like a terrible mistake (156).[30]

In "J. R. R. Tolkien: Narnian Exile," Joe R. Christopher offers an important refinement of this perspective. He says that Tolkien was not bothered so much by the mixing of mythologies as by their *distortion*. In his objection to the work, Tolkien refers specifically to the encounter between Lucy and Tumnus, a faun or satyr. Christopher writes, "Tolkien is thinking in mythological terms—what is a faun? how can one be expected to act? Lewis is reducing Greek mythology to the pleasant level of a child's story, where the faun is just a picturesque exterior of a nice person. In Mr. Tumnus' cave, a door leads from the main room to his bedroom . . . and that door is never, in the story, opened" (41). Again, Christopher writes, "Tolkien was bothered as an artist that Lewis's fauns did not obey their own nature, for (Tolkien thought) they were fixed myths that could be introduced into a Secondary World only as the myth had been established" (*C. S. Lewis* 118). It is certainly true that Tolkien himself mixed elements from different cultural contexts in his own work and even borrowed names from different languages and cultures. But in doing so, Tolkien was careful to honor the essential nature of the materials as they had been established by his sources.

When Lewis first shared his Narnia story with Tolkien, he probably expected a "helpful and sympathetic" response (Sayer, *Jack* 189). Instead, Tolkien thought that it was "about as bad as can be" (qtd. in Sayer, "Recollections" 25). Lewis was taken aback. "He was hurt, astonished, and discouraged when Tolkien said that he thought the book was almost worthless" (*Jack* 189). Sayer explains, "Jack had a high opinion of Tolkien's judgment and was distressed and disconcerted by his harsh response, especially since he himself had little confidence in the merits of his story" (189).

Despite his lack of confidence, Lewis decided to give it one more try. On 10 March 1949, he had dinner with Roger Lancelyn Green, and after dinner, Lewis read him two chapters of *The Lion, the Witch and the Wardrobe*. Green tells us that Lewis stopped reading and remarked that "he had read the story to Tolkien, who had disliked it intensely: was it any good? Green assured him that it was more than good, and Lewis had the completed novel ready to lend him (in the original manuscript) by the end of the month" (Green and Hooper 241). There is every indication that Lewis's question is entirely sincere. Throughout his letters, there are constant inquiries to friends, colleagues, and students asking whether or not a particular story or poem or other project is "any good" or "worth working on." For all of his bluster, Lewis cared deeply about the opinions of others, and he relied a great deal on their encouragement as he worked on his texts. Sayer writes, "Were it not for friends who praised it highly, he might never have published it" (*Jack* 189). In other words, if Lewis had considered Tolkien's response alone, the whole project might have been abandoned after just two or three chapters.

Even after Lewis completed the first book and wrote six more, Tolkien's assessment of The Chronicles of Narnia did not change. Late in his life, at the age of 72, Tolkien writes, "It is sad that 'Narnia' and all that part of C. S. L.'s work should remain outside the range of my sympathy" (*Letters* 352). The regret in his tone is telling: it saddened him that he could not countenance his dear friend's work.

DISPARAGING *THE LORD OF THE RINGS*

Members of the Inklings criticized many different works, and *The Lord of the Rings* was not exempt. Tolkien began writing it in December of 1937, and he completed the typescript in 1949; in other words, Tolkien was writing his "new Hobbit" for most of the active period of the Inklings, and the Inklings were an integral part of the process. The book occupied a considerable place, year after year, in the course of these meetings, and in general, the group was enthusiastic about it. However, there were dissenting voices. John Wain, who complained about a lot of things, complained about this too: "When Tolkien came through the door at a meeting of the Inklings with a bulging jacket pocket, I winced because I knew we were in for a slab of Gandalf and Bilbo Baggins and the rest of it. I wished him no harm, but would have preferred him to keep his daydreams within bounds and not inflict them on us" ("John Wain" 329). When Wain was asked what he thought of Middle-earth, he replied, "The fact is that I don't think anything of it. It has, and had, nothing to say to me. It presents no picture of human life that I can recognize" (329). Others, more or less, arrived at a similar conclusion. Owen Barfield is reported to have said, "I know this wouldn't be a popular thing, but I just can't get into that *Lord of the Rings* trilogy. I cannot finish it. I just can't get through it."[31] R. E. Havard remembers struggling "to pick up the thread of the story" when he first heard *The Lord of the Rings* read out loud ("Philia" 352). He borrowed the typescript copy and found that in reading it at his own pace, he was able to "savor its compulsive character" (352). "Still," he writes, "there have always been those who have found it hard to take" (352).[32]

Wain, Barfield, and Havard all struggled with the book; Hugo Dyson was by far its most outspoken critic. To some extent, this is Dyson's claim to fame. David Bratman puts it strongly: "If Hugo Dyson is remembered for one thing by Inklings readers, it's as the guy who didn't like *The Lord of the Rings*" ("Dyson" 28). Others clearly agree. A. N. Wilson says that Dyson "felt a marked antipathy to Tolkien's writings" (216). And Joe R. Christopher has referred to Dyson as "the anti-resonator."[33] Why such emphatic statements? It is not just that Dyson was loud in his manner and derogatory in his comments. By the spring of 1947, Dyson had become so irritated with *The Lord of the Rings* that he began to exercise a kind of "veto" against any more readings (*Brothers* 200). Stories about Dyson's vehement objection to *The Lord of the Rings* have circulated for years. In his biography of C. S. Lewis, Wilson gives a particularly colorful portrayal of Dyson as veto monger (217). His version of the story is quoted by Bratman in his article about Dyson. Perhaps the best authority is Christopher Tolkien, who describes the conflict this way:

Well, I should mention the very important figure of Hugo Dyson, who was an English don, English Literature at Oxford. Brilliant, vastly entertaining man who didn't like *The Lord of the Rings*. I remember this very vividly, my father's pain, his shyness, which couldn't take Hugo's extremely rumbustious approach. Hugo wanted fun, jokes, witticisms, lots of drink. And Lewis, who I deeply admired and loved—he had a strong, a strong manner. And he would say "Shut up Hugo. [claps hands] Come on Tollers." And *The Lord of the Rings* would begin with Hugo lying on the couch, and lolling and shouting and saying, "Oh God, no more Elves." The Inklings was a bit like that. (*A Film Portrait*)[34]

Despite Lewis's encouragement, things got so bad that if Dyson was present at an Inklings meeting, Tolkien would not read. And if Dyson arrived late, and a reading was already in progress, Tolkien would stop and put the manuscript away. Evidently, Dyson's impact was not popular—Warren Lewis, for example, calls it "unfair"—but the Inklings were not able to do anything about it.

Tolkien persisted, of course, so while Dyson managed to slow things down, his carping made little difference to *The Lord of the Rings*. However, it did change the Inklings. Duriez writes, "Less than three years after Dyson began to veto Tolkien's reading, the literary meetings of the group foundered" (*Gift* 129). It is widely held that in attacking these readings, Dyson was attacking the raison d'être of the group; that in impeding the participation of one of its members, Dyson was eroding its spirit. Dyson delivered an axe blow to the root of the tree. The Inklings were shaken, and they never quite recovered.

Abandoning *The Noises That Weren't There*

The power of opposition is further illustrated by a series of changes made to one of Charles Williams's novels. The idea for a new book first came to him in May 1943. He writes, "I now lie at night . . . with a kind of ghostly skeleton of a novel, and wake scared and unrefreshed" (*To Michal* 163). He started writing it in mid-June, despite the fact that "nothing much occurs to me for a plot" (163). He explains, "I can't waste any more time before beginning; even if we re-write, we shall have something to re-write" (163). It is a detective story, set against the backdrop of war-torn London. A young girl's body is found in an empty house. The house is said to be haunted, and a clairvoyant is brought in to investigate. Williams called this new novel *The Noises That Weren't There*.

Once he finished the first three chapters, he read them to Lewis and Tolkien and also shared them with his wife.[35] All were unanimous in their dislike of the chapters, so Williams set them aside. On 3 September he writes, "Three quarters of my mind is delighted that we are so at one about my discarded chapters; the other quarter is sad about the wasted work. Two months almost thrown away! But perhaps something better may come" (168).

He started over. By 23 September, he was working on a brand new draft, and by 5 October, he was making good progress. Writing again to Michal, he says, "Waking at one . . . I got on with the novel, & wrote about a thousand words, going to sleep again about four. I hope to do some more this evening" (171). The new work differs significantly from the old, but they do share a number of similar features. In both stories, there is a character whose wife has recently died. In both stories, the protagonist has supernatural experiences or abilities. Both include a character named Jonathan Drayton, a painter who is particularly interested in the effects of light and color. And both deal with the central concept of an evil character who creates human forms out of dust and water. The new novel was entitled *All Hallows' Eve.*

There are several parallel passages in the two books, including this description of one of Drayton's paintings. In *The Noises That Weren't There,* it reads as follows:

> It was part of London—she thought, of the City after a raid. There was a wide stretch of open desolation in front, and a few houses in the background; towards the right a shape which resolved itself as probably St. Paul's, incidental as that might be. The time was early dawn, the sky clear, and the light coming from the yet unrisen sun beyond the group of houses. The light was the most outstanding thing in the painting; indeed, as Clarissa gazed, it seemed that it stood out from the painting and threatened to dominate the room itself. At least it so dominated the painting that all the other elements and details were contained within it, and seemed almost to float in light as does the earth itself. (17)

The description in *All Hallows' Eve* reads like this:

> It was a part of London after a raid—he thought, of the City proper, for a shape on the right reminded him dimly of St. Paul's. At the back were a few houses, but the rest of the painting was a wide stretch of desolation. The time was late dawn; the sky was clear; the light came, it seemed at first, from the yet unrisen sun behind the single group of houses. The light was the most outstanding thing in the painting; presently, as Richard looked, it seemed to stand out from the painting, and almost to dominate

the room itself. At least it so governed the painting that all other details and elements were contained within it. They floated in that imaginary light as the earth does in the sun's. (26–27)

In comparing these two passages, or other parallel passages in the two works, it is apparent that there is very little stylistic difference between the versions. Word choice and syntax are somewhat altered: the change of "dominated" to "governed" eliminates some repetition and provides a more evocative image; removal of the awkward aside "incidental as that might be" lends more seriousness to the scene; the last sentence of the revision is a more powerful expression of the point. In general, the revised material is smoother and it does read better. But these modifications are minor. The key difference between the two novels is structural rather than stylistic. The fragmentary *Noises That Weren't There* is largely an extended explanation of concepts. As Hadfield says, "There is hardly scope to develop a story, and much of the three chapters is an exposition of the working of magic, whereby the noises were not noises but 'a pressure felt in her body and changed by her body into the noise'" (*Charles Williams* 227). *All Hallows' Eve* uses the same underlying ideas, and even some of the same characters and scenes, in the service of the story.[36] In the new novel, narrative portions are increased, conversations and explanations are decreased, and the overall pace is much improved.

As Williams wrote *All Hallows' Eve,* he read it to the Inklings, chapter by chapter, and then revised it in response to their criticism. Most scholars consider it one of Williams's finest works, and the Inklings played a significant role in it from start to finish. Tolkien notes, "I was in fact a sort of assistant midwife at the birth of *All Hallows' Eve,* read aloud to us as it was composed, but the very great changes made in it were I think mainly due to C. S. L." (*Letters* 349). Tolkien modestly characterizes his role as a kind of midwifery, then defers to the even greater influence of Lewis on the work.[37] It is also worth noting that Tolkien gives the group credit for bringing about "very great changes" in Williams's text, and not just minor or insignificant adjustments.

Stephen Medcalf believes that this process of working on *All Hallows' Eve* also played a significant part in a sermon by C. S. Lewis. Medcalf writes, "It seems likely to be more than a coincidence that at the time when Williams was writing this novel, on Whitsunday 28 May 1944, C. S. Lewis, a close friend and at that time very much under his influence, preached a sermon connecting the relation of meaning to sound in speech with the maxim 'not by conversion of the Godhead into flesh: but by taking of the manhood into God.' Lewis called the relation, and the sermon after it, 'Transposition.' The sermon is a remarkable piece of philosophical argument—in my own view, by far Lewis's best philosophical piece" (41). Medcalf devotes a full page of his essay to exploring the connections between Williams's novel and Lewis's sermon.

Dropping the Epilogue

The Noises That Weren't There is not the only example of a text that the Inklings rejected and the author abandoned.[38] Another is found in *The History of Middle-earth*. As Christopher Tolkien has noted, "The words that end *The Lord of the Rings*, "'Well, I'm back,' he said,' were not intended to do so when my father wrote them in the long draft manuscript" (*Sauron* 114). Tolkien wrote an epilogue to the book.[39] Though the events it describes take place sixteen years after Sam returns to the Shire, the epilogue was not composed at a different time or written as a separate document. Christopher Tolkien observes, "It is obvious from the manuscript that the text continued on without break; and there is in fact no indication that my father thought of what he was writing as markedly separate from what preceded" (114). The first version begins with a description of Sam and his children sitting by a fire:

> On a stool beside him sat Elanor, and she was a beautiful child more fair-skinned than most hobbit-maids and more slender, and she was now running up into her 'teens; and there was Frodo-lad on the hearthrug, in spite of his name as good a copy of Sam as you could wish, and Rose, Merry, and Pippin were sitting in chairs much too big for them. Goldilocks had gone to bed, for in this Frodo's foretelling had made a slight error and she came after Pippin, and was still only five and the Red Book rather too much for her yet. But she was not the last of the line, for Sam and Rose seemed likely to rival old Gerontius Took in the number of their children as successfully as Bilbo had passed his age. There was little Ham, and there was Daisie in her cradle. (*Sauron* 114)

Sam has been reading from the Red Book and talking about entwives and Lórien, Legolas and Gimli and Treebeard. The children love these stories and apparently know them well. "I want to hear about the Spider again. I like the parts best where you come in, dad," exclaims Frodo-lad, and Elanor asks, "When can I go and see? I want to see Elves, dad, and I want to see my own flower" (115).

   Two different versions of the epilogue have been published in volume 9 of *The History of Middle-earth.* In both versions, the chapter serves to tie up some loose ends and explain what happens to some of the characters. Both epilogues conclude with a tender exchange of faith and love between Sam and his dear wife, Rose. Christopher Tolkien states with some emphasis, "It cannot be doubted that this was how he intended at that time that *The Lord of the Rings* should end" (119). Here are the concluding paragraphs as they appear in the final draft:

> The stars were shining in a clear dark sky. It was the second day of the bright and cloudless spell that came every year to the Shire towards the end of March, and was every year welcomed and praised as something surprising for the season. All the children were now in bed. It was late, but here and there lights were still glimmering in Hobbiton, and in houses dotted about the night-folded countryside.
>
> Master Samwise stood at the door and looked away eastward. He drew Mistress Rose to him, and set his arm about her.
>
> "March the twenty-fifth!" he said. "This day seventeen years ago, Rose wife, I didn't think I should ever see thee again. But I kept on hoping."
>
> "I never hoped at all, Sam," she said, "not until that very day; and then suddenly I did. About noon it was, and I felt so glad that I began singing. And mother said: 'Quiet, lass! There's ruffians about.' And I said: 'Let them come! Their time will soon be over. Sam's coming back.' And you came."
>
> "I did," said Sam. "To the most belovedest place in all the world. To my Rose and my garden."
>
> They went in, and Sam shut the door. But even as he did so, he heard suddenly, deep and unstilled, the sigh and murmur of the Sea upon the shores of Middle-earth. (127–28)

When *The Lord of the Rings* was published, it contained no epilogue. Tolkien explains that he left it out because those who had read it disliked it: "An epilogue giving a further glimpse (though of a rather exceptional family) has been so universally condemned that I shall not insert it. One must stop somewhere" (*Letters* 179). There is no specific record of the readers Tolkien is referring to here: his comment that the epilogue had been "universally condemned" may be a reference to several individual Inklings, or to the Inklings as a group, or even to a larger circle including his family and his publisher. It is likely that Lewis in particular objected to the epilogue. Tolkien acknowledges that he eliminated several sections dealing with hobbits specifically because Lewis found them "tiresome."[40] Tolkien felt that if Lewis didn't like them, other readers would feel the same (376).

So, against his better judgment, Tolkien made the decision to drop the epilogue. But apparently he regretted this decision afterward. When *The*

Return of the King had been published, Tolkien complained: "I still feel the picture incomplete without something on Samwise and Elanor, but I could not devise anything that would not have destroyed the ending, more than the hints (possibly sufficient) in the appendices" (*Letters* 227). It may be argued that instead of "destroying the ending," this epilogue would have provided a sweet and satisfying close to the story.[41] Apparently Tolkien thought so, but the others disagreed, and so the epilogue, drafted and revised, is not included in the published text.

CONCLUSIONS

Havard tells the story of bringing Christopher Dawson to Magdalen College to meet C. S. Lewis. Dawson was a historian who "had written much on the philosophy and history of religion" ("Philia" 360). The evening was a dismal failure. Though Lewis was in every way gracious, Dawson was very uncomfortable. Havard says that he "shrank from our vigourous humour and casual manners" (360). The frank and informal nature of Inklings conversation did not appeal to everyone, but clearly this was exactly the way they liked it. One reads over and over again of the Inklings asking for feedback, asking for advice, asking for criticism. As Lewis explained to E. M. W. Tillyard,

> A friend of mine once described himself as being 'hungry for rational opposition.' The words seemed to me to hit off very happily the state of a man who has published doctrines which he knows to be controversial, and yet finds no one to voice the general disagreement that he looked for. It was with just such a hunger that I sat down to read your formidable *Rejoinder* to my essay on the *Personal Heresy*. In such matters to find an opponent is almost to find a friend; and I have to thank you very heartily for your kind and candid contribution to the problem. (Tillyard and Lewis 49)

In this chapter, we have looked at a number of criticisms that the Inklings made about one another's work. Some involve little complaints; others are characterized by more extended critiques. There are offhand comments about minor differences, and there are treatises about major differences in philosophy and outlook. In a small number of cases, there is a wholesale lack of sympathy for the work of another Inkling; among these are Wain's struggle with *The Lord of the Rings*, Warren Lewis's problems with *Christian Reflections*, C. S. Lewis's antipathy towards some of Williams's very early poetry, and Tolkien's dismissal of the Narnia stories. But even when the criticism is blunt or harsh, these disagreements occur within the context of genuine friendship, and even the most caustic comments tend to be marked with humor and conducted with charity. The Inklings were "hungry for rational opposition." They were grateful to have found it in each other.

NOTES

1. Oral History Interview with R. E. Havard, conducted by Lyle W. Dorsett for the Marion E. Wade Center (26 July 1984), page 16.

2. Don W. King notes that despite her professed reluctance, Pitter did give Lewis extensive feedback on his poetry. "Lewis often asked Pitter's advice about his own verse, admiring her native ability and appreciating her critical insights. In effect, Pitter became Lewis's mentor as a poet" (*Poet* 225). Pitter's comments on three of Lewis's poems, along with the manuscript source for her quote about the lion's roar, are published on page 790 of Lewis's *Collected Letters*, volume 2. Their mutual influence is discussed in King's book *Hunting the Unicorn*.

Although she claimed to be nervous about criticizing Lewis's poetry, Pitter happily attacked a number of his other works, including *The Lion, the Witch and the Wardrobe*. She explains, "I used sometimes to try and catch Lewis, you know, because his invention, especially in the Narnia stories, is so brilliant and so various" (Oral History Interview with Ruth Pitter, conducted by Lyle W. Dorsett (23 July 1985), page 19. In *C. S. Lewis: A Companion and Guide*, Hooper records the details of one of their conversations, including the rousing conclusion by Warren Lewis:

> RP: The Witch makes it always winter and never summer?
> CS: (In his fine reverberating voice) She does.
> RP: Does she allow any foreign trade?
> CS: She does not.
> RP: Am I allowed to postulate a *deus ex machina*, perhaps on the lines of Santa Claus with the tea-tray? (This is where CS lost the contest. If he had allowed the deus-ex-m., for which Santa gives good precedent, he would have saved himself.)
> CS: You are not.
> RP: Then how could the Beavers have put on the splendid lunch?
> CS: They caught the fish through holes in the ice.
> RP: Quite so, but the dripping to fry them? The potatoes—a plant that perishes at a touch of the frost—the oranges and sugar and suet and flour for the lovely surprise Marmalade Roll—the malt and hops for Mr Beaver's beer—the milk for the children?
> CS: (with great presence of mind) I must refer you to a further study of the text.
> Warnie: Nonsense, Jack; you're stumped and you know it. (722)

3. While the Inklings could be ferocious in their exchanges with one another, they were also capable of enormous grace and sensitivity. For example, Pauline Baynes notes that Lewis was both patient and kind in his criticisms of her drawings for The Chronicles of Narnia:

> When [Lewis] *did* criticize, it was put over so charmingly, that it wasn't a criticism, i.e., I did the drawings as best as I could—(I can't have been much more than 21 and quite untrained) and didn't realize how hideous I had made the children—they were as nice as *I* could get them—and Dr Lewis said, when we were starting on the second book, 'I know you made the children rather plain—*in the interests of realism*—but do you think you could possibly pretty them up a little now?'—was not that charmingly put? (Hooper, *C. S. Lewis* 406–07)

In another instance, a South African student, Peter Philip, explains, "On one occasion, I used the word 'efficacy' in an essay. Unfortunately I did not know how to pronounce it, and my guess proved to be woefully off course. Lewis looked at me and said, 'How interesting that that should be the South African pronunciation. In England we pronounce it "effikasy"'—which I thought was an extremely kind and tactful method of putting me right" (94).

4. Without question, there are times when advice given to Inklings was completely ignored. For example, Lewis's autobiographical *Surprised by Joy* was strongly criticized. According to Havard, Warren Lewis was emphatic that his brother should not publish it: "You can't," Warren said, "you can't publish this. It's not fair to the school." But Lewis "just stuck his heels in and said 'I'm going to.'" Havard also describes another instance: Nevill Coghill "wrote a rather savage little piece of verse about the church as it existed and Lewis thought this shouldn't be published and said so very forcibly and over and over again. But Coghill published it in spite of him" (Oral History Interview with R. E. Havard, conducted by Lyle W. Dorsett for the Marion E. Wade Center (26 July 1984), pages 19–20.

5. The Inklings also criticized their own work with ease. An amusing example is found in Lewis's "Reply to Professor Haldane." Though he takes issue with Haldane's wrong-headed review of his Ransom trilogy, Lewis readily grants that his novels are hardly trouble free. He writes, "If I were briefed to attack my own books I should have pointed out that though Weston, for the sake of the plot, has to be a physicist, his interests seem to be exclusively biological. I should also have asked whether it was credible that such a gas-bag could ever have invented a mouse-trap, let alone a space ship" (72).

6. There is no definitive documentation for the dates of the "Great War." As to the start, Lewis writes, "In the summer of 1922 I finished Greats. . . . The Great War with Barfield had, I think, begun at this time" (*Surprised* 212). As to the finish, Lionel Adey comments that sometime after he returned to the Christian faith, "Lewis lost interest and declined to resume the 'Great War'" (*Great War* 30).

7. The remaining documents are available to researchers at the Marion E. Wade Center. Adey studied these letters and corresponded with Owen Barfield to gain insight into their meaning and to fill in the gaps. His findings are published in *C. S. Lewis's "Great War."* Chapter 11 of his book is particularly useful, for it offers an extended and insightful treatment of the impact of this debate on both participants.

8. Barfield expresses his experience vividly, employing the language of battle. He says that in conversation with Lewis, he felt like he was "wielding a peashooter against a howitzer" (*Owen Barfield* 28). In another description, Barfield's analogy is athletic rather than military: "When one met [Lewis] and had the intention of putting forward something, arguing with him, it was rather like going in to bat in a game of cricket against a very swift bowler. You were so terrified as you walked toward the wicket that every idea in your head completely vanished except that at all costs you must keep a straight bat" (9–10).

9. When Barfield expanded *Poetic Diction,* he added consideration of three main ideas: first, a definition of poetic criticism as midwifery; second, the possibility that by tracing words to their "figurative origins" we can "unthink" the distinction between poetry and science; and third, a strong and elaborated distinction between "man as creator and knower" (Adey, *Great War* 32).

10. Flieger is making a distinction between The Silmarillion, meaning Tolkien's mythology in general, and *The Silmarillion,* meaning only those portions of the early material collected, edited, and published in the 1977 book by that title. Scholars make an effort to maintain this distinction even though Tolkien himself was not consistent on the matter.

11. Warren Lewis is referring to some of the Barfield material that Christopher Derrick added when he adapted Warren Lewis's biography of C. S. Lewis. Warren Lewis was angry about many aspects of this unfortunate transformation. "This busybody Derrick has performed the most ruthless surgery on it," he complained. But the "worst outrage" was that Derrick had added in several "unintelligible" contributions from Barfield (*Brothers* 256–57).

12. The passage in question comes on pages 64 and 65 of the novel *Perelandra*. Its conclusion reads as follows:

> There was no category in the terrestrial mind which would fit her. Opposites met in her and were fused in a fashion for which we have no images. One way of putting it would be to say that neither our sacred nor our profane art could make her portrait. Beautiful, naked, shameless, young—she was obviously a goddess: but then the face, the face so calm that it escaped insipidity by the very concentration of its mildness, the face that was like the sudden coldness and stillness of a church when we enter it from a hot street—that made her a Madonna. The alert, inner silence which looked out from those eyes overawed him; yet at any moment she might laugh like a child, or run like Artemis or dance like a Mænad. (64)

Lewis was well aware of the difficulty of describing the green lady of *Perelandra*. In a letter dated 9 November 1941, he writes,

> I've got Ransom to Venus and through his first conversation with the "Eve" of that world: a difficult chapter. I hadn't realised till I came to write it all the *Ave-Eva* business. I may have embarked on the impossible. This woman has got to combine characteristics which the Fall has put poles apart—she's got to be in some ways like a Pagan goddess and in other ways like the Blessed Virgin. But if one can get even a fraction of it into words it is worth doing. (*Collected Letters* 2: 496)

13. There are three versions of these comments by Barfield: "C. S. Lewis in Conversation," published in *Owen Barfield on C. S. Lewis;* "In Conversation," published in Carolyn Keefe's *C. S. Lewis: Speaker and Teacher;* and a talk Barfield gave at Wheaton College, the transcription of which is housed at the Wade Center. There are modest differences among these versions, as one might expect. The long quotation here is taken from the Wheaton transcription because in this version Barfield is somewhat more precise about the content of his criticism.

14. Owen Barfield tells us that "'take that grin' etc. [is] an allusion (see *Surprised by Joy*) to the ways of bygone Wyvern Bloods" (*Owen Barfield* 38).

15. Derek Brewer explains that close attention to stylistic matters was an important part of Lewis's approach in tutorials. Brewer describes his experience this way: "As I read my essay, he made notes. Many of these were minute points of verbal structure—rhythm, clarity, and precision—which he raised when I finished reading" (123). He elaborates: "After the general comment on the essay, he usually pointed out the small-scale deficiencies, not at all in a captious way. Then we discussed the principal points made and any other things to be said about the texts. This was almost always delightfully interesting. He had a vivid response to the most various literature, expressed in ready penetrating comment and wit. One of his most notable characteristics as a man as well as a tutor was his magnanimity, his generous acceptance of variety and difference, sure of his own standards but tolerant of others,' and of others' failings" (125).

16. Oral History Interview with R. E. Havard, conducted by Lyle W. Dorsett for the Marion E. Wade Center (26 July 1984), page 19.

17. There is no such thing as an "Inklings style," nor are there any stylistic traits that the Inklings universally praise or condemn. Still, one rhetorical offense that is attacked frequently is obscurity, and one recommendation that appears over and over again is to clarify. In tutorials, Lewis urged his students to write clearly. Edmonds explains, "I had a turgid style and [Lewis] constantly urged me to simplify it" (48). Lewis expresses the same idea in a number of his letters. In giving a young correspondent his rules for good writing, three out of five urge clarity. Rule number two is this: "Always prefer the plain direct word to the long, vague one. Don't *implement* promises, but *keep* them" (*Letters to Children* 64).

Most of the Inklings complain about the issue of obscurity and plead for the virtue of clarity somewhere in their writing. Havard emphasizes that the Inklings as a group placed considerable importance on this trait: "[C. S. Lewis] advised writers, especially beginners, to avoid ornament, but to set down as simply and clearly as possible what it was they had to say, then to go through it and remove all purple passages or anything that seemed to be particularly fine writing. All the Inklings had learned by experience that passages valued most by the writer appealed least to the reader. It is a hard saying but worth remembering" ("Philia" 357).

18. Unpublished letter, 25 September 1942, from T. S. Eliot to Charles Williams.

19. Warren Lewis uses the idea of a "butter bath" memorably in his diary entry of 11 November 1947. Nevill Coghill had talked with him right before a concert, saying, "I always like to see you at a concert because then I know it's going to be a good one." Warren Lewis writes, "Of course it means nothing, but the fact remains that we all like butter, and rightly so, for it *is* a lubricant" (*Brothers* 214).

20. Williams believed his work was improving, particularly in terms of its clarity. In an unpublished letter to Phyllis Potter, Williams notes that he is "glad to think that the SUMMER STARS are more lucid. They ought to be" (qtd. in Schneider 190).

21. In observing this, several cautions are in order. For one thing, Tolkien described himself as "a man of limited sympathies" (*Letters* 349). In another letter, he says bluntly, "My taste is not normal" (34). His preferences were specific and his standards were high; in short, there is a lot of work Tolkien did not particularly care for. Furthermore, many of Tolkien's most critical comments about his fellow Inklings, including Lewis, occur very late in his life. There is strong evidence that his views and attitudes shifted over time. Finally, many of the Inklings, especially Tolkien and Warren Lewis, use their diaries and some of their letter writing to work out their grumbles and frustrations. Therefore, it is wise to treat these comments as a small (albeit significant) part of a much larger story.

22. The letter is not dated. Humphrey Carpenter and Christopher Tolkien assume it was written in 1943, the same year *Christian Behaviour* was published. The letter was never sent. A copy was found "tucked into Tolkien's copy of Lewis's booklet" (*Letters* 59). The fact that this letter was never sent should not be taken as evidence that Tolkien was not earnest about his objections. Tolkien wrote a number of letters, comments, and critiques that he did not send. See, for example, his long response to W. H. Auden's review of *The Return of the King,* published on pages 238–44 of his *Letters.* It may be, however, that Tolkien expressed his views to Lewis at some point. It is clear from looking closely at the texts of *Christian Behaviour* (1943) and *The Four Loves* (1960) that Lewis's views on these issues did change over time. Certainly many different factors contributed to these changes, but it is possible that Tolkien's perspective made some contribution, since Lewis's views shift in the direction of the position Tolkien expresses in his letter.

23. Tolkien in a BBC interview, posted at http://daisy.freeserve.co.uk/jrrt_int.htm and accessed 20 May 2005.

24. Tolkien contributed some research to *Studies in Words;* Lewis incorporated only a small portion of his text. Tolkien explains, "I wrote for him a long analysis of the semantics and formal history of *BHŪ with special reference to Φύσις. All that remains is the first 9 lines of PHUSIS (33–34) with the characteristic Lewisian intrusion of 'beards and cucumbers.' The rest is dismissed on p. 36 with 'we have not a shred of evidence'" (*Letters* 302). Lewis does not credit Tolkien for providing this information. One might expect Tolkien to be upset by this. To the contrary, he writes, "I am deeply relieved to find I am not mentioned" (302).

25. Tolkien's commentary on Lewis's book *Letters to Malcolm* exists in manuscript form in the Bodleian Library. It has been titled "The Ulsterior Motive" and it is not among the Bodleian papers generally available to researchers. Carpenter quotes from it on pages 50, 51–52, 216, and

232 of *The Inklings* (Hammond and Anderson 335). Those who have read it describe it as choppy and redundant. The mood is not bitter, just cranky. John D. Rateliff characterizes it as the sort of letter one would write to a lifelong friend who has just done something that really annoys you (personal correspondence, 20 April 2005).

26. Scott is basing her comment on two conversations with Tolkien during which they specifically discussed The Chronicles of Narnia. Her report and an analysis of it are published in Christopher's "J. R. R. Tolkien, Narnian Exile."

27. The concept of allegory in relation to the work of the Inklings in general and The Chronicles of Narnia in particular is a complex and problematic subject, outside the scope of this present study. Carpenter gives a brief and useful statement on the matter: "The fact that the Narnia stories are 'about' Christianity does not mean that they are allegorical. The characters exist in their own right and are not mere allegorical types. The events of the Christian story are reimagined rather than allegorised, and the reader is left free, as he never is with allegory, to interpret in whatever fashion he pleases" (*Inklings* 223). Hooper elaborates the important differences between allegory, supposal, and symbolism on pages 423–29 of *C. S. Lewis: A Companion and Guide.*

28. Joe R. Christopher has argued against this opinion, stressing that he finds no reliable record that Tolkien ever criticized The Chronicles of Narnia specifically on the basis of its allegorical nature. Christopher also believes that at the time Tolkien expressed this strong negative reaction, he had heard only the first two or three chapters of the book, before the explicitly Christian elements of the story appeared.

29. Tolkien expressed irritation with Lewis's borrowings, but none of his accusations include direct reference to Narnia. His comments span a period of nearly thirty years. In 1938, he writes, "Eldila, in any case, I suspect to be due to the influence of the Eldar in the Silmarillion" (*Letters* 33). In 1945, he complains about references and allusions "creeping" into Lewis's work (113). In 1951, he offers an extended explanation of *Númenóre,* and grumbles that "Lewis derives [the term] from me and cannot be restrained from using, and mis-spelling [it] as Numinor" (151). In 1955, he protests that Lewis has included a reference to Númenóre in *That Hideous Strength* (224). In 1961, he explains to another reader that Lewis's *Numinor* is derived from his *Númenor* (303). In 1965, Tolkien gives the most extended discussion of the issue, calling Lewis's memory "capacious but not infallible" (361). And in 1967, four years after Lewis died, Tolkien describes the history of "The Downfall of Númenor," adding, "This attracted Lewis greatly (as *heard* read), and reference to it occurs in several places in his works: e.g. 'The Last of the Wine,' in his poems" (378).

This point of contention was obviously a matter of great concern to Tolkien. He tells one reader, "Your discovery of 'Numinor' in C. S. L's *That Hideous Strength* is discovery of a plagiarism." But then he softens the statement, explaining, "Well, not that, since he used the word, taken from my legends of the First and Second Ages, in the belief that they would soon appear" (*Letters* 224). In including references to Tolkien's work, Lewis was not trying to be sneaky. He acknowledges in the preface to *That Hideous Strength* that Tolkien is his source, and he laments the fact that Tolkien's book is still in manuscript. He was also not trying to be malicious. He clearly believed that Tolkien's work would soon be published and that his use of Tolkien's material would be viewed with favor, recognized as an indirect tribute or deliberate literary allusion. But whatever Lewis's perceptions or his motives may have been, Tolkien clearly believed some trespass had been committed.

30. M. A. Manzalaoui makes the same point, and in his discussion he provides the following list of Lewis's sources in addition to the obvious Gospel parallels: "Homer, Plato, Virgil, *The Arabian Nights, Beowulf,* the Middle English romances of *Sir Orfeo, Sir Gawain,* and *Havelock,* Malory's *Morte d'Arthur,* at least three of Chaucer's poems, Dante, Shakespeare, Milton, Wagner,

Alice in Wonderland, Huckleberry Finn, Richmond Cromptom's [*sic*] *William,* and Lewis's own friends Charles Williams and Tolkien" (16).

31. Oral History Interview with Stella Aldwinckle, conducted by Lyle W. Dorsett for the Marion E. Wade Center (26 July 1985), page 45. Aldwinckle is describing a conversation she had with Owen Barfield in which he expressed this opinion.

32. Reaction to *The Lord of the Rings* has always varied. Havard summarizes: "At first hearing, its reception was mixed. Lewis himself was loud in its praise, but his view was not shared by everyone" ("Philia" 352). That was true in the beginning, and it continues to this day: the book still receives both praise and scorn. Not all find *The Lord of the Rings* to their liking, but support for the work has steadily increased. Havard notes, "Time has supported Lewis's judgment, and Tolkien has added Hobbits to folklore" (352). But Tolkien himself knew that his mythology was not going to appeal to everyone. He notes, "Those that like this kind of thing at all, like it very much, and cannot get anything like enough of it" (*Letters* 121–22). Putting it more bluntly and lightly, Tolkien quips, *"The Lord of the Rings* / Is one of those things: / If you like it you do: / If you don't, then you boo!" (qtd. in Carpenter, *Tolkien* 223). Or, as W. H. Auden observes, "Nobody *seems* to have a moderate opinion: either, like myself, people find it a masterpiece of its genre or they cannot abide it" ("At the End" 44). Tolkien expected that the number of people who liked the story would be comparatively small (*Letters* 122). In fact, he was genuinely surprised to discover the extent of interest in his story. He writes, "Nothing has astonished me more (and I think my publishers) than the welcome given to *The Lord of the Rings*" (221).

33. Personal correspondence, 12 June 2002.

34. Mike Glyer has speculated that the reason Dyson interrupted readings of *The Lord of the Rings* had nothing to do with elves and hobbits, and everything to do with his own experiences as a soldier. As Lewis says, Dyson was "a burly man, both in mind and body, with the stamp of the war on him" (*Collected Letters* 2: 17). Mike Glyer believes that scoffing about elves may have provided Dyson with "a manly way of avoiding the strife and intensity of the story" (personal correspondence, 4 October 1998).

35. These three chapters have been published in *Mythlore.* The introduction to the material wrongly asserts that this is Williams's last novel, left unfinished at the time of his death in 1945. In fact, *The Noises That Weren't There* immediately precedes *All Hallows' Eve.*

36. This is not to say that *All Hallows' Eve* is either easy or straightforward. In a charitable review, Orville Prescott writes, "There are fascinating aspects to this book, the regal authority with which it presents the world of the spirit, the noble faith with which it cleaves to the essence of ethical problems" (23). Prescott takes Williams to task nonetheless, criticizing (among other things) "his opaque style, his prodigal use of symbols and his deliberate mystification" (23).

37. Tolkien's description of himself as an assistant midwife is well-known. Less known is Lewis's use of a similar label. In a letter to a correspondent about the extent of his influence on Tolkien, Lewis says he acted "as a midwife" (qtd. in Kilby, *Tolkien* 76).

38. Lewis also abandoned a number of works in progress. We have the (controversial) fragment called *The Dark Tower.* He did not finish the poem version of the Cupid and Psyche myth. There is the Lefay fragment, two chapters of a Narnia tale (see Hooper's *Past Watchful Dragons*). He had tried twice to write a book on prayer; on 15 February 1954 he wrote to Sister Penelope saying, "I have had to abandon the book on prayer; it was clearly not for me" (qtd. in Hooper, *C. S. Lewis* 378). There is little conclusive evidence that links any of the Inklings to the abandonment of these manuscripts or to the fact that he later returned to some of them and successfully completed them.

39. Some readers and book sellers refer to Tolkien's *Bilbo's Last Song* as the epilogue to *The Lord of the Rings.* The poem is written in twelve short stanzas, each one a mere 12 to 14 words in length,

and it has been published in a small volume richly illustrated by Pauline Baynes. In it, Bilbo says goodbye to Middle-earth as he journeys to the Grey Havens. While it does concern events that take place at the end of the story, it should not be confused with the epilogue Tolkien intended.

40. On 8 February 1967, for example, Tolkien writes specifically that Lewis found light-hearted hobbit conversation tiresome, and adds, "To tell the truth he never really liked hobbits very much" (*Letters* 376). Even though this was written late in Tolkien's life and must be considered within that context, it does suggest that the extended epilogue may have been an example of the kind of writing Lewis did not care for.

41. Readers remain sharply divided about Tolkien's decision to drop the epilogue. In a recent poll posted on www.sf-fandom.com, readers were asked to vote whether he should have left it in or taken it out, and, at the time of this writing, the results were split exactly 50/50.

5

Editors
Making Changes

I spent much of last night labouring on Witch-craft—*the worst is that I must, I fear, write the last chapter again. But I have drafted most of it.*
    —*Charles Williams*

The Venus book [Perelandra] *is just finished, except that I now find the two first chapters need re-writing.*
    —*C. S. Lewis*

But, of course, such a work as The Lord of the Rings *has been edited.*
    —*J. R. R. Tolkien*

We edit to let the fire show through the smoke.
    —*Arthur Plotnik*

As chapters 3 and 4 have demonstrated, when the members of a writing group serve as resonators and opponents, they establish a rich context where creative work can flourish. They provide structure, create expectations, validate risk, encourage healthy competition, model techniques, provide accountability, promote excellence, generate new projects, redirect talents, sharpen purpose, reconsider direction, and celebrate success.

In this chapter, we will consider the work of the Inklings as editors. While encouragement and criticism tend to be directed at the writer, editing tends to be directed toward the text itself.[1] Editorial feedback may take a variety of forms: verbal or written, brief or extensive, direct or indirect, serious or playful. When the members of a writing group serve as editors, they offer feedback or advice that results in very specific changes.

The Inklings edited one another's work at all levels. Warren Lewis read and corrected the proofs of *The Pilgrim's Regress*. C. S. Lewis read and corrected the proofs of Dyson's *Augustans and Romantics*.[2] Williams did preliminary work on *The Allegory of Love* in his official capacity as an editor at Oxford University Press. Owen Barfield read the manuscript of *Surprised by Joy* to check it for possible legal implications. The Inklings also asked for advice on small details: Tolkien, for example, wrote to Christopher Tolkien asking whether "Shelob" seemed to be a good name for a spider, and, in another letter, he explains that he is in need of specific information on how to stew a rabbit.[3] In addition, a number of the Inklings, notably C. S. Lewis, J. A. W. Bennett, and C. L. Wrenn, served as editors of collections that included essays by other Inklings. We may assume that in the process of preparing these materials they exercised some editorial function.

But when we study the process of editing, we are not limiting our attention to supplying details, correcting errors, copyediting, or reading proofs. Editing includes much more than adjusting word choice or restructuring syntax. It also includes large or global changes that come about as specific comments lead the writer to completely revise or "re-see" the project and take it in a whole new direction. Advice may be offered at various stages of the writing process: when the author is kindling an initial vision, sketching a tentative draft, rewriting a small scene, strengthening the flow of an argument, considering an additional source, polishing the final galleys. The timing itself will have an impact on the changes that result.

In general, the power of editors to affect a text depends on how fixed or fluid the writer considers the text to be. In fact, Gere's research on writing groups shows that textual indeterminacy, that is, a draft open to substantial change and revision, is an essential ingredient in the success of any writing group (75).[4] This helps to explain the effectiveness of the Inklings. As they met and talked about their work, they clearly viewed each manuscript as a work in progress.[5] Even their name—"Inklings"—hints at fleeting notions, half-formed ideas, and rough impressions. Tolkien writes that they did not read polished, publishable drafts to one another, but rather "largely unintelligible fragments of one another's works" (*Letters* 209). They shared rough drafts with one another, fully expecting to revise their texts, sometimes adding, sometimes deleting, and sometimes adjusting the material. They might take all of the advice they were given, or sift through it and take one small part. Sometimes, advice served as a springboard to new ideas; other times it sparked a reaction in direct opposition. The result was constant and significant change.[6] In a comment both matter-of-fact and categorical, Tolkien writes "of course there was a tremendous lot of revision" (qtd. in Duriez, *Gift* 139).

Tolkien in particular is notorious for the amount of revising that characterized his writing process. Since it is often claimed that Tolkien was not influenced by the comments he received, the constantly evolving nature of his work is worth emphasizing. His first drafts tend to be very rough indeed, sometimes nearly illegible, often breaking off into fragmented notes when ideas flowed faster than his hand could write.[7] Having dashed off a draft, he would rewrite and rewrite and rewrite again.[8] According to the Marquette University Library, Tolkien's was "an extraordinary creative process." As many as 18 drafts exist for single chapters. The complete manuscript of *The Lord of the Rings* consists of 7,125 leaves and nearly 10,000 pages.[9]

Christopher Tolkien explains that his father built his manuscripts in stages or waves; he calls them "phases" (*Shadow* 3). Tolkien worked like a painter who first pencils in a rough sketch, then fills in a more detailed drawing, then adds layers of color, working from background to foreground to final details.[10] The earliest drafts were written at great speed, and it is often these earliest drafts, what Christopher Tolkien calls "primary compositions," that Tolkien read to the Inklings (*War* 107).

Tolkien revised not only a lot of his text, but also many different aspects of it. Christopher Tolkien says that the features of his story that changed the most were the "names and relations of the hobbit-families of the Shire," asserting, "In no respect did my father chop and change more copiously" (*Shadow* 35). But names and genealogies are not all Tolkien revised: "[*The Lord of the Rings*] was begun in 1936, and every part has been written many times. Hardly a word in its 600,000 or more has been unconsidered. And the placing, size, style, and contribution to the whole of all the features, incidents, and chapters has been laboriously pondered" (*Letters* 160). Again, Tolkien writes, "The writing of *The Lord of the Rings* is laborious, because I have been doing it as well as I know how, and considering every word" (42).[11] Verlyn Flieger expresses the point succinctly: "Tolkien started, stopped, returned to, reconsidered, revised, and re-revised almost everything he wrote" (*Question* 5–6). And he pressed on even after the entire work had been drafted, reconsidered, and rewritten. Tolkien explains that "when the 'end' had at last been reached the whole story had to be revised, and indeed largely re-written backwards" (*Fellowship* xiv).

It is hard to overstate the case. Describing the section of the story that tells of the journey from Bree to Weathertop, Christopher Tolkien writes, "The manuscript of this chapter is an exceedingly complicated document: pencil overlaid with ink (sometimes remaining partly legible, sometimes not at all), pencil not overlaid but struck through, pencil allowed to stand, and fresh composition in ink, together with riders on slips and complex directions for insertions" (*Shadow* 133). The versions of this particular section of manuscript are so complicated that Christopher Tolkien provides a chart to help readers track the progression of the various threads.

In a description of his father's work on *The Silmarillion*, Christopher Tolkien says, "It was far indeed from being a fixed text, and did not remain unchanged *even in certain fundamental ideas* concerning the world it portrays" (emphasis added). He adds, "As the years passed the changes and variants, both in detail and in larger perspectives, became so complex, so pervasive, and so many-layered that a final and definitive version seemed unattainable" (*Silmarillion* 7). Tolkien was constantly working on his sub-created world. Some of the most foundational aspects of the people, events, and nature of Middle-earth remained in flux all the days of his life.

To what extent did the Inklings contribute to this evolving draft? For one thing, they supported Tolkien's natural impulse to keep polishing and perfecting his work. Lewis writes that Tolkien is "one of those people who is never satisfied with a MS. The mere suggestion of publication provokes the reply 'Yes, I'll just look through it and give it a few finishing touches'—wh. means that he really begins the whole thing over again" (*Collected Letters* 2: 631).[12] Without a doubt, this tendency to rework his text was primarily an expression of Tolkien's personality and a reflection of his established writing habits. But the Inklings reinforced rather than restrained this natural tendency. As Tolkien read his texts aloud at meetings, group members not only encouraged him to revise and improve the work, they also made specific suggestions. Although the Inklings did not generally keep any record of these recommendations, a number of their comments do survive. These serve as important evidence that the Inklings had significant impact on Tolkien's text.

GLOBAL SHIFTS IN *THE LORD OF THE RINGS*

We have seen that Tolkien gratefully acknowledged Lewis for his role as encourager. Tolkien openly credits Lewis for two kinds of help: convincing him that his "private hobby" would be worth sharing with a public audience and urging him to continue working on the book when he wanted to give up. But Lewis also made a number of specific comments that led to modifications in *The Lord of the Rings*.

When Tolkien had finished his rough draft of the beginning chapters, he gave them to C. S. Lewis and to Rayner Unwin, asking for feedback. Responding independently, the two readers made essentially the same observation: the chapters have "too much conversation and 'hobbit talk' which tends to make it lag a little" (*Shadow* 108). On 4 June 1938, Tolkien conveyed his thanks to Rayner Unwin "for bothering to read the tentative chapters, and for his excellent criticism." Tolkien adds, "It agrees strikingly with Mr Lewis,' which is therefore confirmed" (*Letters* 36).

Tolkien plainly appreciated this "excellent criticism." This is particularly interesting since Tolkien himself did not believe the text suffered from too much dialogue. "The trouble is," he says, "that 'hobbit talk' amuses me." The fact is he enjoys it "more than adventures." Despite this personal preference, Tolkien concludes, "I must plainly bow to my two chief (and most well-disposed) critics" (*Letters* 36). As he revised these early sections, Tolkien crossed out lines of dialogue, tightened up conversations, and banished long explanations to the appendices. Tolkien changed his text, and he did it with amazing ease and grace. And it is interesting that in the process, he not only defers to his critics, but also praises them.[13] Since this feedback shaped the earliest chapters of *The Lord of the Rings,* it seems certain that Tolkien kept this advice in mind as he wrote new sections.

Tolkien went back and rewrote the first few chapters, but he did not know what to do next. On 17 February 1938 he writes, "The Hobbit sequel is still where it was, and I have only the vaguest notions of how to proceed" (*Letters* 29). Five months later, on 24 July 1938, he is in exactly the same spot. He says of the story, "It has lost my favour, and I have no idea what to do with it" (*Letters* 38). Although Tolkien offers a number of explanations for his difficulties, it is clear that at this point, he is fundamentally uncertain about the nature of the book. He writes, "I am personally immensely amused by hobbits as such, and can contemplate them eating and making their rather fatuous jokes indefinitely; but I find that is not the case with even my most devoted 'fans'" (*Letters* 38). As this comment shows, Tolkien still saw his *Hobbit* sequel as having the primary characteristics of the first book: aimed at a young audience, built around humor and pranks, and modeled somewhat on the structures of a folk or fairy story. Readers and critics alike have noted that even in the final version, the first three chapters of *The Lord of the Rings* retain something of this quality.

At this point in Tolkien's composing process, on 24 July 1938, Lewis made an important observation. Tolkien records, "Mr Lewis says hobbits are only amusing when in unhobbitlike situations" (*Letters* 38). It appears that as a direct result of this comment, Tolkien began to consider a more ambitious purpose, an "unhobbitlike" seriousness to his new story. There is additional evidence that points to the part Lewis played in nudging the story away from the frivolous and toward a more serious purpose. In a letter to a reader, Lewis makes it plain that he urged Tolkien's story in this specific direction. Lewis writes, "My continued encouragement, carried to the point of nagging, influenced him very much to write at all *with that gravity* and at that length" (qtd. in Kilby, *Tolkien* 76, emphasis added).

The change in tone is clear in Tolkien's revision of a key passage in chapter 3. In the first draft, three hobbits named Bingo, Odo, and Frodo have left Hobbiton and are walking through the Shire. Suddenly, the sound of hoofs draws near, and they all hide in a little hollow beside the road. "Round a turn came a white horse, and on it sat a bundle—or that is what it looked like: a small man wrapped entirely in a great cloak and hood so that only his eyes peered out, and his boots in the stirrups below" (*Shadow* 47).

The horse and rider stop near Bingo. "The figure uncovered its nose and sniffed; and then sat silent as if listening. Suddenly a laugh came from inside the hood." It is Gandalf, who calls out, "Bingo my boy!" as he throws aside his wrappings (*Shadow* 47).

In manuscript, the story breaks off at the bottom of this page, and shortly after Tolkien first drafted it, he went back and rewrote this passage. Here is the same section again, as it appears in *The Fellowship of the Ring*:

> Round the corner came a black horse, no hobbit-pony but a full-sized horse; and on it sat a large man, who seemed to crouch in the saddle, wrapped in a great black cloak and hood, so that only his boots in the high stirrups showed below; his face was shadowed and invisible.
>
> When it reached the tree and was level with Frodo the horse stopped. The riding figure sat quite still with its head bowed, as if listening. From inside the hood came a noise as of someone sniffing to catch an elusive scent. (73)

It is clear that this description of a Black Rider draws extensively from the original description of Gandalf, including the cloak and hood and sniffing sound. But things have shifted radically. Gandalf is gone: a mysterious Black Rider appears instead. The mood is quite altered. Once personal and playful, the feel is now much darker. Frodo's response to this strange figure is an "unreasoning fear" (73).

The sudden appearance of this Black Rider raises two key questions. First, what is the nature and purpose of this evil creature? And second, if this isn't Gandalf, then what could have happened to their friend?[14] Finding answers to these questions will determine the necessary direction of the events that follow. With this new apparition, the tale has turned.

But not only has the hobbit adventure changed, Tolkien's experience as a writer has changed as well. At last Tolkien seems to catch his stride. Soon afterward, he reports that the story "is now flowing along, and getting quite out of hand. It has reached about chapter 7 and progresses towards quite unforeseen goals" (*Letters* 40). There is a clear break from the tentative and uncertain tone of the past. Now the manuscript flows along and has taken on a life of its own—*it* is flowing, *it* progresses, *it* has reached chapter 7, *it* is getting out of hand.[15]

Even the title has changed. It is no longer "The New Hobbit": Tolkien now refers to his story as "The Lord of the Ring [sic]" (*Letters* 40). It is clearly something new, distinct from its predecessor, and moving toward a different purpose. These radical changes occur within a month of Lewis's observation about hobbits.

Less dialogue, more narrative. Less hobbit talk, more danger. It is evident that Lewis's comments influenced the type of narrative Tolkien produced. But there is a much larger issue: to some extent, Lewis and the Inklings were also responsible for the fact that Tolkien produced narrative at all.[16] During the years he worked on the project, Tolkien had a well-documented tendency to stop working on the novel and turn his attention either to his invented languages or to the histories and genealogies of his invented world. He was always reluctant to turn away from these consuming interests. He writes, "I think it is plain that . . . a sequel or successor to The Hobbit is called for. I promise to give this thought and attention. . . . The construction of elaborate and consistent mythology (and two languages) rather occupies the mind" (*Letters* 26). Again he writes, "The most absorbing interest is the Elvish tongues, and the nomenclature based on them; and the alphabets" (247). Tolkien was a philologist through and through. In fact, Kilby noted this with some irritation during his stay with Tolkien in the summer of 1966, remembering, "It would be satisfying to record that I always found him busy at his writing, but that is not true. I did find him sometimes working at his Elvish languages, an activity which seemed endlessly interesting to him" (*Tolkien* 26).

Tolkien observes, "If I had considered my own pleasure more than the stomachs of a possible audience, there would have been a great deal more Elvish in the book" (*Letters* 216). Nonetheless, he once again deferred to his audience. If he had not, the work would have been much different. Writers such as Knight and Carpenter are adamant that Tolkien worked "from great depths within himself" and would have written everything he wrote even if he had "never heard of the group" (Knight 5; Carpenter, *Inklings* 160). To the contrary. Without the Inklings, it is certain that we would have more details of Shire genealogies, more words in the Elvish vocabulary, and fewer stories of the Third Age of Middle-earth.[17]

FINE-TUNING

These examples show several ways in which early comments had an impact on the nature of *The Lord of the Rings*. As he wrote new chapters, Tolkien read them to the Inklings, and Lewis and the others continued to offer advice, much of it very precise. While the major impact of global revision is important, I believe these small editorial changes tell us much about the way this group functioned. These comments may be small leaves, but they are powerfully suggestive of the shape and nature of the tree to which they belong.

One interesting example is a precise change found in *The Two Towers*. In an early draft of the chapter where Merry and Pippin first encounter Treebeard, the shaggy Ent looks at the little hobbits and remarks, "Very odd you are, indeed. Crack my timbers, very odd." In the manuscript, this line is struck out, and underneath Tolkien has written, "queried by Charles Williams—root and twig" (*Treason* 419). The phrase "crack my timbers" is replaced by "root and twig" at two different places in the story (419).[18]

Several other things are significant about this small detail. Some of the Inklings found Tolkien's story tiresome and hard to follow, but Williams paid such close attention that he knew this small interjection was out of character for Treebeard. Perhaps it was too piratical, suggesting Long John Silver or "Shiver me timbers." Or perhaps the hint of violence—a crack or break—seemed somehow out of place in the context of these slow and thoughtful beings.

In addition, it appears that very little pressure was needed to provoke this change. Apparently Williams "queried" its appropriateness; Tolkien took note and made the change. As Rateliff writes, "Tolkien felt no self-consciousness about jotting down that note to himself giving Williams full credit" ("'Something'" 52).

There are two other places in the manuscript of *The Lord of the Rings* where Tolkien makes note of input from another Inkling. In a draft of the chapter "A Short Cut to Mushrooms" in *The Fellowship of the Ring*, an invisible Bingo Baggins puts a scare into Farmer Maggot by draining a beer mug and flinging the good farmer's hat. Christopher Tolkien writes, "In the margin of the manuscript my father wrote: 'Christopher queries—why was not *hat* invisible if Bingo's clothes were?'" (*Shadow* 297). Tolkien responded by substituting a jug for the hat, then eventually dropped the playful but somewhat troublesome scene altogether. Christopher Tolkien notes, "I was much opposed to its loss" (297). He was also opposed to the excision of a hobbit named Odo, a character who played an important part in early drafts of *Fellowship*. "Christopher wants Odo kept," wrote J. R. R. Tolkien in the margin. But Odo was dropped, though the "Odo-element" is absorbed by a number of other characters, particularly Fatty Bolger.[19]

These are not the only places where the name of an Inkling is written in the margin of another Inkling's manuscript. Another example is found in Williams's unfinished "The Figure of Arthur." This work was published together with a long essay by C. S. Lewis under the title *Arthurian Torso*. In one of the more memorable descriptions of a reading by an Inkling, Lewis explains how he and Tolkien heard the first two chapters of this manuscript read aloud.

> Picture to yourself, then, an upstairs sitting-room with windows look-
> ing north into the 'grove' of Magdalen College on a sunshiny Monday
> Morning in vacation at about ten o'clock. The Professor and I, both on
> the chesterfield, lit our pipes and stretched out our legs. Williams in the
> arm-chair opposite to us threw his cigarette into the grate, took up a pile
> of the extremely small, loose sheets on which he habitually wrote—they
> came, I think, from a twopenny pad for memoranda, and began as fol-
> lows:—(Williams and Lewis 2)

In the second chapter of "The Figure of Arthur," Williams discusses the phrase
"Give us this day our daily bread" from the Lord's Prayer. Here, in the margin of the manuscript, the name "Tolkien" has been written in pencil. Lewis
provides a footnote to explain that Tolkien interrupted the reading at this
point and "raised some philological questions about the meaning of ἐπιούσιον
[daily]." Lewis speculates that Williams "intended to discuss the matter with
him more fully on some later occasion" (15).[20] Williams died before he finished the book, so there is no further record of philological conversations or
editorial changes. But the interruption, question, attribution, and intention
are all fully documented.

One Williams penciled another comment in the margins of this manuscript that
can be traced to another interruption by an Inkling. In a section discussing
the sources used by Geoffrey of Monmouth, Williams dismisses the possibility
of "some intermediary tale which is now wholly lost." Lewis writes, "At this
point I interrupted the reading to suggest that the view taken by A. Griscom
(*The Historia Regum Britanniae of Geoffrey of Monmouth,* London, 1929) was
different. The single word 'Griscom' pencilled on the MS. doubtless means that
Williams intended to give the matter further consideration" (Williams and
Lewis 32). Everything about this exchange is typical of the way the Inklings
edited one another's work. The author reads aloud from a rough, handwritten
draft. A listener (in this case, Lewis) interrupts the reading to make a specific
suggestion about the piece.[21] The author jots a quick note on the manuscript.
The note is brief and somewhat cryptic. It is also completely unattributed.[22] We
know that Lewis is the source of this change because Lewis tells us so. These
things are important to keep in mind when we examine marginal notes and
emendations in any of the Inklings' manuscripts.

One further point is worth mentioning. In his description of this event, Lewis
says that he and Tolkien heard only the first two chapters of Williams's book
read aloud. However, this interruption occurs in chapter 3: clearly, there must
have been more interaction among the Inklings than we have specific reference
to. All of this helps paint a picture of how the Inklings interacted when they
gathered, whether in dyads, in triads, or in the larger Thursday meetings.

In considering these three editing changes, we also begin to see the range of feedback these men offered one another. An awkward phrase is corrected, a philological question about a biblical text is raised, and an additional source that offers a contrasting point of view is recommended. As the following illustration will show, this is only a small sample of the kinds of feedback that characterized the mutual work of these writers.

THE LAY OF LEITHIAN

Tolkien began his work on *The Lord of the Rings* in 1937, and by then, the Inklings were meeting frequently. Feedback was extensive, and it was given orally. But earlier, before the habit of regular interaction was established and before the group had grown, Tolkien shared *The Lay of Leithian* with Lewis, and this is one of the few cases where we have an extended *written* commentary from one Inkling to another.[23] In fact, in this case we have an unusually complete record of the poem's development. We can study Tolkien's original rough drafts, we can read Lewis's suggestions, and then we can compare them to Tolkien's revisions. A close look at this exchange shows us much about the ways in which the Inklings edited one another's texts. All citations in this section, unless otherwise noted, are from *The Lay of Leithian* as it has been published in *The Lays of Beleriand*.

The Lay of Leithian is a long narrative poem, more than four thousand lines, written in octosyllabic couplets.[24] In Tolkien's notes, he usually refers to the poem as *Tinúviel*. Christopher Tolkien calls it *The Lay of Leithian*. But its full title, found on page 153, is as follows:

The
GEST
of
BEREN son of BARAHIR
and
LÚTHIEN the FAY
called
TINÚVIEL the NIGHTINGALE
or the
LAY OF LEITHIAN
Release from Bondage

This poem holds a particularly significant place in Inklings history, for it is the one Tolkien showed to Lewis in December 1929, the one that led to the deepening of their friendship and the formation of their regular Monday morning conversations.

After Tolkien and Lewis first discussed the poem, Lewis took the text home and read it with great care. The next day, he wrote a brief and enthusiastic letter to Tolkien, communicating his first impressions. In this first response, Lewis begins, characteristically, with frank praise. He notes two things in particular: it succeeds in presenting a cohesive alternative world, and it has the quality of true myth. He assures Tolkien that he would have appreciated the work even if he had happened upon it in a bookshop "by an unknown author" (151). He insists that the work deserves a wide audience, a kind of encouragement that, as we have seen, meant a great deal to Tolkien.

Sometime later, Lewis responded to *The Lay of Leithian* again. This time, rather than giving a short note or a brief word of encouragement, Lewis wrote fourteen pages of detailed, line-by-line criticism. The form of Lewis's feedback is ingenious, for it is written as if a group of scholarly experts are critiquing variant manuscript versions of an ancient poem. He names his experts Peabody, Pumpernickel, Schuffer, and Schick. These characters offer commentary on the text of the poem using exaggerated academic jargon[25]:

Peabody observes of this whole passage: "The combination of extreme simplicity, with convincing truth of psychology, and the pathos which, without comment, makes us aware that Gorlim is at once pardonable and unpardonable, render this part of the story extremely affecting." (318)

"The latest redactors," says Pumpernickel, "were always needlessly amplifying, as if the imagination of their readers could do nothing for itself, and thus blunting the true force and energy of the *Geste*." (323)

"My own conclusion is that *if* the assonance in the *textus receptus* is correct, the same phenomenon must originally have occurred often, and have been suppressed elsewhere by the scribes." (Schuffer) (328)

Schick's complimentary title of "internal rime" for these cacophonies does not much mend matters. (316)

This form of criticism is especially interesting because by using this technique, Lewis creates multiple voices like those of a writing group. The mock annotation also allows Lewis to claim that the weak passages are not poorly written poetry but unfortunate corruptions of the original manuscript. As Christopher Tolkien notes, this pretense "entertainingly took the sting from some sharply expressed judgements" (151). For example, Lewis writes, "Many scholars have rejected lines 1–8 altogether as unworthy of the poet" (315). This is one of two places where Lewis labels lines as "unworthy": in both cases, as Christopher Tolkien notes, Lewis's "severe criticism" led to complete rewriting of the passage (326).

Lewis also questions Tolkien's use of the phrase "meats were sweet" in the line "his meats were sweet, his dishes dear" (157). He suggests that this is a corrupted reading of variant manuscripts he labels P, R, and K. Lewis writes, "Let any one believe if he can that our author gave such a cacophony." He provides alternative versions from two other theoretical manuscripts, the J version which reads "His drink was sweet his dishes dear," and the L version which reads "His drink was sweet his dish was dear" (315). The J and L of these versions may stand for "Jack" and "Lewis" respectively. In quoting both of these "critics," Lewis creates an opportunity to suggest more than one alternative line.

Lewis's criticisms are often extremely precise. For example, he comments that Tolkien's use of "did" to fill out a line is clumsy. Tolkien eliminates this usage three times in the poem ("did fall," "did flutter," and "did waver"). Lewis also complains that there are too many monosyllabic lines, and the revised versions attest to Tolkien's attempts to eliminate them.

Many specific lines are changed. Here are a few examples:

Lewis called this weak: "who had this king once held in scorn" (317)
Tolkien changed it to this: "who once a prince of Men was born" (161)

Lewis called this "Latinised":   "or ask how she escaping came" (318)
Tolkien changed it to this: "or ask how she escaped and came" (163)

Lewis said the word *halting* was "rubbish":   "its echoes wove a halting spell" (325)
Tolkien changed it to this: "its echoes wove a binding spell" (180)

Lewis criticized Tolkien's poem line by line. But he did even more. He completely rewrote a number of passages, claiming that these alternatives represented the "true" or "authentic" work of the poet. This shows a remarkable boldness. It is one thing to suggest that an author change a weak line or avoid monosyllabic constructions; it is quite another to personally rewrite the verse. Yet that is exactly what Lewis did. And the extent to which Tolkien incorporated Lewis's work is striking.

The following examples show some of these changes step by step. First is the line as Tolkien originally wrote it. Then there is the line as Lewis suggested it ought to be written. Finally, in each case, is the line as it appeared in Tolkien's revision:

Original Tolkien:	"of mortal feaster ever heard" (316)
Lewis suggestion:	"Of mortal men at feast has heard" (316)
Revised Tolkien:	"of mortal Men at feast hath heard" (156)
Original Tolkien:	"his evil legions' marshalled hate" (317)
Lewis suggestion:	"The legions of his marching hate" (317)
Revised Tolkien:	"the legions of his marshalled hate" (161)
Original Tolkien:	"bewildered, enchanted and forlorn" (323)
Lewis suggestion:	"wildered, enchanted and forlorn" (323)
Revised Tolkien:	"enchanted, wildered and forlorn" (177)

In the examples above, Tolkien changed his text in keeping with Lewis's suggestion. In the following examples, Tolkien rewrote the line exactly as Lewis penned it:

Original Tolkien:	"he saw afar the elven-sheen" (324)
Lewis suggestion:	"he saw far off the elven-sheen" (324)
Tolkien revision:	"he saw far off the elven-sheen" (179)
Original Tolkien:	"With gentle hand there she him led" (328)
Lewis suggestion:	"Downward with gentle hand she led" (328)
Revised Tolkien:	"Downward with gentle hand she led" (188)

These lines show the extent to which Tolkien incorporated specific suggestions made by Lewis, sometimes using them exactly, sometimes changing them slightly. In the following longer passage, Tolkien changed his word order and imagery in response to Lewis's proposed alternative:

Original Tolkien:	swift ruin red of fire and sword
	leapt forth on all denied his word,
	and all the lands beyond the hills
	were filled with sorrow and with ills. (317)
Lewis suggestion:	And ruin of red fire and sword
	To all that would not hail him lord
	Came fast, and far beyond the hills
	Spread Northern wail and iron ills. (317)

Revised Tolkien: With fire and sword his ruin red
                        on all that would not bow the head
                        like lightning fell. The Northern land
                        lay groaning neath his ghastly hand. (161)

This is a remarkable exchange of intelligent critique and careful revision.[26] Even more interesting changes appear in the following section, the passage which forms the climax of the narrative. Tolkien's revision closely reflects Lewis's suggestions, and he incorporates the final two and a half lines exactly as Lewis wrote them.

Original Tolkien: His voice such love and longing fill
                        one moment stood she, touched and still;
                        one moment only, but he came
                        and all his heart was burned with flame. (325)

Lewis suggestion: Such love and longing filled his voice
                        That, one moment, without choice,
                        One moment without fear or shame,
                        Tinúviel stood; and like a flame
                        He leapt towards her as she stayed
                        And caught and kissed that elfin maid. (325)

Revised Tolkien: His voice such love and longing filled
                        one moment stood she, fear was stilled;
                        one moment only; like a flame
                        he leaped towards her as she stayed
                        and caught and kissed that elfin maid. (180)[27]

The Lay of Leithian was not published until after Tolkien's death, which complicates the task of assessing the final impact of Lewis's commentary. However, there is a short section of the poem that appears in *The Lord of the Rings*, where it serves as Gimli's song in the Mines of Moria. Tolkien's original draft of Canto I, the one he first gave to Lewis, begins as follows:

A king there was in olden days:
his golden crown did brightly blaze
with ruby red and crystal clear;
his meats were sweet, his dishes dear;
red robes of silk, an ivory throne,

and ancient halls of archéd stone,
and hoarded gold in gleaming grot
all these he had and heeded not. (157–58)

In his commentary on Tolkien's text, Lewis criticizes these lines, then writes the following and offers it as an alternative:

That was long since in ages old
When first the stars in heaven rolled,
There dwelt beyond Broseliand,
While loneliness yet held the land,
A great king comely under crown,
The gold was woven in his gown,
The gold was clasped about his feet,
The gold about his waist did meet.
And in his many-pillared house
Many a gold bee and ivory mouse
And amber chessmen on their field
of copper, many a drinking horn
Dear purchased from shy unicorn
Lay piled, with gold in gleaming grot. (315)

Tolkien considered this suggestion and revised the poem several more times. He ignored Lewis's proposed addition of amber chessmen and ivory mice (316). And he did not add the unicorn, a creature more at home in Narnia than in Middle-earth. He reworked the rhymes and refashioned the descriptions, following Lewis's broad concerns but, in general, not his specific material. Still it is worth noting that the later revisions of the poem retain one specific image introduced by Lewis: a many-pillared house, modified to "hall." And in Gimli's song in *The Lord of the Rings*, Tolkien adapted half a dozen lines that originally referred to Thingol and applied them to Durin:

A king he was on carven throne
In many-pillared halls of stone
With golden roof and silver floor,
And runes of power upon the door.
(*Fellowship* 308)

Tolkien wrote these lines; Gimli sang them; but this notable and enduring image owes much to C. S. Lewis.

In *The Lay of Leithian,* as in other projects, Tolkien worked through multiple adaptations and revisions. In the process, as Christopher Tolkien makes clear, Tolkien took most of Lewis's comments into account and included many of the specific rewrites exactly as Lewis had suggested.[28] Christopher Tolkien writes, "Almost all the verses which Lewis found wanting for one reason or another are marked for revision in the typescript B if not actually rewritten, and in many cases his proposed emendations, or modifications of them, are incorporated into the text" (151).

Nonetheless, he did dispute some of Lewis's suggestions. Lewis advises that internal rhyme is "an infallible mark of corruption" (316). Tolkien retains internal rhyme throughout the poem. Also, Lewis claims that lines 631–32 ("the dizzy moon was twisted grey / in tears, for she had fled away") made use of "half-hearted personification." Next to this criticism in Lewis's letter, Tolkien writes, "Not so!!" adding this explanation: "The moon was dizzy and twisted because of the tears in his eyes" (323). Despite Tolkien's protest and convincing rationale, he still struck the questioned lines from the manuscript.

In another case, Tolkien uses chiasmus, a grammatical inversion in the second of two parallel phrases, near the beginning of a stanza. The lines read,

> 'Where art thou gone? The day is bare,
> the sunlight dark, and cold the air!' (183).

Lewis is critical of this figure of speech, writing "The chiasmus is suspiciously classical" (326). He recommends a straight parallel instead: "Dark is the sun, cold is the air" (326). In the margin Tolkien writes a protest: "But classics did not invent chiasmus!—it is perfectly natural" (327). In this case, no changes were made to the text.

Nor did Tolkien accept Lewis's rather peculiar suggestion that the spelling of labyrinth in line 1075 of the poem be changed to "laborynth" (329).

All in all, the extent to which Tolkien rewrote this text in response to Lewis's commentary is remarkable. Remarkable, too, is the time span involved. Tolkien began the poem in September 1925, and he returned to it in the mid-1950s. Christopher Tolkien writes, "Some of the revisions to the *Lay of Leithian* are at least 30 years later" (152).

THE "SARUMAN PASSAGE"

Tolkien does not mention Lewis's participation in *The Lay of Leithian.* But he does credit Lewis for the significant editing of another work, what he calls the "Saruman passage" in *The Lord of the Rings.* Tolkien says specifically that his revised version is "much better" than his first draft. He also plainly states that in rewriting it, he found Lewis's "detailed criticisms" both fitting and useful (*Letters* 376).

Tolkien identifies this section as "the confrontation between Gandalf and his rival wizard, Saruman, in the ravaged city of Isengard" (*Letters* 376).[29] In *The War of the Ring,* Christopher Tolkien describes innumerable changes to this portion of the manuscript. Here are some that seem to me to be particularly noteworthy:

- A long discourse on tobacco is marked "Put into Foreword" (38).
- In the draft, Théoden laughs loudly. In the revision, the laughter is removed and "his gravity (at least of bearing) was restored" (36).
- In the draft, Gandalf makes an unkind remark to Théoden about his age: "It is long since you listened to tales by the fireside, . . . and in that rather than in white hairs you show your age, without increase in wisdom" (30). This remark is "very firmly struck through on the manuscript" (42).
- In the first draft, Théoden delivers a lengthy discussion about hobbits, explaining that he has heard of *holbytlan,* "half-high folk" who dwell in holes, and he speculates at some length about the origin of their name. This philological excursus was dropped (36).
- In the margin, a question is written, "Shall there be *more* real Ents?" (49).
- A description of Saruman's voice is substantially altered. In an early draft, it is "unpleasant" and "scornful" (62). In the revised version, "Its tone was that of a kindly heart aggrieved by injuries undeserved" (*Two Towers* 564).
- In the original sketch of the scene, Gandalf takes Saruman's staff away from him and breaks it in his hands (*War* 65). In *The Two Towers,* Gandalf "raised his hand, and spoke slowly in a clear cold voice. 'Saruman, your staff is broken.' There was a crack, and the staff split asunder in Saruman's hand, and the head of it fell down at Gandalf's feet" (569).
- In the initial version of the scene, the *palantír* shatters on impact (*War* 65). In the second version, it "splintered on the rock beside the stair" (65). In the final version, "the ball was unharmed: it rolled on down the steps, a globe of crystal, dark, but glowing with a heart of fire. As it bounded away towards a pool Pippin ran after it and picked it up" (*Two Towers* 569).
- The cliché "Set a thief to hinder a thief!" is removed (*War* 66).

I cannot link any of these changes directly to conversations with the Inklings in general or comments made by Lewis in particular. In the history of his father's work on this section, Christopher Tolkien makes no references to any of the Inklings. But, as we saw in chapter 3, Tolkien was "*dead stuck*" at this point in the story, and he plainly credits Lewis for encouraging him to continue and also for providing "detailed criticisms" that led to significant improvement. The specific changes I have listed above—shortening dialogue, removing long expository sections, eliminating a philological commentary, softening a caustic remark, dropping a cliché, adding gravity to Théoden's bearing, envisioning broader possibilities for this *palantír* and asking about further interaction with the Ents—all are consistent with the kinds of suggestions Lewis makes elsewhere. Furthermore, the physical evidence of these changes to the manuscript is exactly what one would expect when an author is responding to the comments and criticisms of a careful reader—a phrase is emphatically struck out, a small slip of paper is attached, a question is scribbled in the margin.

Having said that, it is also important to say that Tolkien's acknowledgment of his debt to Lewis here is direct, but it is also grudging and limited. His comment appears in his lengthy response to an article written for the March 1968 issue of the *Daily Telegraph Magazine*. After Charlotte and Denis Plimmer interviewed him for the article, they sent him a draft. He responded to it with concern: "There are one or two points which I should prefer to see altered, and some inaccuracies and misunderstandings that have, no doubt partly by my own fault, crept into the text" (*Letters* 372).

Following a polite cover letter, Tolkien copied passages from the article, then offered a correction and explanation for each one. The Plimmers write that Lewis would urge Tolkien to improve a section by saying, "Better, Tolkien, please!" and Tolkien would "sit down and write the section over." They explain that this process had an impact on "the Saruman passage" in particular, and claim that Tolkien now considers this section "the best in the book."

Having read this account, Tolkien offers this rather stern correction: "I do not think the Saruman passage 'the best in the book.' It is much better than the first draft, that is all. I mentioned the passage because it is in fact one of the very few places where in the event I found L's detailed criticisms useful and just" (*Letters* 376).

A number of observations about this comment are particularly important to this study. Tolkien affirms that Lewis urged him to rewrite and that he responded to Lewis's urging by writing and rewriting. Also, Tolkien suggests that Lewis offered criticisms with some frequency and that these criticisms were extensive, or "detailed." Finally, this remark shows that Lewis specifically critiqued this passage of Tolkien's book, that Tolkien took Lewis's advice and rewrote the passage, and that he believed the section was "much better" as a result.

However, the odd thing about this attribution is that Tolkien says this is one of "very few places" where he found Lewis's comments "useful and just." This is curious, since elsewhere he readily credits Lewis for his input into the early chapters of the book and repeatedly expresses unqualified enthusiasm for Lewis's encouragement of the project as a whole. A look at the context may shed light on the discrepancy. Tolkien is responding to an article that has misrepresented him. He finds it necessary to write pages and pages of corrections; this concern is just one of them. The grumpy and somewhat defensive tone is certainly understandable given the nature of the document.

But it is more likely that the date rather than the circumstances provide the key to understanding this passage.[30] This was written in 1967, nearly forty years after Lewis and Tolkien began to meet and share their work. As Tolkien got older, he became more likely to deny the participation of others in the creation of his work. As Rateliff and others have made clear, Tolkien's comments about the Inklings were increasingly negative as years went by, particularly as Charles Williams and then Joy Davidman played larger roles in Lewis's life. Tolkien says this is one of the few places that Lewis's detailed criticisms were useful and just. It may be more accurate to say that this is one of the few places where Tolkien specifically acknowledges the careful editing of his friend and colleague.

LEWIS AS REVISER

Lewis's writing process was quite different from Tolkien's. While Tolkien wrote things out in order to discover what he wanted to say, Lewis tended to mull over his ideas before committing anything to paper. While Tolkien produced draft after draft, Lewis generally recorded his material in a fairly complete form. And while Tolkien considered every word on the page, Lewis wrote rapidly once he had settled on a clear idea and the right form to express it.[31] Given Lewis's tendencies, it is commonly believed that when he wrote a book, he just sat down, dashed it off, and sent it in. Hooper, for example, says that if you look at Lewis's manuscripts, "There is next to no evidence of rewriting or of copious changes."[32] He adds, as if with pride, "You don't have a man revising or anything like that" (qtd. in Phillips 113).[33] There is some truth to this, and scholars rightly point to the rapid composition of *The Pilgrim's Regress* and certain gaps and inconsistencies in The Chronicles of Narnia as evidence. But even though this view is commonly held, it is still incomplete.

For one thing, Lewis often tried out his story ideas in more than one form, experimenting by creating several variations of the same work. It is a radical form of revision, one that allowed him to work out key concepts, images, motifs, and phrasing, and paved the way for rapid composition once he discovered the best genre for the work. *Dymer,* for example, was first written in prose form, a second time in verse form, next as a ballad he called "The Red Maid," and then a fourth and final time as a long epic poem in rhyme royal (Hooper, *C. S. Lewis* 145–47). *Till We Have Faces* underwent a similar transformation: in November 1922, Lewis recorded that he hoped to write a masque or play based on the Cupid and Psyche myth. But rather than writing it as a play, he spent the next year to trying to write it as a poem. Then, in 1955, he started all over again and wrote it as a novel. *Perelandra* also went through significant changes. It started out as a short poem that included specific references to floating islands and also "the alien Eve, green-bodied" (*C. S. Lewis* 220). Then, shortly afterward, Lewis abandoned the poem and wrote the story as a novel. In each of these cases, the final version was written rapidly, but it is important to understand that Lewis had been working on the content and expression of these works for a considerable time before he wrote them in their final form.

In addition, there are a number of instances where Lewis did substantially revise his work. The most extensive example is *The Magician's Nephew*.[34] He also rewrote chapter 3 of *Miracles* and produced abridged versions of *Perelandra* and *That Hideous Strength*.[35] He made substantial changes in the drafts of his broadcast talks in order to adjust them for radio audiences and then made further modifications as he prepared them for publication as *Mere Christianity*.[36]

Even after a draft was completed, Lewis often sought feedback. He sent Arthur Greeves all of *The Pilgrim's Regress* along with an extended request for comments, asking particularly for help on any passages "where one word less wd. make all the difference" (*They Stand* 446). He sent Sister Penelope the entire draft of *Perelandra,* saying, "It's uncorrected, so you can exercise your textual criticism on it" (*Collected Letters* 2: 527). He mailed most of his poems to Owen Barfield asking for detailed critique. He talked regularly with Ruth Pitter about the craft of poetry and put high value on her comments about his work.

Lewis was even known to niggle over tiny details and worry over factual inconsistencies in his work. One particularly apt example comes from *The Screwtape Letters*. In the first edition, published in 1942, Uncle Screwtape advises Wormwood that a well-meaning "patient" can be coaxed out of the British Museum and, once he is "on the street," can be distracted by the sight of a newsboy, then the No. 73 bus, and so on. Apparently, numerous readers had written to tell Lewis that such a thing was impossible—one simply couldn't see the No. 73 bus from the street in front of the British Museum.[37] "Drat that Omnibus!" wrote Lewis, and he tried hard to find a solution (Hooper, *C. S. Lewis* 103). In 1959, Lewis began working on what he called *The Whole Screwtape,* a volume which was to include the original *Screwtape Letters* along with "Screwtape Proposes a Toast." The new edition would allow for two other changes: adding an explanatory preface that addressed issues raised by readers, and editing the troublesome first letter so that the problem of the No. 73 bus would no longer attract attention. Lewis listed the possibilities to his publisher, Jocelyn Gibb: "If you can provide the number of any bus that might be seen in some such neighbouring street, and then emend *street* to *streets* in the last line of p. 24, we shall have saved our bacon. If this is impossible then take your choice of *green coach, jeep, fire engine, Rolls, police car, or ambulance*" (*C. S. Lewis* 103–4). Gibb considered the options and made the most modest change possible: he added the single letter "s" to the word "street." The new line read: "Once he was in the streets the battle was won." Lewis was greatly relieved at this elegant solution. "I believe we've got it right," he said. One small change, and, as Hooper notes, "This problem which had nagged at Lewis for over twenty years was solved" (104).

In addition, it is worth noting that Lewis constantly tinkered with his poetry. Hooper writes, "Even after he thought one was completed he might suggest a change here. Then a change there" (Introduction, *Poems* vii–viii). As a result, "It was not always easy to determine his final version of a poem, especially if there were slightly different versions or if the poem had already appeared in print" (vii).[38] Cecil Harwood provides one example: he says that when Lewis was told that a canto from his narrative epic *Dymer* was "not up to standard, he went away and produced another in the space of a few days" (377).[39]

In general, though, Lewis tended to spend a long time developing his ideas, then deliver them quickly. Havard writes that for Lewis, "major works such as books grew from a painful period of gestation. He described this state as being 'in book,' and the process of actual writing as akin to parturition—painful but enlivening" ("Philia" 358). Some of the time that Lewis spent "in book" was reserved for private reflection. But it is a striking feature of Lewis's writing process that he typically involved others as he worked out his ideas. A perfect illustration is found in Lewis's interaction with Clifford Morris. Since Lewis never learned to drive a car, Morris served as his driver, traveling with him "some hundreds of miles," and enjoying "some hundreds of conversations on all sorts of subjects" (Morris 319).[40] Morris describes Lewis's writing process this way:

> There were occasions when Jack used me as a kind of sounding board when he was trying out some new ideas or some new way of putting an old idea or some fresh outline or even, now and again, some striking phrase. As we might be sitting over a glass of beer, or as we were quietly driving along, he would suddenly say, "Friend Morris, listen to this, and tell me if it means anything to you," or, "How does this strike you?" And

if I didn't "catch on" at once, I have known him to scrap the whole idea, phrase, sentence, or whatever it was and then begin all over again from another angle or in another way. (326)

Morris's comments illustrate that Lewis talked over small elements, like phrases, and large elements, like ideas or concepts. Depending on the editorial feedback he got, he would readily adjust or adapt or drop material before he wrote it down.

Another example of this process is the way he came up with title ideas. A letter to Roger Lancelyn Green shows Lewis spinning out possibilities and discussing them with a broad range of readers, including Warren Lewis. Lewis writes to Green specifically to ask for advice on his "immediate problem wh. is the title of the new [Narnia] story" (*Letters* 424). Then he explains that there has been considerable disagreement on the issue: "[Geoffrey] Bles, like you, thinks *The Wild Waste Lands* bad, but he says *Night Under Narnia* is 'gloomy.' George Sayer & my brother say *Gnomes Under N* wd be equally gloomy, but *News under Narnia* wd do. On the other hand my brother & the American writer Joy Davidman (who has been staying with us & is a great reader of fantasy & children's books) both say that *The Wild Waste Lands* is a splendid title. What's a chap to do?" (424). Eventually, every one of these possibilities was rejected. The book was entitled *The Silver Chair.*

In short, Lewis eagerly sought advice as he composed, but since his composing style was largely internal rather than external, there are few written records to examine. But this does not mean he did not solicit feedback as he wrote and then change his work substantially in response to the comments he received. There is every indication that he enjoyed input from others and took their advice seriously. Discussing the impact of his own comments on Lewis's drafts, Douglas Gresham testifies that Lewis was "the kind of man who would listen to what I said" (Foreword 2).[41]

INTO THE WARDROBE

Lewis's habit of asking for feedback also resulted in an interesting modification to the text of *The Lion, the Witch and the Wardrobe.* The full context is uncertain, but apparently Owen Barfield either discussed the manuscript of this book with his wife, Matilda "Maud" Barfield, or else he had taken a manuscript copy home to read and had shared the text with her. Owen Barfield wrote Lewis a letter to convey several concerns. We do not have that letter, but we do have Lewis's response to Maud Barfield. Lewis writes, "Owen has told me about the two main snags, from your angle, in the story. The fur can easily be removed. I am afraid I was not thinking of the fur trade at all, but only of the fact that you wd. almost certainly find fur coats in an old wardrobe. Much more serious is the undesirability of shutting oneself into a cupboard. I might add a caution—or wd. this only make things worse?" (*Collected Letters* 2: 942–43). Even though Lewis says the fur is expendable, the reference to fur is retained in the published version of the story: "Looking into the inside, [Lucy] saw several coats hanging up—mostly long fur coats. There was nothing Lucy liked so much as the smell and feel of fur. She immediately stepped into the wardrobe and got in among the coats and rubbed her face against them" (*Lion* 7).

On the other hand, Lewis did accept the "more serious" suggestion to include something about the danger of wardrobes. In this same passage, we are told that Lucy leaves the door of the wardrobe open "because she knew that it is very foolish to shut oneself into any wardrobe" (*Lion* 7). Not only is the warning spelled out, but the verb also shifts from past tense to present tense, making the point even more emphatic.

The caution is repeated when Lucy enters the wardrobe a second time: "But as soon as she reached it she heard steps in the passage outside, and then there was nothing for it but to jump into the wardrobe and hold the door closed behind her. She did not shut it properly because she knew that it is very silly to shut oneself into a wardrobe, even if it is not a magic one" (*Lion* 27). Again, there is the shift to present tense—it *is* very silly to shut oneself into a wardrobe. And Lewis adds an important point of clarification: be careful not to shut that door, whether the wardrobe is magical or not.[42] Hooper notes that altogether "there are *five* such warnings in the first five chapters of the book" (Lewis, *Collected Letters* 2: 942n.66).

OUT OF THE SILENT PLANET

We have seen a number of changes that Lewis made to his texts in response to reader feedback. He might also take another tack: rather than change the text, he might add to it, directly addressing a question or answering an objection right in his text. He made this a regular practice in the construction of his broadcast talks.[43] This may be at work in a passage that appears near the end of *Prince Caspian*.[44] One of the clearest examples appears in *Essays Presented to Charles Williams*. This collaborative book includes six essays, five of them written by Inklings (Tolkien, Lewis, Barfield, Gervase Mathew, and Warren Lewis) and one by Dorothy L. Sayers. Lewis wrote the preface, and six pages into it, he offers this description of Charles Williams: "Mr. Williams's manners implied a complete *offer* of intimacy without the slightest *imposition* of intimacy. He threw down all his own barriers without even implying that you should lower yours" (x). This was certainly Lewis's experience with Williams, but apparently not everyone agreed with him. At this point in the preface, Lewis writes: "But here one of my collaborators breaks in upon me to say that this is not, after all, the true picture; that he, for his part, always found Williams a reserved man, one in whom, after years of friendship, there remained something elusive and incalculable" (x).

What were the circumstances of this interruption? And who is the "collaborator" Lewis mentions here?[45] Had Lewis been reading a rough draft of this preface aloud at an Inklings meeting when someone interrupted him? Had he been at home at the Kilns with Warren Lewis and turned to talk with him about this description, only to have his brother offer a modified picture? Had he met with Tolkien on a Monday morning, or enjoyed a visit from Barfield, or run into Mathew? We just don't know. But this is an interesting documented case of a text written by an Inkling and then directly modified by another Inkling. Lewis simply adds the vignette right into his text, mentioning both the collaborator and the interruption. He then responds by adding a qualifying statement to balance his own point of view.[46]

The most extensive example of Lewis editing a piece this way is his revision of *Out of the Silent Planet*. We noted in chapter 1 that Tolkien had closely edited the draft of this work. The details are mentioned in Tolkien's letter to Stanley Unwin dated 4 March 1938, which David Downing calls "one of the most perceptive brief treatments of Lewis's strengths and weaknesses as a writer" (*Planets* 35). Tolkien's letter is comparatively brief and indirect—nothing at all on the level of Lewis's lengthy critique of *The Lay of Leithian*. But it shows that Tolkien recognized the book's quality and understood Lewis's writing skills. It also provides a clear example of Lewis making changes in direct response to the critique of his friend.

As was typical of the Inklings, Tolkien's comments are rich in encouragement. He says the book is enthralling, adding he could hardly put it down (*Letters* 32). He commends the language and poetry of Malacandra, saying it is "very well done," and "extremely interesting." Also, in a statement that must be considered high praise from Tolkien, he says "the linguistic inventions and the philology on the whole are more than good enough" (33).

Still, Tolkien does find fault with the story. And he makes it clear that he has expressed his concerns to Lewis. His first criticism is one that still lingers: the book is simply "too short" (*Letters* 32). Tolkien is not saying that he personally would have liked the book better if it were longer, but that he finds the story too short for other reasons. Speaking practically, he says that the book is "rather short for a narrative of this type." Speaking artistically, he says that "the central episode of the visit to Eldilorn [*sic*] is reached too soon" (33).

In Tolkien's opinion, these problems remain. But several of his other criticisms have been addressed. Tolkien took issue with the style, observing "Lewis is always apt to have rather creaking stiff-jointed passages" (*Letters* 32). Tolkien also found a number of details in the plot that struck him as "inconsistent" (32–33). And he says he had some specific qualms about matters of philology, though he does not specify them. According to Tolkien's report, all of these comments have resulted in specific changes to the story.

It is worth noting that Tolkien's criticisms and Lewis's changes occur at three levels: the whole text (plot), the sentence ("creaking" passages), and the word (philology). Every aspect of Lewis's writing is addressed. But it is even more noteworthy to see the extent of Lewis's changes. Tolkien assures Unwin that these problems "have since been corrected to my satisfaction" (*Letters* 32–33). Lewis was by nature far more casual about the details of his fiction than Tolkien, who was thorough and thoroughly fussy. Therefore, if Lewis corrected the text to Tolkien's satisfaction, there must have been significant interaction and substantial change.

But in addition to this process of editing, Lewis changed the novel in another way: he added a postscript.[47] It is illuminating to compare Lewis's comments in the postscript with Tolkien's criticisms about the book. In the conclusion of *Out of the Silent Planet,* we are told that even though the book is cast in fictional form, the events described therein really did happen, and that Lewis had simply been writing down what he had been told by Ransom, the main character. The postscript is written as if Ransom himself has just finished reading the novel, and he is writing to Lewis to tell him that he is quite disappointed with it.

The voice of Ransom and the nature of his concerns sound suspiciously like those of J. R. R. Tolkien. Ransom is irritated, for example, that Lewis has cut the philological parts so ruthlessly. It is not hard to imagine that just as Lewis had demanded more narrative in Tolkien's text, Tolkien may have wanted more philological detail in Lewis's text. Ransom is also annoyed that so little attention has been given to the culture of Malacandra, to calmer circumstances when the texture of daily life is clearly seen. He scolds Lewis for these omissions, then adds his own remembrances of the geography and answers questions about pets, funerals, and the night sky. There is the quick filling in of homely details—of the average temperature of a *hross* and the nature of their droppings and the fact that they don't shed tears but do drink alcohol. Ransom also describes other subspecies, such as the silver *hross* and the red *sorn,* and then apologizes for having given Lewis so little information about the *pfifltriggi.* He says in jest, "I agree, it is a pity I never saw the *pfifltriggi* at home. I know nearly enough about them to 'fake' a visit to them as an episode in the story, but I don't think we ought to introduce any mere fiction" (*Silent Planet* 156–57).

Both of these priorities, an inherent fascination with language and a profound enjoyment of the details of common life, were significant to Tolkien, and these additions may be direct responses to his expressed disappointment that they were treated so superficially. We know that in his critique of the novel, Tolkien wrote that he believed *Out of the Silent Planet* was "too short." It may well be that the postscript provides more of the kind of information he had been hoping for. But its form is certainly unconventional—rather than go back and revise the story itself, as Tolkien would have done, Lewis creates an imaginary situation in which he can register the complaints and tack on an addendum to the story.

In this postscript, Lewis also addresses a logical inconsistency. The spaceship becomes unbearably hot as they near the sun on the return trip. Ransom asks scornfully, "Why must you leave out my account of how the shutter jammed just before our landing on Malacandra? Without this, your description of our sufferings from excessive light on the return journey raises the very obvious question, 'Why didn't they close their shutters?'" (*Silent Planet* 158). Is Lewis poking fun at himself for missing such a conspicuous mistake? Or are the Inklings the ones who asked this "very obvious" question?[48]

Most personal and provocative of all, I think, is the final line of the postscript. The original wager that motivated the book specified that Lewis would write a space travel book, and Tolkien a time travel book. As Rateliff points out, Lewis, having finished his task, seizes the chance to "open the door for Tolkien's book" ("Time Travel" 206). Lewis writes, "Now that 'Weston' has shut the door, the way to the planets lies through the past; if there is to be any more space-travelling, it will have to be time-travelling as well . . . !" (*Silent Planet* 160). Again, Rateliff notes, "Lewis had used the closing lines of *Out of the Silent Planet* to set up what he no doubt saw as its companion volume, Tolkien's time-travel story, *The Lost Road*" ("Time Travel" 206). Specific, challenging, and encouraging all at once, Lewis ends his story with a comment directed to Tolkien and designed to encourage him on his way.[49]

CONCLUSIONS

Each time a writer revises a draft, fresh opportunities arise for comments and questions and even mutual experiences to inspire significant change. In a highly interactive group, especially one with a long history of regular meetings, few of these will be documented at the time. But as this chapter has shown, there are some cases where we can directly trace a change in a text to input from one Inkling to another. The longer I look at the material, the more examples I find. But one must stop somewhere. Perhaps the overall impact of this process of editing and revising can best be perceived through the words of the Inklings themselves[50]:

In *Saving the Appearances,* Barfield thanks Lewis, among others, for "thoughtful comments and practical suggestions, which I have used freely."

In *The Sunset of the Splendid Century,* Warren Lewis thanks Gervase Mathew and C. S. Lewis "for their patience in listening to several chapters of it in manuscript" (x). Warren Lewis also thanks Mathew for reading the manuscript of *Assault on Olympus* and making "useful suggestions."

In *The Parlement of Foules: An Interpretation,* J. A. W. Bennett thanks Lewis and Colin Hardie for "corrections and suggestions" (v).

In *The Allegory of Love,* Lewis thanks Barfield, Dyson, and Tolkien, noting in particular that Tolkien read and commented on the first chapter. In *English Literature in the Sixteenth Century, Excluding Drama,* Lewis thanks Bennett and Dyson "for advice and criticism" (vii).

In *The Court of Richard II,* Mathew acknowledges "pervasive influences" from friends, including Nevill Coghill and C. S. Lewis, and he names Tolkien among those with whom "minor problems" have been discussed (xi). In his article "Justice and Charity in *The Vision of Piers Plowman,*" Mathew thanks Coghill for his input (360n).

In *A Study of Old English Literature,* C. L. Wrenn thanks four of his professional colleagues, including Tolkien, who have "given me not only the benefit of their writings but frequent personal guidance" (vi). In *Beowulf, with the Finnesburg Fragment,* he thanks Tolkien and R. W. Chambers, crediting the two of them for "what is valuable in my approach to *Beowulf*" (5).

In *The Poet Chaucer,* Coghill acknowledges Mathew and Dyson, among others, for "their patient reading of this book before it was printed, and for many wise and learned suggestions they have made and I have adopted" (viii).

As we will see in the next chapters, collaborative works, references in their books and articles, dedications of entire works, and other forms of textual evidence round out the picture of pervasive interaction and significant influence. But in just this quick sampling, we see credit and gratitude expressed by seven different Inklings about eleven different titles, acknowledging thoughtful comments, practical suggestions, advice, criticism, input, guidance, and influence from seven specific Inklings.

In this context, Lewis's straightforward observation about the influence of the group bears mention. In a statement more indicative than comprehensive, Lewis writes, "[Williams's] *All Hallows' Eve* and my own *Perelandra* (as well as Professor Tolkien's unfinished sequel to the *Hobbit*) had all been read aloud, each chapter as it was written." And he adds with certainty, "They owe a good deal to the hard-hitting criticism of the circle" (*Essays Presented* v). It is a sweeping statement, a strong claim. I, for one, believe him.

NOTES

1. Of course, non-Inklings edited the work of the Inklings, and one of the most notable examples is Joy Davidman, C. S. Lewis's wife. She had a hand in several of Warren Lewis's books. She corrected the proofs for *The Sunset of the Splendid Century* (x). She also edited and prepared the index for *Assault on Olympus;* in the foreword, Warren Lewis thanks her for "her patient kindness in pruning the first draft and recommending certain excisions." She also worked on *The Scandalous Regent.* In the foreword of that book, he thanks her "for her kindness in reading my manuscript and for making many valuable suggestions." He dedicated *The Scandalous Regent* "To My Sister-in-Law Joy Davidman."

Davidman was also the first person to read a number of C. S. Lewis's books in manuscript; in fact, she typed several of them in preparation for submission. The household at the Kilns was so focused on their various, intertwining writing projects that Davidman quipped, "We're all hard at work here; the house is practically a book factory" (qtd. in Glyer, "Joy Davidman" 16). For more about Davidman's participation in Lewis's writing, particularly their collaboration on *Till We Have Faces,* see my article "Joy Davidman Lewis."

2. Lewis had a consistently low opinion of his skills as a proofreader. In 1946, he thanks Dorothy L. Sayers "for the errata" that she found in *Out of the Silent Planet* and tells her, "I shall never make a proof reader" (*Collected Letters* 2: 729). Two years later, he writes to her again and observes, "I wish I were a better proof reader, but I'll never learn" (2: 887). In 1961, he thanks Arthur Greeves for noting a misprint in the proof copies of *An Experiment in Criticism,* and says, "I'm v. bad at spotting them" (*They Stand* 555).

3. The question about Shelob appears in *Letters,* page 81, and the one about stewed rabbit appears on page 74. Lewis also sought specific advice on this kind of small detail. An example is found in a letter to his friend Roger Lancelyn Green. One of the most memorable scenes in all of The Chronicles of Narnia occurs in *The Silver Chair,* where Puddleglum the Marshwiggle stamps out a magical fire. On 6 March 1951, Lewis thanks Green for his editorial comments on this section, which helped him to be accurate about the nature of the fire, the fuel, and the hearth: "You are quite right about a wood fire. Wood keeps on glowing red again in the places you have already extinguished—phoenix-like. Even the large webbed feet of a Marshwiggle couldn't do it. Yet it must be a flat hearth, I think. *Does* peat go out easily by treading? As an Irishman I ought to know, but don't. I think it will have to be a coal fire in a flat hearth. After all, Underland might well use coal, whereas wood or charcoal would have to be imported" (qtd. in Hooper, *C. S. Lewis* 404).

4. Anne Ruggles Gere and Ralph Stevens found that "when participants in writing groups read 'finished' writing, the language of the group often became acerbic or vacuous because members felt (perhaps unconsciously) that they had no purpose" (Gere 75). In their collaborative research, they found that cutting remarks, or empty, meaningless ones, are the inevitable result if the group tries to function apart from the expectation of immediate benefit to the current written draft.

Gere elaborates this point by citing a particularly unsuccessful writing group. She observes, "One of the least effective groups I have observed . . . worked in a classroom where the teacher asked students to respond to finished pieces of writing" (106). The students quickly learned that when the text is finished, there is no point in the interaction; where there is no hope of real changes, criticism is a hollow exercise.

Furthermore, Gere has found that in ineffective writing groups, the participants were acutely aware of the problem: "Although they never articulated their complaint, students knew that they didn't have a 'real' task; the comments they made would not shape a revision because the writing was completed" (106). Even students who are critiquing one another's texts under the direct authority of teachers and under the strong motivation of grade books will not persist in making substantial comments on one another's written texts if they see it as a fruitless activity. The expectation of changing and thus improving texts is even more important to those who gather in voluntary writing groups.

5. This pattern of critiquing written drafts is similar in many ways to the structure of the university tutorial. W. J. B. Owen was one of Lewis's students, and he remembers sessions with his tutor quite well. Owen would read his essay aloud, then Lewis would comment. "The praise was brief, a few words only, but always gratifying. The criticism was searching but mildly presented: could that phrase not be recast? would that idea not be better if developed in such a way? and so forth" (59). The supportive mood and the range and specificity of feedback Owen describes are characteristic of the Inklings as well.

6. Warren Lewis was well-acquainted with change and revision, though it was not generally a happy process for him. Prompted by a publisher's request, he shortened *Assault on Olympus* from 120,000 words to 100,000 words and then once more to 90,000. He did not enjoy it, writing, "I made the second cut and typed the damned thing for the *third* time—doing the 90,000 in ten days, and incidentally driving myself into Restholme thereby" (*Brothers* 244).

7. Christopher Tolkien has given us an enormously valuable and endlessly interesting discussion of his father's writing process (and important documentation of the way writers work) in *The History of Middle-earth*. It is impossible to overstate the value of these detailed and cogent books to this present study. Of particular interest are the four volumes—*The Return of the Shadow, The Treason of Isengard, The War of the Ring,* and *Sauron Defeated*—that describe and demonstrate Tolkien's process of writing *The Lord of the Rings.*

Throughout these books, Christopher Tolkien emphasizes the messy and fragmentary nature of his father's manuscripts. There are many passages that elaborate this point; the following is representative:

> The earliest plot-outlines and narrative drafts are often barely legible, and become more difficult as the work proceeded. Using any scrap of the wretched paper of the war years that came to hand—sometimes writing not merely on the backs of examination scripts but across the scripts themselves—my father would dash down elliptically his thoughts for the story to come, and his first formulations of narrative, at tearing speed. In the handwriting that he used for rapid drafts and sketches, not intended to endure long before he turned to them again and gave them a more workable form, letters are so loosely formed that a word which cannot be deduced or guessed at from the context or from later versions can prove perfectly opaque after long examination; and if, as he often did, he used a soft pencil much has now become blurred and faint. (*Shadow* 4)

8. One exception is "Leaf by Niggle." Another is *Smith of Wootton Major.* But in most cases, even when working on translations or writing personal letters, Tolkien tended to be an external processor—that is, he would write things down in order to figure them out, and then revise them, usually extensively.

9. The J. R. R. Tolkien Collection, Marquette University Library, Milwaukee, Wisconsin. Source: http://www.marquette.edu/library/collections/archives/tolkien.html. Accessed 5 September 2004.

10. The comparison to the painting process is apt for a number of reasons. Tolkien was a talented artist and his watercolors deserve serious critical attention. In the autobiographical allegory "Leaf by Niggle," he portrays himself as a painter and *The Lord of the Rings* as an enormous painting. For examples of his work and expert analysis of his art, see Hammond and Scull's *J. R. R. Tolkien: Artist and Illustrator.*

11. Priscilla Tolkien illustrates the extent to which her father's careful attention to detail led him to ongoing revision. She remembers that he rewrote a section of *The Lord of the Rings* "because he had described something as being by full moon and realized on looking back at the time scheme that he was a day in advance, that the moon couldn't have been full until the next day" (*A Film Portrait*). Readers interested in further discussion of these changes are directed to Tolkien, *Letters,* page 80; *The War of the Ring,* pages 270–72; and Hammond and Scull, *The Lord of the Rings: A Reader's Companion,* pages xlv–l.

12. Lewis also says that Tolkien had "only two reactions to criticism: either he begins the whole work over again from the beginning or else takes no notice at all" (*Letters* 481). Scholars have typically used this statement as evidence that the Inklings did not influence Tolkien. Given the consistent testimony of his friends, Tolkien's own description of his writing process, and the heavily emended text of his manuscripts, the evidence suggests that Tolkien was far more likely to enter into a substantial revision than he was to "take no notice" of the advice he was given. This exact point is made in another discussion of Tolkien's writing process: "His standard of self criticism was high and the mere suggestion of publication usually set him upon a revision, in the course of which so many new ideas occurred to him that where his friends had hoped for the final text of an old work they actually got the first draft of a new one" ("Professor J. R. R. Tolkien" 15).

13. Tolkien frequently made changes, or refrained from making changes, in deference to his readers against his personal judgment. For example, in a letter to Christopher Tolkien dated 31 May 1944, he writes, "I am not really satisfied with the surname Gamgee and shd. change it to Goodchild if I thought you would let me" (83). Christopher Tolkien writes, "I replied that I would never wish to see *Gamgee* changed to *Goodchild,* and urged (entirely missing the point) that the name *Gamgee* was for me the essential expression of 'the hobbit peasantry' in their 'slightly comical' aspect, deeply important to the whole work" (*War* 123). Tolkien replied, "As to Sam Gamgee. I quite agree with what you say, and I wouldn't dream of altering his name without your approval; but the object of the alteration was precisely to bring out the comicness, peasantry, and if you will the Englishry of this jewel among the hobbits" (*Letters* 88). The extent to which Tolkien submits control of his text to others, here and elsewhere, is remarkable.

14. These questions are discussed in their larger context in David Bratman's article "Top Ten Rejected Plot Twists," pages 15 and 16.

15. For Tolkien, it was not unusual to have a project take on a life of its own. In a letter to Christopher Tolkien, he describes his tentative thoughts on how *The Lord of the Rings* will end, then adds, "It will probably work out very differently from this plan when it really gets written, as the thing seems to write itself once I get going, as if the truth comes out then, only imperfectly glimpsed in the preliminary sketch" (*Letters* 104). In "Scholar's Melancholy," Lewis also expresses the conviction that writing projects often take a different direction from what one expects:

> . . . we remember vast
> Designs and knowledge gathered, and intent to do
> What we were able then to have done . . . something drew
> A sponge across that slate. The ferly would not last. (*Collected Poems* 98, ellipsis in original)

16. In the preface to Lewis's *On Stories and Other Essays,* Hooper writes, "Professor Tolkien told me that he had been reading various genealogies and appendices to Lewis long before there was any written story. His interests, he told me, were primarily in those aspects of 'Middle Earth' and that it was his friend C. S., or 'Jack,' Lewis who encouraged him to write a story to go with them. 'You know Jack,' he said to me. 'He had to have a *story!* And that story—*The Lord of the Rings*—was written to keep him quiet!' It is, as it was meant to be, a generous and telling tribute" (xx).

17. I hasten to add that there are many fine Elvish linguists who fervently wish Tolkien had in fact spent much more of his available time developing his languages.

18. John D. Rateliff is the first scholar to document this ("'Something'" 52).

19. Attendees will long remember Christopher Tolkien's 1987 lecture at the Mythopoeic Society Conference in Milwaukee where he traced the transformations of Odo before a rapt audience. No recording was made of the talk. The essence of his remarks may be found in *Return of the Shadow.*

20. "Epiousios," found in Matthew 6:11 and Luke 11: 3, is typically translated "daily," but some, including Williams, suggest that the word here means "present" or "substantial." Vine, Unger, and

White explain, "Some would derive the word from *epi*, 'upon', and *eimi*, 'to be', as if to signify '(bread) present', i.e., sufficient bread, but this formation is questionable" (143).

21. Frequent interruptions were standard practice in Inklings meetings. One interesting comment on this is found in Tolkien's fictional account of the Notion Club, where interruptions and critiques are vividly portrayed. Early in the story, for example, the members of the club joke about it, as Lowdham teases Guildford, "You dislike [criticizing] about as much as Philip dislikes interrupting" (*Sauron* 162). The barb about interrupting is intended for Lewis.

22. The difficulty of identifying a source for this kind of small editorial suggestion was underscored for me recently when I purchased an autographed copy of *Old King Coel* by Adam Fox. The inscription reads, "To Mrs. Dockar Drysdale fr. Adam Fox with grateful thanks for 'loped' in I.58. 18.xi.37." Sure enough, stanza number 58 in section one describes "six or seven wolves in ragged rank" who "loped and floundered" on (22). The first of these verbs was apparently suggested to Fox by Drysdale, and that fact is acknowledged only to her, and only in this handwritten, private note.

23. Lewis's presence also made a difference in an academic project that Tolkien undertook: his translation of *Beowulf*. The manuscript is not available as of this writing. However, a small news item mentions that one of Tolkien's *Beowulf* translations "includes hand-written annotations by Tolkien's close friend C.S. Lewis" (http://www.collegenews.org/x1946.xml). We know that Lewis edited Tolkien's fiction; this new evidence shows that he participated by giving feedback on academic work as well.

24. Much of the material in this section was first presented in my article "More Than a Bandersnatch," published under the name Diana Lynne Pavlac in *Proceedings of the J. R. R. Tolkien Centenary Conference 1992*.

25. To speak through fictional characters is not an unusual rhetorical strategy for the Inklings. For example, Lewis used this device in one of his most popular books, *The Screwtape Letters*, and again in one of his last works, *Letters to Malcolm*.

Tolkien's use of persona is both more subtle and more pervasive. He often spoke through retellers, such as the narrators of *The Book of Lost Tales*. Also, it was his habit to speak of his work as if it were a genuine history, based on the "realities" of Middle-earth. Tolkien's use of retellers, personae, and secondary reality is discussed extensively by Verlyn Flieger in *Interrupted Music*. In *Splintered Light,* Flieger notes, "Behind the multiplicity of personas is the man who is all of them, who has conflicting things to say and chooses to say them in conflicting voices" (149).

26. Josh Long and Charles A. Huttar assisted with careful reading and helpful insight into these various poetic versions. I gratefully acknowledge their help.

27. Christopher Tolkien notes that this version now contains a defective couplet, calling this "a hasty revision, based on a criticism of Lewis's" (*Lays* 181).

28. In his biography of Tolkien, Humphrey Carpenter says Tolkien "did not accept any of Lewis's suggested emendations" to *The Lay of Leithian* (145). Sometime later, Carpenter changed his opinion. Christopher Tolkien points out that in *The Inklings*, this view has been "corrected" (*Lays* 315).

29. There are two difficult questions that arise in analyzing this acknowledgement of Lewis's input on this passage. The first is the question of exactly how much of the text Tolkien is referring to. In the earliest draft, what are now chapters 8, 9, and 10 of book 3 of *The Lord of the Rings* were written as a single chapter, and it seems to me that Tolkien is referring to the entire sequence of events from Gandalf's arrival at Orthanc to his departure, and not merely the specific conversation between Gandalf and Saruman. The second question is how many different drafts should be considered. Tolkien says the text is better than the first draft as a result of Lewis's detailed criticisms, suggesting that he means all of the changes made between the first draft and the published version, not just the changes between the first draft and the second.

30. I am grateful to John D. Rateliff for always insisting that in order to properly interpret any comment made by an Inkling, the full context is of paramount importance.

31. Lewis's process for fiction was a little bit different, as he elaborates in "It All Began with a Picture. . . ." Here, Lewis reports that his Narnia stories began with an image and he simply "followed the story," writing it out as images continued to flow. When writing fiction, he, like Tolkien, had the strong sense of the story writing itself.

32. It is of some interest that one of the most common changes in Lewis's actual drafts is that words are crossed out multiple times as Lewis struggled to spell them correctly. Despite his blazing intellect and deservedly famous memory, he had a lot of trouble with spelling.

33. This comment by Hooper is surprisingly protective, as if someone had accused Lewis of being a bad writer because he might be guilty of revising. This negative attitude toward revision is exceedingly common, and completely uncalled for. Most writers revise. Many writers revise more, not less, as they become more accomplished at their craft. The skill or genius of a writer or other artist cannot be correlated with the fluency of first performance.

34. *The Magician's Nephew* went through two major revisions. In *Past Watchful Dragons,* Hooper traces the history of what he calls the Lefay Fragment, a rough draft that Lewis wrote "soon after *The Lion, the Witch and the Wardrobe* and before the final draft of *Prince Caspian*" (67). Hooper compares this fragment to "a fuzzy ball of dandelion seeds." He says, "Some of the seeds, or 'pictures,' found root in other books, and some remained on the parent stem and became the basis for *The Magician's Nephew* as we now have it" (67). Much later, when Lewis had written three-quarters of *The Magician's Nephew,* he showed the draft to Roger Lancelyn Green, who objected to several parts of the story (Hooper, *C. S. Lewis* 405). Lewis "set the book aside for the moment," and when he came back to it nearly two years later, he radically changed it (405).

35. Lewis made fairly drastic changes to *That Hideous Strength.* The abridged version is about a third shorter than the original and has a new title: *The Tortured Planet.* There are, in fact, three different versions of *That Hideous Strength.* For details regarding the variations, see Hooper's *C. S. Lewis,* pages 240–42, and David Lake's article "The Variant Texts of *That Hideous Strength.*"

36. Extensive documentation of Lewis's editing process in response to the specific requests of Eric Fenn, his producer, can be found in *C. S. Lewis at the BBC* by Justin Phillips.

37. Lewis's response to one such reader appears on page 614 of *Collected Letters,* volume 2: "Chestnuts! Whiskers! This bloomer has been pointed out several times already. The higher critics will use it to prove that the book was really written 200 years later by five different 'Hands' as they appropriately call them!"

38. Some scholars, particularly Kathryn Lindskoog, have raised questions about Hooper's interaction with Lewis's poetry. I believe that Hooper rightly asserts that Lewis constantly revised his poems even after they had been published and also that it is difficult to determine the final or authoritative version of Lewis's poems.

39. During their years as students at Oxford, A. C. Harwood, Lewis, and Barfield were close friends, and the three men would regularly critique one another's poetry. A selection of Harwood's essays are collected in *The Voice of Cecil Harwood,* edited by Owen Barfield. An interesting history of the development of *Dymer* and the input of Barfield and Harwood on this poem may be found in Hooper's *C. S. Lewis,* pages 145–49.

40. Clifford Morris wrote a short poem in memory of Lewis, which Warren Lewis included in his diary entry for Friday, 21 July 1967. Morris's poem begins,

My friend is dead,
And I have never missed
A dear friend more. I miss
Him in the town, and in
The countryside. I miss
His face, his voice, his smile, his
Presence by my side. . . . (*Brothers* 276)

Warren Lewis comments, "The simplicity and obvious sincerity of these artless verses I find very comforting, and I wrote this morning to tell Morris how much pleasure he had given me" (277). A slightly different version of the poem is reprinted on page 329 of Morris's article "A Christian Gentleman."

41. It may be that a comment from a child stimulated Lewis's thinking and led to some aspects of the development of *The Magician's Nephew.* Mary Clare Havard reports that Lewis gave her a copy of *The Lion, the Witch and the Wardrobe* to read in typescript, and that she "wrote a solemn criticism for him, saying what I liked about it—and what I didn't. One thing I did not like was the presence of a lamppost when the children first arrived in Narnia; I don't suppose I knew the word anachronistic, but that's what I thought it was." She adds, "I was rather pleased when he explained how the lamppost arrived in Narnia in one of the later books" (qtd. in Hooper, *C. S. Lewis* 759).

42. Linda S. Spitser points out that while neither Lucy nor Peter shut the wardrobe door behind them, Edmund does. "It is another way that Lewis underscores Edmund's foolish and irresponsible nature" (personal correspondence, 11 August 2004).

43. Phillips writes that after the very first talk was broadcast, "letters began to pour in." Phillips commends Lewis for his response: "From the start of the second talk, Lewis weaves the observations received into the broadcasts. Although the original correspondence sent in has not, to my knowledge, survived, there are plenty of indications in the talks themselves as to the points raised" (124).

44. In his article "J. R. R. Tolkien: Narnian Exile," Joe R. Christopher suggests that Lewis responded to Tolkien's criticism of the first two chapters of *The Lion, the Witch and the Wardrobe* by adding a section to the end of *Prince Caspian.* He argues that one of Tolkien's major objections is that Lewis sanitizes or sentimentalizes mythical creatures, taming (and thereby misrepresenting) the nature of characters like the faun or satyr. Late in *Prince Caspian,* there is a wild romp of mythological characters, including Bacchus and Silenus. In the story, Susan observes, "I wouldn't have felt very safe with Bacchus and all his wild girls if we'd met them without Aslan" (*Prince Caspian* 154). As these mythological creatures become part of this story, Lewis argues, their behavior is redeemed. Christopher explains, "That is, Lewis seems to reply to Tolkien, under Christ certain basic impulses can be controlled. . . . under Christ, such things can be kept in bounds" (42). Christopher says of this passage, "It is difficult not to believe that this is a deliberate answer by Lewis to Tolkien" (41).

45. It is possible that the collaborator mentioned here is Tolkien. As was noted in chapter 4, he had a somewhat uneasy relationship with Williams. And in his personal copy of *Essays Presented to Charles Williams,* Tolkien makes two interesting notes in the margin of the preface. Lewis writes that by 1939, Williams "had already become as dear to all my Oxford friends as he was to me" (*Essays Presented* viii). Next to these words, Tolkien wrote the words, "Alas, no!" (qtd. in Carpenter, *Inklings* 120). And Lewis writes, "In every circle that he entered, he gave the whole man" (*Essays Presented* v). Next to these words, Tolkien wrote the words, "No, I think not" (qtd. in Carpenter, *Inklings* 121).

46. Lewis records two similar interruptions in his commentary "Williams and the Arthuriad." In one of them, he is discussing Williams's treatment of Byzantium, and he includes this footnote: "Fr. Gervase Matthew [*sic*], O.S.B., tells me that Williams's picture of Byzantium catches some aspects of the historical reality better than Gibbon's: though Gibbon was at first Williams's only source" (*Essays Presented* 106). The placement and explanation of this note suggest that Mathew had read this section of Lewis's text and offered this comment. Lewis, characteristically, simply attaches this note to his text. In addition, Mathew may be one of the unnamed referents in another footnote earlier in the text. Lewis, commenting on a section of Williams's "The Figure of Arthur," writes, "The sentence is incomplete. In my opinion all that follows probably made part of a separate chapter and there is probably a long hiatus. Others, at least as well qualified as

I to judge, think differently" (78). These "others" may refer to the Inklings, or they may refer to a larger group, including Alice Mary Hadfield, who had permitted Lewis to use her typed copy of "The Figure of Arthur" (2).

47. There is another published instance where Lewis addresses problems in a book by adding a note to the end. *The Personal Heresy* concludes with a four-and-a-half page "note" in which Lewis says that he has reread his share of the book and is "disquieted" by what he now perceives as discrepancies between the first essay and the fifth essay (146). But rather than revise them, he comments on this fact and discusses his concerns. In this particular situation, of course, Lewis could not have gone back and revised the text itself without falsifying the history of his debate with Tillyard.

48. Tolkien may be the one who brought this point to Lewis's attention. If I had to speculate, though, I would guess that Warren Lewis, always one who loved vehicles and transportation of various kinds, may be the one who caught the mistake. This may be part of the reason *Out of the Silent Planet* is dedicated to Warren Lewis, "a life-long critic of the space-and-time story."

49. In his preface to *The Dark Tower and Other Stories,* Hooper theorizes that Lewis "had in mind the possibility of a sequel to *Out of the Silent Planet* in which Ransom would play some part and in which time-travel would figure pretty largely" (8). I find no evidence to suggest that this was part of Lewis's thinking. As Rateliff explains, "It is more likely, given Lewis's characteristic generosity, that he seized this chance to open the door for Tolkien's book" ("Time Travel" 206).

50. Except where otherwise identified, all of these citations are from the acknowledgment pages of the books mentioned. I am grateful for David Bratman's help in verifying many of these important references.

6

Collaborators
Working Together

*Friends are not primarily absorbed in each other.
It is when we are doing things together that
friendship springs up—painting, sailing ships, pray-
ing, philosophizing, fighting shoulder to shoulder.*
—C. S. Lewis

*People should understand that real value in the
sciences, the arts, commerce, and, indeed, one's
personal and professional lives, comes largely from
the process of collaboration.*
—Michael Schrage

As I discussed at the end of chapter 2, LeFevre proposes four specific kinds of interaction that are common when writing is viewed as a social process: encouragement, opposition, editing, and collaboration. There are not very many situations in which two or more Inklings conceive of and then produce a work together. In fact, on several occasions, members of the group attempted to collaborate and simply failed. And yet, as we will see in this chapter, there are significant collaborative projects that included two or more of them. In addition, there are many joint projects, that is, projects assembled sequentially or projects that contain some number, small or large, of connections, conjunctions, intersections, or overlaps. There are also several important activities—what might be called collective actions—that occupied the group and its members.

Many of these projects are not collaborations as the word is typically understood, even though these poems, stories, plays, essays, books, and events show a high degree of interdependence and serve as strong evidence of mutual influence. It is worth noting, however, that in Composition Studies and in sociological approaches to the creative process, the term "collaboration" is generally used to describe a very broad range of activities.[1] In fact, in most of the professional literature since the early 1990s, the idea that creativity is a social process, one involving many different individuals engaged in any single work, has been largely taken for granted. As LeFevre says in her description of the writing process, we no longer view creativity as "the isolated activity of an individual who carries around ideas in a self as she carries money in a wallet and knows before she spends it exactly what it will buy" (64).[2]

Instead, compositionists, sociologists, psychologists, and others who study creativity are increasingly convinced that all creative work is imagined, invented, produced, and distributed within complex social structures. Writing, like other inventive behaviors, is seen as inherently interactive. LeFevre says that in the normal course of events, people "become partners in the process of creating ideas" (62). Scholars commonly refer to all of these participants as collaborators.[3]

BOXEN

The earliest and most reciprocal collaboration relevant to the Inklings is Boxen, the imaginary world created by C. S. Lewis and Warren Lewis when they were boys. In April 1905, the Lewis family moved from Dundela Villas, a house in an inner suburb of Belfast, to Little Lea, a new house on the outskirts of the city. Lewis was six years old at the time, and in his autobiography he describes the impact of this transition: "My father, growing, I suppose, in prosperity, decided to leave the semidetached villa in which I had been born and build himself a much larger house, further out into what was then the country. The 'New House,' as we continued for years to call it, was a large one even by my present standards; to a child it seemed less like a house than a city" (*Surprised* 9–10). The Lewis brothers took over one of the attic rooms, a room they referred to as "the little end room," and this is where Lewis's first stories "were written, and illustrated, with enormous satisfaction" (*Collected Letters* 1: 107; *Surprised* 13).

The stories of Animal-Land were set in medieval times and featured dressed animals, including a frog named Lord Big, a rabbit king named Benjamin VII, and a bear named James Bar.[4] During this early period, 1905–1906, Warren Lewis also wrote stories, yet his stories were very different from his brother's. Warren was interested not in medieval times but in modern times. He was captivated not by dressed animals but by trains and steamships. He did not invent a new country but created an ideal world based on his childhood concept of India.

Warren Lewis was sent to attend Wynyard School in England, and when he came home to Ireland on holiday, he and his brother began merging their imaginary worlds into one. Animal-Land was reconceived as an earlier stage in its history, while India represented the modern period of that same world. With the rough timeline and history accounted for, the boys began work on geography and transportation: "Then Animal-Land had to be geographically related to my brother's India, and India consequently lifted out of its place in the real world. We made it an island, with its north coast running along the back of the Himalayas; between it and Animal-Land my brother rapidly invented the principal steamship routes. Soon there was a whole world and a map of that world which used every color in my paintbox" (*Surprised* 14).[5]

Much of this initial creative collaboration took place over the Christmas holiday of 1908. Having ironed out the details, the boys named this new world Boxen. Stories, maps, plays, drawings, essays: the boys expressed their new world in a wide range of creative modes. It was a beautifully detailed sub-creation. Warren Lewis even published a Boxonian newspaper.

In 1909, Warren was transferred from Wynyard School to Malvern College; Jack stayed at Wynyard, where he had matriculated the previous year. The increased distance between them made it difficult for the boys to stay in regular contact. Instead of working alone on the stories, maps, and illustrations for Boxen, Jack set this collaborative project aside. He began work on "a 'medieval' novel entitled *The Ajimywanian War*."[6] Hooper says it is "unexpectedly dull" (qtd. in C. S. Lewis, *Boxen* 14). This early solo effort lacks the bright energy that characterizes the Lewis brothers' collaborative work.

The stories of Boxen vary greatly in quality; readers who look here for a precursor to Narnia are generally disappointed. Still, the work is clever and engaging. Not only that: it has tremendous value as evidence of the boys' collaborative creative process. Joe R. Christopher notes, "Perhaps Lewis's childhood period of imaginative play (Animal-Land) that was shared by his brother (India) prepared him to be an author who was ready to borrow from his friends" (*C. S. Lewis* 2). In his discussion, Christopher focuses on C. S. Lewis, who began his creative work in daily collaboration with his older brother and continued to work collaboratively with others throughout his life. But the observation applies just as much to Warren Lewis. And, as we shall see later in this chapter, early collaborative experiences are characteristic of other members of the group as well.

Collaborative Poetry

When C. S. Lewis left home and started his undergraduate studies at Oxford, he gained a reputation as a mysterious figure, "a strange fellow who seemed to live an almost secret life and took no part in the social life of the college" (L. Baker 65). Despite this shadowy reputation, a student named R. M. S. Pasley sought him out. Pasley introduced Lewis to Leo Baker; they were soon joined by Owen Barfield, Cecil Harwood, and W. O. Field. A shared passion for poetry forged the connection, and from the beginning, they read each other's original work. Baker emphasizes, "Our initial link was, without question, poetry" (67).

During their first term at Oxford, they "planned some afternoon walks together and the exchange of our poems for mutual comment" (L. Baker 66). These evolved into large-scale walking tours—two or more would commit a week or so to walking across the English countryside with pauses at inns and pubs. They adopted the name "The Cretaceous Perambulators."[7] But sightseeing was not the centerpiece of these excursions. Literature was. Baker remembers, "What did we talk about on those walks? Naturally, of first importance were the poems we had most recently written" (71).

In addition to talking about their poetry, Baker, Barfield, Lewis, and the others composed stories and poems during these excursions.[8] Lewis tells of a walking tour in the spring of 1940: "We had a splendid evening 'telling a story'—an old diversion on these walks in which each player invents a chunk in turn: the natural tendency of each to introduce new characters and complications and then to 'hand the baby' to the next man, produces the fun." On this particular occasion, Hugo Dyson met them for a part of their tour, and Lewis notes that he "proved specially good" at this round-robin storytelling (*Collected Letters* 2: 384–85).

Another time, Lewis, Barfield, Harwood, and Field set out on a walking tour. After a very pleasant start, they encountered some nasty setbacks: strong wind, steep hill, scrubby camp, and bad food, including oranges of the "tough, acrid, unjuicy type, which is useless for thirst and revolting to taste" (*Collected Letters* 1: 689).

Lewis and Barfield responded to this series of challenges by converting their personal frustration into collaborative poetry. Lewis writes, "Barfield and I dropped behind and began composing in Pope-ian couplets a satire on the people who arrange walking tours. Nothing cd have been happier. At a stroke every source of irritation was magically changed into a precious fragment of 'copy'" (*Collected Letters* 1: 689–90). Barfield recalls that the poem included jokes at the expense of their walking companions. They dubbed Harwood, who was fond of cheese, "Philocasius," and Field, who was tall and thin, they renamed "Longus" (*Cretaceous*). Lewis notes that composing poetry had done them both some good: "By the time we had walked three miles we were once more in a position to enjoy the glorious country all round us" (*Collected Letters* 1: 690).

On another occasion, Lewis told Arthur Greeves about a different collaborative project: "That night we slept at Challacombe and composed ex-tempore poetry: telling the story of the Fall between us in the metre of Hiawatha" (*They Stand* 352). Barfield also remembers this serial poem and explains that one of the lines contained a reference to "the mystical caboodle" (*Cretaceous*).

And again, on 30 June 1922, Lewis records a poem he and Barfield composed together: "On the way back we started a burlesque poem in *terza rima* composing a line each in turn: we continued it later, with paper, by candle light. It was very good nonsense. We entitled it 'The Button Moulder's story' and went to bed" (*All My Road* 60).[9]

"The Button Moulder's story" was never published, and I could find no trace of the paper copied by candlelight. Like the other poems mentioned here, it was apparently a light-hearted narrative poem with a strong scheme of rhyme and meter. Composing poems and stories to pass the time, to mythologize their experiences, to provide mental exercise, or to amuse one another was a natural part of walking tours, and a common feature of Lewis and Barfield's friendship.[10]

This habit extended across the years. But despite this long history of mutual composition, only one Barfield/Lewis poetic collaboration has been published. This poem is titled "Abecedarium Philosophicum," and it appeared in the *Oxford Magazine* on 30 November 1933.[11] It is cheerful nonsense, neatly discussing (and dismissing) thirty philosophers or philosophical ideas in alphabetical order. The poem begins,

> A is the Absolute: none can express it.
> The Absolute, Gentleman! Fill up! God bless it!
> B is for Bergson who said: "Its a crime!
> They've been and forgotten that Time is Time!"
> C is for Croce who said: "Art's a stuff
> That means what it says (and that's little enough!)" (298)

And so it continues through the alphabet, listing Descartes, Elis, Fichte, the Good, Hume, and so on, all with the same light and irreverent touch. If this published work is characteristic of the larger body of unpublished material, it indicates that topics both silly and serious were addressed with gusto in the work that Barfield and Lewis wrote together.

A CRETACEOUS PERAMBULATOR

One of the most unusual collaborations to grow out of these mutual experiences is a booklet titled *A Cretaceous Perambulator*, published in 1983 in a limited edition by the Oxford University C. S. Lewis Society.[12] This little book had its start in April 1936, when Barfield, Harwood, and Lewis scheduled a walking tour. It turned out that Lewis was unable to join them, so, as a joke, Barfield and Harwood conspired to have Lewis make it up to them by taking a mock exam. They modeled their test after the School Certificate exam taken by British students at age 16, and they sternly informed Lewis that he would not be permitted to walk with them ever again unless he passed the test and gained readmittance into the "College of Cretaceous Perambulators."[13]

The booklet contains a five-page introduction by Walter Hooper, two pages of test questions by Barfield and Harwood, three-and-a-half pages of answers by Lewis, and a seven-page commentary written by Hooper based on an interview he conducted with Owen Barfield, who reminisced about the test and its circumstances.

In the introduction, we are told that one of the questions in the first draft of the test was, "Who were: Owen Glendower, Owen Nares, Robert Owen, Owen More, Owen Barfield, Vale Owen, Owain, Ywain, Rowena, Bowen, Rovin,' Sowin,' Growin,' Knowin' and Gloin?" Although this question did not make it into the final version of the test, the questions that did are equally facetious.

The test itself consists of three parts. Sixty minutes are allowed for Part I, which consists of ten short essay questions. These include, "Why are you the best map reader?" "Distinguish carefully between a walking-tour and a walking-race," and "Give the (long) semantic history of the word 'Guiting.'" One of the most interesting questions in this first section is an essay question that asks Lewis to describe "an imaginary walking-tour lasting not less than 4 days with no more than 4 of the following." The list of potential walkers includes Father Ronald Knox, Mahatma Gandhi, G. K. Chesterton, Mary Pickford, Sigmund Freud, Sir William Morris, Lord Olivier, and "Tha Dhali Llama of Thibet" [*sic*].

Forty minutes are allowed for Part II of the test. Six topics are given for an "English Essay." These include "Bredon" and "My Favourite Soaking-machine, and why." In the notes, Hooper quotes a Lewis letter of 11 May 1915 in which Lewis explains that he coined the expression "Soaking-Machine" for "private circulation." He writes, "The word 'soak' means to sit idly or sleepily doing nothing;" therefore, a Soaking-Machine is just a comfortable place to sit and daydream (*They Stand* 71).[14]

Part III of the test is the practical section, requiring that Lewis first "show reasonable proficiency in the game of Darts," and second, "read a Chapter to the satisfaction of a recognised Bishop of the Established Church." The notes explain that none of the Perambulators were proficient at darts. And the request to read a chapter comes from their habit of stopping at any church they came upon. They would then rest in a pew while one of the walkers would read a chapter from the Bible at the lectern.[15]

Lewis's answers to these questions are as light-hearted as the imaginative test deserves, full of schoolboy lapses in taste, imagery, sophistication, and grammar. At one point he deliberately taunts Barfield by indulging in the most blatant form of chronological snobbery.[16] Lewis writes, "It is true that [Aristotle] was not such a good philosopher as Lord Bacon but ought we to laugh at him for that, no We ought to remember that he lived a lot earlier when people were much less civilized."

Lewis invokes Aristotle again in answering the question, "Why are you the best map reader?" Lewis explains:

Aristotles [*sic*] astonishing learning enabled him to discover that there were four Causes—formal, efficient, material and final
e.g.-
i   The formal reason why I am the best map reader is because I have the best map reading faculty.
ii   The efficient is because I read it best
iii   The material is my brains.
iv   The final is that we can find the way

A Cretaceous Perambulator is certainly an unusual collaboration, and it serves to illustrate the robust and energetic spirit that characterized the creative life of the Inklings. Like other Lewis/Barfield collaborations, it has "a peculiarly Oxonian character, a mixture of high seriousness, good humor, and genial fellowship" (Tennyson xvi).

KNIGHTLY BEHAVIOUR

Another short work offers a further glimpse of the Inklings' sense of humor and lively interaction. This book, published in a limited edition of 126 copies, is titled *Mark vs. Tristram: Correspondence between C. S. Lewis and Owen Barfield*. A bit of background is necessary in order to understand this series of letters. In 1947, Eugène Vinaver published *The Works of Sir Thomas Malory*, a three-volume edition of Malory's Arthurian romances that includes a long introduction and extensive critical notes. Vinaver describes the history and importance of his book this way:

In 1931 I was asked by the Delegates of the Clarendon Press to prepare a critical edition of Malory based on the two extant copies of Caxton's volume. My work was nearing completion when, in the early summer of 1934, a startling discovery was made in the Fellows' Library in Winchester College by the then Librarian, Mr. W. F. Oakeshott. While the contents of the library were being examined for another purpose, a fifteenth-century manuscript of Malory's romances unexpectedly came to light. . . . Further inquiry showed that, while the manuscript was not that used by Caxton, it was in many respects more complete and authentic than Caxton's edition and had the first claim to the attention of any future editor of Malory. My task was thus clearly outlined for me. Without undue regret I abandoned my original project and undertook to edit Malory's works from the newly discovered text. (v–vi)

When Vinaver published his edition of Malory based on this hitherto unknown manuscript, it caused an uproar. Marvin D. Hinten explains, "This was a momentous occasion for Medieval literature scholars—roughly the equivalent to Shakespearean scholars discovering a new version of *Hamlet* with an added scene" (287). Some of the academic hue and cry came in response to the brand new text; even more came in reaction to new revelations about Malory. Before this time, the character of its author was largely a matter of speculation. But the new manuscript contained key biographical information, and it was not exactly flattering. Vinaver explains that in 1450, when Malory was over forty, he went from being "a peaceable and presumably well-to-do citizen" to a lawbreaker. "In the course of eighteen months—from January 1450 to July 1451—he was charged with several major crimes, including a robbery, a theft, two cattle-raids, some extortions, a rape, and even an attempted murder" (xvi). The final straw was this: the noble knight, Sir Thomas Malory, had written much of his work in prison.

The problem, of course, was not so much that Malory's reputation had been besmirched; rather, it was the sudden discrepancy between the ideal of virtue set forth in the Arthurian romances and the depths of vice now apparent in the author's personal life. Vinaver notes that Caxton makes plain in his preface that these stories describe "renowned acts of humanity, gentleness, and chivalry" and that they were presented specifically "for our doctrine and for to beware that we fall not to vice or sin, but exercise and follow virtue" (xx).

Lewis entered the fray with a review titled "The *Morte Darthur*," published in the *Times Literary Supplement*. In this brief essay, Lewis questions whether the evidence really proves that Malory was an evil man. He points out that legal procedures were quite different in Malory's time, and, therefore, "there is no need to suppose that Malory did all the things of which he was convicted" (105).

However, continues Lewis, even if Malory had in fact done every one of the things he was accused of, these "crimes" meant something different in his context than they would in our own. The word "rape," for example, simply meant "abduction," and no distinction would have been made between abducting a woman with evil intent and abducting her in order to rescue her out of a dangerous situation. Therefore, it is not appropriate to evaluate Malory's behavior simply on the basis of these labels. The more important question for Lewis is not if Malory's conduct was illegal or if his actions were punished by imprisonment. As Hooper explains in his introduction to *Mark vs. Tristram,* the real question is whether Malory's actions were "unknightly" and whether we should disregard the true character of his tales, which show a reverence for "mercy, humility, graciousness and good faith."

Lewis concludes his case by plucking two characters out of Malory's stories and posing this hypothetical question: "But how different such nobility may be from the virtues of the law-abiding citizen will appear if we imagine the life of Sir Tristram as it would be presented to us by King Mark's solicitors" (*"Morte"* 105).

Owen Barfield, a solicitor by profession, read Lewis's essay and took this casual concluding remark as a personal challenge. Barfield replied to Lewis's essay by sending him a "threatening" letter from the law offices of Barfield and Barfield (his real-life legal partnership) claiming to represent H. M. King Mark I of Cornwall. The letter is addressed to Messrs Inkling and Inkling, who serve as legal representation for the beleaguered Sir Tristram. Lewis found Barfield's feigned legal challenge irresistible and quickly responded in kind.

Mark vs. Tristram collects their correspondence: a total of five fictional letters, three from Barfield on behalf of King Mark and two from Lewis in defense of Sir Tristam.[17] In the first letter, Barfield and Barfield issue the complaint: While Tristram was entrusted with escorting King Mark's fiancée across the Irish channel, "he took advantage of those very circumstances to seduce this unfortunate lady" (Lewis, *Collected Letters* 2: 781). Furthermore, evidence has been found that the illicit relationship between Tristram and Isoud continues. Therefore, write Barfield and Barfield, "We must ask you to let us hear from you within twenty-one days, should your client have any proposal to make for compensating our client—so far as this is now possible—for the grievous injury he has suffered from your client's behaviour, for which we should have thought 'dishonourable' was scarcely an adequate word" (2: 782). The letter concludes by warning Tristram's defense team that any attempt to dismiss these charges by claiming that magic or witchcraft were somehow involved will not be admissible as evidence in a trial by jury.

Lewis responds, and his letter, signed by the legal firm of "Messrs Blaise and Merlin," is also written in mock legal language. Blaise and Merlin are blunt and to the point: they have instructed their client Tristram to ignore the frivolous threat issued in the first letter. Simply put, they say, no misconduct whatsoever has occurred, and furthermore, anyone who has questions about Tristram's conduct should address them directly to the attention of Tristram's overlord, H. M. Arthur of Logres!

Two letters follow from Barfield and Barfield. In the first, they agree to settle the matter through arbitration, and "the arbitrator so appointed is the immediate Lord to whom the Defendant owes allegiance," i.e., King Arthur (2: 784). In the next letter, they backpedal even more, saying, "Our client [Mark] will not in fact take any steps to bring this matter to arbitration provided that your client [Tristram] signs a full and complete *Retractatio* of all the works of the flesh." The plaintiff pushes the issue even further by suggesting that this matter can be settled most conveniently by using the standard legal form "which was approved by the Court in Arthur v. Lancelot" (2: 785).

The fifth and final letter of the sequence, written by Lewis on behalf of "Maistre Bleyse," is written in a mock Middle English, loosely imitating Malory's own writing style. It is addressed to the "lerned clerkes maister barfield and maister barfield" and asserts, "wytte ye well syr tristram of lyones is newlie come ageyne to þis reaulme of logres." This letter explains that "by grete adventure" Tristram has met syr Kaye in a tavern, and syr Kaye has "pleynlie" denied that he ever charged Tristram with wrongdoing (unless, possibly, "he was either dronken or subtilly enchaunted and wiste not what he wrote"). Therefore, without the testimony of this chief witness, the case and the correspondence are both dropped (*Collected Letters* 2: 785).

Maistre Bleyse offers another reason for wanting to bring the matter to a close: their law firm has fallen into disarray. "Merlyon" has suddenly left for London, but before he left, he turned his partner Bleyse into "an Asse." He has since turned him back but unfortunately left him with long ears and hooves (*Collected Letters* 2: 786).

This clever Lewis/Barfield collaboration is one result of Lewis's important review of Vinaver's *Malory.* But another work also emerged from this matter, an important academic project and a substantial collaborative work involving Lewis and another member of the Inklings, J. A. W. Bennett.[18] In 1963, Bennett edited and presented *Essays on Malory.* Though this collection seems to be a simple series of scholarly essays, Bennett's preface makes it clear that in assembling this volume, he is seeking primarily to showcase the dispute between Lewis and Vinaver over Malory's reputation. Bennett introduces their disagreement by praising Vinaver, saying, "Not least of his merits as a critic is his readiness to take account of points of view differing from his own; and this could hardly be better shown than in the debate with Professor Lewis here for the first time set forth" (v).

Essays on Malory begins with a brief descriptive piece: librarian W. F. Oakeshott's essay explaining how he happened upon the new Malory manuscript. Then Lewis opens the debate with "The English Prose *Morte,*" an essay that builds on his earlier review. Lewis, of course, is no stranger to this argumentative format. His defense of the Christian faith in the open forum of the

Socratic Club and in the BBC broadcast "Any Questions?" is well known.[19] Several of his collected essays, including "A Reply to Professor Haldane" and "Rejoinder to Dr Pittenger," are written contributions to public debate. And one of his earliest scholarly works, *The Personal Heresy* (1939), consists of a series of argumentative articles he exchanged with E. M. W. Tillyard.

In his essay for the Bennett volume, Lewis starts as he often does, by laying out the intellectual problems in a succinct list. He lists five paradoxes "thrown up" by the new scholarship, then discusses them, attempting to place each one in the larger context of Malory's success (7).[20] Lewis believes that whatever Malory's own life or motivations may have been, he has in fact presented highly moral stories with a strong sense of both the marvelous and the spiritual. He concludes that Vinaver has done us all a great service by collecting and arranging the stories of Sir Thomas Malory in such a careful and coherent way. Through the entire piece, Lewis's tone is quite congenial. Though he disagrees with Vinaver on a number of points, and often strenuously, he gives Vinaver great credit and sincere praise for his important work.

Vinaver's response is equally courteous. In fact, he presents his entire essay in the form of a letter, beginning with "My Dear Lewis" and concluding "Yours, Eugène Vinaver" (29, 40). He opens by admitting he has a great advantage in the discussion, having been given a copy of Lewis's essay and afforded the opportunity to study it and respond directly to it. "Of all the contributors to this volume I am the most fortunate," he writes. "You have shown me your essay and asked me to write a reply to it or, to quote your own words, 'a development from it.' The privilege is a perilous one, and at first I hesitated to take up the friendly challenge; but the prospect of a dialogue with you on the vital issues you have raised is irresistible" (29). Their frank enjoyment of intellectual challenge is quite evident here. Vinaver is as thoughtful and systematic as his opponent. He answers Lewis point by point, sometimes agreeing, sometimes disagreeing, sometimes simply complicating the questions and assumptions that have been raised.

Bennett's book is 145 pages long; the essays by Lewis and Vinaver combined form roughly a third of it. The other five essays seem tangential to the heart of Bennett's purpose: to call attention to this central discussion in which his fellow Inkling enters into one of the biggest literary debates of their day.

OTHER INKLING COLLABORATIONS

The Inklings made a habit of thinking and talking about collaboration. A number of projects were planned, but for one reason or another, they were never completed. For example, in 1944 Lewis and Tolkien began "to consider writing a book in collaboration on 'Language' (Nature, Origins, Functions)"

(Tolkien, *Letters* 105). Hooper tells us that by 1948, the book "got as far as the title 'Language and Human Nature' and was advertised by the S. P. C. K. [the Society for Promoting Christian Knowledge] as due in 1949" (Lewis, *Letters* 399). In 1949, Chad Walsh published *C. S. Lewis: Apostle to the Skeptics* in which he reported optimistically, "The Student Christian Movement Press, in its recent announcement of forthcoming books, listed a text on semantics, *Language and Human Nature*, to be written jointly by Lewis and his friend, Prof. F. R. R. [*sic*] Tolkien, but I gather that it is still in the blueprint stage" (10).

This book project was apparently serious and substantial enough to warrant promotion by the publisher, and many people knew of it. But the book was never written. In 1950, Lewis grumbled, "My book with Professor Tolkien—any book in collaboration with that great but dilatory and unmethodical man—is dated, I fear, to appear on the Greek Kalends!" (*Letters* 399).

What became of it? In a short piece titled "A Note on an Unpublished (and Probably Unwritten) Collaboration," Joe R. Christopher writes, "But one cannot help wondering what the relationship between language and human nature is—especially one which would interest the Student Christian Movement Press" (29). Christopher speculates about the fate of their material: "Perhaps part of what Lewis would have contributed appears in his *Studies in Words* (Cambridge, England: Cambridge University Press, Second Edition with Three New Chapters, 1967). Perhaps part of what Tolkien would have contributed appears in his 'English and Welsh' in *Angles and Britons* (Cardiff: University of Wales Press, 1963) pp. 1–41" (29).

Lewis and Williams embarked on two collaborative projects, and these, too, were never completed. Reference to one of them is found in a 1946 letter from Lewis to Dorothy L. Sayers, where Lewis describes a proposed series, "a sort of library of Christian knowledge for young people in the top forms at school." He tells her the series will be called *The Thorn Books*, "being elementary as Horn-Books, dealing with thorny questions, from an Anglican point of view." Lewis writes, "C. W. had already talked to me about it and he and I were to collaborate on a short Xtian Dictionary (about 40 Headings) for it" (*Collected Letters* 2: 721–22).

Lewis then asks Sayers if she might be available to contribute a volume to the series. He chides, "Don't blast me. Good books *have* sometimes been begotten by letters like this!" (*Collected Letters* 2: 722). Sayers said no; Barbara Reynolds explains, "Her conscience prevented her from writing for the purpose of edifying readers" (Sayers, *Letters* 3: 252).[21]

The other latent Lewis/Williams collaboration is mentioned in *Essays Presented to Charles Williams* where Lewis explains that Williams "toyed with the idea that he and I should collaborate in a book of animal stories from the

Bible, told by the animals concerned." Lewis describes some of the possible story lines. They could tell the story of Jonah from the point of view of the whale, and the story of Elisha from the point of view of the two she-bears. "The bears were to be convinced that God exists and is good by their sudden meal of children" (xii).

Though nothing came of either the short Christian dictionary or the book of animal stories, Lewis and Williams spent time in conversation planning the nature and content of these two projects and perhaps others as well. And it is interesting that in both of these cases, Williams served as the initiator, and he recruited Lewis to participate.

Only two of the Inklings succeeded in planning and publishing purely collaborative academic books together: Christopher Tolkien and Nevill Coghill. They produced three carefully edited editions of Chaucer's tales as part of Harrap's English Classics series: *The Nun's Priest's Tale, The Pardoner's Tale,* and *The Man of Law's Tale.* In each case, the poem itself is only a small part of the book, 24 or 25 pages in length. Each has a substantial explanatory introduction, more than 60 pages long, and detailed textual notes, appendices, and a glossary. If there is anything remarkable about these three collaborative volumes, it is simply that they are so ordinary. Solid, reliable, and widely respected, they are classic scholarly editions of these three Chaucer works.[22]

THE PROBLEM OF PAIN

Lewis's *The Problem of Pain* may be considered a joint project, one that further illustrates the range of creative interaction among the Inklings. Lewis had taken up the task of writing this book with great reluctance. Ashley Sampson, founder of the Centenary Press and an editor at Geoffrey Bles, had been impressed with *The Pilgrim's Regress,* and he approached Lewis asking him to write a book on the Christian view of pain and suffering. At first Lewis demurred, then he asked if he might "be allowed to write it anonymously" (*Problem* vii).

Lewis finally began the book in the summer of 1939 and completed it by the spring of 1940 (Hooper, *C. S. Lewis* 295). During this time, he read it aloud at meetings of the Inklings. George Sayer writes that Havard and Tolkien in particular "provided many suggestions" (*Jack* 162). Not only did Havard comment on the book as it was written, but Lewis asked him to write an appendix to the book "on the observed effects of pain . . . from clinical experience" (*Problem* 143). Havard says that he "was glad to do so and took some trouble over it." He reports with pride that when Lewis saw the piece, "he seemed pleased" and "one evening read it to the Inklings, winning for me some appreciation" ("Philia" 356–57).[23]

Havard also notes that Lewis extensively revised the work. Havard explains that he had overrun his "allowance," so Lewis shortened it. Lewis also "edited" it, and Havard writes, "I was impressed by the trouble he took to get it right" ("Philia" 356–57). *The Problem of Pain* is Lewis's first important work of Christian apologetics, and it is still one of his most popular. It serves as one of the most comprehensive illustrations of the highly interactive process of drafting, commenting, editing, and collaborating described in these pages. It is, appropriately, dedicated "To The Inklings."

ESSAYS PRESENTED TO CHARLES WILLIAMS

We have seen that a number of Inklings worked together in pairs on several projects and potential projects: Lewis and Barfield, Lewis and Tolkien, Lewis and Williams, Lewis and Bennett, Coghill and Christopher Tolkien, Lewis and Havard. Such pairs were common, but there is only one book the Inklings completed as a group, a collection entitled *Essays Presented to Charles Williams*. As was noted in chapter 1, Williams first came to Oxford when World War II prompted the move of Oxford University Press from London to Oxford. As the war drew to a close, Williams prepared to return to his home and family in London. The Inklings began a book of essays to be published in his honor; Lewis explains that he and Tolkien together took the initiative in proposing the project (*Collected Letters* 2: 649). But in 1945, Williams experienced severe abdominal pains. On the 14th of May, he was taken to the hospital and operated on. He died the next day. The Inklings completed the collection of essays, but with a significant change in purpose. Lewis grimly observes in the preface, "We now offer as a memorial what had been devised as a greeting" (vi). The proceeds of the sale were earmarked for Williams's widow.

There is little information about how the Inklings went about choosing, editing, and ordering the essays. In the book itself, Lewis is nowhere designated as editor, but it is clear that he undertook this function. He wrote the preface and, as we have seen, he read it to his collaborators and altered it in response to their comments. Lewis invited two additional participants, T. S. Eliot and Dorothy L. Sayers, expanding the scope of the project.[24] And Lewis is the one who did substantial editing of the essay Sayers submitted. In one letter to her, he enthuses, "I've romped through your essay for a first reading with v. great delight. There's not a dull moment and some things are superlatively good" (*Collected Letters* 2: 685). He continues with the suggestion that she use English rather than Italian for her quotations from Dante; in the published version, she keeps the Italian but adds English translations. Then Lewis writes, "On a separate sheet I add detailed comments and suggestions" (2: 686). The extent of Lewis's feedback to Sayers not only supports his role as editor of the volume but also suggests that in compiling the volume, Lewis in particular and the Inklings in general offered critique and made revisions to the essays in this book.

Essays Presented to Charles Williams displays the writing skill of Dorothy L. Sayers and five key Inklings: C. S. Lewis, Warren Lewis, Tolkien, Barfield, and Mathew. It demonstrates their range of intellectual vitality. And when it was published, it helped establish the Inklings as "a corporate identity in the public eye" (Carpenter, *Inklings* 224).[25] However one may evaluate its accuracy in representing the group or assess its significance as a statement of "corporate identity," it does stand alone as the only book the Inklings produced together.

OTHER ESSAY COLLECTIONS

There are several other essay collections that deserve brief mention here. Though they were not products of the Inklings as a group, they do include essays by some of the Inklings and, in some cases, there was significant interaction among them as they worked. *Essays Presented to Charles Williams* is one of two Festschrifts that honored Inklings after their death. The other is *Patterns of Love and Courtesy: Essays in Memory of C. S. Lewis,* edited by John Lawlor. Published in 1966, it contains essays by ten writers "who all enjoyed Lewis's friendship." They included four of the Inklings: Colin Hardie, Gervase Mathew, J. A. W. Bennett, and Nevill Coghill. Lawlor explains, "Our hope had been to present this book to Lewis in the year of his retirement" (Preface). Here, as in the essays dedicated to Williams, death forestalled them. One Inkling, Gervase Mathew, participated in both of these memorial volumes.

Happier occasions led to other essay collections. In 1962, Tolkien celebrated his seventieth birthday, and his friends published a Festschrift entitled *English and Medieval Studies: Presented to J. R. R. Tolkien on the Occasion of His Seventieth Birthday.* It was edited by Norman Davis and C. L. Wrenn and included twenty-two contributions, including four essays by Inklings: J. A. W. Bennett, Nevill Coghill, C. S. Lewis, and C. L. Wrenn. When the book was published, the contributors organized a party in his honor. Tolkien specifically wrote to encourage Lewis to attend. He sent his regrets: "I shan't be at the Festschrift dinner. I wear a catheter, live on a low protein diet, and go early to bed. I am, if not a lean, at least a slippered pantaloon. All the best. Yours, Jack" (qtd. in Carpenter, *Inklings* 250). Lewis died one year later.

There are other collections that include contributions by two or more members of the group. There are important primary sources about the group and its members tucked away in these volumes. *Light on C. S. Lewis* was edited by Jocelyn Gibb and published in 1965, two years after Lewis died. The eight essays in this volume do not provide scholarly analysis but rather informal personal reflection. As Gibb explains in the preface to the volume, "This book is no biography. All it does is to present, from several people who knew him and his writings, an answer to the simple question 'C. S. Lewis—how did he strike you?'" (vi). Three of the Inklings—Owen Barfield, J. A. W. Bennett, and Nevill Coghill—contributed articles, and Warren Lewis assisted in editing the volume.

A more recent volume also collects essays and remembrances from people who knew Lewis, and the Inklings are represented there as well.[26] Como's *Remembering C. S. Lewis* is easily the best essay collection about Lewis; in fact, it remains one of the best books of any kind about Lewis as a person. Como has not tried to bring the twenty-four essays into an artificial consistency of style, length, or content, and as a result, the view of Lewis is multifaceted, quirky, and inconsistent. In short, it is both well-rounded and unvarnished. It includes essays by Inklings John Wain, Adam Fox, Gervase Mathew, R. E. Havard, and James Dundas-Grant.

ARTHURIAN TORSO

Another book that contains work by more than one Inkling is *Arthurian Torso*. This combination of Williams's history and Lewis's criticism was first published by Oxford University Press in 1948. "C. Williams & C. S. Lewis" are listed on the cover as co-authors, and the sections authored by Lewis and by Williams are approximately equal in length.

In his introduction to the volume, Lewis describes the unusual origin of this book. Williams died in 1945, leaving two works unfinished: "One was a long lyric cycle on the Arthurian legend of which two instalments had already appeared under the titles of *Taliessin through Logres* (1938) and *The Region of the Summer Stars* (1944). The other was a prose work on the history of the legend which was to have been entitled *The Figure of Arthur*" (Williams and Lewis 1). Lewis was well acquainted with Williams's Arthurian poetry and prose. He writes, "Since I had heard nearly all of it read aloud and expounded by the author and had questioned him closely on his meaning I felt that I might be able to comment on it, though imperfectly, yet usefully" (1). Lewis worked from a number of sources: a typescript of Williams's unfinished essay, his knowledge of Williams as a friend and scholar, their conversations about Arthurian legend in general and Williams's Arthurian writings in particular, and his experience in hearing both the poems and prose Arthuriana read and discussed.[27] Lewis also worked from a long exposition of the poetry written by Williams himself: "His most systematic exposition had been given to me in a long letter which (with that usual folly which forbids us to remember that our friends can die)

I did not preserve; but fortunately I had copied large extracts from it into the margin of my copy of *Taliessin* at the relevant passages" (1).[28] Drawing from these sources, Lewis wrote at length about the work Williams left behind. This extended commentary became the basis for a series of lectures he gave at Oxford in the autumn of 1945. It was given the title "Williams and the Arthuriad" and eventually published together with Williams's unfinished *The Figure of Arthur* as *Arthurian Torso.*

Lewis describes the book as follows: "In [this book] Williams the critic and literary historian provides an introduction to my study of Williams the Arthurian poet; or, if you prefer, I add to Williams's history of the legend an account of the last poet who has contributed to it—namely, Williams himself" (Williams and Lewis 1–2). It is an important contribution to the literature on King Arthur. But more pertinent to this study, it offers further evidence that Lewis and Williams were comfortable and effective in this kind of collaborative mode. Gervase Mathew notes, "It is almost a symbol of the nature of their friendship that the draft and the lectures should weld so perfectly into a single book, although superficially the technique is very different" ("Williams and the Arthuriad" 14). In this one volume, we have literary history and literary criticism, and an important example of a joint project by two of the Inklings.

J. R. R. TOLKIEN AND CHRISTOPHER TOLKIEN AS COLLABORATORS

Of all the examples of Inkling collaboration, none is more extensive or important than the common labor of J. R. R. Tolkien and his son Christopher. In a letter to Stanley Unwin written in 1945, Tolkien says that Christopher "occupied the multiple position of audience, critic, son, student in my department, and my tutorial pupil" (*Letters* 113). Christopher Tolkien's name may be found somewhere on nearly every one of his father's works—the foreword to the fiftieth anniversary edition of *The Hobbit*, the maps in *The Lord of the Rings,* the editing of *The Silmarillion*, and the energy and vision behind all twelve volumes of *The History of Middle-earth.*[29] Their creative interaction is well documented. In another letter to Stanley Unwin, Tolkien calls his son his "chief critic and collaborator" (*Letters* 118).

Chief critic perhaps; chief collaborator without question.[30] Christopher Tolkien's earliest contribution to his father's work was as a primary audience for *The Hobbit*. He was about five years old when he first heard the words, "In a hole in the ground there lived a hobbit" (Foreword, *The Hobbit*). As we have seen, the presence of interested and eager readers is a crucial part of the creative act; this is true of authors in general and of J. R. R. Tolkien in particular.[31]

Christopher Tolkien critiqued both the text and the drawings of *The Hobbit* as the book took shape. Early on, as John Tolkien and Priscilla Tolkien note, "Christopher was always much concerned with the consistency of the story" (*Family Album* 58). In the foreword to the fiftieth anniversary edition, Christopher Tolkien tells about a time when his father was reading to him, and he interrupted to criticize the consistency of the story, saying, "Last time, *you said* Bilbo's front door was blue, and *you said* Thorin had a golden tassel on his hood, but you've just said that Bilbo's front door was green, and the tassel on Thorin's hood was silver." Much annoyed, his father "'strode across the room' to his desk to make a note" (Foreword).

Though J. R. R. Tolkien sometimes found this trait annoying, he quickly learned that Christopher's attention to detail could be used to advantage. In 1938, he writes, "I then put my youngest son, lying in bed with a bad heart, to find any more [errata in the published text of *The Hobbit*] at twopence a time. He did" (*Letters* 28). From a very early age, Christopher Tolkien participated in his father's work as a proofreader and critic.

Their interaction continued as Tolkien worked on *The Lord of the Rings*. John Tolkien and Priscilla Tolkien give a detailed account of the circumstances surrounding the collaboration during this time: "Ronald [Tolkien] kept in very close imaginative contact with Christopher during 1944 and 1945 when Christopher was stationed in South Africa. In these letters (many of which appear in the volume of letters published after J. R. T.'s death) he sent Christopher regular instalments of the book as he wrote them, as well as discussing the ideas and problems he was encountering" (*Family Album* 73). Tolkien looked forward to sending new chapters to his son; in 1944, he expressed his appreciation to Christopher, saying, "This book has come to be more and more addressed to you, so that your opinion matters more than any one else's" (*Letters* 91).[32]

One of the most underappreciated contributions that Christopher Tolkien made to *The Lord of the Rings* is his detailed maps. His careful cartography was based on a large number of rough sketches and contradictory concepts his father had been working from. Christopher's comprehensive maps did not merely adorn the work; the process of mapmaking and storytelling was highly collaborative and each shaped the other. J. R. R. Tolkien writes, "I wisely started with a map, and made the story fit" (*Letters* 177). And again, in an interview on the BBC, he asserts, "If you're going to have a complicated story you *must* work to a map, otherwise you can never make a map of it afterwards" (*Audio Portrait*). The verisimilitude of *The Lord of the Rings* has its roots not only in J. R. R. Tolkien's thoroughness but also in the skill and clarity of Christopher Tolkien's maps. They allowed Tolkien to maintain a "meticulous care for distances," as well as an accurate assessment of travel routes and geography (*Letters* 177).

Although Christopher Tolkien served as an important collaborator during Tolkien's life—audience, editor, critic, commentator, evaluator, typist, and mapmaker—his high level of participation in his father's work is even more evident in the posthumously published work *The Silmarillion*. As Tolkien labored on *The Lord of the Rings*, he often protested that *The Silmarillion* was his real work. In 1938, he emphasized that his mind was "preoccupied with the 'pure' fairy stories or mythologies of the *Silmarillion*," adding, "even Mr Baggins got dragged" into this tale "against my original will" (*Letters* 38). Nearly twenty years later, he was still adamant: "My heart and mind is in the *Silmarillion*" (*Letters* 261). William Cater calls this work "the heart of Tolkien's invented mythology, the scarcely visible roots from which grew the great tree of *The Lord of the Rings*, the source of his invented languages, the origin of his invented peoples, elves, hobbits, ents, dwarves, orcs" (91).

Over the years, Tolkien drafted a vast amount of material for *The Silmarillion*. With the completion of *The Lord of the Rings*, he returned to this project, and after his retirement in 1959, he vowed to give it his full attention. But he quickly became overwhelmed by the task. He found himself easily distracted, and he spent his days writing letters or playing solitaire. By this time, Tolkien had become increasingly isolated, and as a result he found himself increasingly unable to write. Thus, when he died in 1973, he left an enormous amount of material unfinished, unconnected, and unorganized.[33] Christopher observes, "By the time of my father's death the amount of writing in existence on the subject of the Three Ages was huge in quantity (since it extended over a lifetime), disordered, more full of beginnings than of ends, and varying in content from heroic verse in the ancient English alliterative meter to severe historical analysis of his own extremely difficult languages: a vast repository and labyrinth of story, of poetry, of philosophy, and of philology" (*A Brief Account*). Christopher Tolkien decided that rather than present all of the different versions of the poems and stories of *The Silmarillion*, he would select among them, arranging them in the "most coherent and internally self-consistent" way, presenting a "completed and cohesive entity" (*Silmarillion* 8; *Unfinished Tales* 1).

Not only did he select and edit the vast amount of material his father had written, but he also composed sections of the narrative in order to fill in the gaps his father had left. He explains, "Here and there I had to develop the narrative out of notes and rough drafts; I had to make many choices between competing versions and to make many changes of detail; and in the last few chapters (which had been left almost untouched for many years) I had in places to modify the narrative to make it coherent" (*A Brief Account*). Christopher Tolkien acknowledges, "There's a great deal of my own personal literary judgment in the book" (qtd. in Cater 94). Ultimately, the task of creating a

complete, coherent work was so demanding that he called in the assistance of
Guy Gavriel Kay, who worked with him on the project during 1974 and 1975.
The Silmarillion was finally published in 1977.

The Silmarillion was followed by *Unfinished Tales.* Christopher Tolkien
indicates that "the book is no more than a collection of writings, disparate
in form, intent, finish, and date of composition (and in my own treatment
of them), concerned with Númenor and Middle-earth" (*Unfinished Tales* 1).
Whereas the goal of *The Silmarillion* was to produce a "cohesive unity," Christopher Tolkien's purpose in *Unfinished Tales* was to select, order, and present
the series of incomplete narratives untouched, then to add lengthy explanatory
and prefatory material.

After *Unfinished Tales,* Christopher Tolkien continued in his commitment
to his father's work and eventually completed a twelve volume set, *The History
of Middle-earth,* published between 1983 and 1996. *The History of Middle-earth*
includes various drafts and versions, including material Tolkien had deleted,
and stories, poems, sketches, and outlines that were never finished.

In completing this monumental task, Christopher sorted through and
selected among numerous editions and revisions, using the insight and expertise that he alone possessed as one intimately involved in the creation of
the original works. As Douglas A. Anderson wisely emphasizes, Christopher
Tolkien deserves considerable credit simply for the work of deciphering his
father's often cryptic penmanship (247). Christopher provided detailed essays
on the various documents and wrote extensive footnotes and explanations of
the material. As profitable as it is to have Tolkien's previously unpublished
manuscripts, much of the value of these volumes is in Christopher Tolkien's
explanatory notes and interpretive commentary.

In addition to these important contributions to his father's imaginative
world of Middle-earth, Christopher Tolkien also contributed to Tolkien's
scholarly work in Middle English. In 1975, two years after Tolkien's death, Allen
and Unwin decided to issue Tolkien's translations of *Sir Gawain and the Green
Knight, Pearl,* and *Sir Orfeo* in one volume. Christopher Tolkien explains that
his father "wished to provide both a general introduction and a commentary;
and it was largely because he could not decide on the form that these should
take that the translations remained unpublished" (7). Christopher Tolkien
was called upon to gather the translations. He writes, "In choosing between
competing versions I have tried throughout to determine his latest intention,
and that has in most cases been discoverable with fair certainty" (8). He used
his father's notes to compile an introduction for the book.[34] He also prepared
a short glossary, printed in the back of the book.

And there is more. Christopher Tolkien has published a number of brief articles that discuss various aspects of his father's work. He edited the essay collection *The Monsters and the Critics and Other Essays* and worked with Humphrey Carpenter as coeditor of *The Letters of J. R. R. Tolkien.* He prepared notes for *The 1977 The Lord of the Rings Calendar, The 1978 Silmarillion Calendar,* and *The 1979 Tolkien Calendar.* He wrote the foreword and critical notes for *Pictures by J. R. R. Tolkien.* And he supplied a critical introduction to *Tree and Leaf.*

Tolkien left a great deal of his work unfinished when he died. What we have of Tolkien's writing and what we know of Tolkien's sub-created world is due in large part to the insight and effort of Christopher Tolkien. As Rayner Unwin eloquently observes, "In effect one man's imaginative genius has had the benefit of two lifetimes' work" ("Early Days" 6). Without Christopher Tolkien, not only would *The Hobbit* and *The Lord of the Rings* look very different, but so would the face of Tolkien scholarship.

Collective Action

Michael P. Farrell proposes that collaborative circles typically move through seven stages. They are Formation, Rebellion against Authority, Quest, Creative Work, Collective Action, Separation, and Nostalgic Reunion (17–26). While the Inklings show evidence of many of these steps, they fit this stage model somewhat loosely. This is particularly evident in the fifth stage of collaborative circles, the collective action stage. In this stage, the attention of the group shifts. It has been directed inward in order to "mine the creative process"; now the attention of the group "turns outward" with an increased desire to impact society (Farrell 286). Farrell writes, "The collective action stage of a circle begins when the members decide to carry out a group project aimed at winning support for their vision outside their own network. The project could be a journal, an art exhibition, a grant proposal, or some other task that requires interdependent work" (286). The Inklings did not invest much energy in this kind of collective action.[35] Instead, they focused on promoting one another's work to the larger intellectual world: advocating one another's work to publishers and promoting one another's accomplishments through cover blurbs and book reviews. There are exceptions, though. Some of this collective action was frivolous, some serious; some was very successful, and some decidedly not.[36]

As we have seen, when Lewis and Tolkien were new faculty members at Oxford, they joined forces and won a major political coup: the revision of the

English curriculum. Tolkien was the instigator, "reviving an old Oxford quarrel, which had split the Honour School of English Language and Literature ever since its foundation at the end of the nineteenth century" (Carpenter, *Inklings* 24). The debate centered on two key questions: whether the curriculum should focus on pre-Chaucerian literature or survey all periods, and whether early literature should be approached as literature or language study.

Lewis favored the survey approach, and he voted against Tolkien in early faculty debates. But in 1926, Tolkien founded the Coalbiters, a group of dons who met to read Old Norse. By cultivating love for this literature, Tolkien swayed the members of this small but influential group, and in 1931, the faculty adopted Tolkien's reforms for the syllabus (Carpenter, *Inklings* 55).

A political element colored their entire Oxford careers; even when Tolkien and Lewis began their regular Monday morning meetings, they talked school politics as well as literature and theology (Carpenter, *Inklings* 54–55). At one point, Tolkien declared an ambition "to get C.S.L. and myself into the 2 Merton Chairs" (*Letters* 108).

The Coalbiters continued to meet, and a second group was formed: "The English School 'junto' led by Lewis and Tolkien began to hold informal dinners," which included Inklings Coghill and Dyson. Their political ambitions are clear in their choice of name—they called their meetings "Caves," taking their cue from the Cave of Adullam in which David "organised the conspiracy" against King Saul, a story told in chapter 22 of I Samuel. As Carpenter explains, this junto was clearly conspiring against the "reigning party in the English School" (*Inklings* 56).

Ultimately, the Cave was not an effective force for political transformation. Other than the English curricular reform, the only significant victory for the Inklings was engineering the election of Adam Fox to the Oxford Professorship of Poetry in 1938. This Oxford chair is a five-year position, and, unlike other university posts, the Professor of Poetry is elected by popular vote of all the MAs. The position has provoked bitter debate, not only about the holder's literary convictions, but also about the position's purpose: Is the point to provide a platform for a practicing poet or for a scholar of poetry? Wilson observes, "Although there have been some famous poets who occupied this chair (for example Matthew Arnold and W. H. Auden), it has much more commonly been occupied by dons" (156).

In 1938, E. K. Chambers, a distinguished Shakespeare scholar, had been put forth for the position. Though Chambers possessed considerable academic credentials, Adam Fox was surprised to hear that he had been nominated. Fox reports, "When at breakfast one morning I read that Chambers was proposed,

I said without any thought of being taken literally, 'This is simply shocking; they might as well make me Professor of Poetry.'" Lewis, who was seated next to him at the time, said in reply, "Well, we will" ("At the Breakfast Table" 187).

So the Inklings joined forces to oppose Chambers, ostensibly on the grounds that the position should be filled by a practicing poet, and they put forth Fox instead. They lobbied enthusiastically for votes, and Fox was elected on 2 June 1938. Tolkien responded with enthusiasm and pride: "[Fox] was nominated by Lewis and myself, and miraculously elected: our first public victory over established privilege. For Fox is a member of our literary club of *practising poets*" (*Letters* 36). Lewis was more modest and measured: "Another pleasing thing that happened this week was the confirmation of our little party's good judgement in making Fox professor of poetry" (*Collected Letters* 2: 355).[37]

Carpenter argues that the Inklings had little motive for this activity—he believes that it did not pay off for the group in any tangible way. Why do it? Carpenter suspects that the Inklings wanted to demonstrate their power as a group (*Inklings* 163). It seems to me, however, that the motive was less to flex their collective muscles than to promote their collective convictions about what sort of person should or should not hold this position.

The syllabus reform and the election of Fox were triumphs of their collective action. But another political attempt ended less successfully. In 1951, the position of Professor of Poetry was again vacant, and this time the Inklings put forth C. S. Lewis for the position. Lewis ran against Cecil Day Lewis, and he was defeated, with a final vote of 173 to 194 (Hooper, *C. S. Lewis* 56). Many believe that Lewis's strong Christian views were responsible for his defeat. Warren Lewis recorded in his diary, "I'm astonished at the virulence of the anti-Xtian feeling shown here; Hugo [Dyson] told me that one elector whom he canvassed announced his intention of voting for CDL *on the ground that* J had written *Screwtape!*" (*Brothers* 239–40).

But Warren Lewis notes that dinner was "merry" despite "our defeat" (*Brothers* 240). Tolkien corroborates this fact. Correcting the rumor that Lewis had been "cut to the quick" by the defeat, Tolkien explains, "I remember that we had assembled soon after in our accustomed tavern and found C. S. L. sitting there, looking (and since he was no actor at all probably feeling) much at ease. 'Fill up!' he said, 'and stop looking so glum. The only distressing thing about this affair is that my friends seem to be upset'" (*Letters* 351).[38]

One other event deserves brief mention here. After years of vainly hoping for a professorship at Oxford, Lewis was surprised by an offer from another quarter. Early in 1954, Cambridge University announced the creation of a new chair for a Professor of Medieval and Renaissance English. The electors were

F. P. Wilson, Professor Basil Willey, Sir Henry Willink, and J. R. R. Tolkien. They chose Lewis unanimously as the first holder of this coveted position (Hooper, *C. S. Lewis* 66). They wrote to Lewis on 11 May 1954 to tell him so.

Lewis was flattered, but he graciously declined the appointment, citing "domestic necessities" (66). They wrote again, Lewis declined again, and then Tolkien took action. He had a long talk with Lewis, then he wrote to several of the electors. The sticking point was arranging appropriate accommodations: Lewis did not want to sell the Kilns and uproot Warren Lewis and Fred Paxford. Tolkien urged the electors to provide rooms for Lewis so he could live comfortably in Cambridge during the week and still return to Oxford on the weekends. They agreed to these arrangements, and Lewis accepted the position. He was quite clear about the real reason for his acceptance, telling Willink, "Since my last letter to you I have had a conversation with Tolkien which has considerably changed my view" (qtd. in Hooper, *C. S. Lewis* 68). He held the position of professor for eight years, until declining health led to his retirement. It proved a happy move, and Tolkien deserves considerable credit for it. From their early meetings as junior faculty members to these final years of final assignment and retirement, Tolkien and Lewis worked together within the academic environment and effected significant change.

CONCLUSIONS

Of the five categories of interaction and influence considered in this book, collaboration raises some of the most interesting questions about the way we view the writing process. It also reveals many of our biases and difficulties with ideas of influence and interaction. The root of it may lie in the problem of attribution. Acknowledging collaborators can present difficult problems, and these problems can pose a serious hindrance to collaborative scholarship. LeFevre points out that it becomes particularly complicated when one begins to examine the components of a writer's social context. She offers the following examples: "If Y and Z help me revise a manuscript, how should I acknowledge them? Or needn't I? If I thank them in a footnote, will someone think I'm dropping names? Will they be implicated if my book gets negative reviews? Before I acknowledge them, should I ask if they object? If a book evolves from a series of talks Z and I have over lunch, who is the inventor? Who should own the copyright? Is it ethical for me merely to dedicate it 'to Z, without whom . . .'"? (123, ellipsis in original).

LeFevre further illustrates the point by citing the work of novelist John Gardner. In an interview with Joe David Bellamy, Gardner explains that if he has any doubts about "what a character would say or what a room would

look like," he asks his wife, explaining that her imagination "informs everything I do" (Bellamy 189). And that raises questions in Gardner's mind about
attribution:

> Perhaps I should have used "John and Joan Gardner" on the titles all
> along; I may do this in the future. But in modern times such a work is
> regarded as not really art. The notion that art is an individual and unique
> vision is a very unmedieval and unclassical view. In the Middle Ages it
> was very common to have several people work on one thing; the thir-
> teenth-century Vulgate cycle of Arthurian romances had hundreds of
> writers. I feel comfortable with this approach, but I haven't felt comfort-
> able telling people it's what I do. As I get more and more into the medieval
> mode, I'll probably admit how many writers I have. (189–90)

Gardner is exactly right about the medieval mindset. Lewis makes this same
point in his discussion of the contrast between medieval and modern notions of authorship. When dealing with medieval literature, Lewis says, "the
book-author unit, basic for modern criticism, must often be abandoned"
(*Discarded Image* 210). He explains, "One is tempted to say that almost the
typical activity of the medieval author consists in touching up something
that was already there; as Chaucer touched up Boccaccio, as Malory touched
up French prose romances which themselves touched up earlier romances in
verse, as Laȝamon works over Wace, who works over Geoffrey, who works
over no one knows what" (209). As a result, says Lewis, "We should have to
think of the total result chemically rather than arithmetically" (209). Chemically, or perhaps architecturally:

> Some books—if I may use a comparison I have used elsewhere—must
> be regarded more as we regard those cathedrals where work of many dif-
> ferent periods is mixed and produces a total effect, admirable indeed but
> never foreseen nor intended by any one of the successive builders. Many
> generations, each in its own spirit and its own style, have contributed
> to the story of Arthur. It is misleading to think of Malory as an author
> in our modern sense and throw all the earlier work into the category
> of "sources." He is merely the last builder, doing a few demolitions here
> and adding a few features there. (210)

This is true in earlier times, before the cultivation of a concept of literary
property; it is still true in a large percentage of creative work. But despite his
awareness of this tendency, Gardner is very uncomfortable naming his wife

as a collaborator: "I use a lot of people, Joan in particular. She hasn't actually written any lines, because Joan's too lazy for that. But she's willing to answer questions" (Bellamy 190).[39]

As LeFevre points out, this is a delicate and difficult issue that deserves some attention:

> Not everyone who assists invention must be part-author, but there may well be better ways than we have at present to document the various contributions. . . . The complicated question of how to assign credit for a collaborative invention is inextricably tied to a larger question about what "counts" as a significant intellectual contribution to one's community and one's field. (123)

The Inklings wrote collaborative works, designed and assembled mutual projects, and engaged in transforming collective action. In his book *The Four Loves,* Lewis elaborates the pleasure of working with one's colleagues side by side. In fact, he builds his theology of friendship upon this very idea: "You will not find the warrior, the poet, the philosopher or the Christian by staring in his eyes as if he were your mistress: better fight beside him, read with him, argue with him, pray with him" (71). In addition to these examples of warriors who fight, poets who read, philosophers who argue, and Christians who pray, one might add the important and influential interaction of collaborators who write. Together.

NOTES

1. For more on creativity as a social process, see *Creative Collaboration* by Vera John-Steiner; *Collaborative Circles* by Michael P. Farrell; *Multiple Authorship and the Myth of Solitary Genius* by Jack Stillinger; *Art Worlds* by Howard S. Becker; *Organizing Genius* by Warren Bennis and Patricia Ward Biederman; and *Shared Minds* by Michael Schrage. For more on writing as a social process, see *Invention as a Social Act* by Karen Burke LeFevre; *Collaborative Learning* by Kenneth A. Bruffee; *Singular Texts/Plural Authors* by Lisa Ede and Andrea Lunsford; and *New Visions of Collaborative Writing* edited by Janis Forman.

2. LeFevre is drawing from Bakhtin, Kuhn, Rorty, Geertz, and Berger. In using this particular illustration, she is following George Herbert Mead. Owen Barfield expresses much the same idea using a different metaphor. "We ought to be very careful how we talk about words 'having' meanings at all," he warns. "Words do not contain meanings as a cigarette box contains cigarettes" (*Speaker's Meaning* 28). In his discussion of the relationship between language and meaning, and in much of his other work on the subject of language and perception, Barfield anticipates and illuminates significant aspects of social constructionist theory.

3. Jack Stillinger, for one, is expansive in his view of collaborators. He includes the contributions of agents, editors, friends, publishers, sources, and spouses as co-creators of the text. Stillinger explores the work of William Blake as a case in point. Blake is generally viewed as the most independent of creative artists, an author who wrote books, illustrated them, and then published and distributed them all by himself. Therefore, he would seem to deserve claim to

the title "solitary genius" more than any other author we know. But Stillinger argues that even William Blake was not free from a wide range of contextual factors that influenced his thinking, his creative impulse, and his productivity. As Stillinger puts it,

> He was unquestionably an original genius, but like other original geniuses was partly a product of historical and cultural circumstances beyond his control. He was (to use the simplest possible illustrations) a revolutionary at the time of the French Revolution and would have been a different kind of revolutionary had he lived a century earlier or later; he could rail at Newton and Locke, who wrote and became major intellectual forces before he was born, but not at Charles Darwin or Freud, who came afterward; he could rewrite Milton and Swedenborg but not, say, Yeats or Eliot. To separate "pure" authorship from the circumstances of time and place, one would have to lock up not only the manuscripts but the authors themselves (and, in the process, thereby deprive them of, among many other necessities, language itself). (185)

In short, even William Blake, who exercised complete control over every step of his creative work, was not a solitary genius but one who collaborated with other thinkers, historical events, and readers. More typically, writers collaborate with editors, illustrators, typesetters, publishers, and distributors as well. Writing, by its nature, takes place in a highly interactive context.

4. Most critics describe Lewis's childhood writing as "intensely dull" (Green and Hooper 23). These stories reflect his attempt to write about grown-ups, and, as his brother explains, Lewis had come to believe that "grown-up conversation and politics were one and the same thing, and that everything he wrote must therefore be given a political framework" (W. H. Lewis, "Memoir"27). Warren Lewis notes, "In the upper-middle-class society of our Belfast childhood, politics and money were the chief, almost the only subjects of grown-up conversation: and since no visitors came to our house who did not hold precisely the same political views as my father, what we heard was not discussion and the lively clash of minds, but rather an endless and one-sided torrent of grumble and vituperation. Any ordinary parent would have sent us boys off to amuse ourselves, but not my father: we had to sit in silence and endure it" (26).

5. As several others have noticed, the description of Malacandra as "a bright, pale world—a water-colour world out of child's paintbox" echoes this chapter of Lewis's creative life at Little Lea (*Silent Planet* 42).

6. The text of *The Ajimywanian War* is available to researchers at the Marion E. Wade Center. It has been copied into the *Lewis Papers*, volume 3, pages 162–64.

7. The word "cretaceous" comes from the Latin word for chalk, and it refers to the Cretaceous Age, the third and last period of the Mesozoic era. This era ended with the sudden extinction of the dinosaurs. In his address titled "De Descriptione Temporum," given in 1955, Lewis refers to himself as the last of the dinosaurs. Perhaps the idea of identifying himself with the age of the dinosaurs dates from this much earlier time in his life.

8. Lewis also composed stories and poems in close collaboration with others. He and Roger Lancelyn Green talked about works in progress and generated a number of potential projects together. They spoke of working on a novel collaboratively, but nothing came of it.

Lewis also composed poems with his wife, Joy Davidman. One memorable occasion occurred as the two of them toured Greece with Green and his wife, June. Green records that while in Crete, they stopped at a "terrible tourist resort" called The Glass House (Green and Hooper 274). "We were kept waiting hours for a very indifferent meal," records Green, "and the band blared away deafeningly. Joy finally began flicking bread-pellets at the nearest musician" (274). As time dragged on, they amused themselves by composing alternate lines of a poem:

[Jack]   A pub-crawl through the glittering isles of Greece,
[Joy]   I wish it left my ears a moment's peace!

[June]	If once the crashing Cretans ceased to bore,
[Roger]	The drums of England would resist no more.
[Jack]	No more they *can* resist. For mine are broken!
[Roger]	To this Curetes' shields were but a token,
[June]	*Our* cries in silence still above the noise—
[Joy]	He has been hit by a good shot of Joy's!
[Jack]	What aim! What strength! What purpose and what poise! (274)

Apparently this sort of poetic composition was quite common. Douglas Gresham records that his mother and Jack would regularly engage in "rhyming competitions" as they wrote alternating lines of poetry together. One afternoon, they sat at the Trout Inn at Godstow. This pub features a patio overlooking a stream filled with fish known as chavender, or chub. There Jack and Joy composed a serial poem that included the line "Pavender or Pub," giving rise to the Narnian fish known as the pavender, (MereLewis Digest 23 Jan 1997 13:17:42). Paul Ford elaborates the history of the pavender and rhymes concerning it in *Companion to Narnia*, page 308.

9. Verlyn Flieger points out that the Button Moulder is a character from Henrik Ibsen's *Peer Gynt* (personal correspondence, 1 Feb. 2006).

10. One unusual collaboration is mentioned in a letter to Arthur Greeves. Lewis jests that he and Barfield are planning a Bacchic Festival, and that they will write poetry for it and Maud Barfield will "compose a dance" (*They Stand* 367).

11. Don W. King points out that an early draft of this poem appears in the *Lewis Papers*, volume 9, pages 164–65 (*Poet* 367).

12. On pages 116–17 of *Sleuthing C. S. Lewis,* Kathryn Lindskoog raises several questions about the authenticity of this document. I do not find the argument convincing, but I encourage readers to examine the evidence and draw their own conclusions.

13. Lewis would have been very well acquainted with this exam—not only had he been required to take it as a student, he (like Tolkien) supplemented his income by grading piles of them. He did not relish the task. Writing to A. K. Hamilton Jenkin, he complains, "I've been having the hell of a job correcting the English Essays for the Higher Certificate, blue pencil in hand, twelve hours a day. You've no idea what its like" (*Collected Letters* 1: 613).

14. George Sayer offers another perspective on the word "soak": "The routine of the walk was always the same. One of us would shoulder 'the pack.' We would walk for half an hour. If it was warm enough, and somehow it usually was, we would then have a 'soak.' This meant lying or sitting down while Jack smoked a cigarette" (*Jack* 207).

15. Lewis writes memorably of one such occasion in a letter to Arthur Greeves on 29 April 1930.

The descent, largely guided by compass, was even more exciting: specially the suddenness with which a valley broke upon us—one moment nothing but moor and fog: then ghosts of trees all round us: then a roaring of invisible water beneath, and next moment the sight of the stream itself, the blackness of its pools and the whiteness of its rapids seeming to tear holes (as it were) in the neutral grey of the mist. We drank tea at the tiny hamlet of Stoke Pero where there is a little grey church without a tower that holds only about twenty people. Here, according to an excellent custom of our walks, one of the party read us a chapter of Scripture from the lectern while the rest of us sat heavily in the pews and spread out our mackintoshes to let the linings steam off. (*Collected Letters* 1: 893)

16. Throughout his life, Lewis credited Owen Barfield for a number of important insights; one that is mentioned both emphatically and repeatedly is the importance of avoiding chronological snobbery. In his preface to *The Allegory of Love*, for example, Lewis thanks Barfield "above all," for he is the one who "has taught me not to patronize the past, and has trained me to see the present as itself a 'period'" (viii).

17. *Mark vs. Tristram* was published in 1967. The individual letters, Lewis's and Barfield's, have been reprinted in Lewis's *Collected Letters* 2: 781–86.

18. The achievements of yet another Inkling are highlighted in the preface of *Essays on Malory*. Bennett notes that three men deserve special credit for the fact that Malory is "read more widely than ever before, and perhaps with greater sympathy than at any time since Spenser" (vi). The three he mentions are Eugène Vinaver, T. H. White, and Charles Williams.

19. For more on these subjects, see "University Battles" by Christopher W. Mitchell, and *C. S. Lewis at the BBC* by journalist and broadcaster Justin Phillips.

20. The five paradoxes are Malory's character defects, his aversion to the "marvellous," his unraveling of the "Interwoven or Polyphonic" narrative, his evasion of the religious significance of the Grail, and his splintering of the tale's coherence (Bennett, *Essays on Malory* 7).

21. Dorothy L. Sayers addresses this issue at length in three letters to C. S. Lewis. They are in volume 3 of her collected letters and are dated 31 July 1946, 5 August 1946, and 8 August 1946. They form the centerpiece of a key disagreement between them about the appropriate use of talent. As with all of Sayers's writings, they are lively, rich, and provocative. For more about the debate between Sayers and Lewis on the proper use of creative gifts, see Glyer and Simmons, "Dorothy L. Sayers and C. S. Lewis."

22. David Bratman observes,

> It is typical in such collaborations for the co-authors to focus their attention on different aspects of the work, for instance, purely linguistic data versus literary interpretation. Internal evidence suggests that Coghill probably wrote the lengthy introductions, which are unsigned but use the first person singular, while Christopher Tolkien probably contributed the linguistic notes and glossaries. This resembles how E. V. Gordon and J. R. R. Tolkien allocated the work load in their edition of *Sir Gawain and the Green Knight.* (personal correspondence, 13 November 2004)

Another book in the series, *The Knight's Tale,* was edited by another of the Inklings, J. A. W. Bennett. He does not acknowledge any of the Inklings in this work. However, he does recommend fifteen titles for further reading, and three of the fifteen—*Geoffrey Chaucer* and *The Poet Chaucer* by Coghill, and *The Allegory of Love* by Lewis—are by fellow Inklings (208, 164).

23. There is an interesting and unresolved discrepancy in the report of this event. In this quote from "Philia," Havard says Lewis read the appendix to *The Problem of Pain* to the Inklings. But in a letter addressed to Warren Lewis, C. S. Lewis writes that Havard is the one who read the paper "on his clinical experience of the effects of pain, wh. he had written in order that I might use all or part of it as an appendix to my book" (*Letters* 337).

24. There are a number of letters from T. S. Eliot in volume 2 of Lewis's *Collected Letters*. Apparently Eliot planned to participate in *Essays Presented to Charles Williams* but did not submit anything in time to be included. Both Lewis and Eliot express sincere regret that he was not able to participate.

25. Joe R. Christopher writes, "The essay by Gervase Mathew published in *Essays Presented to Charles Williams* is an argument against a position that Lewis presented in *The Allegory of Love*. I don't know if Lewis was accepting Mathew's argument or if he was simply enjoying the argument for its own sake, but it says something about the Inklings—and especially about Lewis in them—that this establishment of their 'corporate identity' did not set them up as a self-praise society" (personal correspondence, 13 May 2005).

26. The Inklings are not the only friends of Lewis who compiled essay collections focusing on him as a person. *In Search of C. S. Lewis* (1983) was edited by Stephen Schofield of the *Canadian C. S. Lewis Journal* and contains interviews, essays, and letters, many of which first appeared in that publication. Schofield writes that the book is "an attempt to shed new light on Lewis, chiefly through friends and pupils. Some have written reminiscences. Others, I have interviewed, and

a few chapters I have written myself, as indicated" (xi). The essays are useful primarily in their picture of Lewis's personality and habits, as opposed to his beliefs or his accomplishments. They are often contradictory, very personal, and strongly biased, both for and against him. The first person thanked on the acknowledgments page is Owen Barfield. Six of the letters included at the end are from Inklings: one by David Cecil, one by John Wain, two by Owen Barfield, and two by Warren Lewis, making this book a (limited) source of primary information about the group.

A second related book is *We Remember C. S. Lewis* (2001). As editor David Graham explains in the introduction, this book is intended as a sequel to *In Search of C. S. Lewis,* and it is motivated at least in part by his bitter disappointment with the publisher's "slovenly approach" to the first book (viii). This second book is also highly personal and largely gleaned from the pages of the *Canadian C. S. Lewis Journal.* It includes one short essay by C. S. Lewis, "What France Means to You," first published in the French journal *LaFrance Libre* 7.42 (15 April 1944) and reprinted in the spring 1995 issue of the *Canadian C. S. Lewis Journal.*

As of this writing, I note that a volume of Tolkien-related interviews and reminiscences, edited by Douglas A. Anderson and Marjorie J. Burns, is forthcoming. I do not have any other information about this collection at this time.

27. In his review of *Arthurian Torso,* fellow Inkling Gervase Mathew stresses the fact that Lewis and Williams were very close friends, and he emphasizes Lewis's suitability to take on this task. Mathew writes, "His particular clarity of phrase, his integrity of thought and his friendship have made him these lyrics' best interpreter. And this is fitting, for in a life of so many friendships Charles Williams had no closer or dearer friend" (14). Mathew also affirms that Lewis has handled Williams's material accurately. Mathew writes, "It is perhaps worth record that there is hardly a positive statement in his notes which I cannot vouch for on the independent authority of Charles Williams" (14).

28. Unbeknownst to Lewis, Williams kept a typescript of this commentary on his Arthurian work, and he distributed a number of copies of it (Ridler 178). One of these typescripts is available to researchers at the Marion E. Wade Center.

29. For a list of Christopher Tolkien's contributions to his father's works and his own works of scholarship, see Douglas A. Anderson's "Christopher Tolkien: A Bibliography" in Flieger and Hostetter's *Tolkien's Legendarium.*

30. In his letters, Tolkien actually refers to three different people as his "chief" critics: C. S. Lewis, Rayner Unwin, and Christopher Tolkien. There is no contradiction here; different individuals were of critical importance during different stages of his composition.

31. The importance of audience is emphasized by Carpenter, who notes that *The Hobbit* sat in Tolkien's study "incomplete and now likely to remain so" for one reason: his children "were growing up and no longer asked for 'Winter Reads,' so there was no reason why *The Hobbit* should ever be finished" (*Tolkien* 180). Much later, when Tolkien was at work on *The Lord of the Rings* and Christopher Tolkien, then aged twenty, was called up into the Royal Air Force, Tolkien said it was "very trying having [his] chief audience Ten Thousand Miles away" (*Letters* 104) and again, "I don't think I should write any more, but for the hope of your seeing it" (94).

32. No one can deny the importance of Christopher Tolkien's contributions to his father's work, yet it is important to remember that Tolkien relied upon a number of people for feedback and assistance throughout the years he worked on *The Lord of the Rings.* Tolkien writes, "The audience that has so far followed The Ring, chapter by chapter, and has re-read it, and clamours for more, contains some odd folk of similar literary tastes: such as C. S. Lewis, the late Charles Williams, and my son Christopher; they are probably a very small and unrequiting minority. But it has included others: a solicitor [Owen Barfield], a doctor (professionally interested in cancer) [R. E. Havard], an elderly army officer [Warren Lewis], an elementary school-mistress,

an artist, and a farmer" (*Letters* 122). It is interesting that the first six people he mentions here are all Inklings. It would be foolish not to recognize the role Christopher Tolkien played in *The Lord of the Rings* during the war years; it would be just as foolish to take J. R. R. Tolkien's praise of Christopher Tolkien out of its larger context.

33. The sheer volume of materials is astonishing. For example, Kilby notes that the manuscript of *The Lord of the Rings* alone "made a stack seven feet high" (*Tolkien* 12).

34. The introduction to *Pearl,* published in this special combined edition, was taken from Tolkien's earlier work in collaboration with E. V. Gordon. Christopher Tolkien explains, "After my father and Professor E. V. Gordon had collaborated in making an edition of *Sir Gawain,* which was published in 1925, they began work on an edition of *Pearl.* In the event, that book was almost entirely the work of Professor Gordon alone, but my father's contribution to it included a small part of the Introduction; and the essay is here reproduced in the form it finally took as the result of their collaboration" (*Sir Gawain* 8). A preface to E. V. Gordon's edition of *Pearl* was written by his widow, Ida L. Gordon. In it, she explains that Gordon and Tolkien began work on an edited edition of *Pearl* in 1925 but "when he found himself unable to give sufficient time to it, Professor Tolkien suggested that my husband should continue the work alone" (iii). Gordon did continue the work, but it remained unfinished at his death in 1938. Ida Gordon completed it, and it was first published in 1953. She writes, "My warmest thanks must go to Professor Tolkien, who had the original typescript for some time and added valuable notes and corrections; he has also responded generously to queries" (iii). By the time these words were published, it had taken three scholars twenty-eight years to prepare this volume for publication.

35. Cultural transformation was never central to the Inklings vision, but it was at the heart of Tolkien's first writing circle, the Tea Club and Barrovian Society (TCBS). John Garth writes,

> Somewhere along the line the TCBS had decided it could change the world. The view had been born on the rugby pitch in the spirited exploits of Wiseman and Tolkien, the Great Twin Brethren. It had grown during the battle to wrest control of school life from boorish-ness and cynicism—a prolonged struggle from which the TCBS had emerged victorious. The ejection of "Tea-Cake" Barnsley and the vapid, irony-obsessed members of the TCBS had left the Council of London free to reaffirm the society's sense of mission. Tolkien had told them that they had a "world-shaking power," and (with the occasional exception of the more cautious Gilson) they all believed it. (137)

36. Early on, Lewis organized an elaborate "anti-Eliot campaign" among four of his college friends, attempting to discredit free verse as a literary form (Carpenter, *Inklings* 21). Lewis was motivated by "burning indignation," but Frank Hardie and Nevill Coghill were "in it for pure fun," and Henry Yorke joined in "chiefly for love of mischief" (*All My Road* 413–14).

They wrote a number of free verse poems collaboratively, trying to imitate Eliot's style as much as they possibly could. They intended to submit them for publication in the *Criterion,* a journal edited by Eliot. To preserve the illusion of authenticity, they used the pseudonym "Rollo and Bridget Considine" and planned to send them via a friend who lived in Vienna (*All My Road* 413). Lewis writes, "We rolled in laughter as we pictured a tea party where the Considines should meet Eliot: Yorke wd. dress up for Bridget and perhaps bring a baby" (413–14). To their considerable disappointment, nothing ever came of the prank.

37. Lewis expressed this opinion some twenty months after the election. Chambers had just given a "portentously dull" guest lecture at Oxford, and this fueled Lewis's conviction that Fox had been the better candidate for Professor of Poetry (*Collected Letters* 2: 355).

38. Lewis took a rather stoic view of such matters. In a letter to his godson Laurence Harwood, Lewis writes, "I think life is rather like a bumpy bed in a bad hotel. At first you can't imagine how you can lie on it, much less sleep in it. But presently one finds the right position

and finally one is snoring away. By the time one is called it seems a very good bed and one is loth to leave it" ("The Godfather" 55).

39. John Gardner's comment that his wife's contribution has minimal value since she has "written no lines" may be usefully contrasted to C. S. Lewis's view that Vinaver had been an important collaborator in telling the tales of King Arthur despite the fact that "his chisel has touched no stone of the building" (*"Morte"* 27). Lewis explains, "Beyond question, Professor Vinaver has shown the cathedral from a new angle; placed the modern pilgrim where he will enjoy it best" (28).

7

Referents
Writing about
Each Other

Did I ever mention that Weston, Devine, Frost, Wither, Curry and Miss Hardcastle were all portraits of you? (If I didn't, that may have been because it isn't true. By gum, tho,' wait till I write another story.)
—C. S. Lewis to Owen Barfield

I've just been having mumps. Humphrey kept on quoting bits out of The Problem of Pain, *which I call a bit thick.*
—C. S. Lewis to George Sayer

I often find strange things attributed to me in [Lewis's] works.
—J. R. R. Tolkien

Creativity is the ability to respond to all that goes on around us, to choose from the hundreds of possibilities of thought, feeling, action, and reaction and to put these together in a unique response.
—Clarissa Pinkola Estes

Being friends with an artist can be a dangerous thing—artists have a way of using everything and anything as raw material for creative expression. Artists portray their friends in poems and plays, sculpt their likenesses into clay and marble, work their images into the colors of a painting, and weave their deepest dreams into the lyrics of a song. The Inklings took great pleasure in writing about one another in various forms. They based some of their fictional characters on each other. They wrote poems fine and foolish about one another. They dedicated books to each other, and they included frequent references to each other in their publications. They also produced a large number of works specifically for and about one another, including book reviews, poems, memoirs, and obituaries.

These texts show close friendships and significant and sustained interaction. And yet referential writing is typically neglected in discussions of influence. Even Karen Burke LeFevre, who provided the theoretical model used in this study, does not mention it in her book. Literary reference is a form of influence in its purest sense: without the presence of the other individual, these allusions, tributes, character studies, and works would not exist. In some ways, editing and collaboration, or even encouragement and disagreement, are more readily recognized as forms of literary influence. But it is important to look at this written evidence also, giving appropriate attention to the presence of the Inklings not only in each other's lives but also quite literally in one another's work.

THE INKLINGS AS CHARACTERS

The Inklings make frequent appearances as fictional characters, depicting themselves and one another in their writing. As seen in chapter 6, the Lewis brothers collaborated on an imaginary world called Boxen, and, writing about it much later, C. S. Lewis makes it clear that the key characters in this childhood fantasy bear a strong resemblance to the members of the Lewis family. "The reader will divine a certain resemblance between the life of the two kings under Lord Big and our own life under our father. He will be right" (*Surprised* 80). Lewis elaborates, "The two sovereigns who allowed themselves to be dominated by Lord Big were King Benjamin VIII of Animal-Land and Rajah Hawki (I think, VI) of India. They had much in common with my brother and myself" (81).

Lewis depicted himself again more than twenty years later in his book *The Pilgrim's Regress.* In it, he tells of his own search for joy, and there is nothing particularly subtle or vague about his identification with John, the main character. Even the main character's name is indicative; as Kathryn Lindskoog points out, Jack is a nickname for John, and Lewis had gone by the name Jack since he was four years old (*Finding* 2). Owen Barfield shows up in this book too, as the figure of History. Barfield notes that Lewis once "casually remarked" to him that "in limning that figure, he had me somewhere at the back of his mind" (*Owen Barfield* 73).

Lewis puts himself into other works as well. He serves as the narrator in *Out of the Silent Planet* and *Perelandra.* Tolkien believed that Mr. Bultitude, the bear in *That Hideous Strength,* was a portrait of Lewis.[1] And there are aspects of The Chronicles of Narnia that have precise biographical parallels.[2] Hooper offers one example: "The Narnian character closest to Lewis himself is the 'old Professor' we meet in *The Lion,* and who appears again as Lord Digory in *The Last Battle*" (*C. S. Lewis* 427). And it is easy to see other parallels in the description of the big drafty house (rather like Little Lea), the prominent wardrobe (Lewis had several in his home), and the children who are evacuated to a country home for safety during war time.[3]

Like Lewis, Charles Williams based some of his invented characters loosely on himself. In *Shadows of Ecstasy,* Roger Ingram is "recognisable as bearing a superficial resemblance to Williams" (Carpenter, *Inklings* 93). Ingram holds the title of Professor of Applied Literature at London University, a designation that incorporates several of Williams's great loves: literature, learning, and the city of London.

Williams appears in another novel, too. Williams used the pen name Peter Stanhope for his play *Judgement at Chelmsford;* Stanhope appears as the main character, a playwright, in *Descent into Hell,* one of Williams's most vivid and moving novels. Carpenter calls Stanhope "a character undoubtedly based on what Williams would have liked to be" (*Inklings* 107). Stanhope reflects many aspects of Williams's personality: he is creative, intense, mystical, and daring. He is also misunderstood and underappreciated. And there are parallels to certain personal events as well. Bernadette Lynn Bosky observes that the mentorly side of the love Williams felt for his coworker Phyllis Jones is directly reflected in the relationship between Stanhope and a character named Pauline (14).[4]

Though he is best known for his poetry and novels and recognized for his insightful nonfiction works such as *The Descent of the Dove, The Figure of Beatrice,* and *Poetry at Present,* Williams also wrote a large number of plays. Some of these, like *Thomas Cranmer of Canterbury* and *Judgement at Chelmsford,* were written for a general audience. Others, like *The Masque of the Manuscript,* were written and performed in the more personal setting of the publishing house where he worked.[5] In these plays, which reflect life, work, and relationships within Amen House at Oxford University Press, Williams blurs the lines between life and art in interesting ways.[6]

Tolkien also appreciated the dynamic interplay between life and art, fact and fiction. In particular, he recognized his own reflection in the characters he is best known for. In an often quoted passage, Tolkien writes, "I am in fact a *Hobbit* (in all but size). I like gardens, trees and unmechanized farmlands; I smoke a pipe, and like good plain food (unrefrigerated), but detest French cooking; I like, and even dare to wear in these dull days, ornamental waistcoats. I am fond of mushrooms (out of a field); have a very simple sense of humour (which even my appreciative critics find tiresome); I go to bed late and get up late (when possible). I do not travel much" (*Letters* 288–89).[7] In another letter, Tolkien writes, "I resemble a hobbit at any rate in being moderately and cheerfully domesticated, though no cook."[8] Late in his life, he referred to himself as an "elderly hobbit" (*Letters* 315). As Carpenter points out, Tolkien makes this personal connection even more explicit in choosing the name "Bag End" for Bilbo Baggins's house, "which was what the local people called his Aunt Jane's Worcestershire farm" (*Tolkien* 176). This strengthens the identification not only between Tolkien and hobbits in general, but also between Tolkien and

Bilbo in particular. Certainly one need not strain too hard to see something of Tolkien in the depiction of a hobbit who spent his finest days in Rivendell writing tales of hobbit adventures.

As we saw in chapter 3, there are also strong parallels between Tolkien's relationship with his wife, Edith, and the transforming love of his characters Beren and Lúthien. In a letter written in the last year of his life, he writes of meeting her for the first time, calling her "the Lúthien Tinúviel of my own personal 'romance' with her long dark hair, fair face and starry eyes, and beautiful voice." He continues, "But now she has gone before Beren, leaving him indeed one-handed" (*Letters* 417). Their tombstones in Wolvercote Cemetery read, "John Ronald Reuel Tolkien / Beren / 1892–1973" and "Edith Mary Tolkien / Lúthien / 1889–1971."

There are other personal references in *The Lord of the Rings*. For example, the character Tom Bombadil is based on a Dutch doll that belonged to Tolkien's son Michael (Carpenter, *Tolkien* 162). Another familial connection is found in *The Lost Road*. Christopher Tolkien makes this clear in his description of one of the main characters: "Alboin's biography sketched in these chapters is in many respects closely modelled on my father's own life" (53). Duriez and Porter propose that the story does more than just reflect certain events of Tolkien's life; they suggest that the father/son relationship described in *The Lost Road* reflects the "great affinity" Tolkien felt for his son Christopher (210).

Finally, poignant parallels exist between Tolkien and his character Niggle, the protagonist in the short allegory "Leaf by Niggle." Tolkien explains that the story arose from his "pre-occupation with *The Lord of the Rings,* the knowledge that it would be finished in great detail or not at all, and the fear (near certainty) that it would be 'not at all'"(*Letters* 257). Tolkien was struggling and anxious about his book when he "woke up with a short story in his head" (Carpenter, *Tolkien* 196). He wrote the story quickly, with unusual ease. Describing Niggle's work as a painter, and his own work as a novelist, Tolkien writes,

> He was the sort of painter who can paint leaves better than trees. He used to spend a long time on a single leaf, trying to catch its shape, and its sheen, and the glistening of dewdrops on its edges. Yet he wanted to paint a whole tree, with all of its leaves in the same style, and all of them different.
>
> There was one picture in particular which bothered him. It had begun with a leaf caught in the wind, and it became a tree; and the tree grew, sending out innumerable branches, and thrusting out the most fantastic roots. Strange birds came and settled on the twigs and had to be attended

to. Then all round the Tree, and behind it, through the gaps in the leaves and boughs, a country began to open out. ("Leaf by Niggle" 75–76)

The impetus for the story was Tolkien's anxiety; its setting was Tolkien's neighborhood. He explains that one of his sources was a large poplar tree he could see from his bedroom window (*Tree* 6). We also know that about this time, Tolkien had injured his leg and limped, as Niggle does in the story. There are numerous parallels between the fantastic roots and strange birds of Niggle's painting and the mythologies and characters of Tolkien's Middle-earth. The most important parallel between life and art was the therapeutic result of the story. The ease with which he wrote it proved reassuring, helping Tolkien overcome a host of doubts. Or, as Carpenter puts it, as he wrote "Leaf by Niggle," Tolkien "expressed his worst fears for his mythological Tree" (*Tolkien* 196). Writing it helped alleviate his fears and renew his efforts to complete *The Lord of the Rings*.

Traveler from the Silent Planet

Tolkien bears a notable resemblance to his own fictional characters Bilbo, Beren, Alboin, and Niggle. He can also be said to resemble the protagonist in the first book of Lewis's science fiction trilogy. This is Elwin Ransom, a fellow of a Cambridge college who finds himself an unwitting traveler to Mars. The name "Elwin" is a variation of the Old English "Ælfwine," meaning "elf friend" (*Lost Road* 37–38).[9] As it happens, Ransom's academic specialty is philology, and Tolkien himself observes, "As a philologist I may have some part in him." The likeness goes beyond name and profession, for Tolkien says he recognizes that many of his own "opinions and ideas" have been "Lewisified" in this central character. Tolkien's daughter, Priscilla, was at one time convinced that Ransom was based on her father (Tolkien, *Letters* 89). This is particularly appropriate considering that the motivation for *Out of the Silent Planet* was a wager between Lewis and Tolkien—a challenge to write more of the kind of books they liked. It is entirely characteristic of Lewis to start his story with an affectionate portrait of his friend, a traveler embarking on an uncertain, open-ended venture.

On the other hand, one could argue that the similarities between Tolkien and Ransom are quite superficial and that these early details serve as little more than literary scaffolding to get Lewis started on his story. Lewis explains that his reasons for making Ransom a philologist were not personal, but practical: in order for the narrative to move forward with due speed, Ransom must acclimate quickly to the Martian language and culture (Glover 77).

David Downing and others have made a more obvious connection: Ransom resembles Lewis himself. He is "tall, but a little round-shouldered, about thirty-five to forty years of age, and dressed with that particular kind of shabbiness which marks a member of the intelligentsia on a holiday" (*Silent Planet* 7). Furthermore, "the opening pages of *Out of the Silent Planet* describe experiences that Lewis might have had on any one of his walking tours" (Downing, *Planets* 102).[10]

The connection between Lewis and Ransom is even stronger in *Perelandra,* the second book of the series. Downing notes that Lewis was "passionately fond of water," and in this book, enthusiastic descriptions of the look and feel of water are absolutely everywhere (*Planets* 111). Also, Lewis "referred to the second novel of the trilogy several times as his favorite book," which adds strength to the connection between Lewis and Ransom, and "sometimes as evening fell, he was known to look up at the evening star and exclaim, 'Perelandra!'" (120). Downing maintains that Lewis "created in Ransom a character whose convictions and consciousness largely resemble his own" (102). Others, notably George Sayer, agree.

And yet Elwin Ransom is transformed in the course of the trilogy, changing from "a well-intentioned but untested Pedestrian" to "the pendragon and the fisher-king" (Downing, *Planets* 120). By the end of the story, "Ransom has reached a level of spiritual refinement that Lewis would never presume to have attained" (118).[11] Now Ransom resembles neither Lewis nor Tolkien, but another one of the Inklings: Charles Williams. Carpenter observes, "In a sense Charles Williams himself was in it, in the character of Ransom *as now portrayed:* a man of great spiritual strength, a man who easily earns obedience from his followers but is aware that this obedience may be dangerously seductive, a man of quietness and at the same time of great vigour" (*Inklings* 198, emphasis added). Mathew also links the later Ransom with Williams. Hooper notes, "Gervase Mathew was close to both men, and being in a position to observe Williams' profound influence on Lewis, sees the Ransom of the last two romances as having grown into a kind of idealized Williams—but a Williams, I should venture to guess, underpinned by the steady brilliance and philological genius of Lewis's other great friends, Owen Barfield and J. R. R. Tolkien" (*Dark Tower* 96).

Lewis himself is vague on the shifting identity of Elwin Ransom, only admitting that the hero of these books is "a fancy portrait of a man I know." He quickly adds, "but not of me" ("Reply to Professor Haldane" 73).

Lewis's Ransom trilogy contains other characters easily recognized as Inklings. When the need for a physician arises in *Perelandra,* the narrator asks, "Would Humphrey do?" Ransom replies, "The very man" (28). So R. E. "Humphrey" Havard, Lewis's own physician and a faithful member of the Inklings, enters the story. Some hint of Tolkien is there as well, in the character of Dimble, a don with a special vision for England's mythology and a protective concern for trees (*Hideous Strength* 370, 29–30). Also, Lewis refers to Owen Barfield twice in the trilogy: once obliquely as an anthroposophist called B. in *Perelandra* (32) and again directly in *That Hideous Strength* (261). In the second instance, Lewis specifically mentions Barfield's influential theory of ancient semantic unity.[12] The Ransom trilogy is a particularly rich example of a text created in community and crafted to reflect the values and personalities of that community.

Portraits of Lewis

Several of the Inklings incorporate Lewis in their fiction. Tolkien, for example, alludes to his friend in *The Lord of the Rings*: Treebeard's characteristic "*Hrum, Hroom*" is an attempt to capture "the booming voice of C. S. Lewis" (Carpenter, *Tolkien* 194). The identification of Lewis with this wise and ancient tree-man is no small accolade. Tolkien's love for trees is evident throughout his writing.

A strong tribute to Lewis and Lewis's influence is found in another significant detail. On a page of penciled notes regarding the nature of Ents, Tolkien asks himself the question, "Are the Tree-folk ('Lone-walkers') *hnau* that have gone tree-like, or trees that have become *hnau?*" (*Treason* 411). His use of Lewis's invented term for sapient beings in this context is particularly interesting because it is completely natural and unattributed. He also uses the term *hnau* in *The Notion Club Papers* (207).

Though Lewis figures minimally in Tolkien's fiction, he plays a major part in a number of stories by Owen Barfield. For one, Lewis appears as Jak in Barfield's short story "Night Operation." This tale is a self-conscious allegory that takes place in a future world where people live in underground cities. The main character, Jon, resembles Barfield in many ways, particularly in his "insatiable curiosity about—and love of—words and their meanings" (Hunter 129). Jon develops a close friendship with Jak and Peet: "There was a triangle of affinity here, which showed itself in those shared tastes and inclinations that cannot only transcend sharp differences of opinion but may even render them interesting and fruitful instead of irritating and divisive" ("Night Operation" 146). This depiction is quite similar to the way Lewis describes a "Second Friend." Jon and Jak are constantly discussing words and their technical meanings at great length and with enormous satisfaction.

In the story, the three boys manage to escape from their world Underground and make their way to the surface, discovering their true home Aboveground. They love it there and want to stay but soon realize they must return to and devote themselves to helping "as many at least as are not too far gone to come—to return to Aboveground and *live* there" ("Night Operation"

170). In a clear allusion to Plato, the three boys "re-enter the mouth of the cave," descending the "crumbling steps and the slippery slopes," and return to Underground (172).[13] The story ends with this sentence: "What happened after that, how far they maintained their joint resolution, what influence they were able to exert, and what effect, if any, it had on the destiny of that closed society of sickness and the smell of sickness, from which they had momentarily emerged, is a tale that cannot be told for the sufficient reason that it is not yet known" (172). The young men in "Night Operation," through persistent acts of courage, question the assumptions of the world around them. They achieve an evolution of consciousness by immersing themselves in language study, paying close attention to how the meanings of words change over time. As a result, Jak, Peet, and Jon come to see things in a completely new way. Rather than merely enjoying this insight, they use it to seek a better world for themselves and then to reach out to help others. The story expresses some of Barfield's most cherished ideals, including the conviction that language study leads to higher levels of perception, and the belief that a small group of men might change the world.

Lewis also appears as a character in Barfield's novel *Worlds Apart*. This book purports to be the transcript of a three-day conversation among eight friends gathered for a weekend in Dorsetshire. They cover topics ranging from space travel to human nature to the relationship between language and consciousness—in other words, many of Barfield's personal interests. They draw on the ideas of Rudolf Steiner and, at one point, make fun of the fact that they are doing so. Their main subject, to the extent they have one, is that contemporary thinkers are too isolated and their ideas too compartmentalized. One of the academy's greatest needs, they argue, is more communication among intellectuals in various fields.

It is worth noting that the goal of the three-day event described in this book is not to discover common ground but rather to clarify differences by juxtaposing their very different points of view. In this fictional work, Barfield provides his model of the ideal intellectual world, "where the thread is picked up over and over again" and the contestants continue this way "for days or even weeks or months on end" (*Worlds* 10).

In some ways, this book also provides Barfield's vision of an ideal Inklings meeting, and the eight men he describes may be loosely linked with various members of the group. Barfield narrates the story as Burgeon, a solicitor with philological interests. Lewis is present as Hunter, a professor of historical theology and ethics who often turns the conversation toward matters of religion. Hunter occasionally quotes long passages in Latin or Greek, and the others insist, with some irritation, that he translate them. He also quotes freely from Aquinas and the book of Genesis. He has a knack for being both down-to-earth and esoteric. At one point, he complains of a stomachache, then he turns and uses that fact as an illustration of the relationship between perception and reality.

Barfield and Lewis also appear as characters in *This Ever Diverse Pair,* a novel about the daily life of two lawyers in partnership. The main characters are Burgeon and Burden; they express two thinly disguised aspects of Barfield himself.[14] Burgeon, the poet and dreamer, finds himself in necessary but uncomfortable partnership with Burden, the practical man. Together they endure the irritations of a thriving legal practice in order to make a living. The structure of the novel is quite straightforward: each chapter tells the story of one typical case in a lawyer's day. Barfield covers such situations as divorce and title disputes, trust deeds and wills. In chapter 6, Barfield describes a legal case concerning complications with income taxes. The client's name is Ramsden, and elsewhere Barfield states expressly that this character and this specific case depict an actual situation that involved Lewis.[15] In fact, in the prefatory material to the book, Barfield gives the following disclaimer: "With the exception of one chapter, which is with permission (and even encouragement) founded irresponsibly on fact, all the events and characters portrayed in this book are entirely imaginary." Besides the clear admission that one of the chapters is based on a true event and a true character, Barfield also indicates that his subject not only gave him permission but also encouragement to include him in the story.

Barfield takes advantage of the situation to express praise, and a little irritation. When Burgeon receives a letter from Ramsden, for example, he emphasizes, "I am blessed with a number of exceptionally good friends. From all of them I like getting letters; but there is only one whose handwriting on an unopened envelope still gives me the authentic *thrill* of youthful friendship, and that is Ramsden" (*Diverse Pair* 60). What is it about these letters that thrills him so? Simply this: in any letter, even a brief one, Ramsden will invariably include "at least one quotation, philosophical quillet, gibe or cryptic allusion, to the eye of any third party either meaningless or idiotic, but pregnant symbols to us of a period of intellectual intercourse long since woven into the stuff of our lives and taken up into whatever we can claim of wisdom and insight" (60–61).

Ramsden's giftedness as a writer has occasioned this letter and created the legal problem that is the focus of the chapter. Burgeon explains, "During the first twenty years of our acquaintance the writings of Ramsden remained, like my own, a purely and decently literary phenomenon" (*Diverse Pair* 62). In other words, up to this point both Barfield and Lewis had been prolific writers, and their early work, including such books as Barfield's *The Silver Trumpet* (1925), *History in English Words* (1926), and *Poetic Diction* (1928), and Lewis's *Spirits in*

Bondage (1919), *Dymer* (1926), *The Pilgrim's Regress* (1933), *The Allegory of Love* (1936), and *Out of the Silent Planet* (1938), had not sold particularly well.

But then things changed. Burgeon explains that one of Ramsden's books "(not by any means the one I should have chosen) began for some incomprehensible reason to sell to the general public. It was followed quickly by another, the first impression of which disappeared from the stocks like a plate of buttered scones" (62). The Lewis titles that best fit this description would be *The Problem of Pain* (1940) and then, quickly thereafter, *The Screwtape Letters* (1942).[16] Barfield's combination of admiration and irritation are wonderfully evident. Though he does not exactly regret his friend's popularity, he can't resist emphasizing the distinction between being a literary artist and being a popular one. And he simply can't account for the mysterious reason the public rushes to buy these books.

Lewis's sudden popularity and wealth have created the current plight. Lewis frequently offered financial support to needy individuals, and he did so by giving away the royalty income he earned from his books. Unfortunately, he did so without paying any taxes on this income. When Barfield looked at Lewis's financial records, he was appalled; Lewis owed an enormous amount in back taxes. They used the next batch of royalty checks to pay off the debt, then established a charitable trust to be used to make future donations non-taxable.[17] This they dubbed the "Agapony" or "Agapargyry," that is, the agape fund or love fund (Hooper, *C. S. Lewis* 747). This resolved the problem and provided a captivating chapter for Barfield's book.

In addition to these fictionalized versions of Lewis as Jak, Hunter, and Ramsden, Barfield wrote five poems either addressed to Lewis or including reference to some aspect of him. The longest of these is "The Mother of Pegasus," later retitled "Riders on Pegasus."[18] It is a narrative poem, written in seven sections, in which Barfield uses the characters of Perseus and Bellerophon to explore his impression of "living with, not one, but two Lewises" (*Owen Barfield* 22). Barfield explains,

> This experience gradually became something like an obsession with me, and it must have been somewhere about 1950 (when I was still concerned to write verse) that I made it part of the emotional base for a long narrative poem. There were other things I felt the need of unloading as well, and I ended by meditating at some length, and ultimately writing, a sort of extension and combination of two well-known Greek myths in such a way that the characters and events should symbolize, at different levels, a good many matters which I liked to think were still at a "pre-logical" stage in my mind . . . questions to which I did not yet know the answers

and knew that, for the purposes of the poem, it was better that I should not know them. (22)

Another unpublished poem written by Barfield about Lewis is particularly interesting, for it is written entirely in Greek. In a note appended to the manuscript, Barfield explains that he is not certain of the date and estimates that he wrote it sometime between 1941 and 1946. He adds, "I don't think I ever showed it to [Lewis], though I felt a strong impulse to do so. If I did, then he paid scant attention to it; if I didn't, it was because I was afraid of his paying scant attention to it." Barfield is clearly more concerned about being ignored than he is about being criticized. In a translation by Gerald F. Hawthorne, the poem reads as follows:

C. S. L.
Biographia Theologia

Behold, there was a certain philosopher!
And the philosopher knew himself that he is one.
And the Word, having become in the philosopher,
    was One God.
And the Word was the Light of his philosophy,
And the Light was shining in his philosophy,
    and the philosopher knew it not.
The Light was in the philosopher,
And his philosophy came into being through the Light,
and the philosopher knew it not.
The philosopher said that no one
    under any circumstance could ever behold that Light.
And when he had beheld that Light, the philosopher insisted
    that its name was LORD.
And his philosophy bore witness
    about the light,
        that it is the Word and the Life of mankind;
    and about the philosopher,
        that he was not born of the flesh,
        nor of the will of the flesh,
        nor of the will of man,
        nor through a command of the Lord,
        but of God.
And, the philosopher did not receive the witness.[19]

In this "theological biography" of C. S. Lewis, Barfield expresses conflicting emotions: he is glad that Lewis had come to recognize the Lord, and he is disappointed that there remained so many aspects of the Christian faith that, from Barfield's point of view, Lewis persistently failed to grasp.

Another poem about Lewis has been published in the collection *Owen Barfield on C. S. Lewis.* It is entitled "Envoi" and is addressed "To the Author of *The Allegory of Love.*" The editor of the collection, G. B. Tennyson, explains that it was written between 1946 and 1950, not long after "C. S. L. / Biographia Theologia." "Envoi" was part of the cover letter to a collection of poems Barfield was sending to Lewis "for a critical evaluation"; it was intended to "dispose Lewis not to judge too harshly the collection of poems he was receiving." He calls Lewis "Benignant Uncle of the Rose" and describes him as "one who knows / What waters both delight and drown not." His request that Lewis be kind is stated quite baldly as the poet tells Jack, "frown not, / To hear tap on your window-pane / This swiftly-sprung September beanstalk!" Following the name "Jack," in a parenthetical clause, the poet poses the question, "Do you love me, Master?" (162).

Barfield also wrote a memorial poem entitled "Moira"; it is a "reflection on the death of C. S. Lewis one year after that event." The poem opens by asking Death directly, "You came to him: when will you come to me?" and this line is repeated again in the fourth of five stanzas. Three times the poet observes (with slight variation), "He knows what matters now, what matters not" (*Owen Barfield* 163).

What is most remarkable about Barfield's work on Lewis is simply that there is so much of it. As we have seen, Lewis appears as a major character in one short story and two novels, and he is the intended audience and/or subject of at least five poems. Barfield dedicated two of his books to Lewis, collaborated with him in writing poetry, produced two series of literary letters—the "Great War" and *Mark vs. Tristram*—and contributed to the mock exam for the Cretaceous Perambulators. Barfield acknowledges a debt to Lewis in the introductory material of *Poetic Diction, Saving the Appearances,* and *Orpheus.* Furthermore, he wrote more than a dozen essays, lectures, and articles about Lewis. It would be hard to find any other Inkling who devoted so much creative energy to another in such a variety of forms over so significant a period of time.

VERSE

Though Lewis abandoned his plan to make a name for himself through his work as a poet, he never stopped writing poetry and he always took a great deal of pleasure in it. He often wrote from the events of daily life. One example is "The

Small Man Orders His Wedding," written for his fellow Inkling John Wain. There are three holograph versions of this poem, and one of them bears the title "An Epithalamium for John Wain feigned to be spoken in his person giving orders for his wedding" (D. King, *Poet* 344).[20] In this poem of seven stanzas, the bridegroom arranges an exceedingly complicated wedding, coordinating the activities of soldiers, dancing maidens, and a chariot drawn by lions. The rhythms are exaggerated and the pace is lively. King calls attention to its "percussive" nature, that is, its emphasis on bright, sharp sounds such as tambourines, church bells, and trumpets (172). The poem ends suffused in "Aphrodite's saffron light," as the happy newlyweds "lie drowned in dreaming weariness" (*Collected Poems* 47).[21]

On the one hand, like much of Lewis's poetry, this poem was carefully crafted and painstakingly revised. On the other hand, some of Lewis's poetry is more direct, personal, and spontaneous, using his writing talents in the art of daily life. For example, in a 1935 letter to Barfield, Lewis writes, "I hope to arrive at Rudyard (wh. on nearer acquaintance wth. guidebooks turns out to be Rudyard Lake) at 3.13 on Monday," then he breaks into verse:

> Where reservoys ripple
> And sun-shadows stipple
>> The beard of the corn,
> We'll meet and we'll kipple
> We'll carp and then kipple
> At Rudyard we'll Kipple
>> From evening to morn. (qtd. in D. King, *Poet* 295)[22]

The poem continues with more personal references and jokes. In the next stanza, Lewis expresses their intent to discuss Barfield's play *Orpheus* "till fettered by Morpheus" at Chapel-en-le-Frith, a stop they had planned. Walking together and discussing literature are both celebrated in this clever verse.

Lewis used a similar tone in another letter to Barfield, this one written several years earlier.[23] Lewis begins:

> Long at lectures
> On Monday morning
> I work till one! Hoike!!

He asks Barfield to come and pick him up:

> Can your car
> So swiftly over

Earth's back wander
From Oxford to London between one and 5.45?

Then he breaks out with "Walawei? Hoo-ruddy-rah!!!! / Ho-hei!!!!!" The poem ends on a very practical note, suggesting that Barfield remain at Magdalen College until Tuesday night, then join Lewis and Dyson for dinner (qtd. in D. King, *Poet* 294–95).

In the early 1930s, Lewis wrote a humorous poem in the *Beowulf* meter about a time when he served along with Tolkien and E. V. Gordon as examiners in a viva voce session for the English School:

Two at the table in their talk borrowed
Gargantua's mouth. Gordon and Tolkien
Had will to repeat well-nigh the whole
That they of Verner's law and of vowel sorrows,
Cares of consonants, and case endings,
Heard by hearsay.
    Never at board I heard
Viler vivas. (qtd. in Carpenter, *Inklings* 55)

The event described in that short poem really happened, but another Lewis poem features an imaginary situation.[24] Lewis wrote it to illustrate a particular pattern of alliterative meter:

We were TALKing of DRAGONS, | TOLkien and I
In a BERKshire BAR. | The BIG WORKman
Who had SAT SILent | and SUCKED his PIPE
ALL the EVEning, | from his EMPTy MUG
With GLEAMing EYE | GLANCED toWARDS us;
'I SEEN 'em mySELF,' | he SAID FIERCEly. (*Rehabilitations* 122)

The poem was originally published in a journal called *Lysistrata* and later republished in an early Lewis collection, *Rehabilitations and Other Essays.* Both times, the poem was printed with this idiomatic capitalization in order to draw attention to the rhythmic pattern of "Lifts and Dips."

Lewis is the subject of another unusual poem, this one written by fellow Inkling Nevill Coghill. The two men were students together in George Gordon's discussion class, and "it had been decided at the outset that the minutes of Professor Gordon's class were to be kept in Chaucerian verse" (*Literary Es-*

says x). Thus Coghill wrote a long poem about a paper Lewis presented on 9 February 1923. In part, the poem reads

> In Oxenford some clerkes of degree
> Were gadréd in a goodlye companye
> And I was oon, and here will yow devise
> Our felaweshipe that worthy was and wys . . .
> *Sir Lewis* was ther; a good philosópher
> He hadde a noble paper for to offer.
> Wel couthe he speken in the Greeké tongue;
> And yet, his countenance was swythé yong. (x)

Another short and humorous poem that features Lewis is this one, which serves as the dedication and epigraph to *Owen Barfield on C. S. Lewis:*

> To C. S. Lewis
> My public, though select and small,
> Is crammed with taste and knowledge.
> It's somewhat stout and fairly tall
> And lives at Magdalen College.

Tolkien is so well known for the epic *The Lord of the Rings* that it is easy to forget that he produced a good many other things, including poems (*Bilbo's Last Song, The Adventures of Tom Bombadil*), children's stories (*Mr. Bliss, Roverandom, Letters from Father Christmas*), linguistic studies (*A Middle English Vocabulary,* "Chaucer as a Philologist"), stories (*Farmer Giles of Ham, Smith of Wootton Major,* "Leaf by Niggle"), academic essays ("On Fairy-Stories," "Beowulf: The Monsters and the Critics"), translations (*The Old English Exodus*), and scholarly editions (*Sir Gawain and the Green Knight, Ancrene Wisse*). It is also easy to overlook the light touch and delightful sense of humor that shines through much of his work, *The Lord of the Rings* included. That sense of humor is clear and strong in a series of clerihews Tolkien wrote about the Inklings.[25] One of them, about Charles Williams, has already been quoted in chapter 3. He wrote this one about Gervase Mathew:

> The Rev. Mathew (Gervase)
> Made inaudible surveys
> Of little-read sages
> In the dark Middle Ages. (qtd. in Carpenter, *Inklings* 186)[26]

And of Owen Barfield, Tolkien writes,

> Mr Owen Barfield's
> Habit of turning cartwheels
> Made some say: 'He's been drinking!'
> It was only 'conscientious thinking.' (qtd. in Carpenter, *Inklings* 177)

Whether or not Barfield was in the habit of turning cartwheels, he was a trained dancer, and, as such, he was certainly strong and agile. That may be the reference Tolkien intends here. Carpenter adds the explanation that "conscientious thinking" was "one of Barfield's terms for the thought processes related to Anthroposophy" (*Inklings* 177).

Tolkien also wrote a poem about "Humphrey" Havard, whose work as a physician gave rise to his nickname "U. Q." or "Useless Quack:"

> Dr U. Q. Humphrey
> Made poultices of comfrey.
> If you didn't pay his bills
> He gave you doses of squills. (qtd. in Carpenter, *Inklings* 177)

In 1965, W. H. Auden asked Tolkien to contribute something to a Festschrift that he was putting together in honor of Coghill's retirement. Tolkien felt "grieved" that he did not have anything to offer, adding that the only thing he had ever written about Coghill was the following short poem:

> Mr Neville Judson Coghill
> Wrote a deal of dangerous doggerill.
> Practical, progressive men
> Called him Little Poison-pen. (*Letters* 359)

Tolkien continues with this explanation: "That was at a time when under the name of Judson he was writing what I thought very good and funny verses lampooning forward-looking men" (*Letters* 359).

Finally, Tolkien wrote a clerihew about himself. Like his poem about Coghill, this one has appeared only in his letters:

> J. R. R. Tolkien
> had a cat called Grimalkin:
> once a familiar of Herr Grimm
> now he spoke the law to him. (*Letters* 398)

Tolkien wrote clerihews about Williams, Mathew, Barfield, Coghill, and himself, but it seems he did not write one specifically about Lewis. However, he did celebrate Lewis in another short piece, this one gentler in tone and written entirely in Old English. In chapter 1, I discussed the first part of his poem, which begins "Hwæt! we Inclinga." Following the rousing description of the group as a whole, the poem continues, "þara wæs Hloðuig sum, hæleða dyrost, / brad ond beorhtword." Translated, the lines read, "One of them was Hlothwig, dearest of men, broad and bright of word." Carpenter explains that "'Hlothwig' was the Anglo-Saxon form of the Germanic name from which 'Lewis' was ultimately derived" (*Inklings* 176–77).

This is not the only poem written by Tolkien that honors Lewis. "Mythopoeia" is a remarkable and important poem, 148 lines long.[27] Christopher Tolkien notes that it developed through seven versions, each a little longer than the one before. One copy of the poem is marked "J. R. R. T. for C. S. L." (introduction, *Tree* 7).

Tolkien's "Mythopoeia" was inspired by the 19 September 1931 conversation in which Tolkien and Dyson convinced Lewis that the Christian story is a myth that *"really happened"* (Lewis, *Collected Letters* 1: 977). The poem bears this introduction: "To one who said that myths were lies and therefore worthless, even though 'breathed through silver'" ("Mythopoeia" 97). The dedication "Philomythus to Misomythus" (Lover of Myth to Hater of Myth) follows. The poem opens in second person: "You look at trees and label them just so" (97). We know from various accounts of the conversation that in this poem, Tolkien is recapitulating not only the issues discussed that evening but also many of the exact phrases as well. Evidently, their conversation solidified Tolkien's own ideas on the nature of sub-creation, and this poem contains his most clear and elegant expression of this concept:

> The heart of man is not compound of lies,
> but draws some wisdom from the only Wise,
> and still recalls him. Though now long estranged,
> man is not wholly lost nor wholly changed.
> Dis-graced he may be, yet is not dethroned,
> and keeps the rags of lordship once he owned,
> his world-dominion by creative act:
> not his to worship the great Artefact,
> man, sub-creator, the refracted light
> through whom is splintered from a single White
> to many hues, and endlessly combined
> in living shapes that move from mind to mind. (98–99)

On 29 November 1943, Tolkien quoted two lines of this poem in a letter to another Inkling, Christopher Tolkien, who was then in training at an RAF base in Manchester. Tolkien writes, "We were born in a dark age out of due time (for us). But there is this comfort: otherwise we should not *know*, or so much love, what we do love. . . . Also we have still small swords to use. 'I will not bow before the Iron Crown, nor cast my own small golden sceptre down'" (*Letters* 64).

Fourteen lines from the poem were also quoted by Tolkien in "On Fairy-Stories," an essay first composed as an Andrew Lang Lecture and delivered on 8 March 1939 in the University of St Andrews (5–6). That essay also builds upon the conversation between Tolkien, Lewis, and Dyson. It has another Inkling connection, too: it was first published as Tolkien's contribution to *Essays Presented to Charles Williams*.

Tolkien's longest poem about a single Inkling is not a clerihew or a Middle English pastiche or a philosophical declaration. It is a reflective piece written entirely about Charles Williams, published in *The Inklings* by Humphrey Carpenter. It begins "Our dear Charles Williams many guises shows" (123). Tolkien admits that reading Williams can be a challenge: "I find his prose / obscure at times. Not easily it flows" (123). But despite the challenge, there is much that is worthy, and Tolkien says explicitly that he has come "to praise our Charles" (125).

He expresses particular admiration for Williams's skill at discerning and describing the supernatural. Williams understands and exposes the wiles of evil powers: "When Charles is on his trail the devil squeals, / for cloven feet have vulnerable heels" (123). Williams also offers insight into higher realms: "But heavenly footsteps, too, can Williams trace, / and after Dante, plunging, soaring, race / up to the threshold of Eternal Grace" (123).

Then Tolkien turns his attention to the *Taliessin* poems and confesses that he is "bogged in tangled rhymes" (124). He finds the "dark flux of symbol and event" beyond his scope and he says that in Williams's poetry, "fable, faith, and faërie are blent / with half-guessed meanings to some great intent / I cannot grasp" (124).

But it is not Tolkien's purpose here to describe or critique this difficult poem cycle. He has "wandered" from his point. Addressing Williams directly, he concludes,

> When your fag is wagging and spectacles are twinkling,
> when tea is brewing or the glasses tinkling,
> then of your meaning often I've an inkling,
> your virtues and your wisdom glimpse. Your laugh

in my heart echoes, when with you I quaff
the pint that goes down quicker than a half,
because you're near. So, heed me not! I swear
when you with tattered papers take the chair
and read (for hours maybe), I would be there. (126)

Tolkien's conclusion returns our attention to his intended purpose: to affirm Williams as a gifted writer and to acknowledge his important place in their circle. Tolkien also reasserts his personal commitment to supporting Williams's work.

THE NOTION CLUB PAPERS

Much of the firsthand information that we have about the Inklings comes from letters written by the members and from the diaries of Warren Lewis. There is another unusual, interesting, and profoundly important source of information about the group: the draft of an incomplete novel written by Tolkien in the late 1940s. *The Notion Club Papers* purports to be the minute book of an informal literary group meeting regularly sometime in the 1980s.[28] Christopher Tolkien suggests that the work may have been begun simply to amuse the Inklings, as "no more than a *jeu d'esprit*" for their entertainment (149).

In the first draft, Tolkien lists some of the members of this writing group and assigns them rough Inkling equivalents—for example, Franks (later "Frankley") is identified as Lewis, Loudham or Lowdham is Dyson, Ramer is Tolkien, and Dolbear is Havard. But through subsequent drafts, the names and identities switch back and forth, and, in a number of cases, an Inkling serves as the model for more than one character. Some of the specifics are very obviously taken from the Inklings themselves—there are references to the titles of Lewis's works, a comment on Tolkien's essay "On Fairy-Stories," and the description of Dolbear as a red-bearded man nicknamed "Ruthless Rufus." There is even a joking reference to Christopher Tolkien writing "little books of memoirs" with the titles *In the Roaring Forties* and *The Inns and Outs of Oxford* (*Notion Club* 219).

Other, less significant, characters are also described. There is a monk named Dom Jonathan Markison, possibly a portrait of Father Mathew. There is a "sceptical and rather superior onlooker" named Ranulph Stainer, an allusion to Rudolf Steiner. He may represent Owen Barfield or perhaps the presence of Steiner's anthroposophy as a kind of participant in the group (*Notion Club* 151). Two of the minor characters share the last name Rashbold, which is a translation of the German "Toll-kühn" (151). The younger, John Jethro Rashbold, is an "apparently speechless undergraduate." The elder is an Anglo-Saxon scholar. At one point in the story, Lowdham dismisses old Professor Rashbold as a "grumpy old bear" (256).

But despite these obvious connections, Tolkien issues a stern warning that these fictionalized portraits are not meant to represent any individual too closely. Manuscript B contains a "Preface to the Inklings." It begins, "While listening to this fantasia (if you do), I beg of the present company not to look for their own faces in this mirror" (*Notion Club* 148).[29] The characters in the story are intended to be conglomerations. As Tolkien puts it, "At the best you will only see your countenances distorted, and adorned maybe with noses (and other features) that are not your own, but belong to other members of the company—if to anybody" (148–49).

Though the characterization is somewhat oblique, there is no doubt that *The Notion Club Papers* depicts the spirit of the Inklings. The participants read aloud from drafts in progress, including fiction, poetry, and scholarship. They argue, joke, and quip. And they discuss their works quite candidly. The opening scene sounds like it could be a transcript of an actual meeting. Ramer, "one of our oldest members," is having a difficult time: "To-night he read hastily, boggling and stumbling. So much so that Frankley made him read several sentences over again" (161). Here, one cannot help but see an insistent Lewis encouraging a reluctant Tolkien to read and reread an unclear passage.

In another segment of the story, Ramer describes the group's response to his text. He records, "When I had finished reading my story, we sat in silence for a while. 'Well?' I said. 'What do you think of it? Will it do?' Nobody answered, and I felt the air charged with disapproval, as it often is in our circle, though on this occasion the critical interruptions had been fewer than usual. 'Oh, come on. What have *you* got to say? I may as well get the worst over,' I urged turning to Latimer. He is not a flatterer" (*Notion Club* 212). The personal connection is emphasized in this particular instance, for Tolkien has written the word "self" under "Ramer" at the top of this page (212). Tolkien revised this section extensively, and the new version is much milder than the one quoted above. While the revision may be closer to what actually occurred in an Inklings meeting, the first draft may be a more accurate description of Tolkien's emotional experience.

The Notion Club Papers offers us a picture of the Inklings as seen through Tolkien's eyes. In addition to readings and critiques, the members of the Notion Club enjoy in-depth discussion about language and, appropriately, reflect both Tolkien's interests and his point of view.[30] For example, at one point Frankley insists, "Languages are *not* jungles. They are gardens, in which sounds selected from the savage wilderness of Brute Noise are turned into words, grown, trained, and endued with the scents of significance" (225–26).

The members of the Notion Club meet to read and talk, but the story itself is ultimately unsatisfying. The narrative about group meetings gradually gives way to an extended description (more than thirty pages long) by Ramer of his dream-visions as a form of time/space travel. Then two of the members of the group, Arry Lowdham and Wilfrid Jeremy, begin to open themselves to actually experience the kinds of visions that Ramer has described. At this point, the story changes, and the minute book of the Notion Club is left far behind. Tolkien himself realizes that things are heading in a completely new direction. On a slip of paper, he notes, "Do the Atlantis story and abandon Eriol-Saga, with Loudham, Jeremy, Guildford and Ramer taking part" (*Notion Club* 281). Eventually, Tolkien makes the creative leap from one plan to another. The unfolding material dealing with the Atlantis myth has become far more engrossing than the comparatively mundane descriptions of the group members and their interaction.[31] But this new story, like the ongoing account of the activities of the Notion Club, was never completed.

DEDICATIONS

The Inklings express deep appreciation for one another throughout their work, particularly in the dedication pages of their books. Warren Lewis dedicated *The Splendid Century* to his brother, and C. S. Lewis dedicated *Out of the Silent Planet* to Warren Lewis. C. S. Lewis dedicated *The Allegory of Love* to Owen Barfield, "wisest and best of my unofficial teachers." He elaborates his appreciation in lengthy prefatory remarks, praising Barfield again and explaining that he is the one who taught him "not to patronize the past" (viii). Lewis dedicated *The Screwtape Letters* to Tolkien. When he gave Tolkien a copy, he inscribed it "In token payment of a great debt" (Carpenter, *Inklings* 174). And he dedicated *Rehabilitations and Other Essays* to Hugo Dyson. Four of the seven books in The Chronicles of Narnia are dedicated to the children of Inklings members.[32]

Lewis's longest and most tender dedication is the one he wrote to Charles Williams in *A Preface to Paradise Lost*. Lewis had made arrangements for Williams to give a series of lectures at Oxford, and Williams spoke on Milton to a sizable audience. As we saw earlier, Lewis wrote at length to his brother about the impact of the occasion, saying, "I have at last, if only for once, seen a university doing what it was founded to do: teaching Wisdom" (*Collected Letters* 2: 346). Lewis was more than transfixed by the event; he was deeply influenced by it.

188 THE COMPANY THEY KEEP

In his own book on Milton, he gives Williams full credit for "the recovery of a true critical tradition after more than a hundred years of laborious misunderstanding" (*Preface* v). Lewis acknowledges that Williams "partly anticipated, partly confirmed, and most of all clarified and matured, what I had long been thinking about Milton" (v). He encourages others as well: "Apparently, the door of the prison was really unlocked all the time; but it was only you who thought of trying the handle. Now we can all come out" (vi).[33]

For his part, Barfield dedicated *Poetic Diction* to Lewis. In the preface to the second edition of this book, written twenty-four years later, he retained exactly the same dedication, with this addition, "in celebration of nearly half a lifetime's priceless friendship" (38).

And there are others. Wain dedicated *Weep before God,* a collection of original poetry, to Nevill Coghill. Gervase Mathew dedicated *The Court of Richard II* to Nevill Coghill and to the memory of Sir Maurice Powicke, acknowledging "pervasive influences" from friends including C. S. Lewis and J. R. R. Tolkien. Coghill dedicated *Shakespeare's Professional Skills,* his published version of the 1959 Clark Lectures delivered at Cambridge, to Hugo Dyson and Patrick Coghill.

Finally, three books by Inklings are dedicated to the Inklings as a group. Williams dedicated *The Forgiveness of Sins* to the Inklings. Lewis dedicated *The Problem of Pain,* his first work of Christian apologetics, to the Inklings. And a most ringing and powerful dedication, one that clearly expresses the part the Inklings played in Tolkien's work, appeared in the foreword to the first edition of *The Lord of the Rings:* "I dedicate the book to all admirers of Bilbo, but especially to my sons and my daughter, and to my friends the Inklings. To the Inklings, because they have already listened to it with a patience, and indeed with an interest, that almost leads me to suspect that they have hobbit-blood in their venerable ancestry. To my sons and my daughter for the same reason, and also because they have all helped me in the labours of composition" (*Peoples* 25).[34] These pages tell a compelling story. A total of seventeen books by Inklings are specifically dedicated to the group as a whole, to individual Inklings, or to family members of Inklings.

References to Each Other

If one were to compile a comprehensive list of all of the written references that any of the Inklings made to other Inklings and their works, the result would be a book-length study in itself. Here I merely want to observe that such references are very common and note a select few in order to illustrate the kinds of things the Inklings said about one another. These pervasive references are another important indication of strong mutual influence.[35]

The largest body of references is found in Lewis's nonfiction; in fact, it is difficult to find any nonfiction book by Lewis that does not refer to one or more of the Inklings. They are mentioned in his autobiographical writing, including *The Pilgrim's Regress* and *Surprised by Joy.* He refers to them in his literary criticism as well; he cites Tolkien's *The Lord of the Rings* and "On Fairy-Stories" in *An Experiment in Criticism.* He also mentions Tolkien in *The Discarded Image.* Lewis quotes Williams often—for example, in *The Four Loves, Miracles, Reflections on the Psalms,* and *Letters to Malcolm.* Barfield is mentioned frequently, too: references to him appear in *The Discarded Image, An Experiment in Criticism,* and *Letters to Malcolm.* Lewis quotes a phrase from an unpublished Barfield poem, "The Tower," in two of his works: once in an essay titled "Talking about Bicycles" (71) and then again in *Letters to Malcolm* (122).[36] Two lengthy sections in chapter 10 of *Miracles* expound Barfield's beliefs; in one of these, Lewis explains that two books—Barfield's *Poetic Diction* and Edwyn Bevan's *Symbolism and Belief*—are the starting point for his entire discussion (*Miracles* 86). Without a doubt, the Barfield book that impacted Lewis the most is *Poetic Diction:* Lewis refers to it by name in seven of his books.[37] Carpenter writes, "Lewis often referred to [*Poetic Diction*] and to Barfield's notions about myth and language in his lectures and in his own published writings, so often indeed that it became a jest among his pupils that Barfield was actually an *alter ego,* a figment of Lewis's imagination to whom Lewis chose to ascribe some of his own opinions" (*Inklings* 64).

Tolkien makes fewer references to the Inklings. One appears in the essay "English and Welsh," in which Tolkien bolsters his premise with this: "Mr C. S. Lewis, addressing students of literature, has asserted that the man who does not know Old English literature 'remains all his life a child among real students of English'" (163). Tolkien cites Lewis in other works, most extensively in his landmark lecture "Beowulf: The Monsters and the Critics." Answering those who would dismiss *Beowulf* as a wild folktale simply because it includes a dragon, Tolkien writes, "But a dragon is not an idle or a silly tale. Whatever dire origins it has in prehistoric fact, the dragon is as we have it one of the most moving creations of the imagination, richer in meaning than his barrow is in golden treasure" (*Beowulf and the Critics* 55). Tolkien illustrates the enduring fascination writers have with the "worm" by quoting two dragon poems in their entirety. The first is "Iúmonna Gold Galdre Bewunden," a poem by Tolkien that was first published in the Leeds literary magazine *Gryphon* (200). The other poem is Lewis's "The Northern Dragon," first published in *The Pilgrim's Regress.* Tolkien argues that "the two together for all their defects (especially the first I shall quote) seem to me more important for *Beowulf*-criticism, for which they were not written, than very much that has been written with that purpose" (55–56).

There are many, many others. In *He Came Down From Heaven,* for example, Williams refers to Lewis's *The Allegory of Love* as "one of the most important critical books of our time" (86). Another of the Inklings praised this work as well: in a footnote in the introduction to his translation of *The Canterbury Tales,* Coghill recommends it enthusiastically, and in an essay he calls it "the most trenchant and authoritative description of allegory I know" (*Canterbury Tales* 10; *Collected Papers* 201). Coghill also mentions Lewis's scholarship favorably in several other books.

Though some references to Inklings by other Inklings are direct, naming names and spelling out titles, others are vague, using descriptors like "a man" or citations like "once said." There is generally no hint that these are the words of a friend or colleague; the material is acknowledged with appropriate scholarly respect. But occasionally there is a note of familiarity, as in "On Fairy-Stories," where Tolkien corrects Lewis's early, misguided view of myth, softening the blow by calling him "kind" and "confused" (50). And sometimes there is gentle teasing, as when Lewis remarks, "One gets the impression that medieval people, like Professor Tolkien's Hobbits, enjoyed books which told them what they already knew" (*Discarded* 200). All told, these references are notable for the natural and unaffected way in which they have been thoroughly incorporated into each other's work.

TEACHING AND LEARNING

The overwhelming impression one gets from such examples is that the Inklings have learned a great deal from one another and are thankful. But it goes far beyond details and specifics. They also provided models and paradigms that had broad implications for the way they went about thinking, writing, and teaching. They learned foundational concepts from each other, concepts that shifted the course of their basic beliefs and led to fresh insights in their fields.

We have already touched on many examples of this kind of influence. Lewis's religious conversion following his long talk with Dyson and Tolkien is one example. Tolkien's incorporation of Barfield's seminal theories of language into his fiction is another. We have seen how Tolkien and Dyson changed the way Lewis saw the concept of *myth,* how Williams "clarified and matured" Lewis's inchoate thoughts about Milton, how Lewis expressed gratitude to Barfield for teaching him to avoid chronological snobbery, and how Tolkien convinced Lewis of the value of a different approach to education, resulting in a revised English syllabus.

In Tolkien's letters, we find another example of a central idea he learned from Lewis. Tolkien praises Lewis's essay "Myth Became Fact" and then explains that Lewis played a part in clarifying his view of the Bible and of the Christian story, most of all for showing him how worthwhile the story itself was "as mental nourishment." Tolkien writes, "Partly as a development of my own thought on my lines and work (technical and literary), partly in contact with C. S. L., and in various ways not least the firm guiding hand of Alma Mater Ecclesia, I do not now feel either ashamed or dubious on the Eden 'myth.' It has not, of course, historicity of the same kind as the NT, which are virtually contemporary documents, while Genesis is separated by we do not know how many sad exiled generations from the Fall, but certainly there was an Eden on this very unhappy earth." He concludes, "We all long for it, and we are constantly glimpsing it: our whole nature at its best and least corrupted, its gentlest and most humane, is still soaked with the sense of 'exile'" (*Letters* 109).

Another example of teaching and learning comes from C. S. Lewis. In an early conversation with Barfield, Lewis expressed "the point of view that it was unworthy to want things badly." Barfield remembers his sharp reply: "I rapped out without thinking, 'Nonsense, a man must have his *Sehnsucht!*' (I also remember his quoting this later in a way that revealed it had sunk in.) I took the point of view that, yes, you ought to be trying to identify yourself with the macrocosm, but that *your yearning and wanting things badly was really part of your being.* I was rather full of the word *Sehnsucht,* having read so much of Novalis" (emphasis added). Barfield concludes, "Now if you read Lewis's work, you will see that he made a lot of use of *Sehnsucht*—which is German for longing, yearning—he was rather struck by it" (*Owen Barfield* 129). That is an understatement. Before this conversation with Barfield, Lewis thought longings were "unworthy." Following this conversation, Lewis declared, "Our best havings are wantings" (*Letters* 441). The concept of longing is a key part of Lewis's essay "The Weight of Glory," a key image in *The Pilgrim's Regress,*" a key theme in *Reflections on the Psalms,* a key topic in *The Four Loves,* a key issue in *The Problem of Pain,* a key argument in *Mere Christianity,* and a key virtue in The Chronicles of Narnia. It became an inseparable part of his discussion of romantic poetry. And those who have read *Surprised by Joy* know that "an unsatisfied desire which is itself more desirable than any other satisfaction" became the intellectual scaffolding that Lewis used to make sense of his entire life journey. Lewis writes, "In a sense, the central story of my life is about nothing else" (*Surprised* 17–18).

Another powerful idea can also be traced to Barfield's influence. In 1928, Lewis wrote Barfield a letter to tell him what great impact his ideas had had on Tolkien. Lewis reports, "You might like to know that when Tolkien dined with me the other night he said *à propos* of something quite different that your conception of the ancient semantic unity had modified his whole outlook and that he was always just going to say something in a lecture when your conception stopped him in time. 'It's one of those things,' he said 'that when you've once seen it there are all sorts of things you can never say again'" (qtd. in Carpenter, *Inklings* 42). There are undoubtedly dozens—perhaps hundreds—of other examples that deserve recognition and fuller development.[38] There was profound mutual influence among the Inklings even at the level of their most fundamental ideas.

REVIEWS

The Inklings wrote more than forty book reviews to promote one another's work.[39] Williams in particular wrote quite a number of reviews of the works of fellow Inklings, including two different reviews of *The Screwtape Letters*. One was published in the *Dublin Review*. Williams explains that he wants to lend his voice to "reinforce the general recommendation" of Lewis's book. He adds that he not only admires the skill of the book, but also finds it edifying: he recommends it "with the personal sincerity of one who has found himself warned and enlightened" (170). The other review was published in *Time and Tide*, and it is written in imitation of Lewis's devilish letters. Williams's review begins, "My dearest Scorpuscle," and in the last paragraph he warns his readers, "It is a dangerous book, heavenly-dangerous. I hate it, this give-away of hell." Williams signs the review "Your sincere friend, Snigsozzle." Then he adds this menacing postscript: "You will send someone to see after Lewis?—some very clever fiend?" ("Letters in Hell" 245–46).

Williams shows a similar blend of humor and insight in his review of *The Problem of Pain*. He has high praise for Lewis's skill as a writer, noting that his style is "what style always is—goodness working on goodness, a lucid and sincere intellect at work on the facts of life or the great statements of other minds" (62). Poking fun at his own tendency toward obscurity, Williams explains that he does not intend to offer the reader a paraphrase of the book: "Mr Lewis's prose is known, and those who know it would not thank me for translating it into mine" (62).

In addition to writing about *The Screwtape Letters* and *The Problem of Pain*, Williams commented favorably on *Beyond Personality*. He also reviewed David Cecil's *Hardy the Novelist* and Owen Barfield's *Romanticism Comes of Age*. These reviews were written and published after Williams became an active member of the Inklings. But perhaps Williams's most interesting Inkling review is the one he wrote of his own scholarly work *Reason and Beauty in the Poetic Mind*. He candidly admits that he finds himself "in profound agreement" with the "main discourse" of the book. Nonetheless, Williams finds that this book poses a particular difficulty: "All of us have authors whom we cannot read properly, and I am sorry that Mr. Charles Williams is one of mine. If his work has any value I shall never know it, for on the rare occasions—and how rare they seem, alas!—when I have discussed it with a friend, we generally appear to be talking about different books. A something in each book, obvious to others, eludes me; but how obvious to me are things my friend never discovers!" (525). In addition to explaining that he is in many ways a poor commentator on his own work, Williams expresses a strong wish for literate friends, for those who, as Lewis said, speak one's own language (*Collected Letters* 1: 653). This wish was expressed in 1933; six years later, in 1939, Williams joined the Inklings. All in all, this autocritical review is so skillful, gracious, witty, and insightful, I find myself wishing that each of the Inklings had attempted such an account of his own work.

Lewis reviewed *The Hobbit* in the *Times Literary Supplement* (2 October 1937), and again in the *Times* (8 October 1937). The first of these was edited and reprinted in *On Stories and Other Essays on Literature*. Lewis praises Tolkien as a sub-creator: "No common recipe for children's stories will give you creatures so rooted in their own soil and history as those of Professor Tolkien." He adds a comment that is part compliment, part encouragement, and perhaps just a little part gibe at his friend's thoroughness: "Professor Tolkien . . . obviously knows much more about them than he needs for this tale" ("The Hobbit" 81). These and other references to the background mythologies of the story testify to Lewis's familiarity with this larger body of material. They also show Lewis giving generous praise to Tolkien in the area where Lewis himself later struggled, the development of a detailed and internally consistent sub-created world.

Lewis also reflects his own conviction about the nature of children's literature, that no book can be said to be good for children unless it is also good for adults: "This is a children's book only in the sense that the first of many readings can be undertaken in the nursery. . . . Only years later, at a tenth or a twentieth reading, will they begin to realise what deft scholarship and profound reflection have gone to make everything in it so ripe, so friendly, and in its own way so true" ("The Hobbit" 82).[40] In the *Times* review, he quips, "It may be years before we produce another author with such a nose for an elf" (20). In short, he predicts, accurately enough, "*The Hobbit* may well prove a classic" ("The Hobbit" 82).

Another Inkling, R. B. McCallum, also published a review of *The Hobbit*. It is a tiny notice, only 211 words long, which appeared in the 1937–38 annual issue of the *Pembroke College Record*. McCallum says that the work is not academic in its nature but is nonetheless the kind of children's tale only an academic man could write, since it is "one of those children's tales which can be read with profit and amusement even by the most mature." McCallum gives a brief synopsis, then adds these apt words of praise: "The whole book is remarkable for the solidity and exactitude of the narrative, a happy and reflective vein of humour and for the sanity of the underlying philosophy" (9).

Lewis published two enthusiastic reviews of *The Lord of the Rings* in *Time and Tide;* they have been combined and published in the collection *On Stories.* His majestic endorsements have been quoted so often that they have become part of the fabric of Tolkien Studies: "Here are beauties which pierce like swords or burn like cold iron; here is a book that will break your heart" (84). To say that Lewis is unabashed in his enthusiasm for this book is a gross understatement: here is a story, he calmly insists, that "will soon take its place among the indispensables" (90).[41] He praises the story's structure, its theology, geography, paleography, languages, and beings. He even relishes the names of the characters: "The names alone are a feast, whether redolent of quiet countryside (Michel Delving, South Farthing), tall and kingly (Boramir [*sic*], Faramir, Elendil), loathsome like Smeagol, who is also Gollum, or frowning in the evil strength of Barad Dur or Gorgoroth; yet best of all (Lothlorien, Gilthoniel, Galadriel) when they embody that piercing, high elvish beauty of which no other prose writer has captured so much" (84).[42]

Lewis also offers the definitive answer to those who think less of this novel because it is fantasy. "'But why,' (some ask), 'why, if you have a serious comment to make on the real life of men, must you do it by talking about a phantasma-goric never-never land of your own?' Because, I take it, one of the main things the author wants to say is that the real life of men is of that mythical and heroic quality" (89). He continues, "The value of the myth is that it takes all the things we know and restores to them the rich significance which has been hidden by 'the veil of familiarity.' The child enjoys his cold meat (otherwise dull to him) by pretending it is buffalo, just killed with his own bow and arrow. And the child is wise. The real meat comes back to him more savoury for having been dipped in a story" (90). In this review, Lewis's writing is at its best; his use of description, metaphor, and the felicitous phrase is simply as good as it gets. For example, he writes, "But in the Tolkienian world you can hardly put your foot down anywhere from Esgaroth to Forlindon or between Ered Mithrin and Khand, without stirring the dust of history" (86). Lewis's writing shows more than mere enthusiasm for this work; he knows it intimately, understands it fully, loves it deeply, explicates it faithfully, defends it fervently. It has touched him bone deep.

Another review by Lewis addresses *The Oxford Book of Christian Verse,* edited by fellow Inkling David Cecil. In this multilayered example, we have a particu-larly high level of interaction. One Inkling is publishing a review of a book by another Inkling, and he complains that a third Inkling has been left out. All in all, it is a very grumpy review. For example, Lewis challenges Cecil's claim that good Christian poetry is rare. Lewis responds curtly, "I am neither convinced of the fact nor satisfied by the explanation" (95). Lewis admits that he and Cecil agree on one thing: "All hymnbooks are full of very bad poems" (96). Even then, Lewis explains that they heartily disagree as to why this is so!

But Lewis's primary complaint is that Cecil has shortchanged Williams, and the world, by failing to include any of the "great odes from *Taliessin*" (95). Lest this reprimand seem overly personal or even petulant, it is important to remember that Williams's poetry was highly esteemed by scholars and critics in his day. Dodds reminds us of his prominence: "Between 1921 and 1931 Williams published seven volumes of poetry and verse drama. They were reviewed—always favorably in the *Times Literary Supplement,* for example. Williams even enjoyed a degree of international recognition, including the award of a Diploma and Bronze Medal by the Olympic Games in 1924. Major poets and critics acclaimed him. As late as 1935, Chesterton himself wrote to Williams expressing 'the profound admiration' he had always had for Williams's 'extremely individual poetry'" (194). Dodds also notes, "Theodore Maynard, in the introduction to *Our Best Poets: English and American,* ranked Williams third among 'the twelve best contemporary English' poets—after Chesterton and Alice Meynell, and ahead of Yeats" (193).

Despite these compelling credentials, when Cecil selected and edited poetry for *The Oxford Book of Christian Verse,* he included only one poem written by Charles Williams. It is a short piece, only five stanzas long, tucked in between a long section on Gilbert Keith Chesterton and an even longer one on Thomas Stearns Eliot.

Lewis also wrote two reviews of Williams's *Taliessin through Logres;* one of them, published in *Theology,* is a full eight pages long. He begins by acknowledging that the work is very hard to read. Lewis accuses Williams flat out of "disobeying" or misusing the English language ("Sacred Poem" 268). And, singling out one passage in particular, he admits, "The obscurities are to me impenetrable and the style is dangerously near a mannerism" (274). However, Lewis offers needed encouragement that despite these problems, it is worth pressing on: "The poem has greatness enough to justify the intensive study it exacts" (274).[43] He praises the work chiefly for its "combination of jagged weight and soaring movement, its ability to narrate while remaining lyric, and (above all) its prevailing quality of glory—its blaze," and for its "golden, noonday vitality" (268, 275).

The review makes the same point repeatedly: this poem is exceedingly difficult but well worth the effort. While Lewis elaborates and explains this idea with excerpts and descriptions of the themes and symbols, he ultimately shifts to a more personal approach in order to promote the work to the reader. He tells how the poem won him over:

> But what finally convinced me that [Williams] has written a great poem was a transformation which my judgment underwent in reading it. I liked its "flavour" from the first, but found it so idiosyncratic that I thought the book might be what Lamb called a "favourite," a thing not for all days or all palates. . . . But as I went on I found bit after bit of my "real world" falling into its place within the poem. I found pair after pair of opposites harmoniously reconciled. I began to see that what had seemed a deliciously private universe was the common universe after all: that this apparently romantic and even wilful poem was really "classic" and central. I do not think this can happen in a minor work. ("Sacred Poem" 275)

It is typical of Lewis to offer a sound explanation for the greatness of the poem, but then to justify it primarily on the basis of his subjective experience. In short, the poem is great because of what reading it has done to him.

As a whole, reviews of the Inklings by the Inklings balance description with measured praise and appropriate criticism. Lewis wrote and published the largest number of these reviews: a total of nine. John Wain and Charles Williams each wrote seven, and Bennett is close behind with six. While it is difficult to generalize, most of them serve in one way or another to underscore the point that the book they are discussing is worthy of earnest attention.

Memorial Articles, Memoirs, and Obituaries

Reviews are one specific kind of public discourse; the Inklings also wrote about one another in more personal and reflective ways, including memoirs and final tributes.[44] In May 1945, Lewis wrote an obituary of Charles Williams for the *Oxford Magazine.* Calling him an "extraordinary gift," Lewis commends Williams's work as a critic, more as a novelist, but most of all as a poet (265). In a brief and elegant summary, he ventures to guess that Williams will stand as "the great English poet of this age" (265). It may be said that in offering this magnificent compliment, Lewis's gift for friendship is more in evidence than his gift for prophecy.

As we have seen, his introduction to *Essays Presented to Charles Williams* must be viewed as a memorial essay. We have also looked at the course of lectures that, substantially edited, became "Williams and the Arthuriad" in *Arthurian Torso.* One of Lewis's most poignant and powerful poems is "To

Charles Williams," in which he struggles to make sense of the way all things have changed since Williams's death.[45] "It's a larger world / Than I once thought it" he writes. Then he wonders, "Is it the first sting of the great winter, the world-waning?" Or might it be "the cold of spring?" Having wrestled with the unexpected impact of this event, the poet is left with many unanswered questions. And the final irony is this: the only person he can think of who could talk with him about this struggle is Williams himself (*Collected Poems* 119).[46]

Ten years after Williams died, Lewis was still working to keep his memory alive. He joined with Dorothy L. Sayers and published this letter to the editor of the *Times* of London: "Sir.—Sunday, May 15, will be the tenth anniversary of the death of Charles Williams. In his lifetime he became an outstanding figure in the world of English letters. Since his death, his reputation and influence have grown so much that there must be thousands who to-day acknowledge him as a formative influence in their thinking, whether literary or religious" (9). The letter continues by encouraging those who remember Williams to honor his memory by getting together, announcing that special meetings have been scheduled in London, Oxford, and Cambridge.

When Lewis died in 1963, Owen Barfield honored him in two obituaries. The first was published in the *Report of the Royal Society of Literature* and focuses appropriately on his literary accomplishments. Barfield emphasizes that when Lewis was a young man, his "ruling passion" was poetry. He summarizes Lewis's literary achievement as "at once imaginative and learned" (21). He singles out *Till We Have Faces* for special mention, calling it "muscular and strongly imagined" and "a striking product of genuinely mythopoeic imagination." He ends by suggesting that this novel is "perhaps, as he felt himself, his greatest achievement" (22).

In the second obituary, written for the *Oxford Magazine* and published in January 1964, Barfield describes the life and legacy of Lewis in much broader terms. He was known "first and foremost" as a Christian apologist, next as an author of children's books, and then as "the originator of a new type of science fiction." But Barfield puts a greater emphasis on Lewis's scholarship, noting, "Even if he had none of these achievements to his credit, his work as a lecturer, literary critic and historian would alone ensure him a distinguished niche in the world of letters" (155). Barfield concludes his comments by describing the profound effects of Lewis's conversion to Christianity, and his ability to submit to God's benevolent direction, "at first indignantly but with increasing delight as he found his energy grow only greater and more effectual" (156).

Throughout this piece, Barfield characterizes Lewis as one who cared profoundly for the needs of others. He mentions his anonymous gifts of financial support to the needy and the sacrificial way he fought against his personal distaste for letter writing in order to offer counsel to hundreds of people he would never meet. Barfield writes, "I could speak of the strength he was given to lighten the burdens of a whole army of less fortunate or weaker brethren. But there is not space to do so, and I will only add that, as I see it, it is to that delight, that energy, that strength that we owe the almost uninterrupted stream of wisdom, piety, erudition, zest and good sense that flowed from the pen of C. S. Lewis from then on to the end of his life" (156).

Other important tributes to Lewis are collected and published in James Como's *Remembering C. S. Lewis.* As we saw in chapter 6, Como's book includes twenty-four essays, including five from Inklings Wain, Fox, Havard, Mathew, and Dundas-Grant. The result is an incredibly valuable primary resource and multivoiced work. In "A Great Clerke," for example, Wain describes Lewis as a man with a hard outer self, "brisk, challenging, argumentative, full of an overwhelming physical energy and confidence," and a soft inner self "as tender and as well hidden as a crab's" (155).[47] In this memorial essay as elsewhere, Wain does not shy away from criticizing Lewis: he finds his personal writing "lame and unconvincing" (155), he dismisses his novels as "simply bad" (160), and he accuses him of giving place to a "silly-truculent mood" (161). Despite this harsh assessment, the overall effect of the piece clearly communicates both affection and admiration.

Havard's most important writing about the Inklings appears in Como's book also. In "Philia: Jack at Ease," he tells of meeting with Lewis to treat his influenza and then staying to enjoy a long discussion of ethics and philosophy. Havard was struck from the beginning by their contrasting backgrounds: "Lewis was something of a Berkeleyan and had returned to Christianity via idealism, as he describes in his autobiography, whereas I, as a scientist of sorts, had been attracted to the realism of St. Thomas Aquinas" (350). Havard and Lewis, like Barfield and Lewis, relished these fundamental differences, asserting that their friendships were not marred by them but rather based upon them. Havard's article is substantial, particular, and highly personal. He does not idealize Lewis by any means; for example, he writes, "He could be intolerant, he could be abusive, and he made enemies." Such frank comments are balanced by the warm tone. Havard clearly accepted Lewis on his own terms. He writes, "Seeing him so regularly two or three times a week, I came to know him well in all his moods." And, as one who knew him well, Havard concludes, "He was a 'magnanimous' man in the Aristotelian sense of the word" (363).

Tolkien died in 1973.[48] Nevill Coghill wrote a powerful and perceptive obituary for him. He traces Tolkien's early years, then summarizes his scholarly achievements with as much clarity as compactness, emphasizing four of his greatest achievements: *A Middle English Vocabulary,* his collaboration with

Gordon on *Sir Gawain and the Green Knight,* and two critical essays "which, perhaps no one else in the world could have written, namely 'Chaucer as a Philologist' . . . and his masterpiece of critical interpretation: 'Beowulf: The Monsters and the Critics'" (30–31). Coghill praises his important translation work and also notes his skillful editing of the *Ancrene Wisse.*

But the obituary does not merely outline Tolkien's scholarly accomplishments; it also attempts to capture his character. Coghill tells of a time when Tolkien "donned a green robe, turban and liripipe, parted his beard centrally and gave a reading in the original pronunciation of *The Nun's Priest's Tale* at the Oxford Summer Diversions of 1942." He "had a taste for mild mischief," we are told, and Coghill finds that Chaucer's self-description suits Tolkien too: "He semeth elvyssh by his contenaunce" (31).

Having elaborated Tolkien's appetite for serious scholarship and illustrated his sense of play, Coghill discusses his accomplishments as a poet and teacher. Then he mentions *The Lord of the Rings,* offering less a tribute than a rationale for the work. He writes, "It has to be admitted that the reading world is sharply divided between those who are beguiled by these wonderful romances, and those who find them entirely unreadable. The disapprovers reinforce their taste by moral arguments picked out of Freud and elsewhere, and they adopt towards us addicts a '*more adult than thou*' attitude, as if they had never read Coleridge on the 'willing suspension of disbelief which constitutes poetic faith.'" Coghill adds this rhetorical question, "But Tolkien's romances give delight and hurt not, and after all if we are allowed to enjoy a magic island and 'believe' in an Ariel and a Caliban, why may we not suspend our disbelief (if we are not too 'adult' to know how) in barrow-wights and Lothlorien?" (32). Then he concludes, characterizing Tolkien as modest, friendly, helpful, and delightful, and describing him as one who "spoke in sharp bursts at express speed." Talking with Tolkien, he says, was like holding a conversation with "a muted machine-gun, absolutely on target" (33).

After Coghill died in 1980, two of the Inklings wrote memorial essays to commemorate him. David Cecil composed a brief tribute that begins with the admission that Coghill was "not a typical choice" to ascend to the position of Merton Professor of English Language and Literature at Oxford, particularly since he was "better known in Oxford as a personality than as an academic." But Cecil gently enumerates various accomplishments that marked Coghill's contribution to the university: his passion for past authors made them come alive, his understanding of history helped others understand important writers in their context, and his Christian perspective shed light on the moral and spiritual values that are foundational to so many great works. Furthermore, Coghill consistently brought the same passion and insight to his drama productions as he did to the literary page. In conclusion, Cecil tells us, "Oxford and her School of English Literature have reason to be proud" (1334).

John Wain also wrote a memoir of Coghill, capturing the essence of a man whose "whole face had a slightly rough, knocked-about quality, like a chipped statue," but who was totally courteous, a gentleman through and through (*Dear Shadows* 13). The quality that Wain finds most striking and elaborates most ecstatically is Coghill's joie de vivre. He writes, "Nevill was a great celebrator. His heart was naturally full of the emotion of gratitude. The greatness of a Shakespeare or a Mozart or a Cézanne was to him simply an instance of the bounty of God, like the rain and the sun" (19).

In contrast to Cecil, who is restrained in his affirmation of Coghill, Wain is blunt and zealous: "Nevill was the best Merton Professor Oxford had ever had or was likely to have" (*Dear Shadows* 25). He praises Coghill for his extraordinary professional qualities and his scholarly work with *Piers Plowman* and *The Canterbury Tales*. But ultimately, his tribute to Coghill is quite personal. Wain asserts, "He was never my teacher—officially, that is—though I learnt more from him than from almost anyone" (15).

Conclusions

The Inklings show up regularly in the texts of one another's work, from brief quotations in academic writing to character sketches in their fiction, from references in their early poetry to final tributes in obituaries. The examples discussed in this chapter are merely representative. Throughout their novels, essays, poems, and plays, we see the same combination of praise and criticism, gratitude and insight, enthusiasm and witty banter that we read about in their personal lives. There is enough significant interaction woven into these pages to dispel any lingering notion that the Inklings were nothing more than a loose-knit circle of friends. Not only did they work together as they wrote books, poems, and scholarly studies—they also contributed personality to fictional characters, inspired poems, enlivened articles, generated reviews, and, in a thousand other ways, seen and unseen, still speak directly from the pages of one another's texts.

NOTES

1. Lewis denied it, saying, "That is too high a compliment" (*Collected Letters* 2: 682).

2. One of Lewis's most well-known and beloved characters, Puddleglum the Marshwiggle, is also one of his clearest adaptations of a real person into fictional form. Puddleglum is based on Lewis's gardener, Fred Paxford, "an inwardly optimistic, outwardly pessimistic, dear, frustrating, shrewd countryman of immense integrity" (Hooper, *Past Watchful Dragons* 81). Paxford had a gift for making gloomy pronouncements. Doug Gresham writes that a typical conversation would start like this: "'Good morning, Fred,' I might say. 'Ah, looks loike rain afore lunch though, if'n

it doan't snow,'" he would reply (*Lenten Lands* 98). Paxford served the Lewis household from 1930 to 1963, growing vegetables, making repairs, raising chickens, shopping for groceries, and doing some of the cooking on weekends.

3. Hooper explains, "During the Second World War a number of children from schools near the blitzed areas of London were evacuated to Oxford and other parts of the country. All the evacuees accepted by Mrs Moore and Lewis were girls. There were usually three children there at a time, most of whom stayed for several months" (Lewis, *Collected Letters* 2: 270n). Two of the evacuees have written about their experience of living at the Kilns: Margaret Leyland, writing in *The Lamp-post,* and Jill Flewett Freud, writing in *In Search of C. S. Lewis.* Both of the Lewis brothers mention the evacuees briefly in their writing. C. S. Lewis, for example, calls them "very nice, unaffected creatures and all most flatteringly delighted with their new surroundings" (*Collected Letters* 2: 270).

4. Williams is also fictionalized in a novel titled *Nor Fish nor Flesh,* which was written by his friend and coworker Gerard Hopkins. It depicts an uneasy relationship among characters clearly based on Williams, Hopkins, and Jones. Hadfield notes that when the book appeared, Charles Williams was "staggered" (*Charles Williams* 117).

5. Williams's three "publishing house" plays—light, entertaining, and very personal dramas—were published in 2000 as *The Masques of Amen House.*

6. Tolkien also used the power of drama to express his life circumstances. In 1912, at Christmastime, he wrote and starred in a play titled "The Bloodhound, the Chef, and the Suffragette." The story line concerned "Professor Joseph Quilter, M.A., B.A., A.B.C., alias world-wide detective Sexton Q. Blake-Holmes, the Bloodhound." Paralleling Tolkien's own courtship of Edith Bratt, Blake-Holmes has undertaken a search for Gwendolyn Goodchild. "She meanwhile has fallen in love with a penniless student whom she meets while they are living in the same lodging-house, and she has to remain undiscovered by her father until her twenty-first birthday in two days' time, after which she will be free to marry" (Carpenter, *Tolkien* 59).

7. The reference here to "appreciative critics" who find Tolkien's sense of humor "tiresome" is undoubtedly a reference to the Inklings in general and C. S. Lewis in particular.

8. This excerpt comes from an unpublished letter from Tolkien to George Sayer. This line appeared in a news article about the sale of these letters, which was posted at www.theonering.net/perl/newsview/6/1004723086 and accessed August 2004.

9. Tolkien himself had a character named Ælfwine in his early mythology, one iteration of the questing mariner who seeks the elves.

10. The opening scene in *Out of the Silent Planet* may be drawn from a specific incident that happened in 1928. Lewis records in a letter to Warren Lewis: "This time we committed the folly of selecting a billeting *area* for the night instead of one good town: i.e. we said 'Well here are four villages within a mile of one another and the map marks an inn in each, so we shall be sure to get in somewhere.' Your imagination can suggest what this results in by about eight o'clock of an evening, after twenty miles of walking, when one is just turning away from the first unsuccessful attempt and a thin cold rain is beginning to fall" (*Collected Letters* 1: 757).

11. Dorothy L. Sayers noticed the change in Ransom's character, and although she liked *That Hideous Strength* very much, she did not much care for the transformation of the protagonist. Sayers writes, "I'm afraid I don't like Ransom quite so well since he took to being golden-haired and interesting on a sofa like the Heir of Redclyffe" (*Letters* 3: 177).

12. Though the evidence for it is quite slim, some have made the claim that Ramandu, the "retired star" in *The Voyage of the "Dawn Treader,"* is also modeled on Owen Barfield. Ramandu explains his existence on the island by positing a kind of reincarnation; Barfield believed in reincarnation, finding it entirely compatible with his belief in Christ.

13. It is impossible to ignore the strong parallels between the conversation of the boys about the existence of Aboveground in Barfield's "Night Operation" and the conversation between Puddleglum and the White Witch about the existence of the Overworld in chapter 12 of Lewis's *The Silver Chair.*

14. Barfield uses the characters Burden and Burgeon to describe two contradictory aspects of his personality in *This Ever Diverse Pair* (1950) and again in *Unancestral Voice* (1965). Barfield has expressed the conviction in a number of essays that Lewis was a divided man: there are two Lewises (in *Owen Barfield on C.S. Lewis*), three Lewises (in "Lewis, Truth, and Imagination"), or five Lewises (in Edwards's *The Taste of the Pineapple*). These descriptions have often been taken much too seriously. The habit of identifying contrasting aspects of a single individual was a common way for Barfield to describe the normal human personality, including his own.

15. See Tennyson's comments on page 153 of Barfield's *Owen Barfield on C. S. Lewis*.

16. Barfield gives a different account of these events in his introduction to Gibb, *Light on C. S. Lewis*: "I had written and published two books which, in their limited sphere, could both be regarded as successes. He on the other hand had only *Spirits in Bondage* and *Dymer* to his credit and, if my puny sales were only in four figures, his were still in three. This remained the position until the *Pilgrim's Regress* appeared in 1935, after which he never looked back, but appeared to my dazzled eyes to go on for the rest of his life writing more and more successful books at shorter and shorter intervals" (xii–xiii). Gareth Knight credits Williams for this transformation: "It would seem that Lewis and Williams had a strong catalytic effect upon each other, for it is after their meeting that we find a spark entering C. S. Lewis's writing that transformed him from a little-known academic to a popular literary figure" (8).

17. I am unable to find any reliable information on how much money Lewis owed or exactly how the problem of back taxes was addressed. In the novel we are told that Ramsden had given away a total of £1,500 without having paid any taxes. As it happens, a royalty check in the amount of £2,003 is due to arrive. Burden studies the situation at length, and then tells Burgeon, "We have just agreed that the whole of the £2,003, after paying income tax and surtax on itself, will be used up in paying income tax and surtax on the royalties Ramsden has already given away. It should come out almost exactly right. A pure coincidence, of course, but rather neat!" (*Diverse Pair* 64).

18. Both "The Mother of Pegasus" and "Riders on Pegasus" are available to researchers at the Marion E. Wade Center.

19. Barfield's poem "C. S. L. / Biographia Theologia" (in the original Greek and in translation) is available to researchers at the Marion E. Wade Center. It is published here for the first time by the kind permission of G. B. Tennyson on behalf of the Barfield Literary Estate, all rights reserved.

20. MS. Eng. c. 2724, fol. 55 in the Bodleian Library.

21. I am indebted to Joe R. Christopher for bringing this poem to my attention.

22. This poem is published in two places—appendix 3 of Don W. King's *C. S. Lewis, Poet*, page 295, and *C. S. Lewis: Collected Letters*, volume 2, page 158, edited by Walter Hooper. The version in *Collected Letters* includes several changes from the poem as it appears in the manuscript held at the Wade Center and in King's book. Hooper has changed "carp" in line 5 to "camp" and "yus!" in line 8 to "yes!"

23. The letter is undated, though internal evidence suggests it was written in mid-1930. David Bratman notes that it includes an invitation for Barfield to meet Dyson; Lewis and Dyson apparently did not become friends until summer of 1930 (personal correspondence, 14 November 2004).

24. Tolkien wrote a brief comment on this poem, observing that the metrical devices are not "entirely accurate" and speculating about the source of the incident Lewis describes (*Letters* 389).

25. In "J. R. R. Tolkien and the Clerihew," Joe R. Christopher offers a brief history of this poetic form and a selection of clerihews by Tolkien and about him.

26. Joe R. Christopher makes an interesting observation about this poem. In an essay by Luke Rigby titled "A Solid Man," Rigby attributes this poem to Lewis, quoting it as follows:

Father Gervase
Makes inaudible surveys
On little-known sages
Of the Middle Ages. (114)

Christopher speculates that Lewis may have "heard the verse from Tolkien and quoted it in some public situation—and it was thereafter repeated as by him" (Clerihew" 269).

27. In his essay "Tolkien's Lyric Poetry," Joe R. Christopher argues that Tolkien's "Death of St. Brendan" may also be identified with C. S. Lewis (153–54). The poem has been published on pages 261–64 of *Sauron Defeated;* it also appears in a revised version entitled "Imram" on pages 296–99.

28. In its initial conception, the work is directed more or less toward Lewis, and it was intended to be a "vehicle of criticism and discussion of aspects of Lewis's 'planetary' novels" (*Notion Club* 149). The third draft of the work begins, "Beyond Probability / Or / Out of the Talkative Planet," with obvious and playful reference to two Lewis titles (148). Christopher Tolkien believes that Tolkien's use of fictional scholars in *The Notion Club Papers* was influenced by the form of Lewis's pseudo-scholarly commentary of *The Lay of Leithian* (149).

29. I find the parenthetical comment "if you do" to be particularly interesting: Tolkien may be expressing reluctance to share this work with the group. Or this comment may hearken back to criticism that he received from the group in general and Dyson in particular. Tolkien did in fact read *The Notion Club Papers* at Inklings meetings. In his diary entry of 22 August 1946, Warren Lewis writes that Tolkien read "a magnificent myth which is to knit up . . . his Papers of the Notions Club" (*Brothers* 194). Presumably Warren Lewis is referring to *The Drowning of Anadûnê,* published in *Sauron Defeated.*

30. *The Notion Club Papers* may be seen as an idealized Inklings meeting from Tolkien's point of view; *Worlds Apart* may be seen as an idealized Inklings meeting from Barfield's point of view.

31. To some extent, the progress of *The Notion Club Papers* is similar to that of *The Lord of the Rings:* the early segments are light and comical, but these soon give way to more serious, more weighty, more complex narratives. The differences are notable, too. Tolkien never finished *The Notion Club Papers,* even though the raw material he developed here became important and useful to other work.

32. *The Lion, the Witch and the Wardrobe* is dedicated to Lucy Barfield, daughter of Owen Barfield, and Lewis's godchild. *The Voyage of the "Dawn Treader"* is dedicated to Geoffrey Corbett, foster son of Owen Barfield. In later printings, his name is given as Geoffrey Barfield. *Prince Caspian* is dedicated to Mary Clare Havard, daughter of R. E. Havard. *The Silver Chair* is dedicated to Nicholas Hardie, son of Colin Hardie.

33. Williams's response to this dedication is somewhat complex. He was initially quite positive. In an unpublished letter to Raymond Hunt dated 29 November 1941, Williams writes,

> Lewis has just written a book on Milton; I haven't read it but it is sure to be pretty sound; and has charmingly dedicated it to me. I gather that he says that Milton criticism between Johnson and me is practically negligible. Only he says he wishes I had written more because he cannot keep on saying: "As Mr. Williams has remarked to me in private conversation," and the result will be (we fear) that he will get all the credit. But I should never have written the book, & in scholarship he is far more competent than I; and after all, he was struggling toward the truth when I was flung across his path.

Williams is clearly pleased that, first and foremost, Milton is being awarded his proper due. He also admits that he never would have written down his own thoughts on Milton, and that Lewis was well suited to do this important work. But Williams's concern that Lewis would "get all the credit" proved prophetic: the public overlooked Lewis's long and eloquent dedication giving Williams all the glory. Carpenter notes, "The reviews treated Lewis rather than Williams himself as the critic who was restoring [*Paradise Lost*] to its former place." And when Williams realized the full extent of this situation, he became "a little distressed" (*Inklings* 181).

34. Tolkien wrote an earlier version of this dedication in which he mentions the Inklings three times, stating in particular that as a group they "endured" the story with patience. It is published on pages 19–20 of *The Peoples of Middle-earth.*

35. Another way the Inklings were involved in one another's lives is in the space they occupied on each other's bookshelves. It is impossible to track down much information on this fascinating question, but we do have some facts about C. S. Lewis. His personal library included approximately 2,360 volumes, including the following books written by other Inklings:

Owen Barfield: *Law, Association, and the Trade Union Movement* (pamphlet, 1938); *The Silver Trumpet* (1925)
J. A. W. Bennett: *The Parlement of Foules: An Interpretation* (1957)
David Cecil: *Early Victorian Novelists* (1934, 1948 printing); *Jane Austen* (essay, 1936); *Reading as One of the Fine Arts* (essay, 1949); *The Stricken Deer* (1929, 1946 printing); *Two Quiet Lives* (1948)
Nevill Coghill: *Geoffrey Chaucer* (1956); *The Pardon of Piers Plowman* (essay, 1945); *The Poet Chaucer* (1949)
Adam Fox: *Dominus Virtutum* (1936); *Old King Coel* (1937)
Colin Hardie: "Homer and the Odyssey" (offprint, 1942); "The Myth of Oedipus" (unidentified, probably an offprint)
C. S. Lewis: Many copies of his own books, especially recent publications and translations
J. R. R. Tolkien: *Ancrene Wisse* (1962); *The Lord of the Rings* (1954–55); *Sir Gawain and the Green Knight,* ed. Tolkien and Gordon (1925)
John Wain: *Anthology of Modern Poetry* (1963); *Contemporary Reviews of Romantic Poetry* (1953); *Essays on Literature and Ideas* (1963); *Sprightly Running* (1962)
Charles Williams: *The Image of the City* (1958); *James I* (1934); *A Myth of Shakespeare* (1929); *The New Christian Year* (1941); *Poems of Conformity* (1917); *Selected Writings* (1961); *Thomas Cranmer of Canterbury* (1936); "The Way of Exchange" (1941) (a pamphlet in the *New Foundations* series)
C. L. Wrenn: *The English Language* (1949).

This list, compiled by David Bratman, is derived from the bibliography in *C. S. Lewis: A Living Library* by Margaret Anne Rogers, an unpublished MA thesis, Farleigh Dickinson University, 1970. The list records Lewis's library as it was at that time, including some books lost since then, and information on others that have been removed from Lewis's shelves.

36. The phrase is "a whisper / Which Memory will warehouse as a shout."

37. I gratefully acknowledge the help of Douglas Beyer in locating specific citations in the works of C. S. Lewis.

38. A full discussion of these examples and others would require chapters in their own right; in fact, a book-length study of the ways the Inklings impacted one another's thinking would serve as an important contribution to Inklings Studies and an invaluable companion to this book. Here, I hope to draw attention to this aspect of mutual influence and highlight a few of the most important concepts the Inklings learned from one another.

39. A list of these reviews has been compiled by David Bratman and may be accessed at http://home.earthlink.net/~dbratman.

40. See Lewis's essay "On Three Ways of Writing for Children" in *On Stories.*

41. Lewis also wrote a blurb for the dust jacket. Only a portion of it was actually used; I give it here in full:

It would be almost safe to say that no book like this has ever been written. If Ariosto rivalled it in invention (in fact he does not) he would still lack its heroic seriousness. No imaginary world has been projected which is at once so multifarious and so true to its own inner laws; none so seemingly objective, so disinfected from the taint of an author's merely individual psychology; none so relevant to the actual human situation yet so free from allegory. And what fine shading there is in the variations of style to meet the almost endless diversity of scenes and characters—comic, homely, epic, monstrous, or diabolic! (qtd. in *Priestman* 62)

42. Lewis was not a consistent speller; the misspelling of "Boramir" here, like his misspelling of Númenor elsewhere, may point to his enthusiasm while hearing the work read aloud.

43. Throughout this review, Lewis refers to *Taliessin through Logres* as "the poem," even though it is a series of poems or a poem cycle.

44. The list of memorial essays and memoirs discussed here is quite selective. For a more complete list, see http://home.earthlink.net/~dbratman.

45. A different poem may also have a link to Williams. According to Hooper, the one published in Lewis's *Poems* and *Collected Poems* under the title "To a Friend" was "originally written 'To C. W.' and later published (1942) as 'To G. M.'" (*Poems* viii). The poem under the original title appears on pages 726–27 of Lewis's *Collected Letters*, volume 2.

46. This poem written by one Inkling in honor of another was apparently inspired by the poetic invention of a third. Describing "To Charles Williams," Lewis explains, "It was an experiment in a metre invented by my friend Barfield, an 8-stressed line with the first six stresses coming in pairs (roughly u- - u- - u- - u- u-) and underlined (to taste) by internal rhymes (call, all – truly, new l[ight] -) consonances (once, wince) or both mixed (can't, cont[tour], slant)." This quote appears in an autographed copy of *Arthurian Torso*, listed for sale in Catalogue Fifty-Nine issued by Nigel Williams Rare Books.

47. Wain adds that everyone who knew Lewis was aware of this "strange dichotomy" ("Great Clerke" 155); Barfield, too, makes a great deal of these aspects of Lewis's character. But I think David Cecil is closer to the mark: he states that "Lewis was by nature a mixture," combining stern intellectualism with boyish romanticism, with hyper-sensitiveness and independence of character ("C. S. Lewis Unmasked" 11).

48. An obituary for Tolkien published in the *Times,* Monday, 3 September 1973, has caused some controversy. In *Tolkien: A Biography,* Carpenter states that the *Times* obituary was "undoubtedly written by C. S. Lewis long before Tolkien's death" (133). But others disagree; the preponderance of evidence supports the conclusion that Carpenter was mistaken. While this obituary appeared in early versions of Hooper's comprehensive bibliography of the works of Lewis, it has since been removed. The obituary has been reprinted in Salu and Farrell under the title "Professor J. R. R. Tolkien: Creator of Hobbits and Inventor of a New Mythology."

8

Creativity
Appreciating
Interaction

*I wish to claim that such multiple authorship—
the collaborative authorship of writings that we
routinely consider the work of a single author—
is quite common, and . . . can be found virtually
anywhere we care to look in English and American
literature of the last two centuries.*
—Jack Stillinger

*By the labour and valour of many I have come into
my inheritance.*
—Aragorn

What I owe to them all is incalculable.
—C. S. Lewis

Throughout these chapters, we have studied selections from diaries, letters, manuscripts, essays, articles, and books to show how the Inklings worked together and influenced each other. I have tried to focus the discussion on the Inklings themselves. However, if writers really do depend on one another in helpful, joyful, and significant ways, as I have argued throughout this book, then one would expect to find each of the Inklings not only interacting with other Inklings, but also embedded in a series of other important creative collaborations. When we look at the larger picture, it is immediately apparent that this is the case.

Of all the Inklings, Tolkien provides the best example of lifelong creative collaboration, and this is true despite the persistent characterization of him as a markedly independent writer. We have already considered the importance of his family members, particularly his son Christopher. Tolkien also valued the participation of his wife, Edith. As Carpenter explains, "She inevitably shared in the family's interest when he was writing *The Hobbit* and *The Lord of the Rings,* and although she was not well acquainted with the details of his books and did not have a deep understanding of them, he did not shut her out from this side of his life." He adds, "Indeed she was the first person to whom he showed two of his stories, *Leaf by Niggle* and *Smith of Wootton Major*; and he was always warmed and encouraged by her approval." Carpenter also notes that the early pages of *The Book of Lost Tales* are copied in Edith's handwriting (*Tolkien* 158).

These influences are commonly acknowledged, but Tolkien's early involvement with the Tea Club and Barrovian Society (TCBS) and his membership in a large number of other literary groups is generally overlooked and underappreciated. The TCBS began in 1911, when Tolkien was 19 years old and a student at King Edward's, an all-boys school in Birmingham.[1] Three of the senior boys—Tolkien, Christopher Wiseman, and Robert Q. Gilson—worked in the school library, and together they formed the nucleus of a clique that met in the library for tea (Carpenter, *Tolkien* 46). Garth notes, "Theirs was an unlikely partnership, but all the richer for it. They discovered that they could argue with an incandescence few friendships could survive, and their disputes only served to seal the intensely strong bond between them" (5).

The TCBS rallied around the challenge of preparing and enjoying tea on the library premises. However, the TCBS took on an increasingly literary nature when Geoffrey Bache Smith joined their ranks. Smith was a bit younger than the others, but he was "a practising poet of some competence" (Carpenter, *Tolkien* 47). And it was "under the influence" of Smith that the club in general and Tolkien in particular "began to wake up to the significance of poetry" (47).

This small but enthusiastic group had a significant impact on Tolkien: they modeled the behavior of poets and storytellers, provided feedback on his drafts in progress, helped him develop his own critical faculties, recommended reading material that supported and shaped his imagination, and suggested that certain pieces be started, reworked, completed, or submitted for publication. It is no small matter that all of this early influence took place within a highly interactive group setting.

When Tolkien arrived as a student at Oxford, he promptly founded a new literary society, the Apolausticks. According to Carpenter, "It was chiefly composed of freshmen like himself. There were papers, discussions, and debates, and there were also large and extravagant dinners" (*Tolkien* 53). In addition, Tolkien and Colin Cullis started a group they called the Chequers, a small group that met for dinner on Saturday nights (69).

There is no evidence that the Apolausticks or the Chequers provided any encouragement for Tolkien's writing. But at about the same time, he joined another club that did: the Essay Club. In a letter dated 27 November 1914, he reports that his poem "The Voyage of Éarendel the Evening Star," was well received and "well criticised" by the members of this group (*Letters* 8). Just as his poetry had thrived at King Edward's School with the TCBS, so now at Oxford his work continued to be produced in the context of interested readers.

The pattern continued. As Tolkien began his teaching career at the University of Leeds, he joined with his colleague E. V. Gordon to establish the Viking Club, a gathering of undergraduates devoted to reading sagas and translating songs and children's tales into Anglo-Saxon and Old Norse. Later, when Tolkien took a position at Oxford, he founded the Coalbiters, a group that consisted not of undergraduates but college dons; as we have seen, it was through the Coalbiters that Tolkien and Lewis became friends.

Much more could be said. Carpenter's biography of Tolkien and Garth's book on Tolkien's early years paint a compelling picture. Tolkien's involvement in groups is impressive; his leadership in founding and developing them is significant; the extent to which his creative imagination was nurtured in them is extraordinary. In short, participation with the Inklings was not an isolated happenstance in Tolkien's life, but rather the continuation of a long-established pattern of working with others. Furthermore, he continued to work in a context of creative interaction even after the Inklings ceased to meet. One particularly compelling example is Tolkien's communication with Clyde S. Kilby as he struggled to complete the work of his heart, *The Silmarillion.*[2] Kilby, a professor of English at Wheaton College, wrote to Tolkien in 1965, expressing his desire to help with *The Silmarillion*:

> I hope you will not feel me impertinent if I make you the following offer: Being eager to see *The Silmarillion* published, I should like to come over to Oxford next summer and render you any help I can. I am 1) a good typist 2) a bit of a literary critic, having written for the largest newspapers in this country 3) an enthusiast for your writings, having conducted last semester a seminar on them at my college, and 4) for many years I have been used to handling every sort of correspondence. I mention these four rather disparate things with the notion of persuading you I could fit in somewhere. (unpublished letter, 19 November 1965)

Kilby wrote to offer practical help, professional expertise, and enthusiastic support. Tolkien saw the need for it and accepted Kilby's offer in a letter written on 18 December 1965: "If I had the assistance of a scholar at once sympathetic and yet critical, such as yourself, I feel I might make some of it publishable. It needs the actual *presence* of a friend and adviser at one's side, which is just what you offer" (*Letters* 366). Tolkien is clearly grateful for the offer of help, but even more so for the physical presence of an interested reader, a friend and adviser, a resonator who comes alongside.

Kilby worked closely with Tolkien in the summer of 1966. He typed up suggestions, doled out encouragement, and helped impose order on the disordered versions of the manuscripts. But in one summer's time, he was able to accomplish little to bring the book closer to publication. Still, Tolkien appreciated the help. Kilby writes, "He kept saying I was doing him a great deal of good."[3] This episode clearly conveys Tolkien's hunger for the presence of others.

Though Charles Williams's history with writing groups and creative collaborators is less consistent than Tolkien's, his writing is also embedded in a long history of influential relationships. Williams produced his earliest poetry under the encouragement and correction of his father. They took long walks when Williams was young, and during that time they talked of many things, including poetry. In an early poem, he describes his father as the one who "taught me all the good I knew" (Hadfield, *Charles Williams* 9). He continues the poetic stanza, praising his father for his help:

What early verse of mine you chid,
Rebuked the use of *doth* and *did,*
    Measuring the rhythm's beat;
Or read with me how Caesar passed,
On the March Ides, to hold his last
    Senate at Pompey's feet! (10)

Williams's first experiences with writing took place with a sympathetic yet critical reader at his side. Other works, especially his poetry and plays, were strongly influenced by other friendships and relationships, especially with his coworkers at Amen House. And later in his life, he frequently gave credit to his wife, Michal, for the inestimable part she played in his work. As Roma King explains, she was as much as anything "the inspiration that kept him on course lest he ascend to heaven in a chariot of fire" (*To Michal* 6). Williams himself put it more simply when he wrote to remind her, "I always told you I needed you at my back to do anything" (18). But she did more than motivate and inspire; she was a severe critic of his work. Williams praises her for her part as editor, taking note of her "slightly surgical knife-way" of putting things (162).

As discussed in chapter 6, C. S. Lewis began his creative life in collaboration with his older brother. As a young college student, Lewis exchanged manuscripts with Owen Barfield and A. C. Harwood, asking for feedback on poems in progress. Lewis also worked with Arthur Greeves, and his debt to Greeves is strikingly evident in an early book, *The Pilgrim's Regress*. In August 1932, Lewis spent two weeks in Belfast with Greeves, and during that time, he drafted all of *The Pilgrim's Regress.* In a letter, he tells Greeves that he will dedicate the book to him: "It is yours by every right—written in your house, read to you as it was written" (*They Stand* 452). In that same letter, he notes that in the process of revising the manuscript, he incorporated many of Greeves's corrections, or at least made alterations at the points where Greeves raised objections (452). Lewis tells him, "So if the book is a ghastly failure I shall always say 'Ah it's this Arthur business'" (452).

Throughout his life, Lewis habitually generated ideas and received feedback from others. In chapter 5, I mentioned his literary interaction with Clifford Morris, his driver, and Douglas Gresham, his stepson. John Wain remembers that as Lewis worked on his monumental contribution to the *Oxford History of English Literature,* he "showed various chapters in typescript to friends who might advise him" ("Great Clerke" 162). He also worked closely with Joy Davidman on a number of projects. He helped her revise her draft of *Smoke on the Mountain,* a study of the Ten Commandments.[4] She gave him feedback on his poetry, collaborated with him on *Till We Have Faces,* and had a significant influence on *The Four Loves* and *Reflections on the Psalms.*[5] As Don W. King notes, it is also likely that she collaborated with Lewis on the Horatian satire "Evolutionary Hymn" and that the two of them "sang it as a parody of *Joyful, Joyful We Adore Thee* or *Lead Us, Heavenly Father, Lead Us*" (*Poet* 345).

Another person who had a strong impact on Lewis's writing is Roger Lancelyn Green. His influence is particularly evident in The Chronicles of Narnia; in fact, Green provided the name for the cycle, inspired by Andrew Lang's Chronicles of Pantouflia (Green and Hooper 245). Green became involved in the project quite early; he read two chapters of *The Lion, the Witch and the Wardrobe* in March 1949 and declared that they were "very good indeed, though a trifle self-conscious" (qtd. in Hooper, *C. S. Lewis* 402).

Green read all seven of the books in manuscript, and his encouragement and criticism shaped the series in a number of ways. He edited the work, removing some stiffness and clichés and "an occasional forced jocularity" (Green and Hooper 241, 256). More substantially, he helped Lewis address the stories to children, for in this period there were very few children in Lewis's life. Lewis had used a lot of slang from his own childhood which by then had become completely obsolete: "Being rather more in touch with contemporary children, Green was able to suggest a number of small alterations and improvements, ranging from the deletion of 'Crikey!' as a common exclamation among the young ('the word "Crikey!" fell from more than one pair of lips,' as Oswald Bastable says in *The Treasure Seekers*) to the omission of bird's-nesting from among the Pevensie children's occupations—Lewis being unaware of the revolution against 'egg-collectors' achieved by Arthur Ransome" (Green and Hooper 242).

Green's most substantial contribution to the series was his objection to a long section in the draft of *The Magician's Nephew.* He visited Lewis when he had completed about three-quarters of this novel. "Green was unhappy about one section of the story: in this section Digory paid several visits to the dying world of Charn, during which he stayed in a farm cottage with an old countryman called Piers and his wife. Green thought they spoke with too laboured a 'Loamshire' accent, and the whole part seemed to him 'too simple and honest and far too long-winded' but most of all 'seemed to him quite out of harmony with the rest of the book'" (Hooper, *C. S. Lewis* 405). Hooper tells us that initially Lewis "was not convinced" by Green's criticism. Lewis set it aside for about two years while he worked on *English Literature in the Sixteenth Century,* bringing that mammoth effort to completion. Then he wrote *The Last Battle.* After that, he revised *The Magician's Nephew,* chopping the entire section about Piers the Plowman from the original draft and recasting what remained. Green heartily approved, writing, "It's a single unity now, and irresistibly gripping and compelling" (qtd. in Hooper, *C. S. Lewis* 405). Lewis later thanked Green for his input, writing, "You can always feel a paternal interest in this tale, for it owes more than half its merit to your shrewdness in discerning and honesty in pointing out, the fatal 'sag' in the original draft" (Green and Hooper 248).

Green worked with Lewis on a number of projects, and Lewis frequently records having read his latest work to Green. Late in his life, Lewis read him the first chapter of *After Ten Years,* the novel he was working on when he died.[6] During that time, Green also records, "He planned to collaborate with me in a new version of my story *The Wood that Time Forgot* which I had written about 1950 and which Lewis always said was my best" (qtd. in Lewis, *Dark Tower* 155–56). Their interaction illustrates that Lewis, like Tolkien and Williams, constantly relied on others as he wrote.

PROFESSIONAL COLLABORATORS

The Inklings worked closely with others throughout their creative lives, and most of them worked collaboratively in their professional lives as well. Charles Williams produced several anthologies with others. He and V. H. Collins compiled *Poems of Home and Overseas.* Williams worked with associate editors David Cecil, Ernest De Selincourt, and E. M. W. Tillyard on *The New Book of English Verse,* and he provided the notes to Edward A. Parker's *A Book of Longer Modern Verse.* And in H. S. Milford's 1928 edition of *The Oxford Book of Regency Verse,* Milford writes, "The selection is at least equally the work of the editor's two friends and collaborators, Mr. Frederick Page and Mr. Charles Williams" (qtd. in Ridler 198). Williams most collaborative work may be his plays, three of which were written and two of which were staged within the context of Amen House. As J. W. Miller observes, "The theatre, of course, is the most collaborative of all the arts" (qtd. in Ede and Lunsford 68).

Lewis was a contributor to two major collaborative undertakings. He participated on the committee to produce an updated version of *Hymns Ancient and Modern.*[7] He also served on the Commission to Revise the Psalms (Hooper, *C. S. Lewis* 93). He worked on the latter with T. S. Eliot, and he came to appreciate him as a colleague and fellow Christian through this collaborative work.[8] Warren Lewis attempted a collaboration with Joy Davidman, a biography of Mme. De Maintenon called *Queen Cinderella.*[9] Adam Fox compiled *English Well Used* with Andrew Claye and compiled *Sacred and Secular: A Companion* with Gareth and Georgina Keene. Dyson's only published book, *Augustans and Romantics,* was written as a joint project with John Butt.[10] Even Havard did much of his medical research as part of a team; he published more than 35 articles, most of them presented under more than one name.[11]

But again, of all the Inklings, Tolkien is perhaps the best example, for professional collaboration can be found throughout his lifetime. Tolkien served on the staff of *The Oxford English Dictionary* "from late 1918 until the spring of 1920" (Hammond and Anderson 278). There he worked on words that begin with the letter W. "At least *wag, walrus, wampum, warm, wasp, water, wick (lamp),* and *winter* were researched by him" (278). Peter M. Gilliver describes the highly collaborative process of dictionary work: "When Tolkien arrived there remained three teams of lexicographers proceeding through separate swathes of the alphabet, each headed by an Editor" (173).[12] Tolkien always spoke with pride of his work on the *OED.* He said that he "learned more in those two years than in any other equal period" of his life, and two of his works of fiction, *Farmer Giles of Ham* and *The Notion Club Papers,* contain references to the work (Carpenter, *Tolkien* 101; Gilliver 174).[13]

Tolkien's next two academic accomplishments were also philological, and collaborative. In 1922, he published *A Middle English Vocabulary,* a small book designed to be used alongside Sisam's *Fourteenth-Century Verse and Prose.* A total of 2,000 copies were printed. Some were bound together with Sisam's volume; others were issued separately (Hammond and Anderson 1). In 1925, Tolkien published a carefully edited edition of *Sir Gawain and the Green Knight,* prepared in collaboration with E. V. Gordon. "Tolkien was responsible for the text and glossary [177 pages], and E. V. Gordon for the greater part of the notes [53 pages]" (Hammond and Anderson 285).

This acclaimed edition is not the only Tolkien/Gordon collaboration. They also coauthored a booklet entitled *Songs for the Philologists.* It contains verses written by Tolkien and Gordon, "as well as modern and traditional songs, chiefly in Old and Modern English, Gothic, Icelandic, and Latin" (Hammond and Anderson 293).[14] There are thirty songs in all, many set to the tunes of popular songs such as "Polly Put the Kettle On" and "Twinkle, Twinkle Little Star" (294).[15]

The publishing history of this booklet is most unusual. It had been privately circulated in typescript, and Dr. A. H. Smith gave a copy to some of his students "to print at their private press as an exercise." When Smith realized he had not asked for permission, he refrained from distributing the booklets. Most of the copies remained at the press, and most of those were burned when the building caught fire (Hammond and Anderson 293).

The complete record of Tolkien's collaborative scholarship is too long to list here; as Hammond and Anderson observe, "He was generous with his time and scholarship in the aid of others, often at the expense of the writings which appeared (or failed to appear) under his own name" (278).[16] One of his most important collaborators is Simonne d'Ardenne, a student who worked with him on her BLitt. degree in Middle English. Her most significant work of scholarship is an edition of *The Life and Passion of St. Juliana;* scholars are unanimous in observing that it "paradoxically contains more of his views on early Middle English than anything he ever published under his own name" (Carpenter, *Tolkien* 140). Hammond and Anderson report "d'Ardenne admitted privately that the book should have been published as a joint work; but published under her name, as her academic thesis, it entitled her to be elected as a university professor" (278). Tolkien and d'Ardenne planned other joint projects, including an edition of another Western Middle English text called *Katerine.* "But the war intervened" (Carpenter, *Tolkien* 140).[17]

Another of Tolkien's professional collaborations is his work on *The Jerusalem Bible.* Hammond and Anderson explain that Tolkien's participation is "nowhere definitively described" (278). Tolkien prepared the original draft of the translation of Jonah (279). It is also reported that he prepared the original draft of the translation of Job (279). He (characteristically) downplayed his role, writing, "I was consulted on one or two points of style, and criticized some contributions of others. I was originally assigned a large amount of text to translate, but after doing some necessary preliminary work I was obliged to resign owing to pressure of other work" (*Letters* 378). Nonetheless, he is named one of the "principal collaborators" on the project.

Creativity in Community

The examples of encouragement, conflict, editing, collaborating, and referencing described in this book are not intended to form a comprehensive or exhaustive list; rather, they have been selected and organized as typical illustrations of the mutual interdependence of these authors. Though we have considered a great deal of material, there is much more written evidence to be explored. The Inklings were prolific writers: there are thousands of pages of manuscripts and piles of letters, notes, and diary entries. In sifting through the pages, we often find only fragmentary evidence of change—a scribbled note on a manuscript, a sentence in a letter, a reference in a diary page—and we are left to fill in the gaps as best we can.

But it is important to remember that even an exhaustive look at every bit of written evidence will not give us the entire picture. There is also the rich context of ongoing conversation: the comments, questions, and suggestions casually shared as the Inklings went about their work. The full extent of encouragement, collaboration, and correction can never be completely known; nonetheless, the written evidence that does remain serves as an outward and visible expression of a much larger and much more complex pattern of creative interaction. And their experience points to a larger reality: creativity thrives in community.

This is true of the Inklings. It is also characteristic, to a greater or lesser extent, of all collaborative circles, including clusters of scientists, journalists, politicians, educators, social reformers, and engineers.[18] When individuals work together, they shape each other's work in various ways. For the Inklings, this included providing inspiration to embark on new projects; offering support in times of discouragement and confusion; shaping texts for proportion, mood, and direction; criticizing drafts so severely that projects were abandoned and sections of documents were deleted; competing in ways that motivated them to continue writing; editing both rough drafts and finished texts; working together to produce joint projects, large and small; creating fictionalized characters based on one another; writing poems about each another; reviewing books and articles written by one another; and including specific references to one another in their work.

There is clear evidence that dozens of different works were significantly changed by the input of this group.[19] Nonetheless, scholars have generally followed in Carpenter's footsteps, asserting that the word "influence" makes "little sense" when discussing the Inklings. I am persuaded that the number of changes and the many different types of changes indicate otherwise. The benefits of their interaction are many and the results highly significant.

In addition to specific alterations made to their texts, it is certain that the overall productivity of the members and the quality of their writing were greatly enhanced by the fact that they worked together. In his discussion of the creative process, Henry James argues that the best things come from "the talents that are members of a group" (25). James continues with a summary of the nature and importance of this kind of creative interaction: "Great things, of course, have been done by solitary workers; but they have usually been done with double the pains they would have cost if they had been produced in more genial circumstances. The solitary worker loses the profit of example and discussion; he is apt to make awkward experiments; he is in the nature of the case more or less of an empiric" (25). Charles Williams articulates this same principle: "Much was possible to a man in solitude. . . . But some things were possible only to a man in companionship, and of these the most important was balance. No mind was so good that it did not need another mind to counter and equal it, and to save it from conceit and blindness and bigotry and folly" (*Place of the Lion* 187).

Both Williams and James observe that though much is possible to those who work alone, the presence of others ameliorates problems, brings balance, provides inspiration, and increases productivity. LeFevre is wise in emphasizing that such creative interaction may do much more than merely help the writer to become more efficient. Her insight is worth repeating: "Certain acts of invention—or certain phases of inventive acts—are best understood if we think of them as being *made possible* by other people" (65, emphasis added). The wording is important: in many cases resonators, opponents, editors, and collaborators do not merely help a project along, prevent mistakes, eliminate false trails, or quicken the pace. Often, these important companions are crucial participants in a project's very existence. Farrell also writes of the transforming power of creative work in community: "Those who are merely good at their discipline become masters, and, working together, very ordinary people make extraordinary advances in their field" (2). In short, none of the Inklings would have written the same things in the same ways if it had not been for the influence of this group.

Attitudes toward Influence

The kind of creative interaction and mutual influence described in these pages is widespread; it characterized the Inklings and it is common in many other times and places. Despite its prevalence, there is a tendency among some scholars to view the discovery of influence as an indication of moral or artistic failure. When it is found, people often feel cheated or at least vaguely disappointed.

These negative attitudes are apparent in our language—even the metaphors we use to describe influence are highly value-laden. We use loaded expressions: the author *echoes* another's phrases, she *overlaps* another's interests, he is *haunted* by another's themes. We use words like *follows, imitates, reflects, mirrors,* and *derives from,* and these terms suggest a deficiency of strength and an inherent lack of wholeness.

The most common words used to describe influence use an economic metaphor: borrow, owe, debt, indebted, debtor. We say *borrow,* as in "borrow an image" or "borrow a stylistic device." Or we talk about one artist's *great debt* to another or to another's work. Hermerén emphasizes, "The economic metaphors used in these questions have normative implications; at least, they do when they are used literally. If X owes 20 dollars to Y, then X ought to pay Y back 20 dollars" (133).

As a result of these prevailing attitudes, studies of influence are frequently marked by disillusionment. It is as if we are saying, "Gee, isn't it a pity. That poor fellow couldn't manage to complete his work all by himself. He had to go and find someone who could help him out." In many cases, influence is viewed as a watered-down form of plagiarism, and the writer or artist who has "succumbed to influence" is seen as somehow weak, wicked, or wanting.[20]

Again, Hermerén's work is critically important in bringing this problem into focus. He agrees that the negative connotations of these words and phrases are really implied accusations and he explains that is why comparative studies often give offense. He writes: "Research into influences has sometimes been strongly resented by artists and writers themselves, and occasionally led them to deny rather obvious influences. Even if the scholar did not intend to make any implications of this sort, statements to the effect that one work of art was influenced by another have frequently been understood as implying accusations of unimaginativeness, lack of originality, plagiarism, theft, and so forth" (133).

Hermerén illustrates his point by citing an article by Fritz Lugt, who argues that Rembrandt's work exhibits strong ties to established artistic traditions and, on this basis, calls Rembrandt's status into question. Hermerén summarizes this misguided line of reasoning this way: Most people think Rembrandt is a great artist. But Lugt is arguing that Rembrandt borrowed from established artistic traditions. If Lugt is right, then Rembrandt must not be as great as is commonly thought (138).[21]

In study after study of influence in visual arts, performance arts, and literary arts, this pattern of erroneous thinking is endemic. This negative view of influence, so common in academic work, shows up in popular literature as well. For example, a 1997 *Newsweek* article reported that a professor at the University of Northern Iowa had just discovered that Wolfgang Amadeus Mozart "worked as a collaborator." David Buch found copies of "two little-known Viennese operas" dating from 1790 and 1791 that "bear Mozart's name on several sections." Astonishment and dismay—the discovery that Mozart was not a solitary genius (their phrase) warranted a notice on *Newsweek*'s Newsmakers page and bore the sarcastic headline, "Wolfgang, Can You Help Me Out Here?" (55).

Harold Bloom has dealt extensively with this attitude, labeling it "the anxiety of influence." In his discussion of the privileging of originality, he emphasizes that in each generation, "every major aesthetic consciousness seems peculiarly more gifted at denying obligation" (6). According to Bloom, the study of influence can be reduced to the "study of the only guilt that matters to a poet, the guilt of indebtedness" (117). If each poet's ultimate guilt is indebtedness, then each poet's ultimate fear is that "no proper work remains for him to perform" (148). To be free of influence is to be free of "the chill of being darkened by a precursor's shadow" (50). Although Bloom focuses his discussion on the anxiety that the artist feels in relation to her or his predecessors, the same anxiety is evident throughout comparative literary studies, even when the interaction of contemporaries is being discussed.

In the introduction to this book, I explain that most of the books and articles written about the Inklings, and even some of the statements made by the Inklings themselves, include emphatic denial of mutual influence. Why is there such a vigorous attempt to deny, or at least minimize, the possibility of influence? As we saw in chapter 2, much of it must be understood as a tendency to confuse influence with imitation. In claiming that Tolkien was not influenced by Lewis, for example, scholars typically mean that his sub-created world does not resemble Malacandra and his creative aesthetic is different from that which envisioned Narnia. Many of the statements made by Inklings scholars, and by the Inklings themselves, deny imitation or similarity rather than influence per se. Lewis's long letter to Charles Moorman is a case in point. An entire generation of scholars has been discouraged from studying or asserting mutual influence as a result of what appears to be the last word on the question: Moorman writes to ask about influence among the Inklings, and Lewis warns him not to "waste time" on a "barren field" (*Letters* 481). But Lewis is clearly talking about similarities, for if you look at his concluding statement, he is not talking about influence but reflecting on when and how they came to hold a "common point of view" (481). Had Moorman recast his question to include encouragement, or opposition, or collaboration, he might have received quite a different reply.

Other denials of influence also make more sense when we examine the exact wording or consider the entire context. For example, as we saw in chapter 5, Tolkien's comments about Lewis's impact on the Saruman passage are easier to understand when the full circumstances are considered. The same thing is true of Lewis's infamous bandersnatch comment. Lewis does say, "No one ever influenced Tolkien—you might as well try to influence a bandersnatch." But his comment is *immediately* qualified: "He has only two reactions to criticism: either he begins the whole work over again from the beginning or else takes no notice at all" (*Letters* 481). Lewis is not saying, as he is often interpreted as saying, that Tolkien could not be changed and that his work could not be influenced. He is saying that Tolkien's creative imagination could not be led about on a leash, calmly pulled step by step in this direction or that. Instead, like a frumious bandersnatch, it would balk and bolt with a mind of its own. But that is far different from the claim that the encouragement, opposition, and suggestions of others made no difference whatsoever.

While misinterpretations of a comment or false assumptions about influence explain some of these denials, another factor helps to account for the pervasiveness and vehemence of these statements. Such defensiveness is often motivated by a desire to protect the worth of individual accomplishment. In other words, to insist that a work is original may, at the heart of it, simply be a way of saying that a work is really good. Defending originality is a way of defending quality. However, the more we come to realize that creativity normally takes place within supportive communities and that creative work is inherently collaborative in nature, the need for such defensiveness is lessened. Or even eliminated.

It may be easier to view influence in a more open, less hostile way if we understand something about its history. A negative attitude toward influence is so prevalent, and the deniers of influence are so adamant, that it may be difficult to see that this attitude is a relatively modern construct. Bloom blames the Cartesian concept of the individual and the "post-Enlightenment passion for Genius and the Sublime" for creating the anxiety of influence (27).[22] Prior to the Enlightenment, the prevailing attitude toward literary influence was quite different from that widely assumed today. It was largely taken for granted, viewed as a necessary and enriching factor in all creative endeavors. For example, rather than using vocabulary that suggests debt and or theft, Ben Jonson defines influence quite matter-of-factly as the ability of the poet to "convert the substance or riches of another poet to his own use" (qtd. in Bloom 27). Later authors shared this point of view. Johann Wolfgang von Goethe took the pervasiveness of influence utterly for granted, writing, "As soon as we are born the world begins to influence us, and this goes on till we die" (qtd. in Bloom 52). Goethe pushes this idea even further. He sees the accomplishments of the past as vital resources for those of the present, asking, "Do not all the achievements of a poet's predecessors and contemporaries rightfully belong to him? Why should he shrink from picking flowers where he finds them? Only by making the riches of the others our own do we bring anything great into being" (qtd. in Bloom 52).

The same view is evident in the following statement about influence from Percy Bysshe Shelley. Shelley not only takes influence for granted, he also offers one of the broadest possible perspectives on the factors that legitimately affect a writer: "Every man's mind is, in this respect, modified by all the objects of nature and art; *by every word and every suggestion which he ever admitted to act upon his consciousness*" (qtd. in Bloom 104, emphasis added).

These positive views of creativity and influence are not particularly radical or far fetched. In fact, they have been prevalent through much of human history. Barfield discusses this idea at some length, and, characteristically, he approaches the subject in light of the evolution of language. He explains that the concept of independent creativity emerges well after the Renaissance in "the story of a superindividual psychology" (*Speaker's Meaning* 78). He uses the history of the word "genius" to illustrate. Before the Renaissance, "genius" is a spirit-being "other than the poet himself," and the poet partners with or is accompanied or inspired by that genius (78). Barfield explains that they would say, "He *has* a genius." After the Renaissance, the inspiration is seen as a part of the poet himself. We now say, "He *is* a genius." The way we use the term demonstrates a significant change in our underlying assumptions.

Lewis explores similar ideas, but he approaches the question historically rather than linguistically. He explains that the current attitude toward originality would be completely foreign to a medieval artist, who might ask, "Spin something out of one's own head when the world teems with so many noble deeds, wholesome examples, pitiful tragedies, strange adventures, and merry jests which have never yet been set forth quite so well as they deserve? The originality which we regard as a sign of wealth might have seemed to them a confession of poverty. Why make things for oneself like the lonely Robinson Crusoe when there is riches all about you to be had for the taking?" (*Discarded* 211). Lewis continues by pointing out this paradox: "It is just this abdication of originality which brings out the originality they really possess" (211–12).[23]

Tolkien also clearly understood this view of creative expression. The true artist does not create something out of nothing; the wise artist understands, even celebrates, this fact. Tolkien uses a particularly potent metaphor as he articulates the writing process: "One writes . . . not out of the leaves of trees still to be observed, nor by means of botany and soil-science; but it grows like a seed in the dark out of the leaf-mould of the mind: out of all that has been seen or thought or read, that has long ago been forgotten, descending into the deeps" (qtd. in Carpenter, *Tolkien* 126).[24]

Jonson, Goethe, and Shelley all celebrate the poet as one who invents within the rich, supportive context of other writers and other works. Tolkien, Barfield, and Lewis align themselves with this long-established view. And here and there other modern and even contemporary writers raise their voices passionately in support of creativity in community. In a recent speech given when he won the Sunburst Award, Cory Doctorow said,

> No writer is an island, no idea is original, no effort is a solo effort. We stand upon the shoulders of giants, we collaborate with our colleagues and with the immortal words of our dead literary ancestors. Literature—indeed, all human endeavor—is dignified and uplifted through collaboration and cooperation. We sit atop a great erected infrastructure of human invention and effort, all of it embodied in the bricks and boards that surround us, and, most importantly, in the traditional knowledge that allows each generation to improve upon the bricks and boards of the last one.[25]

Doctorow, like Tolkien and Shelley before him, is not suspicious of influence but acknowledges it as valuable, welcomes it as typical, and even celebrates it as invigorating. All three appreciate the contribution of "every word and every suggestion" and enjoy the process of incorporating in renewed form "all that has been seen or thought or read." In short, in the normal course of events, all artists work "in the center of a network of cooperating people, all of whose work is essential to the final outcome" (H. Becker 25).

T. S. Eliot takes the same idea one step further. Eliot does not merely see influence as widespread and inevitable; he insists that the poet must make a deliberate and serious effort to seek it out. The result will be a sense of tradition that compels the poet "to write not merely with his own generation in his bones, but with a feeling that the whole of the literature of Europe from Homer and within it the whole of the literature of his own country has a simultaneous existence and composes a simultaneous order" (761).

Furthermore, having urged the poet to immerse himself in tradition, Eliot reproves those critics who reserve their highest praise for those aspects of a poet's work "in which he least resembles anyone else." Eliot argues that it is wiser to do the exact opposite: "If we approach a poet without this prejudice we shall often find that not only the best, but the most individual parts of his work may be those in which the dead poets, his ancestors, assert their immortality most vigorously" (761).

Lewis would agree, arguing that "an author should never conceive himself as bringing into existence beauty or wisdom which did not exist before, but simply and solely as trying to embody in terms of his own art some reflection of eternal Beauty and Wisdom" ("Christianity and Literature" 7). That work which most reflects others is most grounded, most evocative, most valuable, and most praiseworthy. Rather than viewing influence as an indication of moral or artistic failure, those who adopt a positive attitude toward influence welcome the rich contributions of other texts and invite the ongoing participation of other people, past and present, into the creative process. Rather than suspecting that the interdependence of the Inklings somehow lessens the ultimate value of their accomplishments, those who understand the social and collaborative dimensions inherent in all creative processes will appreciate the rich, supportive environment within which these writers worked. To embrace this understanding of the creative process yields a clearer view of the Inklings and a more accurate picture of how writers and other creative people generally go about their work.

Widening Circles

Several important thinkers have used powerful images to express this idea. Michael Oakeshott imagines an ongoing discussion that spans across time, what he calls "The Conversation of Mankind." Michel Foucault articulates a similar vision: "At the moment of speaking, I would like to have perceived a nameless voice, long preceding me, leaving me merely to enmesh myself in it, taking up its cadence, and to lodge myself, when no one was looking, in its interstices as if it had paused an instant, in suspense, to beckon to me. There would have been no beginnings: instead, speech would proceed from me, while I stood in its path—a slender gap—the point of its possible disappearance" (215). Perhaps the best known word picture that captures this perspective is that of Kenneth Burke's "unending conversation":

> Imagine that you enter a parlor. You come late. When you arrive, others have long preceded you, and they are engaged in a heated discussion, a discussion too heated for them to pause and tell you exactly what it is about. In fact, the discussion had already begun long before any of them got there, so that no one present is qualified to retrace for you all the steps that had gone before. You listen for a while, until you decide that you have caught the tenor of the argument; then you put in your oar. Someone answers; you answer him; another comes to your defense; another aligns himself against you. . . . However, the discussion is interminable. The hour grows late, you must depart. And you do depart, with the discussion still rigorously in progress. (110–11)

This description illustrates the extent to which each utterance is embedded in an ongoing exchange, simply one small part of an intergenerational dialogue.

While Burke's expression of this idea may be the best known, the same idea is articulated with particular beauty and ringing clarity by Dorothy L. Sayers. Scorning those scholars who have left Dante "enthroned in a vacuum," she stresses the need to rescue him from the "exalted isolation in which reverential awe has placed him" (*Further Papers* v). This kind of contextual shift is vital to all literary scholarship: "Poets do not merely pass on the torch in a relay race; they toss the ball to one another, to and fro, across the centuries. Dante would have been different if Virgil had never been, but if Dante had never been we should know Virgil differently; across both their heads Ezekiel calls to Blake, and Milton to Homer" (v).

Lewis, Tolkien, and the other Inklings all place significant value on continuity as an essential attribute of the creative process. Tolkien uses three different images in his essay "On Fairy-Stories" that express three facets of this concept. First, Tolkien uses the image of a single tree, what he calls the "Tree of Tales," on which stories exist as branches "intricately knotted" (22). Second, he conceives of all stories everywhere existing as parts of a tapestry or web, an image that implies the work of many hands, many colors, many times, all contributing to one enormous, seamless, single work. In describing this intricate web, "beyond all skill but that of the elves to unravel," he emphasizes the complex relationships among stories, as well as their interdependence (23). Finally and most powerfully, he uses the image of a cauldron: "Speaking of the history of stories and especially of fairy-stories we may say that the Pot of Soup, the Cauldron of Story, has always been boiling, and to it have continually been added new bits, dainty and undainty" (28). By selecting these specific metaphors—tree, tapestry, web, and cauldron—Tolkien emphasizes that each individual creative act is a participant in something large, complex, and beautiful.

Tolkien illustrates this idea in practical terms when he answers a letter from Carey Blyton, who asks for permission to compose a *Hobbit Overture*. Rather than bristling at the idea, expressing some sort of proprietary privilege, Tolkien responds to the request with generosity and graciousness: "You certainly have my permission to compose any work that you wished based on *The Hobbit*." He not only enthusiastically grants permission, he leaves the nature of the work completely unrestricted. His open-handed attitude is further clarified as he adds, "As an author I am honoured to hear that I have inspired a composer. I have long hoped to do so" (*Letters* 350). In fact, Tolkien cherished this idea early in his creative process, writing that in imagining a mythology for England, his plan was to "leave scope for other minds and hands, wielding paint and music and drama" (145).[26]

C. S. Lewis's invitation to other writers to carry on with his Narnia stories takes the idea of creative continuity a step further. Having created this fantasy world and written seven books of adventures that take place there, Lewis encouraged his readers to take up where he left off and continue the conversation.[27] For example, when Lewis writes to young Sydney on 14 February 1962, he explains, "I'm afraid I've said all I had to say about Narnia, and there will be no more of these stories. But why don't you try to write one yourself? I was writing stories before I was your age, and if you try, I'm sure you would find it great fun. Do!" (*Letters to Children* 101–2).

Sydney isn't the only one invited into the conversation. Lewis asks Jonathan, "Why don't *you* try writing some Narnian tales? I began to write when I was about your age, and it was the greatest fun. Do try!" (*Letters to Children* 99). And here is a third example, written to another child later that same year:

Dear Denise

I am delighted to hear that you liked the Narnian books, and it was nice of you to write and tell me. There *is* a map at the end of some of them in some editions. But why not do one yourself! And why not write stories for yourself to fill up the gaps in Narnian history? I've left you plenty of hints—especially where Lucy and the Unicorn are talking in *The Last Battle*. I feel *I* have done all I can! (104)

"The powerful play goes on," as Walt Whitman would say, and here Lewis invites Sydney, Jonathan, and Denise to contribute their part. To be sure, he is writing to children here, children who are unlikely to publish these works or find a way to profit from them. Still, the mood is indicative. Far from a closed sense of finished text, or a proprietary sense of ownership, Lewis sees his work as open to these participants.

The Inklings emphasize participation in their reflections on creativity and in their creative work as well. No one expresses this idea better than Tolkien, who illustrates this powerfully in a scene central to his work on Middle-earth. In *The Return of the King*, as Frodo is wrapping up his estate before leaving the Shire for good, he goes through his papers with Sam Gamgee and hands him his keys (1003). Frodo also passes on another "key." In addition to inheriting Frodo's house and his treasure, Sam stands in line to inherit something far more important: "There was a big book with plain red leather covers; its tall pages were now almost filled. At the beginning there were many leaves covered with Bilbo's thin wandering hand; but most of it was written in Frodo's firm flowing script. It was divided into chapters but Chapter 80 was unfinished, and after that were some blank leaves" (1003–4). The big book is the Red Book of Westmarch. It was begun a generation earlier as a record of Bilbo's memoirs: "There and Back Again, a Hobbit's Holiday" (*Hobbit* 316). To this, Frodo has added his own account of the War of the Ring, "with the aid of his friends' recollections" (Tyler 486). At this point, Tolkien tells us, the "title page had many titles on it" (*Return* 1004). There are seven to be exact, each drafted, then reconsidered, then crossed out. There has been a great deal of editing and revision along the way. Frodo has settled on the current title, now calling the book

THE DOWNFALL

OF THE

LORD OF THE RINGS

AND THE

RETURN OF THE KING

(as seen by the Little People; being the memoirs of Bilbo and Frodo of the Shire, supplemented by the accounts of their friends and the learning of the Wise.) Together with extracts from Books of Lore translated by Bilbo in Rivendell. (1004)

As Frodo gives him the large red book, Sam looks down at it in wonder. "Why, you have nearly finished it, Mr. Frodo!" he exclaims.

Frodo's answer is gentle, but certain: "I have quite finished, Sam," he says. Then he adds, "The last pages are for you" (1004).

The Red Book that tells the story of the Third Age of Middle-earth is a great collaborative work, based on ancient manuscripts and built upon stories told by Bilbo and Frodo and Sam in turn. The Red Book of Westmarch, like the adventure it describes, is shaped collaboratively.[28]

CONCLUSION

Ultimately, confidence in an ongoing, interdependent creative community has a strong foundation in the Christian faith, a vital link that the Inklings had in common. It is reflected, for example, in the doctrine of the communion of the saints, a central tenet of the Anglican Church, to which Lewis, Williams, Dyson, Coghill, and Fox belonged. It is expressed in the closing prayer of Compline in *The Book of Common Prayer,* which includes this petition: "Grant that we may never forget that our common life depends upon each other's toil" (34).

Accepting the pervasiveness of mutual influence and mutual interdependence is also consistent with Williams's most foundational beliefs, co-inherence and exchange. Co-inherence is a term used by early church fathers to express the unity within the Trinity, the unity of all Christian believers, and the unity of divine and human in the incarnation of Jesus Christ. It was a term of particular significance to Samuel Taylor Coleridge and the other romantic poets. Hadfield describes co-inherence this way: "Christ gave his life for us, and his risen life is in each one if we will to accept it. Simply as men and women, without being self-conscious or portentous, we can share in this life within the divine co-inherence of the Trinity, and in so doing live as members one of another. In our degrees of power, intelligence, love or suffering, we are not divided from God or each other, for Christ's nature is not divided" (*Charles Williams* 32). The idea of co-inherence is not unique to Williams or to the Inklings.[29] Helen Tyrrell Wheeler observes that co-inherence was so important in the 1940s that it "seemed to be the banner word of the time." She hypothesizes that the reason students flocked to hear the lectures given by Williams and Lewis was "to have revealed the *coinherence* of the most disparate texts, times, dilemmas, and ideas" (50).

Williams also used the term "exchange" to describe what it means to live as members of one another. As Roma King explains, Williams "assumes that the whole cosmos is an organism in which all parts are interrelated, inter-dependent, co-inhering, matter and spirit, body and soul" (*Pattern* 18).

Thomas Howard offers the following overview of Williams's theories, and his discussion is particularly helpful since it puts the ideas of Charles Williams and the concept of writers working in community in a larger perspective:

> [Williams] realized that the peace and well-being he enjoyed in England were due to the sacrifices being made by the young men in the trenches of France. In other words, everyone in England owed his life to these men who were laying down theirs.
>
> It seemed to Williams that here was a principle. Everyone, all the time, owes his life to others. It is not only in war that this is true. We cannot eat breakfast without being nourished by some life that has been laid down. If our breakfast is cereal or toast, then it is the life of grains of wheat that have gone into the ground and died that we might have food. If it is bacon, then the blood of some pig has been shed for the sake of my nourishment. All day long I live on this basis: some farmer's labor has produced this wheat and someone else's has brought it to market and so on. . . .
>
> Williams coupled this idea of exchange with two other ideas, namely, "substitution" and "co-inherence," but they all come to the same thing. There is no such thing as life that does not owe itself to the life and la-bor of someone else. It is true all the way up and down the scale of life, from our conception which owes itself to the self-giving of a man and

a woman to each other; through my daily life where I find courtesies such as a door held open if I have a package; . . . to the highest mystery of all in which a life was laid down so that we might all have eternal life. (11–12)

From the death of a grain of wheat to the death of his Lord Jesus Christ, Williams saw all of life as interdependent on the sacrifices and support of one another.[30] Williams was convinced that the nature of heaven was the fulfillment of life in community, and that the tragedy of hell was the isolation of individual from individual, as well as individual from God.

From these philosophical foundations flows the conviction that each author's work is embedded in the work of others, and each author's life is intertwined with the lives of others. It is a perspective that stands in sharp contrast to the common view that creativity is the achievement of a solo author, a solo discoverer, a solo genius.

I am persuaded that writers do not create text out of thin air in a fit of personal inspiration. I believe that the most common and natural expressions of creativity occur as part of an ongoing dialogue between writers, readers, texts, and contexts. This truth is exemplified by the weekly meetings of the Inklings. It is manifest in their relationships with family, friends, colleagues, and acquaintances. And it is expressed in many of their own statements about the creative process. As Williams reminds us, an emphasis on isolated individuals must give way to an interactive view of life, culture, and creativity. Explaining Williams's view, Roma King summarizes, "The parts are so related that the slightest vibration in one is felt throughout the whole, and a break in one is a break in the organism. Each filament exists for the web and not the web for the filament" (*Pattern* 18–19). Like filaments joined together in a web, writers work as members of larger communities. As they work, they influence and are influenced by the company they keep.

NOTES

1. In *Tolkien and the Great War,* John Garth gives an extensive account of the TCBS and its important role in Tolkien's development as a writer.

2. Kilby's description of their time together is recounted in a slim book titled *Tolkien and The Silmarillion.*

3. This comment is found on page 7 of an article by Clyde S. Kilby published in the January 1980 edition of *The Minas-Tirith Evening Star.*

4. Joy Davidman dedicated this book to C. S. Lewis; he wrote the foreword to the British edition.

5. Dorsett gives the following account of their work on *Till We Have Faces:* "While Lewis was on break from Cambridge, he and Warnie invited Joy to visit. During this week at the Kilns she was writing, Warnie was writing, and Jack was mentally paralyzed" (*And God* 116). C. S. Lewis and Joy Davidman settled into the living room and began to work together. Davidman

reports, "We kicked a few ideas around till one came to life. Then we had another whiskey each and bounced it back and forth between us" (116). The idea that "came to life" was to explore the Cupid and Psyche myth. Davidman writes, "The next day, without further planning, he wrote the first chapter! I read it and made some criticisms." Then Lewis "did it over and went on with the next" (116–17). The book continued in this way, writing, critiquing, rewriting, chapter by chapter. She describes her part this way: "I can tell him how to write more like himself! He is now about three-quarters of the way through his new book . . . and says he finds my advice indispensable" (117). For more on their relationship and mutual influence, see my article "Joy Davidman Lewis."

6. Five chapters of this novel, which is set at the end of the Trojan War, can be found in Lewis's *Of Other Worlds* (1966) and *The Dark Tower* (1977).

7. In a letter dated 24 November 1944, Tolkien remarks that Lewis "has been on the Committee revising Ancient and Modern Hymns," and that this involvement led to a discussion of the nature of hymns in an Inklings meeting (103).

8. Lewis's opinion of T. S. Eliot is generally oversimplified and his appreciation for Eliot's work underestimated. For a helpful corrective to these persistent misperceptions, see Charles A. Huttar's "C. S. Lewis, T. S. Eliot, and the Milton Legacy."

9. There are a number of references to *Queen Cinderella* in Joy Davidman's (unpublished) letters. In his "Memoir of C. S. Lewis," Warren Lewis explains that "several books of notes and an explanatory preface" were completed prior to Davidman's death (45).

10. According to the reviews (there is no specific evidence in the book itself), Dyson wrote the text and Butt compiled the bibliography.

11. In medical papers and other scientific research, there is already a strong (and enviable) tradition of attributing the publication to all of those who participated in collaborative research, not just to the individual who either headed the project or drafted the final report. Havard published medical research in two phases: approximately fifteen papers during his medical research career, 1925–35, and more than twenty as part of the Army Malaria Research Unit during World War II. Only five of them appear under Havard's name alone. Bratman clarifies, "Brian Maegraith is the chief author of most of the Malaria Research Unit papers, so they can be seen as collaborative scientific work (not writing work: the writing was probably done by just one of them) done by the group under his direction" (personal correspondence, 23 November 2004).

12. Peter M. Gilliver's "At the Wordface" details Tolkien's work on the *OED*. Gilliver worked on the *OED* as a lexicographer, bringing an insider's understanding of this great collaboration. His article includes several facsimiles of handwritten working notes and actual dictionary entries. He also lists more than thirty words that he believes Tolkien worked on.

13. Tolkien felt a strong investment in the *OED*. McClusky writes, "When his publishers pointed out that 'dwarves' was actually spelled 'dwarfs,' using the *Oxford English Dictionary* as its source, Tolkien not only refused to change it but added, 'After all, I *wrote* the *Oxford English Dictionary*'" (36). John Tolkien and Priscilla Tolkien offer a version of this same story on page 42 of *The Tolkien Family Album*.

14. These humorous verses are unsigned; Tolkien identifies himself as the author of thirteen of them. One of them, "The Root of the Boot," is an early version of Tolkien's poem "The Stone Troll" (Hammond and Anderson 294).

15. Four of these poems (three in Old English and one in Gothic) have been reprinted with translations in appendix A of T. A. Shippey's *The Road to Middle-Earth*.

16. Those interested in knowing more about Tolkien's collaborative works will find them listed in Hammond and Anderson's *J. R. R. Tolkien*. Another Tolkien academic book has a small but interesting Inklings tie. When Alan Bliss edited Tolkien's Finn and Hengest lectures, J. A. W. Bennett lent Bliss his notes on Tolkien's lectures to use as a reference point (Bliss ix).

17. D'Ardenne has written a brief memoir of her work with Tolkien, published in Salu and Farrell's *J. R. R. Tolkien, Scholar and Storyteller*.

18. See Michael J. Farrell's important book *Collaborative Circles* for a readable and wide-ranging discussion of collaboration in psychology, politics, and literature.

19. David Bratman and I have compiled a list of close to fifty titles by Inklings that are known to have been read by other Inklings prior to publication. This list may be accessed at http://home. apu.edu/~dglyer/.

20. In the appendix to his book *Multiple Authorship,* Jack Stillinger lists ninety-six British and American writers who worked collaboratively. His list includes Wordsworth, Coleridge, Austen, Byron, Keats, Dickens, Hardy, Wilde, Shaw, Joyce, Lawrence, Orwell, Beckett, Pym, Irving, Emerson, Hawthorne, Melville, Dickinson, Twain, Dreiser, Crane, Sinclair, Stevens, Eliot, O'Neill, Buck, Hammett, Cummings, Faulkner, Hemingway, Wolfe, Hurston, Stone, Wright, Vonnegut, Updike, Plath, and even Jack Kerouac, Stephen King, and Jacqueline Susann. He emphasizes that his list is representative rather than exhaustive, and it contains only those works "for which there exists some kind of extrinsic (biographical or other documentary) evidence" (204).

21. Kath Filmer attacks Lewis in exactly this way in *C. S. Lewis: Mask and Mirror.* She lists the following sources for his fiction: *The Pilgrim's Regress* is based on *The Pilgrim's Progress; Out of the Silent Planet* draws from *The First Men in the Moon; Perelandra* imitates *Paradise Lost; That Hideous Strength* is inspired by G. K. Chesterton and Charles Williams; The Chronicles of Narnia "echo" Edith Nesbit, Beatrice Potter [*sic*], and Lewis Carroll (6). Filmer is quick to reassure her readers that "none of this necessarily means, of course, that Lewis's work lacks value." Nonetheless, she uses this long list of texts to make this point: "The tendency to rely on deconstructing and reconstructing the work of other authors betrays in Lewis qualities of reticence and insecurity" (6). I question her list of "sources," and I disagree with her conclusion.

22. Both Bloom and Hermerén cite Edward Young's "Conjectures on Original Composition," published in 1759, as the strongest critical statement to blatantly privilege originality, or freedom from influence. Young foreshadows the Romantic temperament, encouraging the poet to reject the accomplishments of the past and be completely himself: "Dive deep into thy bosom; learn the depth, extent, bias, and full forte of thy mind" (336).

Young cites three great reasons to refuse the "taint" of imitation: first, it is impossible for a poet to outdo a predecessor just as it is impossible for a pyramid to overreach its base or a stream to rise higher than its spring; second, to copy something is to thwart Nature herself (who brings forth only originals, no two minds or two faces alike) and to replace high human achievement with the mimicry of a monkey; third, writers who imitate think little and write much, producing fat portfolios which are "little better than more reputable cushions to promote our repose" (334). Instead, Young insists that the true poet must reject "the soft fetters of easy imitation" (331), must not shade his writing from "the beams of [his] own genius; for nothing original can rise, nothing immortal, can ripen, in any other sun" (331). Even the most excellent imitator shares his applause and divides his crown. The imitator builds on another's foundation, and therefore "his debt is, at least, equal to his glory; which therefore, on the balance, cannot be very great" (330).

Young is an early and energetic proponent of this view, but he is by no means the only one. Wordsworth, Coleridge, Keats, Schopenhauer, Baudelaire, and others would, to a greater or lesser extent, agree with him. Bloom lists the following individuals among what he calls the "great deniers" of influence: Nietzsche and Mann in Germany; Emerson and Thoreau in America; Blake and Lawrence in England; and Rousseau and Hugo in France (56). It is not coincidental that these men largely subscribe to the Romantic view of individual, inspired Genius, a point of view criticized by LeFevre, Ede and Lunsford, and other compositionists cited above. Nonetheless, this attitude of suspicion remains common in studies of artistic and literary influence, obscuring our ability to perceive influences and dominating our interpretation of them when they are found.

23. Austin Farrer's description of C. S. Lewis provides a telling illustration of this principle: "Everything went into that amazing capacity of mind, his living friends as much as the authors on his shelves. Not to name those who are still with us, his debts in personal wisdom and in literary inspiration to his wife and to Charles Williams were visible to all. He had no affectation of originality. He did not need it" (385).

24. Tolkien also uses the idea of the "leaf-mould of the mind" in a letter to a reader about the origin of the names Gamgee and Gondor. Tolkien explains, "One's mind is, of course, stored with a 'leaf-mould' of memories (submerged) of names, and these rise up to the surface at times, and may provide with modification the bases of 'invented' names" (*Letters* 409).

25. In 2004, Cory Doctorow received the Sunburst award for best Canadian Science Fiction Book for *A Place So Foreign and Eight More*. My thanks to David Bratman for locating this quotation at http://www.boingboing.net/2004/09/24/corys_sunburst_accep.html (accessed 29 April 2006) and bringing it to my attention.

26. Tolkien supported Carey Blyton's artistic interpretation wholeheartedly. We see the same generosity expressed some time later in his dealing with Donald Swann, who set some of Tolkien's poems to music in a song cycle he called *The Road Goes Ever On*. However, he did not countenance anyone who tampered with his stories, proposed sequels to his work, or hoped to publish new stories that used the same characters or were set in the same world. For Tolkien, that was another matter entirely. In the list of creative works he hoped to inspire, he allowed for "paint and music and drama," but he made no such allowance for other literary arts such as poetry or fiction. I am grateful to Joe R. Christopher for bringing this important quotation to my attention.

27. Apparently such requests for more of Narnia continued long after C. S. Lewis had died. In a 1971 letter to Edward Allen, Warren Lewis writes, "I'm not up to date myself with my brother's sales, but last time I saw any figures, the Narnian romances were the big money spinners; certainly I get more fan mail about them than about any of the others. A sad business children from all over America continue to write to my brother begging him to write another Narnain [*sic*] story; I doubt if the death of CSL made the American papers at all, for it was the same day that Kennedy was killed that he died" (unpublished letter, 8 Jan. 1971).

28. In *The New Tolkien Companion*, J. E. A. Tyler offers a 251-word history of the book as it continues from Samwise to Elanor and then on to others. The fact that such a lengthy history has been so carefully articulated, offers compelling testimony to Tolkien's view of story in general, and this story in particular.

29. T. S. Eliot also explored the concept of co-inherence. For an insightful discussion, see chapter 4 of *A Purgatorial Flame* by Sebastian Knowles.

30. This perspective is also expressed memorably by Martin Luther King Jr.: "We are everlasting debtors to known and unknown men and women. When we arise in the morning, we go into the bathroom and reach for a sponge provided for us by a Pacific islander. We reach for soap that is created for us by a European. Then at the table we drink coffee which is provided for us by a South American, or tea by a Chinese, or cocoa by a West African. Before we leave for our jobs we are already beholden to more than half the world" (211).

The Inklings
Their Lives and Works

by David Bratman

The brief essays that follow are intended to introduce the reader to the lives, scholarly interests, and major works of each of the nineteen "canonical" Inklings listed by Humphrey Carpenter in *The Inklings* (255–59). Many of them did not write fiction, but their scholarship, memoirs, essays, and letters are of interest to those exploring the thought of the Inklings.

Some of the Inklings were quite prolific, and not all their published books are included here. For the three central Inklings, C. S. Lewis, J. R. R. Tolkien, and Charles Williams, whose major works are well known and for whom extensive guidebooks are available, the listings here are particularly abbreviated. The books listed are selected for their importance and interest for the student of the Inklings. Dates are of first publication in book form; some important revisions are noted. Shorter works, such as journal articles, and unpublished works are generally not listed, though some of these are of considerable interest.

Humphrey Carpenter describes his list as consisting of those men "who often came to the Thursday evening gatherings at Magdalen" (*Inklings* 255–59). Strictly defined, they are the attendees who are identified as having been present in a regular, "member" capacity. Others known to have attended Thursday evening gatherings as guests or occasional visitors included H. S. (Stanley) Bennett, Roy Campbell, E. R. Eddison, Warfield M. Firor, Gerard Hopkins, Raymond Hunt, Gwyn Jones, and George Sayer. A number of others attended only Inklings pub sessions.

For readers interested in further information, full bibliographies and useful overviews (books or articles) of an Inkling's life and work are noted when they exist. Further bibliographical details and complete handlists of each Inkling's books are available on my website at http://home.earthlink.net/~dbratman/inklings.html.

BARFIELD, OWEN (1898–1997)

Arthur Owen Barfield met C. S. Lewis when they were both undergraduates at Oxford, probably in late 1919. He read English at Wadham College from 1919 to 1921, when he received his BA. He then wrote a BLitt thesis, which became his book *Poetic Diction* (1928). During the 1920s, Barfield lived outside Oxford and was in regular contact with Lewis both in person and by mail. This was the period in which they engaged in the "Great War." In 1930, Barfield moved to London to begin work as a lawyer. From this time his friendship with Lewis had to subsist on correspondence, occasional visits, and continuations of their annual walking tours made in company with mostly non-Inklings friends.

Barfield attended the Inklings rarely enough that he considered himself a visitor rather than a member ("Inklings Remembered" 549). But he was one of Lewis's closest friends, and his early philosophical work had a great effect on both Lewis and Tolkien, so most scholars consider him one of the most important Inklings. He did most of his writing during the 1920s, before becoming a lawyer, and in the 1960s and 1970s after his retirement.

Barfield was a philosopher of language, interested in the role of language in the perception of reality, whose work is particularly difficult to divide between fiction and non-fiction. He published only one book that is unambiguously a novel, a children's story in the tradition of George MacDonald titled *The Silver Trumpet* (1925). But several of his philosophic works are in semi-fictionalized narrative or dialogue form and can also be considered novels. *This Ever Diverse Pair* (1950) is a somewhat whimsical parable separating the two halves of the author's life—the dull but dependable lawyer and the impractical poet and philosopher—into two personalities who compete for attention. *Worlds Apart: A Dialogue of the 1960s* (1963) and *Unancestral Voice* (1965) are mixtures of narrative and dialogue presenting symposia among a number of characters—some of them based on the author and his friends—offering differing viewpoints on philosophical issues. Barfield's sole published play is *Orpheus: A Poetic Drama,* edited by John C. Ulreich Jr. (1983), a retelling of myth first performed in 1948. The collection *A Barfield Sampler: Poetry and Fiction,* edited by Jeanne Clayton Hunter and Thomas Kranidas (1993), contains poems, a few short stories, and an excerpt from his unpublished novel *English People.*

Barfield claimed that his books say the same thing over and over again, so it may be difficult to identify his most important non-fiction. But many readers point to *Poetic Diction: A Study in Meaning* (1928) as his most fundamental work; it is unquestionably the work that made the greatest contribution to the thinking of his fellow Inklings. In it, he argues that the history of human consciousness may be traced in the history of language, and that separations between the metaphorical and the literal, the spiritual and the mundane, disappear in early thought. *History in English Words* (1926) provides specific examples of the general thesis. *Saving the Appearances: A Study in Idolatry* (1957) argues that what we call "reality" is in large part a result of our subjective perceptions.

The essays in *Romanticism Comes of Age* (1944, rev. 1967) are mostly literary studies reflected through Barfield's interest in anthroposophy. A second collection, *The Rediscovery of Meaning and Other Essays* (1977), includes the important essay "The Rediscovery of Allegory" and Barfield's contribution to *Essays Presented to Charles Williams* (1947), "Poetic Diction and Legal Fiction." Barfield wrote a great deal about Lewis and their friendship; a selection of this work is published in *Owen Barfield on C. S. Lewis,* edited by G. B. Tennyson (1989).

Barfield's unpublished works include two novels (*English People* and *Eager Spring*), a play on Medea, and many poems, including the long poem, *The Mother of Pegasus*. Some of this work is held at the Marion E. Wade Center.

Several books discuss the influence of Barfield's philosophy. Three are of particular interest to Inklings readers: *C. S. Lewis's "Great War" with Owen Barfield* by Lionel Adey (1978), an account of their 1920s philosophical debate; *Splintered Light: Logos and Language in Tolkien's World* by Verlyn Flieger (1983, rev. 2003); and *Romantic Religion: A Study of Barfield, Lewis, Williams and Tolkien* by R. J. Reilly (1971). A complete bibliography of Barfield's published work up to 1974 is in a Festschrift: "A Bibliography of the Works of Owen Barfield" by G. B. Tennyson, in *Evolution of Consciousness: Studies in Polarity,* edited by Shirley Sugerman (1976).

BENNETT, J. A. W. (1911–1981)

Jack Arthur Walter Bennett, known as Jack or occasionally Jaw, came to Oxford from New Zealand in 1933 to study English at Merton College. He attended lectures by J. R. R. Tolkien and C. L. Wrenn and received his PhD in 1938 (Hooper, *C. S. Lewis* 627). He continued as a junior research fellow at Queen's College, interrupted by a period working for British Information Services in the U. S. during World War II. The only record of his attending the Inklings is of two Thursday meetings in 1946 (W. H. Lewis, *Brothers* 193–94). In 1947 Bennett was elected a fellow and tutor in English Language at Magdalen College, where he assisted C. S. Lewis, and he attended faculty and private dinners with Lewis and other Inklings. He succeeded Lewis as Professor of Medieval and Renaissance Literature at Cambridge in 1964, delivering a notable tribute to his predecessor in his inaugural lecture.

Bennett became a distinguished scholar of Middle English literature, specializing in Chaucer. He wrote three major studies of that author, the latter two in the form of lecture series: *The Parlement of Foules: An Interpretation* (1957), *Chaucer's Book of Fame: An Exposition of "The House of Fame"* (1960), and *Chaucer at Oxford and at Cambridge* (1974). He edited Chaucer's *The Knight's Tale* for Harrap's English Classics series (1954). He also prepared editions of works by John Gower, William Langland, and other authors. His *Early Middle English Verse and Prose,* edited with G. V. Smithers (1966), became a standard textbook. He assembled a collection of *Essays on Malory* (1963), which includes a contribution by C. S. Lewis. From 1957 to his death in 1981 he was editor of the journal *Medium Aevum,* to which several Inklings contributed.

A collection of Bennett's essays was published soon after his death as *The Humane Medievalist and Other Essays in English Literature and Learning, from Chaucer to Eliot,* edited by Piero Boitani (1982). The title essay is his inaugural lecture as Professor of Medieval and Renaissance Literature at Cambridge. Bennett's last major project, the volume for the Oxford History of English Literature on *Middle English Literature,* was completed after his death by Douglas Gray and published in 1986.

A complete bibliography of Bennett's published work to 1980 is in a Festschrift: "A List of the Published Writings of J. A. W. Bennett" by P. L. Heyworth, in *Medieval Studies for J. A. W. Bennett,* edited by Heyworth (1981). This volume also contains memoirs of Bennett's life and work.

CECIL, LORD DAVID (1902–1986)

Edward Christian David Gascoyne-Cecil, younger son of the 4th Marquess of Salisbury, read history at Christ Church, Oxford, from 1920. He received his BA in 1924 and became a fellow and lecturer in Modern History at Wadham College, until he resigned in 1930 to become a full-time writer. He returned to Oxford in 1939 as a fellow and tutor in English at New College, becoming the first Goldsmiths' Professor of English there in 1948. He retired in 1969.

Cecil published a few poems in his youth, but his other published work is all non-fiction. He was an evaluative and appreciative critic rather than a textual scholar as many of the other Inklings were. His specialty was late-eighteenth- and early-nineteenth-century literature; he felt a particular affinity to Jane Austen and published *A Portrait of Jane Austen* (1978). He also published studies on *Early Victorian Novelists: Essays in Revaluation* (1934) and *Hardy the Novelist: An Essay in Criticism* (1943). His training as an historian emerged in several biographies, of which *Melbourne* (on Lord Melbourne, Queen Victoria's first prime minister, first published in two parts in 1939 and 1954) and *Max: A Biography* (on Sir Max Beerbohm, the Edwardian satirist and caricaturist, published 1964) remain most renowned. His *Two Quiet Lives* (on Dorothy Osborne and Thomas Gray, published 1948) was read to the Inklings.

Cecil published two essay collections, *Poets and Story-Tellers: A Book of Critical Essays* (1949) and *The Fine Art of Reading and Other Literary Studies* (1957). His edited volumes include *The Oxford Book of Christian Verse* (1940) and a commonplace book, *Library Looking-Glass: A Personal Anthology* (1975).

J. R. R. Tolkien comments that Cecil's wide "interests would seem to be far removed" from those of the Inklings (*Letters* 122). Humphrey Carpenter does not see Cecil as "spiritually an Inkling," but describes him as a distinguished and "most welcome visitor" (*Inklings* 187). Cecil was more than a once or twice visitor, however. He attended Thursday Inklings throughout the 1940s and Tuesday morning pub sessions at least through the end of the decade. He formed personal friendships with Coghill, Lewis, Williams, and Tolkien. In later years he saw Lewis most frequently in the company of their mutual friend Ruth Pitter. He discussed the Inklings as a group in a conversation with Rachel Trickett transcribed as "Is There an Oxford 'School' of Writing?" in *Twentieth Century* 157 (1955): 559–70.

The fullest description of Cecil's personality and work is *David Cecil: A Portrait by His Friends*, edited by Hannah Cranborne (1990). A Festschrift has been published as *Essays and Poems Presented to Lord David Cecil*, edited by W. W. Robson (1970).

COGHILL, NEVILL (1899–1980)

Nevill Henry Kendal Aylmer Coghill was of Anglo-Irish birth. He read History and English at Exeter College, Oxford, from 1919, receiving his BA in 1923. As secretary of the college Essay Club in 1920, he invited Tolkien to read a paper. He met C. S. Lewis when they took a class together in 1923, and the two quickly became friends. After a year teaching at the Royal Naval College, Coghill became a research fellow at Exeter in 1924 and a regular fellow and tutor in English the following year. He remained there until becoming Merton Professor of English Literature in 1957, a position he held until his retirement in 1966.

Coghill was one of the founding members of the Coalbiters in 1926. He also participated in The Cave. From these clubs he naturally became an early member of the Inklings. Barfield recalled at least one nascent Inklings meeting in the 1920s that Coghill attended (Barfield, "Inklings Remembered" 548). Coghill introduced Lewis to Hugo Dyson in 1930, and he introduced Lewis to the work of Charles Williams by lending him a copy of *The Place of the Lion* in 1936. By the war years, other interests had come to occupy Coghill's time and he ceased attending Thursday Inklings. He did visit Tuesday pub sessions for some time, however, and he maintained his friendships with Lewis, Dyson, and others.

Coghill's main scholarly interests were Shakespeare, Chaucer, and Langland, but his true specialty was drama as a genre rather than any specific author or period. He gained some renown and taught himself a great deal by producing plays—especially Shakespeare—for the Oxford University Dramatic Society. Undergraduates including John Wain and Roger Lancelyn Green performed in these. In 1967, Coghill adapted Marlowe's *Doctor Faustus* for the screen and co-directed the film with the leading actor, Richard Burton, another former pupil. After receiving several requests to recite Chaucer's poetry for special occasions, he translated the whole of *The Canterbury Tales* (1951), *Troilus and Criseyde* (1971), and *A Choice of Chaucer's Verse* (1972) into informal modern English verse. He made several recordings reading Chaucer and other poets. In collaboration with Christopher Tolkien, he edited the original texts of three of the *Canterbury Tales* for Harrap's English Classics: *The Pardoner's Tale* (1958), *The Nun's Priest's Tale* (1959), and *The Man of Law's Tale* (1969).

This work—plus some original plays in early-modern pastiche verse, satirical rhymes in the 1930s for the *Oxford Magazine* under the name of Judson, and class notes written up in pastiche verse in the 1920s—made Coghill quite a prolific poet, but in later years he disclaimed any talent for verse ("Men, Poets and Machines" 136). One of his verse plays appeared in book form, an allegorical masque titled *The Masque of Hope*, on a theme devised by Glynne Wickham, performed and published for a visit to Oxford by the future Queen Elizabeth II in 1948.

Coghill wrote a number of scholarly papers, focusing especially on Shakespearean stagecraft, gathered as *The Collected Papers of Nevill Coghill*, edited by Douglas Gray (1988), and one full-length book on Shakespeare as a dramatist, *Shakespeare's Professional Skills* (1964), but his students claimed that his talents at lecturing and directing did not come across on the page.

A memoir of Coghill by his pupil and fellow Inkling John Wain has been published: "Nevill Coghill: A Memoir," in the *Times Educational Supplement* (24 Dec. 1982: 20) and reprinted in Wain's *Dear Shadows* (1986). A Festschrift with a small amount of personal material has been published: *To Nevill Coghill from Friends*, edited by John Lawlor and W. H. Auden (1966).

DUNDAS-GRANT, JAMES (1896–1985)

James Harold Dundas-Grant, known as Jim and, to the Inklings, as D. G., was a reserve officer in the Royal Navy who came to Oxford in 1944 as commander of the Oxford University Naval Division, housed at Magdalen College, where he met C. S. Lewis. After the war he became the landlord of a house for Catholic undergraduates.

D. G. was a regular attendee of Tuesday Inklings pub sessions after the war. W. H. Lewis, in a 1948 diary entry, records that D. G. was not even considered as an invitee to an Inklings ham supper, though he did attend one in 1950 (*Brothers* 219, 235). But according to D. G.'s own account, invitations to ham suppers in Lewis's rooms, presumably the Inklings but not specifically identified as such, began early in his acquaintanceship with Lewis and preceded his invitation to the Eagle and Child pub sessions.

D. G.'s only known publication is "From an 'Outsider,'" a memoir of his friendship with Lewis, in *Remembering C. S. Lewis: Recollections of Those Who Knew Him*, edited by James T. Como (2005).

DYSON, H. V. D. (1896–1975)

Henry Victor Dyson Dyson, known as Hugo, read English at Exeter College from 1919. As an undergraduate in 1920, he attended the Exeter College essay club meeting at which Tolkien read "The Fall of Gondolin." He received his BA in 1921 and a BLitt in 1924, after which he taught English literature as a don at Reading University. He maintained a connection with Oxford, however, visiting frequently and evaluating examinations for the English School. In 1930, Nevill Coghill, whom Dyson had known from undergraduate days, introduced him to C. S. Lewis. Dyson and Lewis quickly became friends, and Dyson became a central and permanent member of the Inklings, attending whenever he could make it to Oxford, where he had many other friends, including Tolkien. Lewis visited Dyson in Reading on occasion.

In 1945 Dyson moved to Oxford when he became a fellow and tutor in English at Merton College. At the Inklings, which he continued attending frequently but not invariably, he was known to prefer talking to reading. He attended Eagle and Child pub sessions only occasionally, but was frequently at the supplementary pub sessions at the King's Arms in the late 1940s. He retired from his Merton post in 1963.

Dyson was a noted lecturer who published very little. His special interest covered the period from the Elizabethans through the eighteenth century. Of his two books, one is an edition of works of Pope titled *Poetry and Prose* (1933), with introduction and notes by Dyson; the other, *Augustans and Romantics, 1689–1830* (1940) is a survey of English literature of the period, with a bibliography by John Butt. Dyson's British Academy lecture of 1950, "The Emergence of Shakespeare's Tragedy," is his only other extensive published work. It appeared in the Academy's *Proceedings* for 1950 (36: 69–93) and was also published in pamphlet form. Dyson appeared on television as a lecturer several times in his later years. Some of his talks were transcribed for the BBC magazine *The Listener*. In 1965 he performed in a small role in John Schlesinger's feature film *Darling*.

A survey of Dyson's life and work has been published: "Hugo Dyson: Inkling, Teacher, *Bon Vivant*," by David Bratman, in *Mythlore* 21.4 (whole no. 82, Winter 1997): 19–34.

FOX, ADAM (1883–1977)

Adam Fox, the oldest Inkling, was an undergraduate at University College, Oxford, from 1902, receiving his BA in 1906. He was a schoolmaster in England and South Africa for many years, returning to Oxford as a fellow and Dean of Divinity at Magdalen College in 1929. He became acquainted with C. S. Lewis as they attended morning prayers in the chapel and breakfasted in the college hall together. Fox was an early regular member of the Inklings. At the instigation of Lewis and the Inklings, he was elected Professor of Poetry in 1938. Fox discusses this controversial incident in "At the Breakfast Table" (186–87), as does John Wain in *Professing Poetry* (U. K. edition only, 15–18).

Fox attended the Inklings regularly up to about 1940 and befriended Charles Williams on his arrival in the city. He was appointed a canon of Westminster Abbey in 1942, and left Oxford for London, where he remained for the rest of his life.

Fox apparently read his poetry regularly to the Inklings, but he is known to have published very little of it, including only one full book, a narrative poem titled *Old King Coel: A Rhymed Tale in Four Books* (1937). As a critic his output was also small: his inaugural lecture as Professor of Poetry was issued as a pamphlet, *Poetry for Pleasure* (1938), but no others appeared. Most of his few articles of poetry criticism date from the 1950s and later. A few of his sermons, from both his Oxford and his Westminster years, have been published.

Fox's greatest scholarly interest was in the Greek and specifically Platonic roots of Christianity. In this field he published *Plato for Pleasure* (1962) and edited *Plato and the Christians: Passages from the Writings of Plato* (1957). His *Meet the Greek Testament: Two Essays and a Dialogue Intended for Those Who Have Little or No Greek* (1952) addresses the subtleties and nuances of the Greek language and compares them with English, especially as it concerns translation of the New Testament. Most of this work is intended for general readers rather than scholars.

A survey of Fox's life and work has been published in German: "Adam Fox (1883–1977): Dichter und christlicher Platoniker," by Thomas Gerold, in *Inklings-Jahrbuch* 19 (2001): 201–14.

HARDIE, COLIN (1906–1998)

Colin Graham Hardie, who sometimes signed his work C. G. Hardie, was the brother of W. F. R. "Frank" Hardie (1902–1990). Both were sometime fellows of Magdalen, and both were friends of C. S. Lewis. Each is often referred to in documents only by surname, so writers on the Inklings occasionally confuse the two.

Colin Hardie was a student at Balliol College, Oxford, from 1924 until receiving his BA in 1928. After a year as a junior research fellow at Balliol, he spent three years as a fellow and tutor in Classics there, then three years as director of the British School in Rome. He became a fellow and tutor in Classics at Magdalen College in 1936, where he remained until his retirement in 1973.

Owen Barfield recalled meeting Hardie in Lewis's company in the 1920s ("Inklings Remembered" 549). But Hardie himself dated his friendship with Lewis to sessions at which they read Dante together, starting just before World War II. Hardie converted to Christianity under Dante's (and Lewis's) influence and became a specialist in Dante. In 1938 he was elected to the exclusive Oxford Dante Society, of which Lewis was already a member, and later became its secretary. While serving in this capacity, he befriended both Williams and Tolkien and arranged for both of them to be elected to the society.

In early 1945 Lewis invited Hardie to join both the Thursday and Tuesday Inklings; he soon became the designated carver at ham suppers. Hardie remained a regular attendee in later years, though he considered himself "only on the fringe of that informal group" (Hardie, "Colleague's Note" 177). He also joined the Socratic Club and gave papers there.

Hardie wrote no full-length books, but his many scholarly papers—most of them on Dante, some on Virgil, and a few on Classical archaeology—are highly technical. His *Times* obituary states that he had "theories about the dating and interpretation of Dante's writings . . . often at odds with accepted views" but also that his work "was always highly scholarly and stimulating" ("Colin Hardie" 21). He edited *Centenary Essays on Dante* by members of the Oxford Dante Society (1965). He published a verse celebration of the Inklings as "'Inklings': British at Oxford and German at Aachen," in *Inklings-Jahrbuch* 1 (1983): 15–18.

In 1967 Hardie became Oxford University's Public Orator, responsible biennially for the Creweian Oration in honor of the university's benefactors and for other public speeches. He kept this post until his retirement. In this capacity, he honored J. R. R. Tolkien on his receipt of an honorary degree in 1972 and John Wain on his election as Professor of Poetry in 1973.

HAVARD, ROBERT E. (1901–1985)

Robert Emlyn Havard, known to the Inklings as Humphrey Havard, read Chemistry at Keble College, Oxford, from 1918. He received his BA in 1921 and later went on to do graduate work in medicine at Queen's College, receiving his MD in 1934. In the meantime, he worked as a medical researcher at various postings in England, writing or co-authoring many papers on phosphate levels and other topics in human biochemistry for medical journals such as *The Biochemical Journal* and *Proceedings of the Physiological Society.*

After receiving his MD, Havard established a general medical practice in Oxford. Among his patients was C. S. Lewis, who invited him to join the Inklings. Havard recalled attending from about 1935 on, but dateable references in his recollections and in a letter by Lewis suggest that he did not actually begin attending until 1940 (*Collected Letters* 2: 343).

Whatever the date, Havard became one of the most central Inklings, if a comparatively quiet one, attending both Thursday and Tuesday gatherings. He contributed the clinical appendix to Lewis's *The Problem of Pain* (1940), which was read to the Inklings. He also gave the paper at the first meeting of the Socratic Club. He remained Lewis's physician and became the Tolkien family doctor as well. In later years, he and Tolkien were neighbors. As a car owner when most of his friends were non-drivers, Havard frequently chauffeured his friends to country inns and pubs for Inklings gatherings.

In 1943 Havard, a naval reserve surgeon, was called to active duty. He was eventually attached to the Army Malaria Research Unit based in Oxford. In this capacity, his name appears on over twenty co-authored papers on mepacrine and other anti-malarial drugs, mostly in *Lancet* and *Annals of Tropical Medicine and Parasitology*. After his retirement from medicine in 1968, he wrote two important memoirs of the Inklings, published in James T. Como's *Remembering C. S. Lewis: Recollections of Those Who Knew Him* (2005, originally published 1979), and *Mythlore* 17.2 (whole no. 64, Winter 1990). Havard also discusses the Inklings extensively in two interviews: one, with Walter Hooper, was published in Hooper's book *Through Joy and Beyond* (1982); the other, with Lyle W. Dorsett in 1984, is held as tape and transcript at the Marion E. Wade Center.

LEWIS, C. S. (1898–1963)

Clive Staples Lewis, known to family and friends as Jack, came from Belfast to University College, Oxford, in 1917. He read Philosophy and English, and—after a break for war service—received his BA in 1923. He then spent a year as a University College tutor in philosophy and in 1925 was chosen a fellow and tutor in English at Magdalen College, where over a nearly thirty-year career he established his literary reputation. In 1954 Lewis became the first Professor of Medieval and Renaissance Literature at Cambridge University, but continued to maintain his home in Oxford. He resigned this post shortly before his death.

In his memoir, *Surprised by Joy: The Shape of My Early Life* (1955), Lewis notes that during his undergraduate and early Magdalen years he made various friends who were all Christians and who facilitated his conversion from atheism to theism and then to Christianity in 1931. They included Owen Barfield, Nevill Coghill, J. R. R. Tolkien, and Hugo Dyson, all of whom became early core members of the Inklings. These four, Barfield and Tolkien in particular, became Lewis's lifelong friends; their meetings as Inklings and in other capacities remained central to his life.

As a writer, Lewis had a broad range of interests. He started out as a poet; the standard posthumous collections of this work are *The Collected Poems of C. S. Lewis* (1994) and *Narrative Poems* (1969), both edited by Walter Hooper. He made his reputation as a scholar in medieval and Renaissance English literature, tending to write broad surveys rather than studies of specific authors. His important works on this subject include *The Allegory of Love: A Study in Medieval Tradition* (1936), *A Preface to Paradise*

Lost (dedicated to Charles Williams, 1942), *The Discarded Image: An Introduction to Medieval and Renaissance Literature* (1964), and a volume in the Oxford History of English Literature, *English Literature in the Sixteenth Century, Excluding Drama* (1954, later re-titled *Poetry and Prose in the Sixteenth Century*). His essays have been published in many posthumous volumes. One titled *On Stories and Other Essays on Literature,* edited by Walter Hooper (1982), collects most of his essays on fiction writing and on the work of his friends and contemporaries. The title essay was Lewis's contribution to *Essays Presented to Charles Williams* (1947).

Lewis became a popular theologian, beginning with *The Problem of Pain* (1940) and earning fame as a BBC broadcaster, with several series of talks on the basics of common Christian belief eventually collected as *Mere Christianity* (1952). Among his other religious and ethical books, *The Four Loves* (1960) is notable for including his thoughts on friendship, a key bonding force among the Inklings, with specific allusions to Williams and Tolkien.

Inspired by the "spiritual thrillers" of Charles Williams and David Lindsay, Lewis began writing fantasy novels carrying theological weight. The Ransom trilogy (1938–1945), *Till We Have Faces* (1956), and the stories collected in *The Dark Tower and Other Stories,* edited by Walter Hooper (1977), are for adults; the seven Chronicles of Narnia (1950–1956) are for children. Lewis also wrote theological semi-fiction, including *The Screwtape Letters* (1942), *The Great Divorce: A Dream* (1945), and the semi-autobiographical *The Pilgrim's Regress: An Allegorical Apology for Christianity, Reason, and Romanticism* (1933, rev. 1943).

Lewis edited two books of Inklings interest: *Essays Presented to Charles Williams* (1947), a festschrift whose contributors were mostly Inklings; and *Arthurian Torso* (1948), a collection of Charles Williams's literary-historical essay "The Figure of Arthur" and Lewis's own commentary on Williams's Arthurian poetry.

Lewis's letters are a major primary source for Inklings history. There are several collections of these. A three-volume *Collected Letters* edited by Walter Hooper began publication in 2000.

A complete bibliography of Lewis's published work is available: "A Bibliography of the Writings of C. S. Lewis" in *C. S. Lewis: A Companion and Guide* by Walter Hooper (1996). This volume is the standard biographical reference source on Lewis. There are many other useful narrative biographies of him and critical studies of his work.

LEWIS, W. H. (1895–1973)

Warren Hamilton Lewis, known as Warren or Warnie and often referred to as "Major Lewis," was C. S. Lewis's elder and only brother. His military career included service in the Royal Army Service Corps during World War I. After retiring as captain in 1932 (he was promoted to major during a brief call-up in 1939–40), he resided with his brother in Oxford. He was a central figure in the Inklings throughout their entire history and provided much of the social glue that held them together.

After organizing and editing several volumes of *Memoirs of the Lewis Family 1850–1930* (never published, held in manuscript at the Marion E. Wade Center), W. H. Lewis devoted himself to writing popular history of late-seventeenth- and early-eighteenth-century France, the period of Louis XIV. He published a collection of essays, still widely read, on the social history of the period, *The Splendid Century: Some Aspects of French Life in the Reign of Louis XIV* (1953). Its chapter on the galleys of France had been his contribution to *Essays Presented to Charles Williams* (1947).

W. H. Lewis followed *The Splendid Century* with five more books that are essentially biographies of major figures of the period. These are *The Sunset of the Splendid Century: The Life and Times of Louis Auguste de Bourbon, Duc du Maine, 1670–1736* (1955); *Assault on Olympus: The Rise of the House of Gramont between 1604 and 1678* (1958); *Louis XIV: An Informal Portrait* (1959); *The Scandalous Regent: A Life of Philippe, Duc d'Orleans, 1674–1723, and of His Family* (1961); and *Levantine Adventurer: The Travels and Missions of the Chevalier d'Arvieux, 1653–1697* (1962). He also prepared an edition of Bayle St. John's translation of *Memoirs of the Duc de Saint-Simon* (1964).

After his brother's death, Major Lewis edited the first collection of *Letters of C. S. Lewis,* with an important personal memoir (1966). His diaries are the most important primary source for Inklings history. The complete diaries are held in manuscript by the Wade Center, and a large selection was published posthumously as *Brothers and Friends: The Diaries of Major Warren Hamilton Lewis,* edited by Clyde S. Kilby and Marjorie Lamp Mead (1982).

A survey of W. H. Lewis's life and works has been published: "W. H. Lewis: Historian of the Inklings and of Seventeenth-Century France," by Richard C. West, in *Seven: An Anglo-American Literary Review* 14 (1997): 74–86.

MATHEW, GERVASE (1905–1976)

Anthony Mathew received the religious name Gervase when he entered the order in 1928. He had come to Balliol College, Oxford, in 1925 to read Modern History. He received his BA in 1928 and from then resided at Blackfriars, the Dominican priory attached to the university. He was ordained in 1934 and in 1937 began lecturing for the university's Modern History, Theology, and English faculties. In 1947 he was appointed university lecturer in Byzantine Studies, and he held this post until he retired in 1971.

Mathew met Charles Williams in 1936 and saw him regularly during the war years when Williams was in Oxford, but it is not clear how well he knew the other Inklings at that time. According to one report, he was present at the Inklings to hear C. S. Lewis read *The Dark Tower* in 1939 or 1940 (Hooper, *C. S. Lewis* 215). But there are no known documentary references to his attending the Inklings before 1946. However, he knew Tolkien at least by 1945, spoke at the Socratic Club that year, and in later years had the reputation of being in touch with influential circles throughout the University (Carpenter, *Inklings* 186). Mathew became a regular, though not a central, figure in both the Thursday and Tuesday Inklings for the rest of their existence. Because of his remarkably wide friendships, he became the group's chief source of university news and gossip.

Mathew's scholarly interests were equally wide. He began writing a few papers in collaboration with his brother David on sixteenth-century English documentary history, then turned to the history and theology of Catholic religious orders, on which his major work is *The Reformation and the Contemplative Life: A Study of the Conflict between the Carthusians and the State* (with David Mathew, 1934). He developed lasting scholarly interests in Byzantine art, publishing *Byzantine Aesthetics* (1963), and also in fourteenth-century English philosophy and society, publishing "Marriage and *Amour Courtois* in Late Fourteenth-Century England" in *Essays Presented to Charles Williams* (1947) and *The Court of Richard II* (1968). About 1950 he became an archaeologist. He made expeditions to the East African coast to excavate early modern Islamic trading cities, studying porcelain shards to determine their trading patterns. He was an expert in the early written history of this region.

A survey of Mathew's life and works, with a fairly full bibliography, appears as a chapter in *Dominican Gallery: Portrait of a Culture* by Aidan Nichols (1997).

McCALLUM, R. B. (1898–1973)

Ronald Buchanan McCallum was born in Paisley, Scotland. He came to Worcester College, Oxford, in 1919 to read Modern History. He received his BA in 1922, spent a year doing graduate study at Princeton University in New Jersey, and another year teaching history at Glasgow University in Scotland. He became a fellow and tutor in History at Pembroke College, Oxford, in 1925, where he remained until his retirement in 1967. He was elected Master, head of the college, in 1955 and served twelve years. His primary achievement as Master, besides fund raising and advancing educational opportunities, was building the new North Quadrangle, by converting existing old buildings into college space rather than tearing them down.

Pembroke was a small college, and McCallum became friends with the new Professor of Anglo-Saxon, J. R. R. Tolkien, who was elected to a Pembroke fellowship at the same time as himself. Tolkien introduced McCallum to the Lewis brothers as early as 1933, when he invited them to dine at Pembroke (W. H. Lewis, *Brothers* 96). But McCallum is not recorded as attending the Inklings until after 1945, the year Tolkien left Pembroke. His attendance seems to have been irregular, but he is recorded as attending a few Thursday meetings in 1948–49. By this time he had also started to attend the pub sessions.

As an historian and college tutor, McCallum specialized in politics. He published three book-length studies in the history of public opinion. One of them, *The British General Election of 1945,* written with Alison Readman (1947), was the first such contemporary scholarly study of an election process. He also wrote on the modern history of the Liberal Party, including a history of Liberal philosophy, *The Liberal Party from Earl Grey to Asquith* (1963).

McCallum devoted a good deal of attention and writing effort to the well-being of his college and the university. He made many contributions to the annual *Pembroke College Record,* including a brief review of Tolkien's *The Hobbit*. He was also actively involved with *The Oxford Magazine,* a small-circulation weekly written by and for an audience of dons, to which several Inklings contributed. McCallum served three separate full terms as editor of the magazine, in 1932–33, 1966–67, and 1972–73, the last one long after his retirement; he also served as emergency editor on a few occasions; he twice reorganized its financial basis after this became precarious; and he wrote copiously for it, especially but not exclusively while serving as editor. Besides serious editorial columns and book reviews, he wrote gentle parodies of Oxford manners and customs, often under the pseudonyms Murripides and Vernon Fork.

A survey of McCallum's life and work has been published: "R. B. McCallum: The Master Inkling," by David Bratman, in *Mythlore* 23.3 (whole no. 89, Summer 2001): 34–42.

STEVENS, C. E. (1905–1976)

Courtenay Edward Stevens, known as Tom (short for Tom Brown), read Greats (Classics, Philosophy, Ancient History) at New College, Oxford, from 1924 and received his BA in 1928. Then, at Oriel College, he undertook a BLitt thesis on the fifth-century Roman Empire, which was completed in 1930 and published as *Sidonius Apollinaris and His Age* in 1933. After completing his thesis, he spent a few years on a fellowship grant studying ancient Irish land tenure in Belfast and then became a fellow and tutor in Ancient History at Magdalen College in 1933. He was away on intelligence work for the Foreign Office during World War II. He retired in 1972.

Stevens is one Inkling whose formal election is recorded in available sources. At a meeting in October 1947, C. S. Lewis "suggested that Stevens should be invited to become an Inkling, and all those present were in favour" (W. H. Lewis, *Brothers* 212). He "made his debut as an Inkling" in a meeting at Merton a month later (*Brothers* 216). Stevens is recorded as attending a few Thursday meetings, and in 1950 he was present at a ham supper. He occasionally appeared at the Eagle and Child pub meetings and the supplementary King's Arms meetings during the same period, but evidently ceased to attend after about 1950.

Stevens was a noted historian specializing in Roman Britain, but he wrote relatively little. His published work up to 1971 is listed in a Festschrift: "A List of the Published Writings of Courtenay Edward Stevens," in *The Ancient Historian and His Materials: Essays in Honour of C. E. Stevens on His Seventieth Birthday*, edited by Barbara Levick (1975). This volume also contains a brief biographical note by the editor.

TOLKIEN, CHRISTOPHER (1924–)

Christopher Reuel Tolkien is the third son of J. R. R. Tolkien. He grew up with his family in Oxford, and as a child he was part of the earliest audience for his father's stories. While ill at the age of thirteen, he reviewed the printed text of *The Hobbit* for typographical errors (J. R. R. Tolkien, *Letters* 28). He transcribed and typed parts of *The Lord of the Rings* and drew the final maps for publication based on his father's, and his own, working maps. The foldout maps are initialed "C. J. R. T." The *J* stands for John, a confirmation name he does not normally use (Anderson 248).

Christopher Tolkien became a student at Trinity College, Oxford, in 1942. After a period of war service he resumed his studies and received his BA in English in 1949, having studied informally with his father and more officially with C. S. Lewis.

Christopher Tolkien was the only regular undergraduate member of the Inklings. After his demobilization in October 1945, the Inklings confirmed his status as an official member (Carpenter, *Inklings* 205). He attended both Thursday night meetings and Tuesday pub sessions throughout the late 1940s and frequently read aloud chapters of his father's *Lord of the Rings:* W. H. Lewis reports that he read "beautifully" (*Brothers* 198).

He became a lecturer in English language and Old Norse at several Oxford colleges, acquiring a fellowship at New College in 1965. In this period he published some editions and studies of Norse sagas, including a translation with notes of *The Saga of King Heidrek the Wise* (1960). He and Nevill Coghill co-edited three of Chaucer's *Canterbury Tales* (1958–69).

After his father's death in 1973, Christopher Tolkien's scholarly career took a major shift into work as his father's literary executor. He resigned his fellowship in 1975 to devote himself to this work full time. Between 1975 and 1996 he edited seventeen new volumes of his father's writings and drawings, and oversaw several other new editions of his father's work. This editing required massive deciphering and organizing of his father's disordered manuscripts. These volumes include *The Silmarillion* (1977), *Unfinished Tales of Númenor and Middle-earth* (1980), *The Monsters and the Critics and Other Essays* (1983), *Pictures by J. R. R. Tolkien* (1979, rev. 1992), a volume of translations of Middle English poetry, *Sir Gawain and the Green Knight, Pearl, and Sir Orfeo* (1975), and the twelve volumes of *The History of Middle-earth* (1983–96).

A complete bibliography of his published work is in a Festschrift: "Christopher Tolkien: A Bibliography," by Douglas A. Anderson, in *Tolkien's Legendarium,* edited by Verlyn Flieger and Carl F. Hostetter (2000).

TOLKIEN, J. R. R. (1892–1973)

John Ronald Reuel Tolkien, known as Ronald in the family and often called Tollers by his friends, came to Exeter College, Oxford, in 1911 and graduated in 1915 with a BA in English. After military service in World War I, he returned to Oxford at the end of 1918 to work as a lexicographer on the *New English Dictionary* (later known as the *Oxford English Dictionary*). During this period, he also taught some university students. In 1920 he read "The Fall of Gondolin" from his unpublished *Book of Lost Tales* to the Exeter College Essay Club, including two undergraduates named Nevill Coghill and Hugo Dyson.

From 1920 Tolkien was reader (and in 1924 became Professor) of English language at the University of Leeds, and in 1925 he returned to Oxford as Rawlinson and Bosworth Professor of Anglo-Saxon with a fellowship at Pembroke College. Tolkien had always been a clubbable man in his social life, and one of his first acts on assuming his post at Oxford was to found the Coalbiters, a club of dons, formed to read Icelandic sagas aloud. At E. Tangye Lean's early 1930s undergraduate Inklings club, Tolkien's poem "Errantry" was one of the works read aloud. Tolkien became a central figure at the succeeding Inklings that met through the 1930s and 1940s. In 1945 he exchanged his previous position for the post of Merton Professor of English Language and Literature; after this date the Inklings met sometimes in his rooms at Merton. Tolkien was a frequent attendee of Inklings pub sessions in the 1940s and continued appearing occasionally later. He retired in 1959 and received an honorary Doctorate in Letters from the university in 1972.

Tolkien's scholarship and creative writing are closely allied. As a scholar he specialized in the language and literature of medieval England, from *Beowulf* to the poems of Chaucer, uniting philological and critical concerns. *The Monsters and the Critics and Other Essays* (1983) is a posthumous collection of his less technical essays, including his pioneering calls for *Beowulf* and fairy-stories to be studied and appreciated for their aesthetic and literary value. The essay "On Fairy-Stories" was first published as Tolkien's contribution to *Essays Presented to Charles Williams* (1947); it also appears in *Tree and Leaf* (1964, rev. 1988). Tolkien prepared textual editions of important manuscripts, of which his *Sir Gawain and the Green Knight,* co-edited with E. V. Gordon (1925, rev. 1967), became and remains a standard in its field. His translation of this and other fourteenth-century poems appear in the volume *Sir Gawain and the Green Knight, Pearl, and Sir Orfeo* (1975).

Tolkien carried his scholarly interests into his creative work, which began as an attempt to express his interest in the dependence of language on myth and to evolve his elaborate invented languages into "a body of more or less connected legend, ranging from the large and cosmogonic, to the level of romantic fairy-story . . . which I could dedicate simply to: to England; to my country" (*Letters* 144). Its first full manifestation was a mythic story cycle called *The Book of Lost Tales,* written between 1916 and 1920 and published 1983–84. Later versions of these stories eventually developed into *The Silmarillion* (never finished; published 1977). Most of Tolkien's other fiction, such as *The Hobbit, or There and Back Again* (1937, rev. 1951 and 1966) and *The Lord of the Rings* (1954–55, rev. 1966), was either drawn into or spun off from this *legendarium.* Another such work, the fragmentary novel *The Notion Club Papers,* published in the collection *Sauron Defeated* (1992), is inspired directly by the Inklings.

Tolkien also painted and wrote poetry; much of this work is also related to the *legendarium.* The largest and most detailed collection and description of Tolkien's artwork is in *J. R. R. Tolkien: Artist and Illustrator,* by Wayne G. Hammond and Christina Scull (1995). His incomplete epic poems on Silmarillion topics are in *The Lays of Beleriand* (1985), with commentary on *The Lay of Leithian* by C. S. Lewis; some smaller poems are in *The Adventures of Tom Bombadil and Other Verses from the Red Book* (1962).

Tolkien was a perfectionist who published few works in his lifetime. His posthumous catalog, mostly edited by his son Christopher, is very large. Besides other books mentioned above, it includes *Unfinished Tales of Númenor and Middle-earth* (1980) and the twelve-volume historical survey *The History of Middle-earth* (1983–96), opened by *The Book of Lost Tales* and *The Lays of Beleriand* mentioned above. *The Letters of J. R. R. Tolkien: A Selection,* edited by Humphrey Carpenter (1981), is very selective but forms an important primary source for Inklings history.

A complete descriptive bibliography of Tolkien's published works to 1992 has been published: *J. R. R. Tolkien: A Descriptive Bibliography,* by Wayne G. Hammond with the assistance of Douglas A. Anderson (1993). A full bibliography is available on the Internet: *A Chronological Bibliography of the Writings of J. R. R. Tolkien,* by Åke Bertenstam, at http://hem.passagen.se/annuvin/tbchron.html. A handlist of Tolkien's works, originally prepared for *J. R. R. Tolkien: A Biography,* by Humphrey Carpenter (1977, also published as *Tolkien: A Biography*), has appeared in revised editions in several subsequent books. Most notable among them is a secondary bibliography: *Tolkien Criticism: An Annotated Checklist,* by Richard C. West (1970, rev. 1981). Carpenter's *Tolkien: A Biography* is the standard life of Tolkien; there are many useful critical books on his work.

WAIN, JOHN (1925–1994)

John Barrington Wain later considered himself a particularly callow youth when he came to St. John's College, Oxford, in 1943 at the age of eighteen to read English. Because of wartime personnel shortages, he was assigned C. S. Lewis of Magdalen College as a tutor; he thrived under Lewis's scholastic regimen. Wain also learned a great deal from Nevill Coghill and the lectures of Charles Williams. As an undergraduate he acted in some of Coghill's Shakespeare productions.

Lewis sometimes invited his pupils or former pupils to the Inklings. Wain was the only one of these who became a frequent attendee. After receiving his BA in 1946 he was a fairly frequent attendee of Thursday Inklings for about three years; in later years he sometimes appeared at morning pub sessions. For the first of his Inklings years, Wain held a research fellowship at St. John's; afterwards he traveled from Reading University, where he taught English Literature until 1955. In later years Wain was a freelance writer living in the Oxford area. He returned to the university in 1971 as a special fellow of Brasenose College, and in 1973 he was elected Professor of Poetry for a five-year term. Some of his lectures in this position were collected as *Professing Poetry* (1977); the U. K. edition includes his comments on Lewis, Adam Fox, and the 1938 election for the post.

Wain shared some of the Inklings' conservative literary values, but was never sympathetic to their love of imagination and fantasy: he once described Tolkien's theory of sub-creation as "manifestly absurd" (*Sprightly* 182). He attended the meetings because he enjoyed the intellectual company of his teachers and others who, like him, always took literature seriously. Wain saw himself as an all-purpose man of letters in the mode of Dr. Johnson, of whom he wrote a biography (*Samuel Johnson,* 1974). Though he is primarily remembered as a novelist, Wain devoted equal attention to being a poet, dramatist, critic, and teacher. Except for some of his criticism, his work is very unlike that of the other Inklings. The writers he is most often associated with are his Oxford undergraduate contemporaries Sir Kingsley Amis and Philip Larkin and the 1950s poetry circle The Movement.

Wain is most important to Inklings Studies as a critic and memoirist. His first memoir, *Sprightly Running: Part of an Autobiography* (1962) contains much of his thought on the Inklings. C. S. Lewis's reaction to the description of the Inklings here, and Wain's response, are in the letter column of *Encounter,* Jan. 1963: 81–82. A second memoir, in *Contemporary Authors Autobiography Series* 4 (1986): 314–32, expands on Wain's account of the Inklings. *Dear Shadows: Portraits from Memory* (1986) is a collection of biographical sketches including one of Nevill Coghill. Neither Wain's full-length studies, *The Living World of Shakespeare* (1964) and a biography of *Samuel Johnson* (1974), nor his essay collections, *Preliminary Essays* (1957), *Essays on Literature and Ideas* (1963), *A House for the Truth* (1972), and *Professing Poetry* (1977), discuss the Inklings' work but they do show a critical mind in the tradition of Lewis.

Wain's fiction is conservative realistic modernism. He published fourteen novels and three short-story collections. His best-known novel is his first, *Hurry on Down* (1953, also published as *Born in Captivity*), a comic picaresque on a footloose graduate. His later novels are more serious. His final trilogy, *Where the Rivers Meet* (1988), *Comedies* (1990), and *Hungry Generations* (1994), is a portrait of Oxford from the 1930s to 1950s through the eyes of a student turned don. Though there is no direct reference to the Inklings, one character, a Shakespeare scholar named Harry Goodenough, is reminiscent of Coghill. Wain's poetry appears in several collections, of which *Poems, 1949–1979* (1980) is the most wide ranging.

A complete bibliography of Wain's published works to 1986 is available: *John Wain: A Bibliography,* by David Gerard (1987). The most complete critical study of his work is *John Wain: A Man of Letters* by Elizabeth Hatziolou (1997), which also has the most biographical material.

WILLIAMS, CHARLES (1886–1945)

Charles Walter Stansby Williams attended University College, London, for a few terms, but had to drop out for financial reasons. He began work at the London offices of the Oxford University Press in 1908 as a proofreader and rose to become a senior literary editor. He wrote poetry, fiction, drama, criticism, and biography, and lectured to adult education classes. In 1936 his novel *The Place of the Lion* (1931) came into the hands of C. S. Lewis, who liked it so much he wrote the author a letter inviting him, if ever in Oxford, to attend a meeting of the Inklings. Williams and Lewis met on several occasions in the next few years, both in Oxford and in London, and Williams became friends with a number of the Inklings.

In September 1939, the London offices of the Press were evacuated to Oxford and Williams became a regular attendee of the Inklings. Meetings were sometimes arranged around his schedule, and he brought friends of his own as guests. He frequently met with the Lewis brothers and Tolkien for a beer and thus became one of the earliest participants in the Inklings' Tuesday morning pub sessions at the Eagle and Child.

Tolkien bore some responsibility for arranging the English Department's wartime lecture schedule, and he and Lewis arranged for Williams to give several lecture series and teach tutorial pupils. They also helped arrange for Williams to receive an honorary MA from the university in 1943. This made Williams eligible for his election the following year to the prestigious Oxford Dante Society, a small club of dons that included Lewis, Tolkien, and Colin Hardie. Williams was the only person of non-academic background who had ever been elected to the society. He was flattered by their attention and in his letters he expresses great pleasure at the opportunity to have detailed learned discussions on the work of a poet who was most meaningful to him.

Williams's interests were in the theological implications of romance and in the interpenetration of the mundane and the spiritual. He expressed these ideas in all his writings. His seven novels are his most widely read works. All of them concern the irruption of the supernatural into modern life. Many readers begin with *War in Heaven* (1930) or *The Place of the Lion* (1931) and go on to *Many Dimensions* (1931) and *The Greater Trumps* (1932). *Descent into Hell* (1937) and *All Hallows' Eve* (1945) are later, richer, and more complex works. *Shadows of Ecstasy* (1933) is an apprentice piece published quite some time after it was written.

Williams's highest achievement is generally considered to be his two late volumes of complex and allusive Arthurian poetry, the cycle *Taliessin through Logres* (1938) and a collection of longer poems, *The Region of the Summer Stars* (1944). The bulk of his drama may be found in *Collected Plays*, edited by John Heath-Stubbs (1963), and *The Masques of Amen House*, edited by David Bratman (2000).

Williams's nonfiction is extensive. After several early books of poetry criticism and sixteenth- and seventeenth-century biography, he turned to theological issues in *He Came Down from Heaven* (1938), *The Descent of the Dove: A Short History of the Holy Spirit in the Church* (1939), *Witchcraft* (1941), and *The Forgiveness of Sins* (1942). His last book of literary criticism, *The Figure of Beatrice: A Study in Dante* (1943), is the most often read. Many of his essays are collected in *The Image of the City and Other Essays*, edited by Anne Ridler (1958). Other posthumous publications include *Outlines of Romantic Theology*, edited by Alice Mary Hadfield (1990), and *The Detective Fiction Reviews of Charles Williams*, edited by Jared C. Lobdell (2003). His wartime letters to his wife, *To Michal from Serge: Letters from Charles Williams to His Wife, Florence, 1939–1945*, edited by Roma A. King Jr. (2001), are a useful primary source on the Inklings.

Williams died after a short illness in May 1945. The Inklings, anticipating his departure from Oxford when the Press returned to London at the war's end, had planned to compile a Festschrift in his honor, but it became a memorial volume: *Essays Presented to Charles Williams* (1947). A complete bibliography of Williams's published work is available: *Charles W. S. Williams: A Checklist*, by Lois Glenn (1975). There are several useful critical studies of his work, and a standard biography with some description of the work: *Charles Williams: An Exploration of His Life and Work*, by Alice Mary Hadfield (1983).

WRENN, C. L. (1895–1969)

Charles Lesley Wrenn, who sometimes signed himself Charles L. Wrenn, read English at Queen's College, Oxford, from 1913 to 1917. After receiving his BA, he became a teacher of English at a series of colleges and universities, spending several years in

India. He returned to Oxford in 1930 as a lecturer in English Language, assisting J. R. R. Tolkien. The two men became friends, and their families even vacationed together. C. S. Lewis also sent pupils to Wrenn for Anglo-Saxon tutoring, at which he was a strict taskmaster.

Wrenn attended some of the first recorded Inklings meetings in 1939 and 1940, but he is not known to have attended during the later war years. He had left his Oxford post for a professorship at the University of London in 1939. He returned to Oxford in 1946 as Tolkien's successor as Rawlinson and Bosworth Professor of Anglo-Saxon. He also resumed attending the Inklings occasionally and went to the Tuesday morning pub sessions as well. Lewis invited him to a ham supper in 1952. One of Lewis's motives was to lure Wrenn away from academic politics (Tolkien, *Letters* 161). But Wrenn spent much of his time in administration in his later years, including helping to organize the International Association of University Professors of English with a conference at Oxford in 1950. He retired in 1963.

Wrenn's scholarly work tends toward explaining the English language and Anglo-Saxon poetry for non-expert readers. These books include *The English Language* (1949), *A Study of Old English Literature* (1967), and *An Old English Grammar,* co-authored with Randolph Quirk (1955, rev. 1957). He edited the 1940 edition of John R. Clark Hall's translation of *Beowulf and the Finnesburg Fragment* to which Tolkien contributed a prefatory essay, and also co-edited with Norman Davis a Festschrift for Tolkien, *English and Medieval Studies Presented to J. R. R. Tolkien on the Occasion of His Seventieth Birthday* (1962).

Wrenn had a wider range of literary interests than some Anglo-Saxonists. He wrote on comparative literature and on later poets, and his collection *Word and Symbol: Studies in English Language* (1967) includes an essay on T. S. Eliot.

Permissions

Permission to use excerpts from published and unpublished material has been granted by the following publishers and bodies:

Excerpts from *Owen Barfield on C. S. Lewis* by Owen Barfield ©1989 and "C. S. L.: Biographia Theologica," a poem by Owen Barfield, are reprinted by the generous permission of G. B. Tennyson on behalf of the Barfield Literary Estate, which retains copyright. All rights reserved.

Excerpts from *The Inklings* by Humphrey Carpenter © 1978 by George Allen & Unwin (Publishers) Ltd. and *Tolkien: A Biography* by Humphrey Carpenter © 1977 by George Allen & Unwin (Publishers) Ltd. are reprinted by permission of Houghton Mifflin Company. U.S. rights. All rights reserved.

Excerpts from *The Inklings* by Humphrey Carpenter copyright © 1979 and *Tolkien: A Biography* by Humphrey Carpenter copyright © 1977 are reprinted by permission of HarperCollins Publishers. World rights. All rights reserved.

Excerpts from *Remembering C. S. Lewis: Recollections of Those Who Knew Him*, ed. James T. Como © 2005 are reprinted by the kind permission of James T. Como. All rights reserved.

The English translation of "C. S. L.: Biographia Theologica," a poem by Owen Barfield, is reprinted by the gracious permission of the translator, Gerald Hawthorne. All rights reserved.

Excerpts from *Invention as a Social Act* by Karen Burke LeFevre © 1987 are reprinted by the gracious permission of The National Council of Teachers of English. All rights reserved.

Excerpts from *C. S. Lewis: Companion and Guide* by Walter Hooper ©1996; *The Collected Letters of C. S. Lewis*, Volume 1 © 2000; *The Collected Letters of C. S. Lewis* Volume 2© 2004; *The Collected Poems of C. S. Lewis* © 1964; and unpublished letters of C. S. Lewis, all copyright C. S. Lewis Pte. Ltd., are reprinted by permission of C. S. Lewis Pte. Ltd. All rights reserved.

Excerpts from *Letters of C. S. Lewis* by C. S. Lewis © 1966 by W. H. Lewis and the Executors of C. S. Lewis and renewed 1994 by C. S. Lewis Pte. Ltd., and *Surprised by Joy: The Shape of My Early Life* by C. S. Lewis © 1956 by C. S. Lewis and renewed 1984 by Arthur Owen Barfield, are reprinted by permission of Harcourt, Inc. U.S. rights. All rights reserved.

Works Cited

Adams, Hazard, ed. *Critical Theory Since Plato*. Rev. ed. Fort Worth, TX: Harcourt Brace Jovanovich, 1992.

Adey, Lionel. *C. S. Lewis's "Great War" with Owen Barfield*. ELS Monograph Series 14. Victoria, BC: University of Victoria, 1978.

———. *C. S. Lewis: Writer, Dreamer, and Mentor*. Grand Rapids, MI: Eerdmans, 1998.

Anderson, Douglas A. "Christopher Tolkien: A Bibliography." Flieger and Hostetter 247–52.

Arieti, Silvano. *Creativity: The Magic Synthesis*. New York: Basic Books, 1976.

Auden, W. H. "At the End of the Quest, Victory." Rev. of *The Return of the King*, by J. R. R. Tolkien. *New York Times Book Review* 22 Jan. 1956: 5. Reprinted in A. Becker 44–48.

———. "The Hero Is a Hobbit." Rev. of *The Fellowship of the Ring*, by J. R. R. Tolkien. *New York Times Book Review* 31 Oct. 1954: 37.

———. Introduction. *The Descent of the Dove*. By Charles Williams. New York: Meridian Books, 1956. v–xii.

Baker, Carlos. *Emerson among the Eccentrics*. New York: Penguin, 1997.

Baker, Leo. "Near the Beginning." Como 65–75.

Barfield, Owen. *A Barfield Reader: Selections from the Writings of Owen Barfield*. Ed. and Intr. G. B. Tennyson. Edinburgh: Floris Books, 1998.

———. *A Barfield Sampler: Poetry and Fiction by Owen Barfield*. Ed. Jeanne Clayton Hunter and Thomas Kranidas. Albany: State University of New York, 1993.

———. "Clive Staples Lewis." Obituary. *Oxford Magazine* (30 Jan. 1964): 155–56.

———. "Clive Staples Lewis." Obituary. *Report of the Royal Society of Literature* (1964): 20–22.

———. "C. S. Lewis and Historicism." *Man's "Natural Powers": Essays for and about C. S. Lewis*. Ed. Raymond P. Tripp Jr. [Denver]: Society for New Language Study, [1975]. 1–8.

———. "Hagar and Ishmael." Hunter and Kranidas 39–44.

———. *History in English Words*. 1926. West Stockbridge, MA: Inner Traditions-Lindisfarne Press, 1985.

———. "The Inklings Remembered." *The World & I* (Apr. 1990): 548–49.

———. Introduction. Gibb ix–xxi.

———. "The Kingdom in Space-Time." Rev. of *Descent into Hell*, by Charles Williams. *New English Weekly* (21 April 1949): 19–20.

———. "Lewis, Truth, and Imagination." *Owen Barfield on C. S. Lewis*. 90–103.

———. "The Meaning of 'Literal.'" *Literary English since Shakespeare.* Ed. George Watson. London: Oxford University Press, 1970. 48–63. Rpt. of "The Meaning of the Word 'Literal.'" *Metaphor and Symbol.* Ed. L. C. Knights and Basil Cottle. London: Butterworths Scientific Publication, 1960.

———. "Night Operation." Hunter and Kranidas, 130–72.

———. *Orpheus: A Poetic Drama.* Ed. and Afterword John C. Ulreich Jr. West Stockbridge, MA: Lindisfarne Press, 1983.

———. *Owen Barfield on C. S. Lewis.* Ed. and Intr. G. B. Tennyson. Middletown, CT: Wesleyan University Press, 1989.

———. *Poetic Diction: A Study in Meaning.* 1928. 2nd ed. Middletown, CT: Wesleyan University Press, 1984.

———. *The Rediscovery of Meaning and Other Essays.* 1977. Paperback ed. Middletown, CT: Wesleyan University Press, 1985.

———. *Romanticism Comes of Age.* 1944, rev. ed. 1967. Middletown, CT: Wesleyan University Press, 1986.

———. *Saving the Appearances: A Study in Idolatry.* 1957. New York: Harvest-HBJ Book-Harcourt Brace Jovanovich, 1965.

———. *The Silver Trumpet.* 1925. Ed. Marjorie L. Mead. Longmont, CO: Bookmakers Guild, 1986.

———. "Some Reflections on *The Great Divorce* of C. S. Lewis." Rev. of *The Great Divorce,* by C. S. Lewis. *Owen Barfield on C. S. Lewis.* 82–89.

———. "The Sound of Friendship." Rev. of *They Stand Together: The Letters of C. S. Lewis to Arthur Greeves,* by C. S. Lewis. *Christian World* 4 May 1979: 13.

———. *Speaker's Meaning.* Middletown, CT: Wesleyan University Press, 1967.

———. *This Ever Diverse Pair.* 1950. Edinburgh: Floris Books, 1985.

———. *Unancestral Voice.* 1965. Middletown, CT: Wesleyan University Press, 1986.

———. "A Visit to Beatrice." *Seven: An Anglo-American Literary Review* 9 (1988): 15–18.

———, ed. *The Voice of Cecil Harwood: A Miscellany.* London: Rudolf Steiner Press, 1979.

———. *What Coleridge Thought.* Middletown, CT: Wesleyan University Press, 1971.

———. *Worlds Apart.* Middletown, CT: Wesleyan University Press, 1963.

Barfield, Owen, and C. S. Lewis. "Abecedarium Philosophicum." *Oxford Magazine* (30 Nov. 1933): 298.

———. *A Cretaceous Perambulator (The Re-examination of).* Ed. Walter Hooper. Oxford: Oxford University C. S. Lewis Society, 1983. N. pag.

Bate, W. Jackson. *The Burden of the Past and the English Poet.* Cambridge: Harvard University Press, 1970.

Bayley, Peter. "From Master to Colleague." Como 164–76.

Beach, Sylvia. *Shakespeare and Company.* 1959. New ed. Lincoln: University of Nebraska Press, 1991.

Becker, Alida, ed. *The Tolkien Scrapbook.* Philadelphia: Running Press, 1978.

Becker, Howard S. *Art Worlds.* Berkeley: University of California Press, 1982.

Bellah, Robert N., Richard Madsen, William M. Sullivan, Ann Swidler, and Steven M. Tipton. *Habits of the Heart: Individualism and Commitment in American Life.* New York: Harper & Row, 1986.

Bellamy, Joe David. "John Gardner." *The New Fiction: Interviews with Innovative American Writers.* Urbana: University of Illinois Press, 1974. 169–93.

Bennett, J. A. W., ed. *Chaucer: The Knight's Tale.* 1954. 2nd ed. Rev. London: Harrap, 1965.

———. "Climates of Opinions." *English and Medieval Studies Presented to J. R. R. Tolkien on the Occasion of His Seventieth Birthday.* Ed. Norman Davis and C. L. Wrenn. London: Allen and Unwin, 1962. 280–305.

———, ed. and Preface. *Essays on Malory.* 1963. Oxford: Clarendon Press, 1965. v–vii.

———. "Gawain Again." Rev. of *Sir Gawain and the Green Knight,* ed. J. R. R. Tolkien and E. V. Gordon. 2nd ed., rev. Norman Davis. *Times Literary Supplement* 25 July 1968: 795.

———. "Gower's 'Honeste Love.'" *Patterns of Love and Courtesy: Essays in Memory of C. S. Lewis.* Ed. John Lawlor. Evanston, IL: Northwestern University Press, 1966. 107–21.

———. "'Grete Clerk.'" Gibb 44–50.

———. "Grete Clerke of Oxford." Rev. of *The Discarded Image,* by C. S. Lewis. *Times Literary Supplement* 16 July 1964: 632.

———. *The Humane Medievalist and Other Essays in English Literature and Learning, from Chaucer to Eliot.* Ed. Piero Boitani. Roma: Edizioni di storia e letteratura, 1982.

———. *The Humane Medievalist: An Inaugural Lecture.* Cambridge: Cambridge University Press, 1965.

———. "Lewis, Clive Staples." *Dictionary of National Biography 1961–1970.* Ed. E. T. Williams and C. S. Nicholls. London: Oxford University Press, 1981. 651–53.

———. *The Parlement of Foules: An Interpretation.* Oxford: Clarendon Press, 1957.

———. *Poetry of the Passion: Studies in Twelve Centuries of English Verse.* Oxford: Clarendon Press, 1982.

———. Rev. of *Letters of C. S. Lewis,* ed. W. H. Lewis. *Magdalene College Magazine and Record* ns 10 (1966): 14–16.

———. Rev. of *A Mind Awake: An Anthology of C. S. Lewis,* ed. Clyde S. Kilby. *New Blackfriars* 50 (1969): 223–24.

———. Rev. of *The Pardon of Piers Plowman,* by Nevill Coghill. *Oxford Magazine* (23 Oct. 1947): 54–55.

———. Rev. of *The Pardon of Piers Plowman,* by Nevill Coghill. *Times Literary Supplement* 6 July 1946: 320.

———. Rev. of *The Poet Chaucer,* by Nevill Coghill. *Landfall* 4 (1950): 246–50.

Bennis, Warren, and Patricia Ward Biederman. *Organizing Genius: The Secrets of Creative Collaboration.* Cambridge, MA: Perseus Books, 1997.

Betjeman, John. Rev. of *All Hallows' Eve,* by Charles Williams. *Daily Herald* [London] 31 Jan. 1945: 2.

Beyond the Movie: The Lord of the Rings: The Fellowship of the Ring. Dir. Lisa Kors. National Geographic, 2002.

Biggs, Blanche. *From Papua with Love.* Sydney: Australian Board of Missions, 1987.

Bliss, Alan, ed. *Finn and Hengest: The Fragment and the Episode.* By J. R. R. Tolkien. Boston: Houghton Mifflin, 1983.

Bloom, Harold. *The Anxiety of Influence: A Theory of Poetry.* London: Oxford University Press, 1975.

The Book of Common Prayer and Administration of the Sacraments and Other Rites and Ceremonies of the Church Together with The Psalter or Psalms of David According to the Use of The Episcopal Church. New York: Oxford University Press, 1990.

Bosky, Bernadette Lynn. Introduction. *The Masques of Amen House: Together with Amen House Poems.* By Charles Williams. Ed. David Bratman. Altadena, CA: Mythopoeic Press, 2000. 1–30.

Bratman, David. "Hugo Dyson: Inkling, Teacher, Bon Vivant." *Mythlore* 21.4 (whole no. 82, Winter 1997): 19–34.

———. "The Literary Value of *The History of Middle-earth.*" Flieger and Hostetter 69–91.

———. "R. B. McCallum: The Master Inkling." *Mythlore* 23.3 (whole no. 89, Spring 2000): 34–42.

———. "Top Ten Rejected Plot Twists from *The Lord of the Rings*: A Textual Excursion into the 'History of *The Lord of the Rings.*'" *Mythlore* 22.4 (whole no. 86, Spring 2000): 13–37.

Bray, Suzanne. "Disseminating Glory: Echoes of Charles Williams in the Works of T. S. Eliot." *Seven: An Anglo-American Literary Review* 14 (1997): 59–73.

Bresland, Ronald W. *The Backward Glance: C. S. Lewis and Ireland.* Belfast: Institute of Irish Studies, Queen's University of Belfast, 1999.

Brewer, Derek. "The Tutor: A Portrait." Como 115–51.

Bruffee, Kenneth A. *Collaborative Learning: Higher Education, Interdependence, and the Authority of Knowledge.* Baltimore: Johns Hopkins University Press, 1993.

Brunsdale, Mitzi. *Dorothy L. Sayers: Solving the Mystery of Wickedness.* New York: Berg Publishers, 1990.

Burke, Kenneth. *The Philosophy of Literary Form.* Rev. ed. New York: Vintage Books, 1957.

Carpenter, Humphrey. *The Brideshead Generation: Evelyn Waugh and His Friends.* Boston: Houghton Mifflin, 1990.

———. *Geniuses Together: American Writers in Paris in the 1920s.* London: Unwin Hyman, 1987.

———. *The Inklings: C. S. Lewis, J. R. R. Tolkien, Charles Williams, and Their Friends.* Boston: Houghton Mifflin, 1979.

———. *The Lord of the Rings: Souvenir Booklet Commemorating Twenty-Five Years of Its Publication.* N. p. Allen and Unwin, 1980.

———. *Tolkien: A Biography.* Boston: Houghton Mifflin, 1977.

Carroll, Lewis. *Alice's Adventures in Wonderland* and *Through the Looking-Glass and What Alice Found There.* 1865; 1872. Oxford: Oxford University Press, 1982.

Carter, Lin. *Imaginary Worlds: The Art of Fantasy.* New York: Ballantine Books, 1973.

———. *Tolkien: A Look behind The Lord of the Rings.* New York: Ballantine Books, 1974.

Cater, William. "The Filial Duty of Christopher Tolkien." A. Becker 90–95.

Cecil, David. *The Cecils of Hatfield House.* London: Constable, 1973.

———. "C. S. Lewis Unmasked." Rev. of *They Stand Together: The Letters of C. S. Lewis to Arthur Greeves,* by C. S. Lewis. *Books and Bookmen* (July 1979): 11–12.

———. *Hardy the Novelist: An Essay in Criticism.* London: Constable, 1944.

———. "Neville [*sic*] Coghill: A Tribute." *Times Literary Supplement* 21 Nov. 1980: 1334.

———, ed. *The Oxford Book of Christian Verse.* Oxford: Clarendon Press, 1951.

———. "Oxford's Magic Circle." Rev. of *The Inklings,* by Humphrey Carpenter. *Books and Bookmen* (Jan. 1979): 10–12.

———. *The Stricken Deer: or The Life of Cowper.* 1929. London: Constable, 1947.

———. *Two Quiet Lives: Dorothy Osborne, Thomas Gray.* Indianapolis: Bobbs-Merrill, 1948.

Chavasse, Claude. "An Irish Setting." Lawlor and Auden 13–21.

Christopher, Joe R. *C. S. Lewis.* Twayne's English Authors Series. Boston: Twayne, 1987.

———. "From the Master's Lips: W. B. Yeats as C. S. Lewis Saw Him." *CSL: The Bulletin of the New York C. S. Lewis Society* 61 (Nov. 1974): 14–19.

———. "J. R. R. Tolkien and the Clerihew." Reynolds and GoodKnight 263–71.

———. "J. R. R. Tolkien, Narnian Exile." *Mythlore* 15.1 (whole no. 55, Autumn 1988): 37–45; 15.2 (whole no. 56, Winter 1988): 17–23.

———. "Letters from C. S. Lewis in the Humanities Research Center, The University of Texas at Austin: A Checklist." *CSL: The Bulletin of the New York C. S. Lewis Society* 133 (Nov. 1980): 1–7.

———. "A Note on an Unpublished (and Probably Unwritten) Collaboration." *Mythlore* 3.2 (whole no. 10, May 1975): 29.

———. "Roy Campbell and the Inklings." *Mythlore* 22.1 (whole no. 83, Autumn 1997): 33–46.

———. "Tolkien's Lyric Poetry." Flieger and Hostetter 143–60.

Coghill, Nevill. "The Approach to English." Gibb 51–66.

———, trans. *The Canterbury Tales.* By Geoffrey Chaucer. Baltimore: Penguin, 1952.

———. *The Collected Papers of Nevill Coghill, Shakespearian and Medievalist.* Ed. and Intr. Douglas Gray. Sussex: Harvester Press, 1988.

———. *Geoffrey Chaucer.* Bibliographical Series of Supplements to *British Book News* on Writers and Their Work. London: Longmans, Green, 1956.

———. "John Ronald Reuel Tolkien." Obituary. *Report of the Royal Society of Literature.* (1973–74 and 1974–75): 30–33.

———. *The Masque of Hope: presented for the entertainment of H. R. H. Princess Elizabeth on the occasion of her visit to University College, 25 May 1948, by the Oxford University Dramatic Society.* London: Oxford University Press, 1948.

———. "Men, Poets, and Machines." *Poetry Review* 56 (1965): 136–47.

———. *The Pardon of Piers Plowman.* London: British Academy, 1945.

———. *The Poet Chaucer.* 1949. 2nd ed. London: Oxford University Press, 1967.

———. *Shakespeare's Professional Skills.* 1959. Cambridge: Cambridge University Press, 1964.

Coghill, Nevill, and Christopher Tolkien, eds. *Chaucer: The Man of Law's Tale.* Harrap's English Classics. London: Harrap, 1969.

———, eds. *Chaucer: The Nun's Priest's Tale.* 1959. Harrap's English Classics. London: Harrap, 1977.

———, eds. *Chaucer: The Pardoner's Tale.* 1958. Harrap's English Classics. London: Harrap, 1980.

Coleridge, Samuel Taylor. *Biographia Literaria; or, Biographical Sketches of My Literary Life and Opinions.* 1817. London: J. M. Dent, 1956.

"Colin Hardie." Obituary. *Times* [London] 20 Oct. 1998: 21.

Como, James T., ed. *Remembering C. S. Lewis: Recollections of Those Who Knew Him.* San Francisco: Ignatius Press, 2005. Rpt. of *C. S. Lewis at the Breakfast Table and Other Reminiscences.* 1979.

Cording, Ruth James. "Links of the Inklings." Pavlac, *Proceedings* 44–47.

Cranborne, Hannah, ed. *David Cecil: A Portrait by His Friends.* 1990. Wimborne, Dorset, UK: Dovecote Press, 1991.

Crispin, Edmund [Bruce Montgomery]. *Swan Song.* 1947. New York: Walker, 1980.

d'Ardenne, Simonne, T. R. O., ed. *Þe Liflade ant te Passiun of Seinte Juliene.* 1936. Early English Text Society 248. London: Oxford University Press, 1961.

———. "The Man and the Scholar." Salu and Farrell 33–37.

Davidman, Joy. *Smoke on the Mountain: An Interpretation of the Ten Commandments.* Philadelphia: Westminster Press, 1954.

Davis, Norman, and C. L. Wrenn, eds. *English and Medieval Studies: Presented to J. R. R. Tolkien on the Occasion of His Seventieth Birthday.* London: Allen and Unwin, 1962.

Delbanco, Nicholas. *Group Portrait.* 1982. New York: Carroll and Graf, 1990.

Dodds, David Llewellyn. "Continuity and Change in the Development of Charles Williams's Poetic Style." Huttar and Schakel 192–214.

Dorsett, Lyle W. *And God Came In.* New York: Macmillan, 1983.

———, ed. and Introduction. *The Essential C. S. Lewis.* 1988. New York: Touchstone–Simon and Schuster, 1996.

———. *Seeking the Secret Place: The Spiritual Formation of C. S. Lewis.* Grand Rapids, MI: Brazos Press, 2004.

Downing, David C. *The Most Reluctant Convert.* Downers Grove, IL: InterVarsity Press, 2002.

———. *Planets in Peril: A Critical Study of C. S. Lewis's Ransom Trilogy.* Amherst: University of Massachusetts Press, 1992.

Dundas-Grant, James. "From an 'Outsider.'" Como 368–74.

Duriez, Colin. *The J. R. R. Tolkien Handbook: A Comprehensive Guide to His Life, Writings, and World of Middle-Earth.* Grand Rapids, MI: Baker Book House, 1992.

———. *Tolkien and C. S. Lewis: The Gift of Friendship.* Mahwah, NJ: HiddenSpring, 2003.

Duriez, Colin, and David Porter. *The Inklings Handbook: A Comprehensive Guide to the Lives, Thought and Writings of C. S. Lewis, J. R. R. Tolkien, Charles Williams, Owen Barfield and Their Friends.* St. Louis: Chalice Press, 2001.

Dyson, H. V. D., and John Butt. *Augustans and Romantics: 1689–1830. Introductions to English Literature* 3. London: Cresset Press, 1961.

Eddison, E. R., ed. and trans. *Egil's Saga: Done into English out of the Icelandic with an Introduction, Notes, and an Essay on Some Principles of Translation.* London: Cambridge University Press, 1930.

———. *A Fish Dinner in Memison:* Book 2, *The Zimiamvian Trilogy.* 1941. New York: Del Rey–Ballantine Books, 1978.

———. *The Mezentian Gate.* Book 3, *The Zimiamvian Trilogy.* 1958. New York: Del Rey–Ballantine Books, 1978.

———. *Mistress of Mistresses.* Book 1, *The Zimiamvian Trilogy.* 1935. New York: Ballantine Books, 1967.

———. *Styrbiorn the Strong.* London: Jonathan Cape, 1926.

———. *The Worm Ouroboros.* 1922. New York: Ballantine Books, 1968.

Ede, Lisa, and Andrea Lunsford. *Singular Texts/Plural Authors: Perspectives on Collaborative Writing.* Carbondale: Southern Illinois University Press, 1990.

Edmonds, E. L. "C. S. Lewis, the Teacher." Schofield 37–51.

Edwards, Bruce L. "*An Experiment in Criticism.*" Schultz and West 159–61.

———. *A Rhetoric of Reading: C. S. Lewis's Defense of Western Literacy.* Values in Literature Monographs 2. Provo, UT: Brigham Young University, 1986.

———, ed. *The Taste of the Pineapple: Essays on C. S. Lewis as Reader, Critic, and Imaginative Writer.* Bowling Green, OH: Bowling Green State University Popular Press, 1988.

Eliot, T. S. "Tradition and the Individual Talent." Adams 761–64.

Evans, David W. "T. S. Eliot, Charles Williams, and the Sense of the Occult." *Accent* 14 (1954): 148–55.

Farrell, Michael P. *Collaborative Circles: Friendship Dynamics and Creative Work.* Chicago: University of Chicago Press, 2001.

Farrer, Austin. "In His Image." Como 383–86.

A Film Portrait of J. R. R. Tolkien. Dir. Derek Bailey. Narr. Judi Dench. Visual Corporation, 1992.

Filmer, Kath. *The Fiction of C. S. Lewis: Mask and Mirror.* London: Macmillan Press; New York: St. Martin's Press, 1993.

Fitch, Noel Riley. *Sylvia Beach and the Lost Generation: A History of Literary Paris in the Twenties and Thirties.* New York: W. W. Norton, 1985.

Flieger, Verlyn. *Interrupted Music: The Making of Tolkien's Mythology.* Kent, OH: Kent State University Press, 2005.

———. *A Question of Time: J. R. R. Tolkien's Road to Faërie.* Kent, OH: Kent State University Press, 1997.

———. *Splintered Light: Logos and Language in Tolkien's World.* Grand Rapids, MI: Eerdmans, 1983.

Flieger, Verlyn, and Carl F. Hostetter, eds. *Tolkien's Legendarium: Essays on The History of Middle-earth.* Contributions to the Study of Science Fiction and Fantasy 86. Westport, CT: Greenwood Press, 2000.

Flower, Linda. "Writer-Based Prose: A Cognitive Basis for Problems in Writing." *College English* 41 (Sept. 1979): 19–37.

Ford, Paul F. "Books of Influence." Schultz and West 102+.

———. *Companion to Narnia.* New York: HarperSanFrancisco-HarperCollins, 1994.

Forman, Janis, ed. *New Visions of Collaborative Writing.* Portsmouth, NH: Boynton/ Cook, 1992.

Foster, Robert. *A Guide to Middle-Earth.* New York: Ballantine Books, 1971.

Foucault, Michel. "The Discourse on Language." *The Archaeology of Knowledge and the Discourse on Language.* Trans. A. M. Sheridan Smith. New York: Pantheon, 1972. 215–37.

Fox, Adam. "At the Breakfast Table." Como 179–88.

———. *Dean Inge.* London: John Murray, 1960.

———. *Old King Coel: A Rhymed Tale in Four Books.* London: Oxford University Press, 1937.

———. *Plato for Pleasure.* London: John Murray, 1962.

———. Rev. of *Terror of Light,* by Charles Williams. *Time and Tide* (18 May 1940): 534.

Fox, Adam, and Andrew Claye, comps. *English Well Used: Prose Passages.* London: John Baker, 1968.

Fox, Adam, Gareth Keene, and Georgina Keene, comps. *Sacred and Secular: A Companion.* Grand Rapids, MI: Eerdmans, 1975.

Fredrick, Candice, and Sam McBride. *Women among the Inklings: Gender, C. S. Lewis, J. R. R. Tolkien, and Charles Williams.* Westport, CT: Greenwood Press, 2001.

Freud, Jill Flewett. "Part B: With Girls at Home." Schofield 55–59.

Fryer, W. R. "Disappointment at Cambridge?" Schofield 29–35.

Garth, John. *Tolkien and the Great War: The Threshold of Middle-earth.* Boston: Houghton Mifflin, 2003.

Gere, Anne Ruggles. *Writing Groups: History, Theory, and Implications.* Carbondale: Southern Illinois University Press, 1987.

Gere, Anne Ruggles, and Laura Jane Roop. "For Profit and Pleasure: Collaboration in Nineteenth-Century Women's Literary Clubs." Forman 1–18.

Gibb, Jocelyn, ed. and Preface. *Light on C. S. Lewis.* Intr. Owen Barfield. 1965. New York: Harcourt, Brace and World, 1966. vi–viii

Gibson, Evan. "Letter to the Editor." *Canadian C. S. Lewis Journal* 80 (Autumn 1992): 12.

Gilbert, Douglas, and Clyde S. Kilby. *C. S. Lewis: Images of His World.* Grand Rapids, MI: Eerdmans, 1973.

Gilliver, Peter M. "At the Wordface: J. R. R. Tolkien's Work on the *Oxford English Dictionary.*" Reynolds and GoodKnight 173–86.

Glover, Donald E. *C. S. Lewis: The Art of Enchantment*. Athens: Ohio University Press, 1981.

Glyer, Diana Pavlac. "Joy Davidman Lewis: Author, Editor, and Collaborator." *Mythlore* 22.2 (whole no. 84 Summer 1998): 10+.

Glyer, Diana Pavlac, and Laura K. Simmons. "Dorothy L. Sayers and C. S. Lewis: Two Approaches to Creativity and Calling." *Seven: An Anglo-American Literary Review* 21 (2004): 31–46.

GoodKnight, Glen, and Bonnie GoodKnight. "Notes of a Journey." *Mythprint* (Oct. 1975): 10+.

Gordon, E. V., ed. *Pearl*. London: Oxford University Press, 1953.

Gordon, Ida L. Preface. E. V. Gordon iii–iv.

Graham, David, ed. *We Remember C. S. Lewis: Essays and Memoirs*. Nashville, TN: Broadman and Holman, 2001.

Gray, Charles Edward. "A Measurement of Creativity in Western Civilization." *American Anthropologist* 68 (1966): 1384–417.

Green, Roger Lancelyn. "Recollections." *Amon Hen* 44 (May 1980): 6–8.

Green, Roger Lancelyn, and Walter Hooper. *C. S. Lewis: A Biography*. San Diego: Harcourt Brace, 1974.

Gresham, Douglas H. *Lenten Lands*. New York: Macmillan, 1988.

———. Foreword. *Letters to Children*. By C. S. Lewis. Ed. Lyle W. Dorsett and Marjorie Lamp Mead. New York: Collier Macmillan, 1985. 1–2.

Grotta, Daniel. *J. R. R. Tolkien: Architect of Middle Earth*. Philadelphia: Running Press, 1992.

Hadfield, Alice Mary. *Charles Williams: An Exploration of His Life and Work*. New York: Oxford University Press, 1983.

———. *An Introduction to Charles Williams*. London: Robert Hale, 1959.

Hammond, Wayne G., and Douglas A. Anderson. *J. R. R. Tolkien: A Descriptive Bibliography*. Winchester Bibliographies of 20th Century Writers. New Castle, DE: Oak Knoll Books, 1993.

Hammond, Wayne G., and Christina Scull. *J. R. R. Tolkien: Artist and Illustrator*. Boston: Houghton Mifflin, 1995.

———. *The Lord of the Rings: A Reader's Companion*. Boston: Houghton Mifflin, 2005.

Hardie, Colin. "A Colleague's Note on C. S. Lewis." *Inklings-Jahrbuch* 3 (1985): 177–82.

———. Rev. of *The Discarded Image*, by C. S. Lewis. *Medium Aevum* 37 (1968): 95–97.

Harwood, A. C. "A Toast to His Memory." Como 377–82.

Hatziolou, Elizabeth. *John Wain, A Man of Letters*. London: Pisces Press, 1997.

Havard, R. E. "Philia: Jack at Ease." Como 349–67.

———. "Professor J. R. R. Tolkien: A Personal Memoir." *Mythlore* 17.2 (whole no. 64, Winter 1990): 61.

Helms, Randel. *Tolkien and the Silmarils*. Boston: Houghton Mifflin, 1981.

Hermerén, Göran. *Influence in Art and Literature*. Princeton: Princeton University Press, 1975.

Hillegas, Mark R., ed. *Shadows of Imagination: The Fantasies of C. S. Lewis, J. R. R. Tolkien, and Charles Williams*. Carbondale: Southern Illinois University Press, 1979.

Hinten, Marvin D. "'The Morte D'Arthur' (Book Review)." Schultz and West 287.

Hooper, Walter, ed. *The Collected Poems of C. S. Lewis*. London: Fount-HarperCollins, 1994.

———. *C. S. Lewis: A Companion and Guide*. N.p.: HarperSanFrancisco, 1996.

———, ed and Preface. *The Dark Tower and Other Stories*. By C. S. Lewis. 7–14.

———. Introduction. *Poems*. By C. S. Lewis. New York: Harcourt Brace Jovanovich, 1964.

———, ed and Introduction. *Letters of C. S. Lewis*. 9–19.

———, ed. and Introduction. *Mark vs. Tristram: Correspondence between C. S. Lewis and Owen Barfield*. Cambridge: Lowell House, 1967. N. pag.

———, ed. *On Stories and Other Essays on Literature*. By C. S. Lewis. New York: Harvest–Harcourt Brace, 1982.

———. "Oxford's Bonny Fighter." Como 241–308.

———. *Past Watchful Dragons: The Narnian Chronicles of C. S. Lewis*. London: Collier-Macmillan, 1979.

———. ed. and Introduction. *Selected Literary Essays*. By C. S. Lewis. vii–xx.

———, ed. *They Stand Together: The Letters of C. S. Lewis to Arthur Greeves (1914–1963)*. New York: Macmillan, 1979.

———. *Through Joy and Beyond: A Pictorial Biography of C. S. Lewis*. New York: Macmillan, 1982.

———. "To the Martlets." Keefe 37–62.

Hopkins, Gerard. "Charles Williams 1886–1945." *Supplement to "The Periodical"* July 1945. Rpt. of article in *The Bookseller* 2059 (24 May 1945). Oxford: Oxford University Press, 1945.

———. *Nor Fish nor Flesh*. London: Gollancz, 1933.

Horne, Brian. "A Peculiar Debt: The Influence of Charles Williams on C. S. Lewis." *A Christian for All Christians: Essays in Honour of C. S. Lewis*. Ed. Andrew Walker and James Patrick. London: Hodder and Stoughton, 1990. 83–97.

Houston, James. "Reminiscences of the Oxford Lewis." Graham 129–43.

Howard, Thomas. *The Novels of Charles Williams*. New York: Oxford University Press, 1983.

Hunter, Jeanne Clayton. "Night Operation." [Commentary]. Hunter and Kranidas 129–30.

Hunter, Jeanne Clayton, and Thomas Kranidas. "Notes to the Poetry." Hunter and Kranidas 177–78.

Hunter, Jeanne Clayton, and Thomas Kranidas, eds. *A Barfield Sampler: Poetry and Fiction by Owen Barfield*. Albany: State University of New York, 1993.

Huttar, Charles A. "C. S. Lewis, T. S. Eliot, and the Milton Legacy: The *Nativity Ode* Revisited." *Texas Studies in Literature and Language* 44 (2002): 324–48.

———. "A Lifelong Love Affair with Language: C. S. Lewis's Poetry." *Word and Story in C. S. Lewis*. Ed. Peter J. Schakel and Charles A. Huttar. Columbia: University of Missouri Press, 1991. 86–108.

Huttar, Charles A. and Peter J. Schakel, eds. *The Rhetoric of Vision: Essays on Charles Williams*. Lewisburg, PA: Bucknell University Press, 1996.

Irwin, W. R. "There and Back Again: The Romances of Williams, Lewis, and Tolkien." *Sewanee Review* 69 (Fall 1961): 566–78.

James, Henry. *Hawthorne*. 1879. Ithaca, NY: Cornell University Press, 1967.

Jeschke, Melanie M. *Inklings*. Fairfax, VA: Xulon Press, 2002.

John-Steiner, Vera. *Creative Collaboration*. New York: Oxford University Press, 2000.

Jones, Siriol Hugh. "Vogue's Spotlight." *Vogue* (Apr. 1947): 75+.

Joosse, Barbara M. *Mama, Do You Love Me?* Illus. Barbara Lavallee. San Francisco: Chronicle Books, 1991.

J. R. R. Tolkien: An Audio Portrait. Presented by Brian Sibley. BBC Worldwide Ltd. 2001.

Keefe, Carolyn, ed. *C. S. Lewis: Speaker and Teacher*. 1971. Grand Rapids, MI: Zondervan, 1980.

Kilby, Clyde S. *Tolkien and The Silmarillion*. Wheaton, IL: Harold Shaw, 1976.

———. "'I'd like to have you come': Clyde Kilby Remembers J. R. R. Tolkien." *Minas Tirith Evening Star* 9.2 (Jan 1980): 5–8.

Kilby, Clyde S., and Marjorie Lamp Mead, eds. and Introduction. *Brothers and Friends: The Diaries of Major Warren Hamilton Lewis.* San Francisco: Harper and Row, 1982.

King, Alec, and Martin Ketley. *The Control of Language.* London: Longmans, Green, 1939.

King, Don W. *C. S. Lewis, Poet: The Legacy of His Poetic Impulse.* Kent, OH: Kent State University Press, 2001.

———. *Hunting the Unicorn: A Critical Biography of Ruth Pitter.* Kent, OH. Kent State University Press, forthcoming.

King, Martin Luther, Jr. *Where Do We Go from Here: Chaos or Community?* New York: Harper and Row, 1967.

King, Roma A., Jr., ed. and Introduction. *To Michal from Serge: Letters from Charles Williams to His Wife, Florence, 1939–1945.* Kent, OH: Kent State University Press, 2002.

———. *The Pattern in the Web: The Mythical Poetry of Charles Williams.* Kent, OH: Kent State University Press, 1990.

Knight, Gareth. *The Magical World of the Inklings: J. R. R. Tolkien, C. S. Lewis, Charles Williams, Owen Barfield.* Longmead, Eng.: Element Books, 1990.

Knowles, Sebastian D. G. *A Purgatorial Flame: Seven British Writers in the Second World War.* Philadelphia: University of Pennsylvania Press, 1990.

Kranidas, Tom. "C. S. Lewis and the Poetry of Owen Barfield." *The Owen Barfield World Wide Website: Barfield Scholarship.* Accessed 17 Nov. 2004. <http://www.owenbarfield.com/>.

Kroeber, A. L. *Configurations of Culture Growth.* Berkeley: University of California Press, 1944.

Lake, David. "The Variant Texts of *That Hideous Strength.*" *Ring Bearer, Journal of the Mythopoeic Literature Society of Australia* 7.1. (Winter 1989): N. pag.

Lasswell, Harold D. "The Social Setting of Creativity." *Creativity and Its Cultivation.* Ed. Harold H. Anderson. New York: Harper & Brothers, 1959. 203–21.

Lawlor, John. *C. S. Lewis: Memories and Reflections.* Dallas: Spence, 1998.

———, ed. *Patterns of Love and Courtesy: Essays in Memory of C. S. Lewis.* London: Edward Arnold, 1966.

Lawlor, John, and W. H. Auden, eds. *To Nevill Coghill from Friends.* London: Faber and Faber, 1966.

Lazo, Andrew. "Gathered Round Northern Fires: The Imaginative Impact of the Kolbítar." *Tolkien and the Invention of Myth: A Reader.* Ed. Jane Chance. Lexington: University Press of Kentucky, 2004. 191–226.

LeFevre, Karen Burke. *Invention as a Social Act.* Carbondale: Southern Illinois University Press, 1987.

Lenander, David. "The Cocktail Party After All Hallows' Eve: All Saints' Day Hangover." Pavlac, *Proceedings* 135–45.

Lewis, C. S. *The Abolition of Man: or Reflections on Education with Special Reference to the Teaching of English in the Upper Forms of Schools.* 1944. N.p.: HarperSanFrancisco-HarperCollins, 2001.

———. *The Allegory of Love: A Study in Medieval Tradition.* 1936. Oxford: Oxford University Press, 1985.

———. *All My Road Before Me: The Diary of C. S. Lewis, 1922–1927.* Ed. Walter Hooper. San Diego: Harcourt Brace Jovanovich, 1991.

———. *Beyond Personality: The Christian Idea of God.* London: Bles-Centenary Press, 1944.

———. *Boxen: The Imaginary World of the Young C. S. Lewis.* Ed. Walter Hooper. New York: Harcourt Brace Jovanovich, 1985.

———. "Charles Walter Stansby Williams (1886–1945)." Obituary. *Oxford Magazine* (24 May 1945): 265.

———. *Christian Behaviour.* 1943. London: Bles-Centenary Press, 1946.

———. "Christianity and Literature." *Christian Reflections* 1–11.

———. *Christian Reflections.* 1967. Ed. Walter Hooper. Grand Rapids, MI: Eerdmans, 1989.

———. *Collected Letters.* Ed. Walter Hooper. 2 vols. to date. London: HarperCollins, 2000–2006.

———. *The Collected Poems of C. S. Lewis.* Ed. Walter Hooper. London: Fount-Harper-Collins, 1994.

———. "Cross-Examination." *God in the Dock* 258–67.

———. *The Dark Tower and Other Stories.* Ed. Walter Hooper. New York: Harvest-Harcourt Brace Jovanovich, 1977.

———. "De Descriptione Temporum." 1955. *Selected Literary Essays* 1–14.

———. "The Dethronement of Power." Rev. of *The Two Towers* and *The Return of the King,* by J. R. R. Tolkien. *Time and Tide* (22 Oct. 1955): 1373–74.

———. *The Discarded Image: An Introduction to Medieval and Renaissance Literature.* 1964. Cambridge: Cambridge University Press, 1967.

———. *Dymer.* 1926. *Narrative Poems.* Ed. Walter Hooper. New York: Harcourt Brace Jovanovich, 1969. 1–91.

———. *English Literature in the Sixteenth Century, Excluding Drama.* 1954. Oxford History of English Literature 3. Oxford: Oxford University Press, 1973.

———. "The English Prose *Morte.*" *Essays on Malory.* Ed. J. A. W. Bennett. Oxford: Clarendon Press, 1963. 7–28.

———. *An Experiment in Criticism.* 1961. Cambridge: Cambridge University Press, 1988.

———. *The Four Loves.* 1960. San Diego: Harvest-Harcourt, 1988.

———. *God in the Dock: Essays on Theology and Ethics.* Ed. Walter Hooper. Grand Rapids, MI: Eerdmans, 1970.

———. "The Godfather." *Oxford Today: The University Magazine* (Michaelmas 1998): 55.

———. "The Gods Return to Earth." Rev. of *The Fellowship of the Ring,* by J. R. R. Tolkien. *Time and Tide* (14 Aug 1954): 1082–83.

———. *The Great Divorce.* 1945. New York: Touchstone-Simon & Schuster, 1996.

———. *A Grief Observed.* 1961. London: Faber and Faber, 1971.

———. "The Hobbit." *On Stories and Other Essays on Literature.* 81–82. Rpt. of "A World for Children." Rev. of *The Hobbit,* by J. R. R. Tolkien. *Times Literary Supplement* 2 Oct. 1937: 714.

———. *The Horse and His Boy.* New York: Macmillan, 1954.

———. "It All Began with a Picture. . . ." *Of Other Worlds* 42.

———. *The Last Battle.* New York: Macmillan, 1956.

———. *Letters of C. S. Lewis.* Ed. and with a Memoir by W. H. Lewis. 1966. Rev. and enl. ed. Walter Hooper. San Diego: Harcourt Brace, 1988.

———. *Letters to an American Lady.* Ed. Clyde S. Kilby. Grand Rapids, MI: Eerdmans, 1967.

———. *Letters to Children.* Ed. Lyle W. Dorsett and Marjorie Lamp Mead. Foreword by Douglas Gresham. New York: Collier-Macmillan, 1985.

———. *Letters to Malcolm: Chiefly on Prayer.* New York: Harcourt Brace and World, 1964.

———. "Life Partners." Rev. of *This Ever Diverse Pair,* by G. A. L. Burgeon (pseud. of Owen Barfield). *Time and Tide* (25 March 1950): 286.

———. *The Lion, the Witch and the Wardrobe*. 1950. New York: Harper Trophy–Harper-Collins, 1994.

———. "The Literary Impact of the Authorised Version." 1950. *Selected Literary Essays* 126–45.

———. *The Magician's Nephew*. New York: Macmillan, 1955.

———. *Mere Christianity: A Revised and Enlarged Edition, with a New Introduction, of the Three Books The Case for Christianity, Christian Behaviour, and Beyond Personality.* 1952. First paperback ed. New York: Collier-Macmillan, 1960.

———. *Miracles: A Preliminary Study*. 1947. Rev. 1960. Restored 1996. New York: Harper-SanFrancisco-HarperCollins, 2001.

———. "Modern Theology and Biblical Criticism." *Christian Reflections* 152–66.

———. "The *Morte Darthur*." Rev. of *The Works of Sir Thomas Malory*, by Eugène Vinaver. *Times Literary Supplement* 7 June 1947: 273–74. Rpt. in *Studies in Medieval and Renaissance Literature*. Ed. Walter Hooper. Cambridge: Cambridge University Press, 1966. 103–10.

———. "Myth Became Fact." *God in the Dock* 63–67.

———. *Of Other Worlds: Essays and Stories*. Ed. Walter Hooper. San Diego: Harvest-Harcourt Brace, 1966.

———. *On Stories and Other Essays on Literature*. Ed. Walter Hooper. New York: Harvest-Harcourt Brace, 1982.

———. "On Three Ways of Writing for Children." *On Stories and Other Essays on Literature* 31–43.

———. *Out of the Silent Planet*. 1938. New York: Macmillan, 1965.

———. *Perelandra: A Novel*. 1943. New York: Scribner Paperback Fiction–Simon and Schuster, 1996.

———. *The Pilgrim's Regress: An Allegorical Apology for Christianity, Reason, and Romanticism*. 1933. Grand Rapids, MI: Eerdmans, 1981.

———. *Poems*. Ed. Walter Hooper. New York: Harcourt Brace Jovanovich, 1964.

———. Preface. *Essays Presented to Charles Williams*. 1947. Grand Rapids, MI: Eerdmans, 1966. v–xiv.

———. *A Preface to Paradise Lost*. 1942. London: Oxford University Press, 1961.

———. *Present Concerns*. Ed. Walter Hooper. San Diego: Harcourt Brace Jovanovich, 1986.

———. *Prince Caspian: The Return to Narnia*. 1951. New York: Collier-Macmillan, 1975.

———. *The Problem of Pain*. 1940. Appendix R. Havard. New York: Macmillan, 1944.

———. *Reflections on the Psalms*. New York: Harcourt Brace Jovanovich, 1958.

———. *Rehabilitations and Other Essays*. London: Oxford University Press, 1939.

———. "Rejoinder to Dr Pittenger." *God in the Dock* 177–83.

———. "A Reply to Professor Haldane." *On Stories and Other Essays on Literature* 69–79.

———. Rev. of *The Oxford Book of Christian Verse*, ed. Lord David Cecil. *Review of English Studies* 17 (1941): 95–102.

———. Rev. of *Taliessin through Logres*, by Charles Williams. *Oxford Magazine* 14 Mar. 1946: 248–50.

———. "A Sacred Poem." Rev. of *Taliessin through Logres*, by Charles Williams. *Theology* 38 (1939): 268–76.

———. *The Screwtape Letters, with "Screwtape Proposes a Toast."* 1942; 1961. New York: HarperSanFrancisco-HarperCollins, 2001.

———. *Selected Literary Essays*. 1969. Ed. Walter Hooper. Cambridge: Cambridge University Press, 1980.

———. *The Silver Chair*. New York: Macmillan, 1953.

——. *Spirits in Bondage: A Cycle of Lyrics*. 1919. *The Collected Poems of C. S. Lewis* 157–223.

——. *Studies in Words*. 1960. 2nd ed. Cambridge: Cambridge University Press, 1967.

——. *Surprised by Joy: The Shape of My Early Life*. New York: Harcourt, Brace and World, 1955.

——. "Talking about Bicycles." *Present Concerns* 67–72.

——. *That Hideous Strength: A Modern Fairy-Tale for Grown-Ups*. 1946. New York: Collier-Macmillan, 1965.

——. *They Stand Together: The Letters of C. S. Lewis to Arthur Greeves (1914–1963)*. Ed. Walter Hooper. New York: Macmillan, 1979.

——. *Till We Have Faces: A Myth Retold*. 1956. New York: Harcourt Brace, 1985.

——. "Tolkien's *The Lord of the Rings*." *On Stories and Other Essays on Literature*. 83–90. Rpt. of "The Gods Return to Earth." and "The Dethronement of Power."

——. *The Tortured Planet*. Abr. ed. of *That Hideous Strength*. New York: Avon Publications, 1946.

——. *The Voyage of the "Dawn Treader."* New York: Macmillan, 1952.

——. *Voyage to Venus (Perelandra)*. 1943. London: Pan Books. 1953.

——. "Wain's Oxford." Letter. *Encounter* (January 1963): 81.

——. *The Weight of Glory and Other Addresses*. 1949. Grand Rapids, MI: Eerdmans, 1979.

——. "'Who gaf me Drink?'" Rev. of *Romanticism Comes of Age*, by Owen Barfield. *Spectator* 9 (Mar. 1945): 224.

——. "Williams and the Arthuriad." *Williams and Lewis* 93–200.

Lewis, C. S., and Owen Barfield. *Mark vs. Tristram: Correspondence between C. S. Lewis and Owen Barfield*. Ed. Walter Hooper. Ltd. ed. 126 copies. Cambridge: Lowell House, 1967. N. pag.

Lewis, C. S., and Dorothy L. Sayers. "Charles Williams." Letter. *Times* [London] 14 May 1955: 9.

Lewis, Warren Hamilton. *Assault on Olympus: The Rise of the House of Gramont between 1604 and 1678*. New York: Harcourt, Brace, 1958.

——. *Brothers and Friends: The Diaries of Major Warren Hamilton Lewis*. Ed. and Intr. Clyde S. Kilby and Marjorie Lamp Mead. San Francisco: Harper and Row, 1982.

——. "Memoir of C. S. Lewis." *Letters of C. S. Lewis* 21–46.

——, ed. *Memoirs of the Duc de Saint-Simon*. 1829–1830. Trans. Bayle St. John. London: B. T. Batsford, 1964.

——. *The Scandalous Regent: A Life of Philippe, Duc d'Orleans 1674–1723, and of His Family*. New York: Harcourt, Brace and World, 1961.

——. *The Splendid Century: Life in the France of Louis XIV*. 1953. New York: Doubleday, 1957.

——. *The Sunset of the Splendid Century: The Life and Times of Louis Auguste de Bourbon, Duc du Maine 1670–1736*. 1955. New York: Doubleday, 1963.

Leyland, Margaret M. "Lewis and the Schoolgirls." *The Lamp-Post of the Southern California C. S. Lewis Society: A Literary Review of Lewis Studies* 1.3 (July 1977): 1–2. Rpt. in *Lamp-post* 12–13 (Dec. 1989): 54–55.

Lindsay, David. *A Voyage to Arcturus*. 1920. New York: Del Rey–Ballantine Books, 1963.

Lindskoog, Kathryn. *The C. S. Lewis Hoax*. Portland, OR: Multnomah Press, 1988.

————. *Finding the Landlord: A Guidebook to C. S. Lewis's Pilgrim's Regress.* Chicago: Cornerstone Press, 1995.

————. *Light in the Shadowlands: Protecting the Real C. S. Lewis.* Sisters, OR: Multnomah Books, 1994.

————. *Sleuthing C. S. Lewis: More Light in the Shadowlands.* Macon, GA: Mercer University Press, 2001.

Macgowan, John. *Infernal Conference: or Dialogues of Devils.* 1772. Pittsburgh, 1832.

Manzalaoui, M. A. "Narnia: The Domain of Lewis's Beliefs." Graham 9–25.

Mathew, Gervase. *The Court of Richard II.* London: Murray, 1968.

————. "Justice and Charity in *The Vision of Piers Plowman.*" *Dominican Studies* 1 (1948): 360–66.

————. "Orator." Rev. of *C. S. Lewis: A Biography,* by Roger Lancelyn Green and Walter Hooper. *New Blackfriars* (1974): 529–30. Rpt., slightly abr. in Como 189–90.

————. "Williams and the Arthuriad." Rev. of *Arthurian Torso,* by Charles Williams and C. S. Lewis. *Time and Tide* (1 Jan. 1949): 14.

Matthews, Janet. "Charles Williams: A Perspective through the Eyes and Works of T. S. Eliot." Pavlac, *Proceedings* 161–94.

McCallum, R. B. Rev. of *The Hobbit,* by J. R. R. Tolkien. *Pembroke College Record* (1937–38): 9.

McClusky, Joan. "J. R. R. Tolkien: A Short Biography." A. Becker 9–42.

McKenna, Stephen. *Confessions of a Well-Meaning Woman.* London: Cassell, 1923.

Medcalf, Stephen. "The Athanasian Principle in Williams's Use of Images." Huttar and Schakel. 27–43.

Milford, Humphrey S., ed., in collaboration with Charles Williams. *The Oxford Book of Regency Verse.* Oxford: Clarendon Press, 1928.

Milligan, B. A. Foreword. Wright N. pag.

Mills, David, ed. *The Pilgrim's Guide: C. S. Lewis and the Art of Witness.* Grand Rapids, MI: Eerdmans, 1998.

Milward, Peter. "From G. K. Chesterton to C. S. Lewis." Graham 65–69.

Mitchell, Christopher W. "Bearing the Weight of Glory: The Cost of C. S. Lewis's Witness." Mills 3–14.

————. "University Battles: C. S. Lewis and the Oxford University Socratic Club." *C. S. Lewis: Lightbearer in the Shadowlands: The Evangelistic Vision of C. S. Lewis.* Ed. Angus J. L. Menuge. Wheaton, IL: Crossway Books, 1997. 329–51.

Moorman, Charles. *Arthurian Triptych: Mythic Materials in Charles Williams, C. S. Lewis, and T. S. Eliot.* Berkeley: University of California Press, 1960.

————. *The Precincts of Felicity: The Augustinian City of the Oxford Christians.* Gainesville: University of Florida Press, 1966.

Morgan, Edwin. Rev. of *The Sunset of the Splendid Century,* by Warren Lewis. *America* 31 Dec. 1955: 383.

Morris, Clifford. "A Christian Gentleman." Como 317–30.

Moynihan, Martin. "I Sleep but My Heart Watcheth." Graham 36–40.

Murray, Robert. "A Tribute to Tolkien." Obituary. *The Tablet* (15 Sept. 1973): 879–80.

Nichols, Aidan. "Gervase Mathew." *Dominican Gallery: Portrait of a Culture.* Leominster: Gracewing, 1997. 268–303.

Oakeshott, Michael. "The Voice of Poetry in the Conversation of Mankind." *Rationalism in Politics.* New York: Basic Books, 1962. 197–247.

Owen, W. J. B. "Splendid Tutor." Graham 59–60.

"The Oxford Dante Society." *Centenary Essays on Dante*. Ed. Colin Hardie. Oxford: Clarendon Press, 1965. 143–47.

Packer, J. I. "The Pilgrim's Regress." Graham 29–31.

Parker, Edward A., ed. *A Book of Longer Modern Verse*. Notes by Charles Williams. Oxford: Clarendon Press, 1926.

Patterson, Nancy-Lou. "'Some Kind of Company:' The Sacred Community in *That Hideous Strength*." Pavlac, *Proceedings* 247–70.

Pavlac, Diana Lynne. "More Than a Bandersnatch: Tolkien as Collaborative Writer." Reynolds and GoodKnight 367–74.

Pavlac, Diana Lynne, ed. *Proceedings of the Sixteenth Annual Convention of the Mythopoeic Society*. Wheaton, IL: Mythcon 16, 1985.

Philip, Peter. "South African View." Schofield 93–96.

Phillips, Justin. *C. S. Lewis at the BBC: Messages of Hope in the Darkness of War*. London, HarperCollins, 2003.

Pitter, Ruth. "Poet to Poet." Schofield 111–15.

Plimmer, Charlotte, and Denis Plimmer. "The Man Who Understands Hobbits." *London Daily Telegraph Magazine* (22 March 1968): 31+.

Plotnik, Arthur. *The Elements of Editing: A Modern Guide for Editors and Journalists*. New York: Macmillan, 1984.

Prescott, Orville. "Books of the Times." *New York Times* 22 Oct. 1948: 23.

Priestman, Judith, comp. *Tolkien: Life and Legend. An Exhibition to Commemorate the Centenary of the Birth of J. R. R. Tolkien (1892–1973)*. Oxford: Bodleian Library, 1992.

"Professor J. R. R. Tolkien." Obituary. *Times* [London] 3 Sept. 1973: 15. Rpt. in Salu and Farrell. 11–15.

Rateliff, John D. "'And Something Yet Remains to be Said': Tolkien and Williams." *Mythlore* 12.3 (whole no. 45, Spring 1986): 48–54.

———. "*The Lost Road, The Dark Tower*, and *The Notion Club Papers*: Tolkien and Lewis's Time Travel Triad." Flieger and Hostetter 199–218.

———. "Owen Barfield: A Short Reading List." *C. S. Lewis, Owen Barfield: A Souvenir Book for the Centenary Celebration Held at Wheaton, Illinois July 15–20, 1998 by the Mythopoeic Society*. Ed. Wayne G. Hammond. N. p., 1998. 22–25.

Ready, William. *The Tolkien Relation*. Chicago: Henry Regnery, 1968.

Renza, Louis A. "Influence." *Critical Terms for Literary Study*. Ed. Frank Lentricchia and Thomas McLaughlin. Chicago: University of Chicago Press, 1990. 186–202.

Reynolds, Patricia, and Glen H. GoodKnight, eds. *Proceedings of the J. R. R. Tolkien Centenary Conference 1992*. Milton Keynes and Altadena, CA: Tolkien Society, Mythopoeic Press, 1995.

Ridler, Anne, ed. and Critical Introduction. *The Image of the City and Other Essays*. By Charles Williams. London: Oxford University Press, 1958.

Rigby, Luke. "A Solid Man." Como 111–14.

Robbins, Rossel Hope. "A Possible Analogue for *The Cocktail Party*." *English Studies* 34 (1953): 165–67.

Rogers, Mary. "Rejected by Oxford." *Oxford Today: The University Magazine* (Michaelmas 1998): 53–55.

Rook, Alan. "The Butcher." Schofield 11–15.

Rosenbaum, S. P., ed. *The Bloomsbury Group: A Collection of Memoirs and Commentary*. Toronto: University of Toronto Press, 1995.

Routley, Erik. "A Prophet." *Como* 105–10.

Sale, Roger. "England's Parnassus: C. S. Lewis, Charles Williams, and J. R. R. Tolkien." *Hudson Review* 17 (Summer 1964): 203–25.

Salu, Mary, and Robert T. Farrell, eds. *J. R. R. Tolkien, Scholar and Storyteller: Essays in Memoriam.* Ithaca, NY: Cornell University Press, 1979.

Sayer, George. "C. S. Lewis: The Man." Schultz and West 246–47.

———. *Jack: C. S. Lewis and His Times.* San Francisco: Harper and Row, 1988.

———. "Recollections of J. R. R. Tolkien." Reynolds and GoodKnight 21–25.

Sayers, Dorothy L. *Further Papers on Dante.* New York: Harper and Brothers, 1957.

———. *Introductory Papers on Dante.* New York: Harper and Brothers, 1954.

———. *The Letters of Dorothy L. Sayers 1944–1950: Vol. 3, A Noble Daring.* Ed. Barbara Reynolds. Cambridge: Dorothy L. Sayers Society, 1998.

———. *The Poetry of Search and the Poetry of Statement.* London: Victor Gollancz, 1963.

Schneider, Angelika. "Coinherent Rhetoric in *Taliessin through Logres.*" Huttar and Schakel 179–91.

Schofield, Stephen, ed. *In Search of C. S. Lewis.* South Plainfield, NJ: Bridge, 1983.

Schrage, Michael. *Shared Minds: The New Technologies of Collaboration.* New York: Knopf, 1990.

Schultz, Jeffrey D., and John G. West Jr. *The C. S. Lewis Readers' Encyclopedia.* Grand Rapids, MI: Zondervan, 1998.

Shippey, T. A. *J. R. R. Tolkien: Author of the Century.* Boston: Houghton Mifflin, 2002.

———. *The Road to Middle-Earth.* 1982. New ed. London: Grafton-HarperCollins, 1992.

Starr, Nathan C. "Good Cheer and Sustenance." *Como* 219–26.

Stillinger, Jack. *Multiple Authorship and the Myth of Solitary Genius.* New York: Oxford University Press, 1991.

Tennyson, G. B., ed. and Introduction. *Owen Barfield on C. S. Lewis.* Middletown, CT: Wesleyan University Press, 1989. xi–xx.

Thisted, Valdemar Adolph. *Letters from Hell.* London: R. Bentley, 1866.

Thrash, Lois G. "A Source for the Redemption Theme in *The Cocktail Party.*" *Texas Studies in Literature and Language* 9 (1968): 547–53.

Tillyard, E. M. W., and C. S. Lewis. *The Personal Heresy: A Controversy.* 1939. London: Oxford University Press, 1965.

Tolkien, Christopher. "The Battle of the Goths and the Huns." *Saga-Book* 14.3. (1955–56): 141–63.

———. Foreword. *The Hobbit, or There and Back Again.* By J. R. R. Tolkien. Special 50th Anniversary Ed. 1987. Boston: Houghton Mifflin, 1966. N. pag.

———. Foreword and notes. *Pictures by J. R. R. Tolkien.* 1979. Boston: Houghton Mifflin, 1992. N. pag.

———. " . . . Future Publishing." *Amon Hen* 63 (Aug. 1983): 4.

———, ed. *The History of Middle-earth.* By J. R. R. Tolkien. 12 vols. Boston: Houghton Mifflin, 1983–96.

———. *The History of Middle-earth Index.* Comp. Helen Armstrong. London: Harper-Collins, 2002.

———. Introduction. *Tree and Leaf.* By J. R. R. Tolkien 5–8.

———, ed. *The Monsters and the Critics and Other Essays.* By J. R. R. Tolkien. London: Allen and Unwin, 1983. Boston: Houghton Mifflin, 1984.

———. "'Moria Gate' . . . Another Look." *Amon Hen* 70 (Nov. 1984): 3.

———. "Notes on the Differences in Editions of *The Hobbit* Cited by Mr. David Cofield." *Beyond Bree*. Tolkien Special Interest Group (July 1986): 1–3.

———. "Notes on the Pictures." *J. R. R. Tolkien Calendar 1979*. London: Allen and Unwin, 1978.

———. "Notes on the Pictures." *The Lord of the Rings 1977 Calendar*. London: Allen and Unwin, 1976.

———. "Notes on the Pictures." *The Silmarillion Calendar 1978*. London: Allen and Unwin, 1977.

———, ed. *Sauron Defeated: The End of the Third Age (The History of The Lord of the Rings Part Four)*. *The History of Middle-earth* 9. London: HarperCollins, 1992.

———, ed. *The Silmarillion*. By J. R. R. Tolkien. Boston: Houghton Mifflin, 1977.

———. *The Silmarillion [by] J. R. R. Tolkien: A Brief Account of the Book and Its Making*. Boston: Houghton Mifflin, 1977. N. pag.

———, ed. and Preface. *Sir Gawain and the Green Knight, Pearl and Sir Orfeo*. Trans. J. R. R. Tolkien. Boston: Houghton Mifflin, 1975. 7–9.

———. "The Tengwar Numerals." *Quettar* 13 (Feb. 1982): 8–9.

———, ed. with Introduction, Commentary, Index, and Maps. *Unfinished Tales of Númenor and Middle-earth*. By J. R. R. Tolkien. Boston: Houghton Mifflin, 1980.

———, ed. *The War of the Ring: The History of The Lord of the Rings Part Three*. *The History of Middle-earth* 8. Boston: Houghton Mifflin, 1990.

Tolkien, John, and Priscilla Tolkien. *The Tolkien Family Album*. Boston: Houghton Mifflin, 1992.

Tolkien, J. R. R. *The Adventures of Tom Bombadil: and other verses from The Red Book*. Boston: Houghton Mifflin, 1962.

———, ed. *Ancrene Wisse: The English Text of the Ancrene Riwle: Ancrene Wisse*. London: Oxford University Press, 1962.

———. *Ainulindalë*. *The Silmarillion*. Ed. Christopher Tolkien. Boston: Houghton Mifflin, 1977.

———. "Beowulf: The Monsters and the Critics." 1936. *The Monsters and the Critics* 5–48.

———. *Beowulf and the Critics*. Ed. Michael D. C. Drout. Medieval and Renaissance Texts and Studies 248. Tempe: Arizona Center for Medieval and Renaissance Studies, 2002.

———. *Bilbo's Last Song (at the Grey Havens)*. 1974. Rev. ed. New York: Knopf, 2002.

———. "Chaucer as a Philologist: The Reeve's Tale." *Transactions of the Philological Society*. London: David Nutt, 1934. 1–70.

———. "English and Welsh." 1963. *The Monsters and the Critics* 162–97.

———. *Farmer Giles of Ham*. 1949. London: Allen and Unwin, 1966.

———. *The Fellowship of the Ring: Being the First Part of The Lord of the Rings*. 1954. Boston: Houghton Mifflin, 1994.

———. *Finn and Hengest: The Fragment and the Episode*. Ed. Alan Bliss. Boston: Houghton Mifflin, 1983.

———. *The Hobbit, or There and Back Again*. Boston: Houghton Mifflin, 1966.

———. "Iþþlen in *Sawles Warde*." *English Studies* 28.6 (Dec. 1947): 168–70.

———. *The Lay of Leithian*. *The Lays of Beleriand* 150–363.

———. "Leaf by Niggle." 1945. *Tree and Leaf* 75–95.

———. *Letters from Father Christmas*. Ed. Baillie Tolkien. 1995. Rev. ed. Boston: Houghton Mifflin, 1999. Enl. ed. of *The Father Christmas Letters*. 1976.

——. *The Letters of J. R. R. Tolkien.* Ed. Humphrey Carpenter with the assistance of Christopher Tolkien. Boston: Houghton Mifflin, 2000.

——. *The Lost Road and Other Writings: Language and Legend before* "The Lord of the Rings." *The History of Middle-earth* 5. Ed. Christopher Tolkien. Boston: Houghton Mifflin, 1987.

——. "Middle English 'Losenger.'" *Essais de Philologie Moderne.* (1951): 63–76.

——. *A Middle English Vocabulary: Fourteenth Century Verse and Prose.* 1922. Ed. Kenneth Sisam. Oxford: Clarendon Press, 1946. N.pag.

——. *The Monsters and the Critics and Other Essays.* Ed. Christopher Tolkien. London: Allen and Unwin, 1983.

——. *Mr. Bliss.* Boston: Houghton Mifflin, 1983.

——. "Mythopoeia." *Tree and Leaf* 97–101.

——. "The Name 'Nodens.'" *Report on the Excavation of the Prehistoric, Roman, and Post-Roman Site in Lydney Park, Gloucestershire.* By R. E. M. Wheeler and T. V. Wheeler. Reports of the Research Committee of the Society of Antiquaries of London 9. Oxford: Oxford University Press, for Society of Antiquaries, Burlington House, London, 1932. 132–37.

——. *The Notion Club Papers. Sauron Defeated* 143-327.

——. "On Fairy-Stories." *Tree and Leaf* 9–73.

——. *The Peoples of Middle-earth. The History of Middle-earth* 12. Ed. Christopher Tolkien. Boston: Houghton Mifflin, 1996.

——. *The Return of the King: Being the Third Part of The Lord of the Rings.* 1955. Boston: Houghton Mifflin, 1994.

——. *The Return of the Shadow: The History of The Lord of the Rings Part One. The History of Middle-earth* 6. Ed. Christopher Tolkien. Boston: Houghton Mifflin, 1988.

——. *Roverandom.* Boston: Houghton Mifflin, 1998.

——. *Sauron Defeated: The End of the Third Age (The History of The Lord of the Rings Part Four). The History of Middle-earth* 9. Ed. Christopher Tolkien. London: HarperCollins, 1992.

——. "Sigelwara Land [Part 1]." *Medium Aevum* 1.3 (1932): 183–96.

——. "Sigelwara Land [Part 2]." *Medium Aevum* 3.2 (1934): 95–111.

——. *The Silmarillion.* Ed. Christopher Tolkien. Boston: Houghton Mifflin, 1977.

——, trans. *Sir Gawain and the Green Knight, Pearl,* and *Sir Orfeo.* Ed. and Pref. Christopher Tolkien. Boston: Houghton Mifflin, 1975.

——. *Smith of Wootton Major.* Boston: Houghton Mifflin, 1967.

——. "Some Contributions to Middle-English Lexicography." *Review of English Studies.* 1 (1925): 210 15.

——. *The Treason of Isengard: The History of The Lord of the Rings Part Two. The History of Middle-earth* 7. Ed. Christopher Tolkien. Boston: Houghton Mifflin, 1989.

——. *Tree and Leaf Including the poem Mythopoeia.* 1964. Intr. Christopher Tolkien. Boston: Houghton Mifflin, 1989.

——. *The Two Towers: Being the Second Part of The Lord of the Rings.* 1954. Boston: Houghton Mifflin, 1994.

——. *Unfinished Tales of Númenor and Middle-earth.* Ed. Christopher Tolkien. Boston: Houghton Mifflin, 1980.

——. *The War of the Ring: The History of The Lord of the Rings Part Three. The History of Middle-earth* 8. Ed. Christopher Tolkien. Boston: Houghton Mifflin, 1990.

Tolkien, J. R. R., E. V. Gordon, and others. *Songs for the Philologists.* London: Privately printed in the Department of English at University College, 1936.

"Tolkien, John Ronald Reuel." *The Concise Encyclopedia of Modern World Literature.* Ed. Geoffrey Grigson. New York: Hawthorn, 1963. 443–44.

Trickett, Rachel, and David Cecil. "Is There an Oxford 'School' of Writing?" *Twentieth Century* (June 1955): 559–70.

Trimbur, John, and Lundy A. Braun. "Laboratory Life and the Determination of Authorship." Forman 19–36.

Tyler, J. E. A. *The New Tolkien Companion.* 2nd. ed. 1st rev. printing. New York: Avon, 1980.

Unwin, Rayner. "Early Days of Elder Days." Flieger and Hostetter 3–6.

Urang, Gunnar. *Shadows of Heaven: Religion and Fantasy in the Writing of C. S. Lewis, Charles Williams, and J. R. R. Tolkien.* Philadelphia: United Church Press, 1971.

Vinaver, Eugène, ed. *The Works of Sir Thomas Malory.* 3 Vols. Oxford: Clarendon Press, 1947.

Vine, W. E., Merrill F. Unger, and William White Jr. *Vine's Complete Expository Dictionary of Old and New Testament Words.* Nashville, TN: Thomas Nelson, 1985.

Wain, John. "Anti-Critic." Rev. of *The Fine Art of Reading,* by Lord David Cecil. *Observer* [London] 21 July 1957, 12.

———. *Arnold Bennett.* Columbia Essays on Modern Writers 23. Irvington, NY: Columbia University Press, 1967.

———. "C. S. Lewis Throws Down a Challenge." Rev. of *An Experiment in Criticism,* by C. S. Lewis. *Observer* [London] 22 Oct. 1961, 31.

———. *Dear Shadows: Portraits from Memory.* London: John Murray, 1986.

———. "Friends and Strangers." Rev. of *The Letters of C. S. Lewis. Observer* [London] 15 May 1966, 26.

———. "A Great Clerke." Como 152–63.

———. "John Wain." *Contemporary Authors.* Autobiography Series 4. Detroit, MI: Gale Research, 1986. 314–32.

———. *Mixed Feelings.* Ltd. ed. of 120 numb. copies. Reading, Eng.: School of Art, University of Reading, 1951.

———. "The Mysterious Women in Lewis's Life." Rev. of *Jack,* by George Sayer. *Canadian C. S. Lewis Journal* 65 (Winter 1989): 6.

———. "New Novels." Rev. of *Till We Have Faces,* by C. S. Lewis; *The Side of the Angels,* by Jean-Louis Ortis; *Homecomings,* by C. P. Snow. *Observer* [London] 9 Dec. 1956: 12.

———. "Pleasure, Controversy, Scholarship." Rev. of *English Literature in the Sixteenth Century, Excluding Drama,* by C. S. Lewis. *Spectator* 1 Oct. 1954: 403–05.

———. *Professing Poetry.* London: Macmillan, 1977.

———. Rev. of *Studies in Words,* by C. S. Lewis. *Twentieth Century* 169 (1961): 86–88.

———. *Sprightly Running: Part of an Autobiography.* New York: St. Martin's Press, 1963.

———. "Wain's Oxford." Reply to Letter by C. S. Lewis. *Encounter* Jan. 1963: 81–82.

———. *Weep before God: Poems.* New York: St. Martin's Press, 1961.

Walsh, Chad. *C. S. Lewis: Apostle to the Skeptics.* New York: Macmillan, 1949.

West, Richard C. "W. H. Lewis: Historian of the Inklings and of Seventeenth-Century France." *Seven: An Anglo-American Literary Review* 14 (1997): 75–86.

Wheeler, Helen Tyrrell. "Wartime Tutor." Graham 48–52.

Williams, Charles. *All Hallows' Eve.* 1945. Grand Rapids, MI: Eerdmans, 1981.

———. *The Arthurian Poems of Charles Williams: Taliessin through Logres and The Region of the Summer Stars.* Woodbridge, Eng: D. S. Brewer-Boydell and Brewer, 1982.

———. *Collected Plays.* Ed. John Heath-Stubbs. New York: Oxford University Press, 1963.

———. *Descent Into Hell.* 1937. Grand Rapids, MI: Eerdmans, 1980.

———. *The Descent of the Dove: A History of the Holy Spirit in the Church.* 1939. New York: Meridian, 1956.

———. "The Figure of Arthur." Williams and Lewis 5–90.

———. *The Figure of Beatrice: A Study in Dante.* 1943. Cambridge, Eng.: D. S. Brewer, 1994.

———. *The Forgiveness of Sins.* 1942. Grand Rapids, MI: Eerdmans, 1984.

———. *The Greater Trumps.* London: Faber and Faber, 1954. Grand Rapids, MI: Eerdmans, 1976.

———. "Hardy." Rev. of *Hardy the Novelist,* by Lord David Cecil. *Time and Tide* (8 May 1943): 380.

———. *He Came Down from Heaven.* 1938. Grand Rapids, MI: Eerdmans, 1984.

———. *Judgement at Chelmsford.* 1939. *Collected Plays* 61–148.

———. "Letters in Hell." Rev. of *The Screwtape Letters,* by C. S. Lewis. *Time and Tide* (21 Mar. 1942): 245–46. Also in *Mythlore* 2.2 (whole no. 6, Autumn 1970): 22.

———. *Letters to Lalage: The Letters of Charles Williams to Lois Lang-Sims.* Kent, OH: Kent State University Press, 1989.

———. *The Masques of Amen House: Together with Amen House Poems and with Selections from the Music for the Masques by Hubert J. Foss.* Ed. David Bratman. Intr. Bernadette Lynn Bosky. Altadena, CA: Mythopoeic Press, 2000.

———, ed., David Cecil, Ernest De Selincourt, and E. M. W. Tillyard, assoc. eds. *The New Book of English Verse.* New York: Macmillan, 1936.

———. "The Noises That Weren't There." *Mythlore* 2.2 (whole no. 6 Autumn 1970): 17–21; 2.3 (no. 7 Winter 1971): 17–23; 2.4 (no. 8 Winter 1972): 21–25.

———. *Outlines of Romantic Theology: With which is reprinted Religion and Love in Dante: The Theology of Romantic Love.* Ed. Alice Mary Hadfield. Grand Rapids, MI: Eerdmans, 1990.

———, ed. *The Passion of Christ: Being the Gospel and Narrative of the Passion with Short Passages Taken from the Saints and Doctors of the Church.* London: Oxford University Press, 1939.

———. *The Place of the Lion.* 1931. Grand Rapids, MI: Eerdmans, 1980.

———. *Poetry at Present.* Oxford: Clarendon Press, 1930.

———. *Reason and Beauty in the Poetic Mind.* Oxford: Clarendon Press, 1933.

———. *The Region of the Summer Stars.* 1944. *The Arthurian Poems of Charles Williams.*

———. Rev. of *Beyond Personality,* by C. S. Lewis; *Light of Christ,* by Evelyn Underhill. *Time and Tide* (16 June 1945): 506.

———. Rev. of *The Problem of Pain,* by C. S. Lewis. *Theology* 42 (Jan. 1941): 62–63.

———. Rev. of *Reason and Beauty in the Poetic Mind,* by Charles Williams. *Week-End Review* (18 Nov. 1933): 525.

———. Rev. of *The Screwtape Letters,* by C. S. Lewis. *Dublin Review* 211 (1942): 170–71.

———. "The Romantic Imagination." Rev. of *Romanticism Comes of Age,* by Owen Barfield. *New English Weekly* (10 May 1945): 33–34.

———. *Seed of Adam.* 1948. *Collected Plays* 149–75.

———. *Shadows of Ecstasy.* 1933. Grand Rapids, MI: Eerdmans, 1980.

———. *The Silver Stair.* London: Herbert & Daniel, 1912.

———. *Taliessin through Logres.* 1938. *The Arthurian Poems of Charles Williams.*

———. *Terror of Light.* 1940. *Collected Plays* 325–74.

———. *Thomas Cranmer of Canterbury.* 1936. *Collected Plays* 1–59.

———. *To Michal from Serge: Letters from Charles Williams to His Wife, Florence, 1939–1945.* Ed. and Introduction Roma A. King Jr. Kent OH: Kent State University Press, 2002.

———. "Uncommon Fairness." Rev. of *Augustans and Romantics, 1689–1830,* by H. P. W. [*sic*] Dyson and John Butt. *Time and Tide* (28 Dec. 1940): 1274–75.

———. *Windows of Night.* Oxford: Oxford University Press, 1924.

———. *Witchcraft.* London: Faber & Faber, 1941.

Williams, Charles, and C. S. Lewis. *Arthurian Torso: Containing the Posthumous Fragment of The Figure of Arthur by Charles Williams and a Commentary on the Arthurian Poems of Charles Williams by C. S. Lewis.* London: Oxford University Press, 1969.

Williams, Charles, and V. H. Collins, comps. *Poems of Home and Overseas.* 1921. Oxford: Clarendon Press, 1930.

Williams, Michal. Appendix. "As I Remember Charles Williams." *To Michal from Serge,* 259–62.

Wilson, A. N. *C. S. Lewis: A Biography.* New York: Norton, 1990.

"Wolfgang, Can You Help Me Out Here?" *Newsweek* (23 June 1997): 55.

Wrenn, C. L., ed. *Beowulf, with the Finnesburg Fragment.* London: Harrap, 1953. 2nd ed., rev. and enlarged. London: Harrap, 1958. 3rd ed., fully rev. W. F. Bolton. London: Harrap, 1973.

———. Rev. of *The Allegory of Love,* by C. S. Lewis. *Oxford Magazine* (25 Feb. 1937): 449–50.

———. *A Study of Old English Literature.* London: Harrap, 1967.

Wright, Marjorie Evelyn. "The Cosmic Kingdom of Myth: A Study in the Myth-Philosophy of Charles Williams, C. S. Lewis, and J. R. R. Tolkien." PhD Diss. University of Illinois, 1960.

Young, Edward. "Conjectures on Original Composition." 1759. Adams 329–37.

Index

Works by the Inklings are indexed under title; other literary works are indexed under author. Fictional characters are indexed under work or author. Scholars are indexed when cited but not for bibliographic references in the text or notes.

Abbreviations: CSL (C. S. Lewis), CT (Christopher Tolkien), CW (Charles Williams), JRRT (J. R. R. Tolkien), OB (Owen Barfield), WHL (Warren Lewis)

"Abecedarium Philosophicum" (OB and CSL), 139

Abolition of Man, The (CSL): *Green Book* in, 38, 44n14

accountability and anticipation, xviii, 64–66, 73n11

acknowledgments, ix–xiii, xviii, 158; in books by Inklings, 98n29, 126–27, 131n22, 164n26, 178, 188. *See also* dedications, editing

Adey, Lionel: on Great War, 79, 95n6–7, 95n9

Adventures of Tom Bombadil, The (JRRT), 74n21, 181

After Ten Years (CSL), 211

Agapony or Agapargyry, 176

aggressive approach (military and athletic analogies), 77–78, 95n8

Ajimywanian War, The (CSL), 137, 161n6

allegory: OB writes, 173; Coghill praises CSL on, 190; CSL on, 35, 190, 205n41; CSL writes, 83, 84–85, 98n27–28; and JRRT as author, 35, 170, 205n41; JRRT dislikes, 83, 84–85

Allegory of Love, The (CSL): acknowledg-

ments in, 127, 162n16; dedicated to OB, 187; OB on, 178; Bennett on, 163n22; Coghill on, 190; Mathew disputes, 163n25; CW on, 69, 190; CW reads and edits, 14–15, 24n31, 101; mentioned, 176, 238

Allen, Edward, 82, 229n27

Allen, Mrs. Edward A., 66

Allen & Unwin (publisher), 1–2, 55, 154. *See also* Unwin, Rayner; Unwin, Stanley

All Hallows' Eve (CW): WHL on, 52; reviewed, 46–47, 99n36; writing of, and read to Inklings, xvi, 17, 30, 89–91, 99n35, 127; mentioned, 36, 247

Amen House: CW's community, 169, 201n4–5, 209, 211–12. *See also* Oxford University Press

Ancrene Wisse (ed. JRRT), 181, 199

Anderson, Douglas A., 154, 212–13

Anglican church, 224; Anglican Revival, 43n4; theology, 146

Anglo-Saxon. *See* Old English

anthroposophy, 6, 79, 182, 185, 231. *See also* Steiner, Rudolf

anticipation. *See* accountability and anticipation

Apolausticks (club), 26n42, 207

Aquinas, Saint Thomas. *See* Thomas Aquinas, Saint

Arabian Nights, The, 98n30

archetypes, 44n13

Ardenne, Simonne (S. R. T. O.) d', 21n3, 213

Arieti, Silvano, 44n13

Aristotle, 141; *De Anima,* 79

Arthurian legend and romances: collaborations, 159, 166n39; influence on Inklings, 28, 35; CSL and OB on, 141–45; CW on, 109, 150–51

The Company They Keep

was designed and composed by Darryl ml Crosby

in 10.5/13.5 Minion Pro with display type in ITC Benguiat;

printed on 55# Writers Natural Hi-Bulk stock

by Sheridan Books, Inc., of Ann Arbor, Michigan;

and published by

THE KENT STATE UNIVERSITY PRESS

Kent, Ohio 44242